The British Library Stu

PROVENANCl
BOOK HISTORY

PROVENANCE RESEARCH IN BOOK HISTORY

A Handbook

DAVID PEARSON

THE BRITISH LIBRARY
&
OAK KNOLL PRESS

For my parents,
with thanks for the earliest bibliographical encouragement

First published 1994 by The British Library
Reprinted with a new Introduction 1998
by The British Library
96 Euston Road
London NW1 2DB
UK

Marketed exclusively in North and South America, including Canada
by Oak Knoll Press
308 Delaware Street
New Castle
DE 19720
USA

ISBN 0 7123 0344 8 (BL cased edition)
ISBN 0 7123 4598 1 (BL paperback edition)
ISBN 1 884718 79 5 (Oak Knoll cased edition)
ISBN 1 884718 80 9 (Oak Knoll paperback edition)

Designed by John Trevitt
Typeset by Norman Tilley Graphics, Northampton
Printed in England by Henry Ling, Dorchester

CONTENTS

PREFACE & ACKNOWLEDGMENTS

This book began life as a list of provenance indexes which I compiled in 1987 and distributed on a self-published basis. Although it was a very modest production, its reception was sufficiently heartening to encourage me to expand the concept, and thus this *Handbook* was born. The original list of published and unpublished provenance indexes has been revised and augmented in various ways, and it now forms chapter VII of the present work.

The aims and objectives of the *Handbook* are set out in the opening pages of the Introduction. It is designed as a reference book, a bibliography, rather than a narrative and interpretative text, with a view to providing assistance to the growing number of people who are interested in the previous ownership of books. Although much of the information in the book can be derived from other sources, there is no comparable guide which brings it all together in one place.

This is a book to be written in and annotated. It is of the nature of bibliographical guides like this to fall out of date even before they are published, as new resources appear and existing ones are augmented. I am also very aware of the fact that different users will perceive different gaps and weaknesses. There are many areas in which lists of examples could be usefully and almost indefinitely extended, and several chapters could easily be expanded to become books in their own right. The questions of inclusion and exclusion, of striking a balance between a manageable overview and a compendium which is sufficiently comprehensive to be useful, are always challenging. The choice of material listed is based very much on a personal selection of reference works which have proved useful to me in pursuing provenance-based research. I will certainly be annotating my own copy, and I will always be glad to receive comments, corrections or additions relating to any part of the text.

This book has been several years in the making and it would have been impossible without the help of a great many people who have given me access to their libraries, answered my letters, or arranged for photography. My information has been gathered partly by visiting libraries, and largely by correspondence, and I am enormously grateful to the many librarians who have patiently answered enquiries about their collections, often at some length. I cannot name them all here; I can only issue general but sincere thanks to all who have helped. There are of course a number of individuals whose assistance or encouragement has been particularly valuable, and for whom a mention here, albeit the best I can offer, is but poor reward. I am especially grateful to John Coast, Arnold Hunt, Brian North Lee, Henry Woudhuysen, and my father, who read part or all of my text in draft form, and whose comments were very useful. I am no less indebted to the following, who all proffered help above and beyond the call of duty: Tom Birrell, who has provided information and encouragement at various points along the way; Sharon Clayton, whose lists helped me to identify the American libraries to whom I should write; my former colleagues in Durham, Ian Doyle, Roger Norris, and Beth Rainey, whose willingness to help never fails; Meg Ford, a tiller of a parallel furrow, whose comments have been much valued; Elisabeth Leedham-Green and Rowan Watson, for palaeographical advice; Roger Lovatt, for generous help and hospitality at the Perne Library; Giles Mandelbrote, for useful discussions and additions to my list of mottoes; Richard Ovenden, who has provided manifold assistance throughout this project; and Michael Perkin, who acted as the initial catalyst to begin the compilation of the book. It should go without saying that none of these people share any responsibility for errors or omissions.

I would also like to express my formal thanks to the following institutions for permission to reproduce pictures of books in their collections:

Aberdeen University Library: fig. 3.31

The British Library: figs. 2.4, 2.18-2.20, 2.23, 2.25-2.26, 2.28, 2.32, 2.42, 3.2-3.3, 3.21, 3.29, 3.32-3.33, 3.35-3.43, 3.47-3.48, 3.50, 3.51-3.54, 4.5, 4.17, 4.28, 8.8-8.9, 8.11-8.18

The British Museum: figs. 3.1, 3.4-3.20

The Syndics of Cambridge University Library: figs. 2.11, 2.13, 2.21, 2.30-2.31, 2.50, 3.34, 3.58, 4.15, 8.6-8.7

The Dean & Chapter of Durham: figs. 2.44, 2.45, 4.14

Durham University Library: figs. 1.3, 2.1, 2.3, 2.15-2.17, 2.24, 2.34-2.41, 2.43, 2.47-2.49, 2.52-2.53, 3.25, 3.44, 3.60, 4.18, 4.20-4.21, 4.23, 8.19

Ushaw College, Durham: fig. 3.30

The Master & Fellows of Emmanuel College, Cambridge: figs. 2.46, 2.51

The Provost & Fellows of King's College, Cambridge: figs. 3.23-3.24

The Archbishop of Canterbury and the Trustees of Lambeth Palace Library: figs. 3.56, 4.30

The Dean & Chapter of Lincoln: fig. 2.12

The Master & Fellows of Magdalen College, Oxford: fig. 4.27

The Director & University Librarian, the John Rylands University Library of Manchester: fig. 2.29

The Faculty of Advocates and the Trustees of the National Library of Scotland: fig. 3.57

The Master & Fellows of Pembroke College, Cambridge: fig. 4.29

The Dean & Chapter of Peterborough: figs. 8.20-8.22

The Master & Fellows of Peterhouse, Cambridge: figs. 2.10, 8.10

The Royal Asiatic Society: fig. 3.62

The Trustees of the Victoria & Albert Museum: figs. 1.1-1.2, 2.2, 2.5-2.8, 2.14, 2.22, 3.45-3.46, 3.59, 4.1-4.4, 4.6-4.13, 4.16, 4.19, 4.22, 4.24-4.26, 4.31, 8.2.

Illustrations of inscriptions and ink stamps have been reproduced actual size as far as possible. Bindings, bookplates and other kinds of illustrations have generally been reduced.

The standard abbreviations for the major bibliographies of British books down to 1801 are used at various points in the text:

STC – A. W. Pollard & G. R. Redgrave, revised by W. A. Jackson, F. S. Ferguson & K. F. Pantzer: *A short-title catalogue of books printed in England, Scotland, and Ireland, and of English books printed abroad 1475-1640*, 3v., London, 1976-91.

Wing – D. Wing, revised by J. Morrison, C. Nelson et al: *Short-title catalogue of books printed in England, Scotland, Ireland, Wales, and British America ... 1641-1700*, 3v., New York, 1982-94.

ESTC – *The Eighteenth-century short title catalogue*, in progress; has been published in microfiche and CD formats, although the most up-to-date version of the file is available on-line through BLAISE and RLIN.

INTRODUCTION
TO THE 1998 REPRINT

'The serious study of private libraries, and of the lessons which can be learned from book ownership, is a growth industry and one which has gained much ground in the recent past.' This statement, from the Introduction to this book, remains as valid today as it was four years ago, and the prediction implicit within it can fairly be said to have come true. There is a steadily growing literature on the ownership and use of books, embracing works on particular private libraries, studies of marginalia, and the new academic vogue for the history of reading. Librarians and booksellers are increasingly noting previous ownership in their catalogue entries. It is therefore inevitable that another of my predictions, that the book would be out of date even before it was published, was equally accurate. There is certainly scope for augmenting it to take recent work on board, quite apart from the need to consider the comments and suggestions which have been helpfully made by reviewers and others.

Thoroughgoing revision must wait for another and later occasion, and the main purpose of the present exercise is to ensure the continuing availability of the original text. Criticisms notwithstanding, it has naturally been heartening to note the generally positive reception which the book has had to date. What follows below is a direct reprint of the 1994 edition but I would like to take the opportunity presented by this reissue to make a few corrections, and to list some resources which have been published over the last few years and which are very pertinent to my original purpose. They are arranged in chapter order with references to page numbers where appropriate.

DAVID PEARSON
April 1998

Chapter II. Inscriptions, mottoes & other manuscript additions
p. 41, painted-in heraldic marks of ownership: see John A. Goodall, 'Heraldry in the decoration of English medieval manuscripts', *The Antiquaries Journal* 77 (1997), 179-220.

Chapter III. Bookplates, book labels and book stamps
p. 71, the Franks catalogue and its limitations: see Brian North Lee's comments in *The Library* 6th ser. 19 (1997), 255-6, in a response to Nigel Ramsay's review of this book in the same volume of that journal, 73-5.
p. 78, Exhibition catalogues: *The world of ex-libris: a historical retrospective/Svet ekslibrisa: istoijska retrospektiva*, 2 vols, Belgrade, 1995 is an internationally and chronologically wide-ranging catalogue, well illustrated.

p. 81, Foreign bookplates, Italy: a major recent reference work on Italian plates, well illustrated, is E. Bragaglia, *Gli ex libris Italiane dalle origini alla fine dell'Ottocento*, 3 vols, Milan, 1993.

Chapter IV. Armorials, other binding stamps & external features
p. 108: see Pamela M. Selwyn, 'An armorial binding of William Cecil, 1st Baron Burghley', in C. W. Marx (ed.), *The Founder's Library, University of Wales* (*Trivium* 29-30), for evidence of donors' arms being used to decorate prizes for students.

p. 113, 'The Franks collection of armorial bookstamps' in the British Library: the material written about by A. W. Pollard in his *Library* article of 1902 is not the scrapbook assemblage of armorials now at L.R.406.i.9, but a collection of *c*. 260 books with armorial stamps collected by Franks and now shelved in the BL at C.67 and C.68.a-e. Although they are still physically together, there is no separate catalogue or index. I am grateful to John Goldfinch for putting the record straight here.

p. 125, labels under horn: the latest example of this practice I have seen, rather later than the 1604 Guildford example cited, is a copy of M. Chemnitz, *Examen Concilii Tridentini*, 1578, now in Trinity College, Oxford (C.10.12), with a label under horn dated 1627 recording the book's donation by James Bingley.

p. 130: questions about the extent to which book purchasers were concerned with the individual characteristics of the bindings they owned are examined, from two rather different viewpoints, in the opening essays of R. Myers and M. Harris (eds.), *Antiquaries, book collectors and the circles of learning*, Winchester, 1996: (i) David Pearson, 'Scholars and bibliophiles: book collectors in Oxford, 1550-1650', pp. 1-26; (ii) Mirjam Foot, 'Scholar-collectors and their bindings', pp. 27-44.

Chapter IV. Sale catalogues
The December 1995 issue of *Papers of the Bibliographical Society of America* (vol. 89 no. 4) was devoted to 'Book catalogues, today and tomorrow: reports and presentations from the 1995 BSA Conference'. It contains many important articles which supplement information in this chapter, covering the bibliography, location and use of sale catalogues.

Although the emphasis throughout this chapter lies with British catalogues, it may be worth mentioning the existence of an important recent history of early French auction catalogues: F. Bléchet, *Les ventes publiques de livres en France 1630-1750: répertoire des catalogues conservés à la Bibliothèque Nationale*, Oxford (Voltaire Foundation), 1991.

p. 158, Francis Edwards: the firm's reference library, including their master set of marked-up Edwards catalogues, was sold by Maggs in 1985 (their catalogue 1062); this set was acquired by the Grolier Club in New York.

p. 161, J. J. Leighton: the firm's ledgers and stock books, 1896-1918, are in the British Library (Add. MSS 45161-45175).

p. 170, works on the history of second-hand bookselling: the essays in R. Myers and M. Harris (eds.), *A genius for letters: booksellers and bookselling from the 16th to the 20th century*, contain several articles pertinent to this theme; see especially C. Edwards, 'Antiquarian bookselling in Britain in 1725: the nature of the evidence' (pp. 85-102) and G. Mandelbrote, 'From the warehouse to the counting-house: booksellers and bookshops in late 17th-century London' (pp. 49-84).

Chapter VII. Provenance indexes

This is the area in which the original text is most liable not only to need supplementing, but to have fallen out of date. The information given here about library catalogues and the state of their indexing is based on original surveys carried out in 1992-3 and it is inevitable that many will have progressed significantly since then. Increasingly, manual catalogues are being converted to automated versions which may be available over the Internet with web interfaces. The most obvious example is perhaps the British Library catalogue, cited in the 1994 book in its printed and CD-ROM versions, now available as OPAC97 via the Library's web site. The range of provenance information in this case has so far remained much the same, but numerous other automated cataloguing projects are in train which will more quickly open up new data on ownership. There is also a burgeoning growth in world wide web sites which contain descriptions of collections, or catalogues and bibliographies, which include provenance information.

I have not tried to chart these new resources, and although that might be a useful exercise, the results would more suitably live in an electronic form that a printed one. My aim here is only to list a selected number of publications which have appeared recently, which fit the criteria of this chapter, and which contain appreciable quantities of provenance information.

p. 191, Jesus College, Cambridge: see L. Warner, 'Fellows, students, and their gifts to Jesus College Library', *Transactions of the Cambridge Bibliographical Society* 11 (1996), 1-48.

p. 199, Cambridge University Library: add to this entry, J. H. Baker and J. S. Ringrose, *A catalogue of English legal manuscripts in Cambridge University Library*, Woodbridge, 1996. Provenances noted in the text, with separate index and notes on provenance in the introduction (pp. xlv-lv).

p. 211, Hereford Cathedral Library: Bannister's catalogue is now superseded by R. A. B. Mynors and R. M. Thomson, *Catalogue of the manuscripts of Hereford Cathedral Library*, Woodbridge, 1993; provenances are noted in the text, and indexed under 'Owners' in the general index.

p. 247, private collections: add D. G. Selwyn, *The library of Thomas Cranmer*, Oxford Bibliographical Society Publications 3rd ser. 1, Oxford, 1996. Provenances, before and after Cranmer, noted in the text; separate provenance indexes.

p. 253, Yale University Library: add B. M. Rosenthal, *The Rosenthal Collection of printed books with manuscript annotations*, New Haven, 1997. A catalogue of

242 early printed books collected for their extensive or distinctive ms annotation; provenances noted and indexed.

p. 259, Harvard University Library: five volumes of the *Catalogue of the fifteenth-century printed books* by J. E. Walsh have now been published, 1991-7.

p. 271, private collections: add Kevin J. Hayes, *The library of William Byrd of Westover*, Madison, 1997. William Byrd (d. 1744) amassed what was, during his lifetime, the largest private library in colonial America, running to nearly 2500 volumes. Although subsequently dispersed it was documented in several early catalogues and this book presents an edited reconstruction of the library, based on these lists, identifying several hundred surviving books. Provenances are noted in the text and included in the index.

Chapter VIII. Heraldry; palaeography; biography, etc.

p. 303, Lawyers: G. Holborn, 'Sources of biographical information on past lawyers', *The Law Librarian* 23 (1992), 75-90 and 119-35, is an extensive list of 332 separate works containing biographical listings of lawyers and related people. It is arranged by categories (e.g. Inns of Court, civilian lawyers, judiciary) with introductory sections on the surviving records.

p. 308, articles on the study and use of provenance: the December 1997 issue of *Papers of the Bibliographical Society of America* (91: 4) was devoted to 'Marks in books: proceedings of the 1997 BSA Conference' and contains many articles on different aspects of provenance research, and work in progress.

p. 308, studies of book collecting and book collectors: James P. Carley and Colin C. G. Tite (eds.), *Books and collectors 1200-1700: essays presented to Andrew Watson*, London, 1997, contains numerous essays on particular collections and collectors, with an emphasis on the monastic libraries and their subsequent dispersals.

p. 311, add J. Glomski, 'Book collecting and bookselling in the seventeenth century: notions of rarity and identification of value', *Publishing History* 39 (1996), 5-21. This article looks at questions of desirability and value in the English book market of the seventeenth century, an important topic which is very little considered elsewhere in the literature.

p. 312, add D. E. Rhodes, 'Some English, Welsh, Scottish and Irish book-collectors in Italy, 1467-1850', in D. E. Rhodes (ed.), *Bookbindings and other bibliophily: essays in honour of Anthony Hobson*, Verona, 1994, pp. 247-76.

Appendix: describing provenance in catalogues

The Library Association Rare Books Group *Guidelines for the cataloguing of rare books*, London, 1997, are particularly concerned with ways of recording copy-specific evidence in catalogue records, and suggest standard formats for recording provenance and binding data, according to various optional levels of sophistication.

I
INTRODUCTION

This *Handbook* is intended to provide a basic reference source for people who are concerned with the provenance – the previous ownership – of printed books and manuscripts. More specifically, its aim is to help researchers who are either:

a) trying to identify owners from inscriptions, bookplates, binding stamps or other marks found in particular books; or

b) trying to trace the present whereabouts or prior existence of books once owned by a particular individual.

It should also be of relevance to anyone who is interested in book ownership generally; those who are studying it as a branch of historical bibliography, those who are pursuing the history of reading and the use of books, and those who wish to trace the circulation of particular texts by identifying the people who once owned them.

This book is first and foremost a bibliography, a listing of other books and sources of information which will help the provenance researcher. It is neither an encyclopaedia nor a history of book collecting or book collectors. In describing the various categories of evidence which may be encountered in early books, a number of representative examples and illustrations have been chosen, but these are never meant to comprise a comprehensive survey of those categories. The aim has always been to provide an overview, and to point the way to further reading, or to material which will help to elucidate a problem. Although the range of books which may be relevant to provenance research is potentially limitless, there is a core of basic material which should be familiar to anyone working in this area, and it is the compiler's hope that this core will be found described within these pages.

The *Handbook* is focussed primarily upon British book ownership from the end of the fifteenth century to the beginning of the nineteenth, or, to put it another way, from the introduction of printing to the time when the introduction of mechanised production techniques brought about great changes in the ways in which books were made and distributed. The medieval era is not excluded but is less of a central concern, not least because medievalists are more advanced than post-Renaissance scholars in mapping out the patterns of book ownership within their period, with the aid of *Medieval libraries of Great Britain* and similar tools. The xenophobic concentration on British book ownership will rightly be criticised as too narrow, on a variety of counts: books originally in British ownership are now found in libraries overseas, books originally in foreign ownership have been migrating into British libraries for many centuries, and the whole notion of a one-country approach is out of place when considering a book trade which has always been international. The different methods of marking book ownership used by British collectors down the centuries have been mirrored or influenced by similar habits overseas, particularly in continental Europe. Recognising these points, an attempt has been made to incorporate some of the more important and more accessible works relating to foreign provenance, and the list of provenance indexes takes in North American libraries as well as British ones. But a truly multi-national bibliography would be an ambitious venture and, if desirable, might best be undertaken as a collaborative project.

THE STUDY OF PROVENANCE

The serious study of private libraries, and of the lessons which can be learned from book ownership, is a growth industry and one which has gained much ground in the recent past. In one sense, an interest in provenance is nothing new; books associated with distinguished people have long been regarded as desirable and noteworthy objects. The gospel-book which reputedly belonged to St. Cuthbert (d.687) was treasured during the middle ages as one of the precious relics of Durham Cathedral.[1] The importance of 'association' in adding value to a book has been recognised and exploited by booksellers, and has featured increasingly in their catalogues since the beginning of the nineteenth century. But there is a difference between venerating a book as a precious relic, and approaching the evidence of previous ownership with a view to asking serious questions about what it can teach us. The study of provenance allows us to assess the size and contents of particular libraries, and to compare them with other collections of their time. It allows us to build up wider pictures of the patterns of book ownership through the centuries, and to see how those patterns change in terms of size, composition, language, subject, or origin. These observations lead on to yield information about the history of the book trade, and about the importance of books in society. The study of an individual private library shows up the interests and tastes of the owner, and the texts which may have influenced his thinking. If he annotated his books, his comments may be valuable as evidence of contemporary reaction to the ideas they contain. An examination of a large number of libraries of one period may show which books were popular and which were not, cutting through the

---

1 C. F. Battiscombe (ed.): *The relics of St. Cuthbert*, Oxford, 1956, p. 360.

distorting veil of several centuries of changing fashion. Ownership evidence may also play an important part in assigning dates to undated books, or in helping to localise and date bindings,. Students of medieval manuscripts have long valued the information which the inscriptions of subsequent owners may yield about the previous history of those manuscripts, and about the ways in which pre-Reformation libraries were dispersed.[2]

All these different avenues are increasingly being explored and a growing corpus of published work is being produced. There have been numerous studies of particular collectors and their libraries, and studies of the uses of private library history in a wider frame. Individual libraries have been reconstructed from various kinds of evidence – lists and catalogues, probate inventories, surviving books, citations of texts in published works – and detailed research has been carried out on the marginal annotations of particular owners. Librarians and booksellers are increasingly inclined to record provenance information in the catalogues they produce. The emphasis of British bibliographical studies, which have focussed for much of the twentieth century on listing the output of the printing presses and producing short-title catalogues, is changing; the primacy of enumerative bibliography is being replaced by the broader concept of the history of the book. Now that the historical lists of published books are established, we are increasingly interested in the ways in which those books were circulated, regarded, and used. The history of reading is gaining ground as an academic discipline. A fuller survey of these developments, with extensive references to some of the publications which have resulted, has been written by David McKitterick and will be found in the volume of essays published to mark the Centenary of the Bibliographical Society.[3]

PROBLEMS OF PROVENANCE RESEARCH

The student of provenance is beset by many problems. Inscriptions in books may be illegible, damaged, defaced, or removed altogether. Bookplates, similarly, may be partly or wholly torn out, or may have other bookplates pasted on top. Although a bookplate might be thought to offer a more substantial target for identification than an inscription, many bookplates hide their owners' identities behind anonymity, initials, or monograms. Many marks of ownership in early books rely on heraldry, an ancient discipline whose arcane codes and terminology are not immediately accessible to many people today. Problems of heraldic interpretation are compounded by the tendency of earlier generations to make questionable and pretentious assumptions about their genealogy.

---

2 See C. E. Wright: The dispersal of the libraries in the sixteenth century in F. Wormald & C. E. Wright (eds.), *The English library before 1700*, London, 1958, 148-175, p. 159.
3 D. McKitterick: Book catalogues, their varieties and uses in P. Davison (ed.), *The book encompassed*, Cambridge, 1992, 161-175.

Mutilation and effacement are perennial problems. Those who have benefited the provenance researcher by clearly inscribing their books have often countered their good deeds by being just as anxious to eradicate all evidence of ownership prior to themselves. Fig. 1.1 shows a book from Ben Jonson's library in which Jonson's characteristic inscription 'Sum Ben Jonsonij', and his motto 'Tanquam explorator', have been firmly obliterated by a later seventeenth-century owner; there is just enough left to identify it. Obliteration like this is slightly better than physical mutilation, which is another common phenomenon; anyone who has spent much time looking at early books will be familiar with the sight of titlepages with neat rectangular patches cut out, where an offending ownership signature has been removed. Fig. 1.2 illustrates a more moderate, but equally frustrating, variation in which the surname only has been mostly snipped out.

Bookbinders have, over the centuries, removed vast quantities of provenance

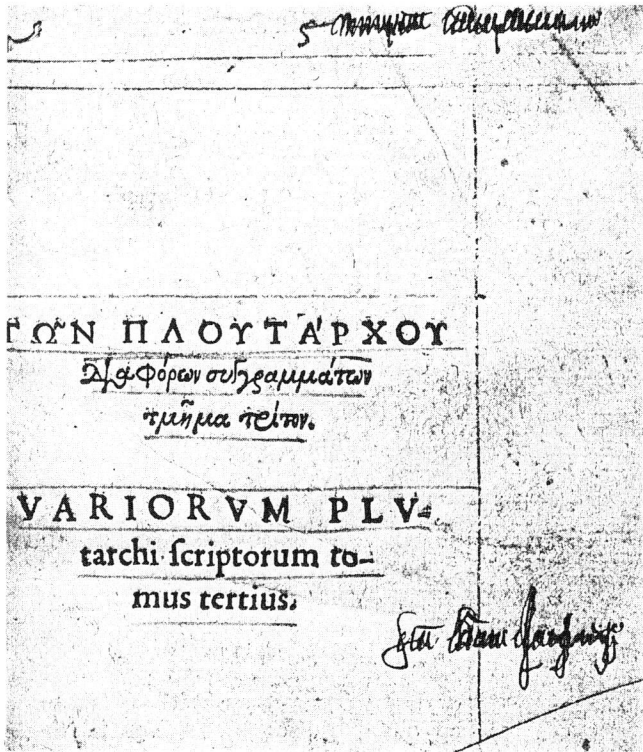

Fig. 1.1 An example of early obliteration: the motto 'Tanquam explorator' and inscription 'Su[m] Ben Jonsonij' of Ben Jonson have been crossed out by a later seventeenth-century owner. National Art Library Clements P19: *Variorum Plutarchi scriptorum tomus tertius*, 1572.

evidence. This is a problem associated with both institutional and private libraries; the former have wished to make their books sound and serviceable, the latter have wished to make them beautiful according to the fashion of the day. Successive rebinding has often involved re-cropping of the edges by the binder's plough, slicing away inscriptions in the manner shown in fig. 1.3. Here, there is enough left of the motto and inscription of Edmund Hastings to make decipherment possible, but this is more by chance than design. Boards carrying names, initials, or armorial stamps have been freely discarded, as have end-papers with inscriptions. Inscriptions elsewhere have been washed out as part of the process of removing the 'blemishes' and making the book fit for the discerning collector. Books have been dismembered in the interests of 'perfecting' other copies. The general tendency nowadays is to exercise restraint, when books are repaired, and to ensure that physical evidence is retained or at least recorded, but this is a very recent development and the practice is still not universal.

Books have been mutilated for other reasons. Bookplate collectors have done no end of damage by removing plates and labels from the books in which they belong, to mount in their albums. Autograph collectors have similarly defaced title pages; the rectagular holes mentioned above may be the work of such people. It is not uncommon to find examples like that shown at fig. 1.4 in the catalogues of dealers in autographs and manuscripts. An early practitioner of this type of vandalism was Thomas Rawlinson (1681-1725); his albums of signatures cut from title pages survive today in the Bodleian Library.[4] People have, similarly, removed title pages, illustrations, devices or colophons; the best-known exponents are John Bagford (1650-1716) and Joseph Ames (1689-1759), whose collections of title pages and other fragments survive in the British Library. Both Bagford and Ames had worthy motives, and it can rightly be pointed out that they saved material which was likely to be discarded anyway – better a title page preserved than nothing at all – but the ultimate judgment of posterity is that it would have been preferable to save the books in their entirety. This kind of vandalism is not, of course, restricted to printed books; medieval manuscripts have been cheerfully chopped up or taken apart for many centuries, particularly if they are illuminated. The dismemberment of the *Tres belles heures de Notre-Dame, du Duc Jean de Berry* began as early as the fifteenth century.[5] Richard Hegge, writing about the sorry state of Durham Cathedral Library in 1625 ('once a little Vatican of choise manuscripts'), lamented the fact that 'bookes were wounded with pen-knifes for their pictures'.[6] As late as 1854, John Ruskin could note in his diary that he had spent an evening cutting up a

4 Rawlinson mss.D.1386-7; see A. N. L. Munby: *The cult of the autograph letter*, London, 1962, p. 4.
5 V. Candea: Dismembered illuminated manuscripts in *An illustrated inventory of famous dismembered works of art*, UNESCO, Paris, 1974 (which see for other examples of manuscript mutilation), 188-193, p. 190.
6 B. R. [i.e. R. Hegge, ed. by R. Baddeley]: *The legend of St. Cuthbert*, London, 1663, pp. 43-44.

Of the Houſes of *P A R L I A M E N T*, made on Munday the 7. of *Novem.* And read in *Guild-hall* on Tuefday the 8. of *Novem.* 1642.

William ✿✿✿✿ *B.* —*r*

Fig. 1.2 The surname of an early owner has been cut out by a subsequent owner. National Art Library Forster 1597: *Three speeches spoken in Guild-Hall*, 1642.

Fig. 1.3 Cropped early seventeenth-century inscription of Edmund Hastings: Bamburgh Library, Durham, O.II.14, *A collection in English, of the statutes*, 1611.

141. **LUTTRELL, NARCISSUS** (1657-1732:annalyst & bibliographer). Piece cut from the flyleaf of a book bearing autogr. inscription— *"Nar.Luttrell His Book. 1680"*.(stained).   £20

Fig. 1.4 From Henry Bristow catalogue 312 (1993).

missal ('hard work').[7] Illuminated manuscripts were often mutilated for their miniatures and decorated initials, which were collected as works of art in their own right, and a trade in fragments of this kind still flourishes, although, as a rule, manuscripts are no longer cut up. Ruskin, like Ames, was motivated by higher aims than mere conoisseurship – he believed in the educative value of portfolios of choice fragments – and there is also a long tradition of compiling

---

7 J. Ruskin: *The diaries*, ed. J. Evans and J. H. Whitehouse, v.2, Oxford, 1958, p. 488.

albums of manuscript fragments for palaeographical study.[8] Many nineteenth-
and twentieth-century collections like this have been put together from binding
fragments – often with no record of the binding from which they were taken –
and there can be no doubt that zeal for the garnering of such specimens has
prompted more than a little rebinding work. Portfolios of fragments may also be
less innocently gathered; the Dean and Chapter of Durham in 1700 saw fit to
mutilate two of their eighth-century gospel books to provide specimens of early
handwriting for Samuel Pepys's calligraphical albums.[9]

This piecemeal mutilation is probably insignificant when compared with the
wholesale destruction of vast quantities of books which has taken place over the
centuries. They have been burnt, torn up, recycled, or simply thrown away as a
consequence of accidental fire, war, heavy use, censorship, or indifference.
There have been a number of watershed periods or major disasters when book
destruction was particularly heavy; the middle years of the sixteenth century,
when the Reformation brought sweeping changes in doctrine and teaching
curricula, saw many library shelves cleared out of older material.[10] There is a
well-known account of the leaves of dismembered manuscripts of Duns Scotus
blowing round the quadrangle of New College, Oxford in the 1530s.[11] The
Civil War was another time of upheaval and library dispersal; and the Great
Fire of London in 1666 devoured many thousands of books. There are
numerous specific examples of libraries destroyed by fire: Ben Jonson lost many
of his books this way in 1623; the library of Henry Hyde, Earl of Rochester was
burnt in 1721; the Cotton Library fire of 1731 is well known as one of the
nation's bibliographical disasters; the Hafod Library of Thomas Johnes was lost
in 1807.[12] Countless books have been thrown away simply because they were
worn out or unwanted; school books and text books are the most frequently
cited cases but they are only the most obvious examples of a common
phenomenon. Waste paper, and waste vellum, was much valued by earlier
generations for a variety of domestic uses and books have been a prime source –
'martyrs of pies, and reliques of the bum', as Dryden put it.[13] The manuscript
leaves blowing round New College were reportedly being gathered up to be
turned into scarecrows. According to John Bale, one mid sixteenth-century
merchant 'bought the contents of two noble lybraryes for XL shyllynges' to turn
into wrapping paper.[14] William Blades, in his treatise on *The enemies of books*

8 See M. McC. Gatch: Fragmenta manuscripta and Varia at Missouri and Cambridge,
Transactions of the Cambridge Bibliographical Society 9 (1990) 434-475, p. 435ff.

9 See R. Latham (ed.): *Catalogue of the Pepys Library at Magdalene College, Cambridge. Volume IV: Music, maps and calligraphy*, Woodbridge, 1989, p. 6.

10 See K. W. Humphreys: The loss of books in sixteenth century England, *Libri* 36 (1986), 249-58.

11 Wormald & Wright, p. 165.

12 D. McPherson, *Ben Jonson's library and marginalia. Studies in philology* 71 (5) (1974), pp. 5-6; W. C. Hazlitt, *A roll of honour*, London, 1908, p. 119; A. Esdaile, *The British Museum Library*, London, 1946, p. 229; *Dictionary of national biography* (Johnes).

13 J. Dryden, Mac Flecknoe, line 101.

14 Humphreys, pp. 250-1.

(London, 1888), describes the discovery of the last few leaves of a rare early sixteenth-century book from the press of Wynkyn de Worde hanging up in a lavatory in Brighton.[15]

Blades's book is a catalogue of examples of destruction which have consumed book collections over the centuries. The present-day reader of his horror stories may reflect that all of this is, at least, in the past, but it is worth pointing out that the century which has elapsed since Blades wrote has not been free of continuing stories of destruction. 120 books, from the parish library of Lanteglos in Cornwall (originally the personal collection of an early eighteenth-century rector) were burnt around 1940 because they were assessed as worthless by the Bishop of Truro.[16] The surviving portion of the parish library of Coniston, Lancashire (founded in 1699) was destroyed circa 1957 because the books were 'dirty and unread'.[17] The bombs which fell during the Second World War destroyed books in London, Liverpool and elsewhere, and further harm was done through the pulping of books for war salvage. There is a copy of Jeremiah Seed's *Discourses on several important subjects* (Dublin, 1752) in Lambeth Palace Library which has a note on the flyleaf, dated 1941: 'Saved from 16th Lambeth Scouts waste paper collection and presented to the Lambeth Palace Library by the assistant scout master'. It is now the only copy of this edition recorded throughout the United Kingdom by the *Eighteenth-Century Short Title Catalogue*, despite its trawl of several hundred libraries. The loss of books through war salvage is a story which has yet to be chronicled.

It is therefore important for the provenance researcher to remember that the respect for early books which is now taken for granted is a fairly recent development. Vast numbers of books have perished utterly and books which are described in old lists and catalogues may no longer exist. Many collections of the past are no longer reconstructable.

A separate kind of problem for the student of provenance, but one which is no less profound, centres round the extent to which owners have marked their books. There are numerous ways in which this may be done – such as inscriptions, bookplates, armorial stamps – and much of this book is devoted to the interpretation of these signs. Although many owners *have* marked their books, for reasons of security, vanity, or both, many more have not, and countless books have passed through various hands without being marked in any way. This applies not only to people who owned only one or two books, but also to substantial collectors. Francis Dee, for example, Bishop of Peterborough (d.1638) bequeathed his personal library of nearly 200 books to St. John's College, Cambridge; they can be identified from a contemporary list and from

---

15 Blades, p. 53. On this theme, see also J. L. Clifford, *Dictionary Johnson*, London, 1979, pp. 20-21. For a fuller and more picturesque overview of the various ways in which books have been destroyed, see the section on 'The misfortunes of books' in H. Jackson, *The anatomy of bibliomania*, new edn, London, 1950, 407-429.

16 N. Ker: *The parochial libraries of the Church of England*, London, 1959, p. 85.

17 *Ibid.*, pp. 74-5.

the fact that a printed gift-label was placed in the books subsequent to their receipt by the College, but not from Dee's personal markings; on the whole, he did not inscribe his books. John Cosin (1594-1672), a more substantial seventeenth-century collector, left a library of about 5500 volumes to the diocese of Durham, but in many cases we can tell that a book belonged to his collection only because it has been kept together since his death. Cosin used a few cryptic markings in some of his books (see fig. 2.10 below), and had a few books marked with an armorial stamp late in life, but he very rarely wrote his name in and many of his books carry no personal ownership mark. This problem generates two obvious consequences. Firstly, there must be book owners of the past, and possibly quite major collectors, whose identity will never be known because their libraries were dispersed without a surviving record and the books were unmarked. Secondly, we may be able to identify people who are likely to have had appreciable libraries, but be unable to confirm one way or the other the influence which personal book ownership had on their activities, as their books cannot be identified even if they still exist. A study of bishops' libraries of the first half of the seventeenth century noted several scholars of the period who probably owned books, whose collections, if they existed, are completely untraceable today; this may be the reason.[18] Experience suggests that, in any old-established English library today (e.g. a cathedral or collegiate library), at least half the books are likely to bear no indication of any previous ownership.

THE ARRANGEMENT OF THIS BOOK

Despite the problems outlined above, a great deal of evidence of former book ownership does survive, and the first three chapters which follow are devoted to the different forms which this evidence may take, and to its elucidation. Provenance evidence may be divided into that which is found inside books, and that which is placed outside, on the covers; the former sort may be further subdivided into manuscript evidence of various kinds, and evidence which is pasted or stamped in (bookplates, labels and stamps). Chapter II is devoted to manuscript evidence, and chapter III deals with bookplates and related phenomena. Chapter IV is concerned with external evidence: armorial and personalised binding stamps, and other marks of ownership which may be found on the outsides of books.

The two chapters which follow on from there deal with lists and catalogues of books, other than library catalogues, which constitute vital secondary sources (the books themselves being the primary sources) in provenance research. Chapter V concentrates on sale catalogues, from auction houses and book-sellers, which contain vast amounts of provenance information. Chapter VI

18 D. Pearson: The libraries of English bishops 1600-40, *The Library* 6th ser 14 (1992), 221-257.

describes other kinds of catalogues, in printed and manuscript form, which list the contents of private libraries.

Chapter VII focusses on library catalogues, both published and unpublished, which include information on the previous ownership of books. Provenance indexes comprise a growing and increasingly important means of discovering the whereabouts of books from dispersed collections. The final chapter is devoted to the bibliography of book collecting and library history, and to reference sources in a range of related subject areas which are of essential relevance to provenance research. An appendix considers the development of the treatment of provenance information in library catalogues, and provides some suggested guidelines in this area, in which standards have yet to be established.

This subdivision of an integrated subject into convenient discrete parts has meant that a certain amount of repetition between chapters is unavoidable. Some reference sources relate to the subjects of several chapters and these books will be found cited more than once in the body of the text, with differing emphasis as appropriate.

HOW TO USE THIS BOOK

In conclusion, this section offers a series of standard questions relating to provenance research, with suggested strategies for using the information in this book to help to solve them. The list is not exhaustive and it is not presented with any wish to pre-empt the choices of the reader; it is intended only as a set of signposts to the many byways of information contained in the book, which, it is hoped, will not look too much like a maze.

I am trying to decipher an inscription
Use the palaeography section in ch. VIII, and see the examples in ch. II.

I am trying to identify a bookplate/book label/book stamp
Use the resources listed in ch. III.

I am trying to identify an armorial book stamp
Use the resources listed in ch. IV.

I am trying to identify an owner whose name I have from an inscription, bookplate, or other evidence
Use the biography section in ch. VIII.

How can I find out about the books of a particular individual?
His library may have been studied and written about: check the Bibliographies covering book collecting and collectors, the Studies of book collecting and book collectors, and the biographical resources, listed in ch. VIII.

His books may survive as a collection somewhere: check the Directories of library collections in ch. VII.

His library may have been sold, and a catalogue may survive: check the Lists and indexes of sale catalogues in ch. V.

His books may be mentioned in his will: see the sections on Probate inventories and Wills in ch. VI.

Some other contemporary list of his collection may have survived: see the resources listed in ch. VI.

His books may be scattered around various libraries today: use the provenance indexes listed in ch. VII.

Where can I locate a copy of a sale catalogue to which I have a reference?

See the sections on Auctioneers' and Booksellers' catalogues, and on Lists and indexes of catalogues, in ch. V.

I am looking for a history of book ownership in a particular period

See the bibliography of Studies of book collecting and book collectors in ch. VIII.

How should I record provenance in my catalogue?

See the Appendix.

II

INSCRIPTIONS, MOTTOES &
OTHER MANUSCRIPT ADDITIONS

INSCRIPTIONS IN BOOKS

The easiest and most common way to indicate ownership of a book is to write one's name in it. Hand-written inscriptions on title pages or flyleaves form the most frequently encountered evidence of provenance; the practice has been general in this country since at least the twelfth century, and it remains so today. As well as writing their name, some book owners have habitually added their qualifications or profession, their place of residence, the price they paid, or the source of the book; others have added mottoes or monograms, or developed distinctive ways of marking particular pages.

In its most basic form, an inscription consists merely of the name of the owner, or a simple sentence meaning, in one way or another, 'X owns this book':

James Watkins his book
Anne Withypoll owth thys booke
Patience Grymes her lybray
Ex libris Laurentii Traves
Ex opibus Gulielmus Watson
Bridgwateri liber
Sum Gulielmi Voii
Liber Fran. Quarles
Ioannis Broci codex
Wagge me tenet
Joannes Frithus me iure tenet
Harisonne me vindicat

Such inscriptions are commonly written on title pages or front flyleaves, but they may also be found at the end of a text, on the rear flyleaves, or elsewhere within the body of a book. There is considerable scope for variety and eccentricity. A seventeenth-century owner called S. Deane chose to indicate his possession of the 1610 edition of St. Gregory by writing his name in tiny capitals in the larger letters of the title page (fig. 2.1).

Many English owners used the vernacular for their inscriptions in books, but Latin, whose influence on the English educational system remained important until well into the nineteenth century, was commonly used until at least the middle of the eighteenth. English names are often Latinised – William Watson becomes Gulielmus Watsonus, John Brock becomes Joannes Brocus, John Frith becomes Joannes Frithus, etc. – and it is common to find degrees given not as B.A. or M.A. as we know them today, but in their Latin forms, A.B. (Artium Baccalaureus) or A.M. (Artium Magister). The early eighteenth-century example of George Oldham (d.1734), fellow of St. John's College, Cambridge (Collegii Divi Joannis Evangelistae Cantabrigiensis Socius) is typical of the kind of inscription commonly used by university-based owners (fig. 2.2). Scholarly owners sometimes wrote their inscriptions in Greek, particularly in Greek books; see, for example, the late sixteenth-century Greek inscription of William Chark (d.1617) in fig. 2.3, or that of John Partridge, fig. 2.4. Greek characters may be used to represent numerical values – a Greek dictionary will show the numbers associated with each letter – and the four final characters in Partridge's inscription, αψκε, stand for the date 1725. Some owners varied the form of their inscription according to the language of the book concerned; for example, John Morris (1580?-1658), most of whose books were absorbed into the Old Royal Library under Charles II, often wrote 'Iohannes Mauritius' in his Latin books, 'Jean Maurice' in his French books, and 'Giovanni Maurizio' in his Italian books.[1] Chark is another example – he used Greek only in Greek texts, and normally inscribed his name in Latin. Fig. 2.5 shows an instance of two languages on the same title page: Augustine Stywarde (or Steward, as his name is normally standardised today; d.1597) has written his name both in the vernacular, and in a Latinised form ('sum Augustini Senascalli liber').

An important point to bear in mind when interpreting inscriptions is the fluid approach to spelling which prevailed in earlier generations. The notion that every word has one correct form in which it should be written is a relatively modern one; in the sixteenth century, and earlier, it was common practice to use various spellings for any particular word, and it is perfectly normal to find documents of this period, written by one person, in which words appear with different spellings at different points in the text. The tendency to standardisation was a gradual development, partly helped by the spread of the printed word, but it was not until the middle or end of the eighteenth century that the process was complete; Samuel Johnson's *Dictionary*, published in 1755, is traditionally considered to have been an important influence here. This flexible approach to spelling also extended to names, and people were not consistent in spelling either their own names, or those of other people; this applies to both Christian names and surnames. When looking at inscriptions in books, therefore, one must expect to see surnames which would today conform to a standard spelling in various forms – Curtis, for example, as Courtis, Curtes, Curteis, Curtesse, Curteys, Curtice, Curtise (and more), or Mountford as

---

1 T. A. Birrell, *The library of John Morris*, London, 1976, p. xx.

Sancti

GREGORII

NAZIANZENI

Fig. 2.1 Inscription of S. Deane: Bamburgh Library, Durham C.IV.21, St. Gregory Nazianzenus, *In Iulianum invectivae duae*, 1610.

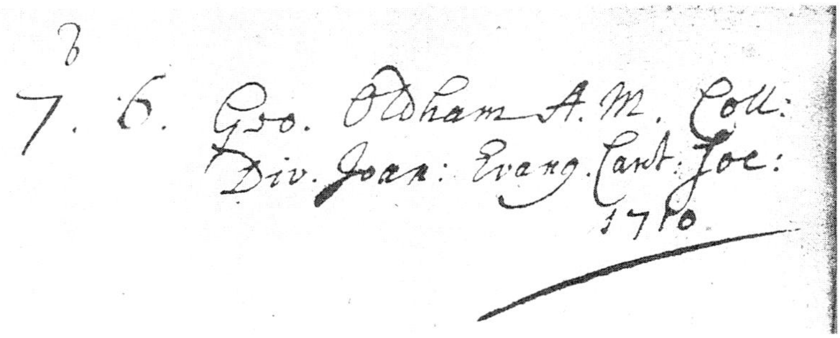

Fig. 2.2 Inscription of George Oldham, Fellow of St. John's College, Cambridge: National Art Library Dyce 7288, J. Pearson, *Opera*, 1688.

Fig. 2.3 The Greek inscription of William Chark: Cosin's Library, Durham R.V.26, G. Codinus, *Selecta de originibus Constantinopolitanis*, 1596.

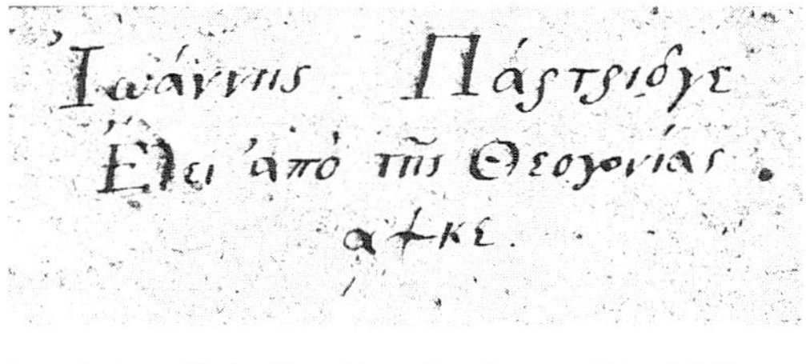

Fig. 2.4 The Greek inscription of John Partridge, dated 1725: British Library 1473.dd.13, J. Harrington, *Horae consecratae*, 1682.

14

Momforth, Mondeford, Monford, Moundeford, Mountfort, Mumford, Mundford, etc. The point is well illustrated by William Stebbing in his biography of Sir Walter Raleigh; he cites over 50 different ways in which the name was written by Raleigh and his contemporaries.[2] In practice, the majority of individual collectors adopted a particular spelling and stuck to it when writing their names in books, but this is not always the case. This is an important point to bear in mind when trying to trace people in biographical dictionaries; it may be necessary to check in several places, using variant spellings.

Many inscriptions consist of a name alone, but owners have often added details of the place or date of purchase, or of their degree, college, or profession; such details are obviously important in the process of identification:

Ra. Neville e Coll. Mer.
[*Ralph Neville of Merton College, Oxford*]
Will. Ashe Coll. Wad. Oxon. 1735
[*William Ashe, Wadham College, Oxford, 1735*]
Liber Henrici Harvei Cantabrig.
[*The book of Henry Harvey, of Cambridge: may mean the book was bought in Cambridge, or may mean only that Harvey lives there*]
Tho. Tounshend pretium 18s. 1678 Norwic.
[*Thomas Tounshend, price 18s., Norwich 1678*]
Thomas Emerson vicarii de Wisebeche
[*Thomas Emerson, Vicar of Wisbech*]

The gift of a book from one person to another will often be recorded in an inscription; again, this can be useful for identifying the people involved, as a search for a link between the two names may narrow down the possibilities:

Tho. Fouli ex dono Gul. Clarei 1614
[*Thomas Fowle, given by William Clare, 1614*]
Rachel Gurdon her book giving by my father Sir Thomas Abdy September the 26 1679
Clarissimo doctissimoque viro Dn. Is. Casaubono Car. Labbaeus D.D.
[*given by Charles Labbe to 'the most illustrious and learned' Isaac Casaubon; the D.D. stands for dono dedit*]

Other forms of inscription involving two names include borrowings, and the certifying of ownership by an associate (the latter is not uncommon in schoolboy and undergraduate inscriptions):

Robert Banfords book borowed by mee Ric. Kilby
William Tranter is the true owner of this book witness John Thorneton

There are, naturally, endless variations on the forms given as examples above, and more eccentric inscriptions will sometimes be found:

---

2 W. Stebbings, *Sir Walter Ralegh*, Oxford, 1891, pp. 30-31. A standard reference work on the development of British surnames and the different spellings through which they have mutated is P. H. Reaney, *A dictionary of British surnames*, London, 1958.

Edward Jackson mislyketh this penne

John Barcllay This booke ise mine he that steles this booke frome me he shaal be hanged on a trie

This booke if yu read out 6 pages a day may be read out in 5 months & 19 dayes N. Hookes

Many owners, in all periods, have included in their inscriptions a note of the price paid for a book; fig. 2.6 shows a typical and randomly selected example from the eighteenth century (see also figs. 8.6 and 8.20 below). Such inscriptions provide an indicator of book prices down the ages, and they become particularly useful when they include, as well as the price, some information on the source of purchase. The chain of provenance can thus be extended backwards. Some collectors, particularly in the late eighteenth and nineteenth centuries, who bought books at auction were in the habit of noting down details of the sale and sometimes the lot number or previous owner. We can therefore make reference to the sale catalogue, if it can be traced, which may help to fill out the picture. A number of major bibliophiles, such as Michael Wodhull (1740-1816) and Richard Heber (1773-1833) are well known for their characteristic notes of this kind[3]; fig. 2.7 shows one in the hand of Alexander Dyce (1789-1869). This example illustrates a caveat to be borne in mind when interpreting auction price lists and marked-up sale catalogues: collectors sometimes use pseudonyms to hide their identity. Inscriptions like this may relate to booksellers' catalogues as well as auction sales, as for example the note by Philip Bliss (1787-1857), shown in fig. 2.8. Such inscriptions can reveal provenance which would otherwise be undetected, because the previous owner has left no mark; some books from the collection of Samuel Johnson (1709-84), recently discovered in the British Library, are identifiable as such only because Charles Burney (1757-1817), who bought them at the auction sale of Johnson's library in 1785, noted this fact on the flyleaves.[4] The inscription from a century earlier, shown in fig. 2.9, is interesting not because it reveals previous ownership, but because it documents the existence of an early book sale which is otherwise unrecorded, as no catalogue has survived; unfortunately, in this case, the writer of the inscription is anonymous.

A number of book owners have favoured **monograms** or **ciphers**, incorporating their initials or the letters of their name, which they would write in their books (for the distinction between a monogram and a cipher, see p. 64 below). Andrew Perne, for example (Master of Peterhouse, Cambridge, d.1589) rarely wrote his name in his books, but regularly inscribed his monogram, combining his initials A P, at the foot of the title page (see fig. 2.10). A contemporary of his, Thomas Byng (Master of Clare College, Cambridge, d.1599), favoured a similar device, sometimes writing his name on title pages, sometimes an abbreviation of his initials T B (fig. 2.11). Michael Honywood, Dean of Lincoln

3 See S. de Ricci, *English collectors of books and manuscripts*, Cambridge, 1930, pp. 81-83, 104.
4 D. Pearson, Unrecorded books from Samuel Johnson's library, *Factotum* 32 (1990), 13-14.

Fig. 2.5 English and Latin inscription of Augustine Steward: National Art Library Clements Dr.3, *Biblia*, 1527.

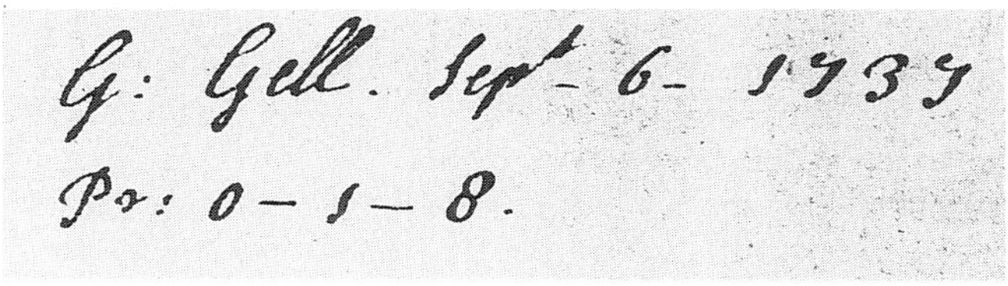

Fig. 2.6 Inscription of G. Gell, with date and price: National Art Library Dyce 951, R. Bentley, *The folly and unreasonableness of atheism*, 1693.

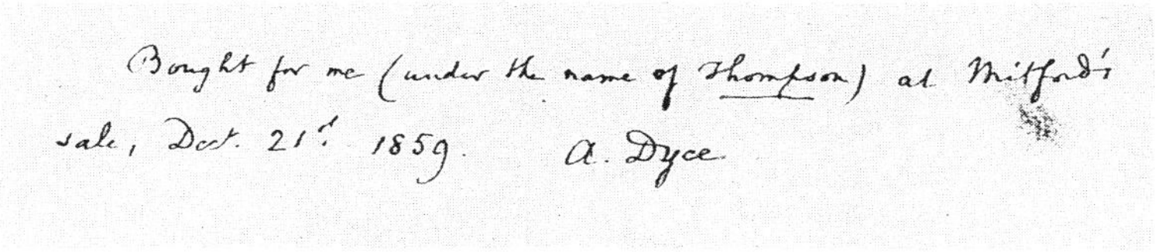

Fig. 2.7 Purchase note by Alexander Dyce: National Art Library Dyce 4963, Horace, [*Opera*], 1728.

Fig. 2.8 Purchase note by Philip Bliss: National Art Library Dyce 4463, A. W. Hare, *A letter to George Martin*, [1814?].

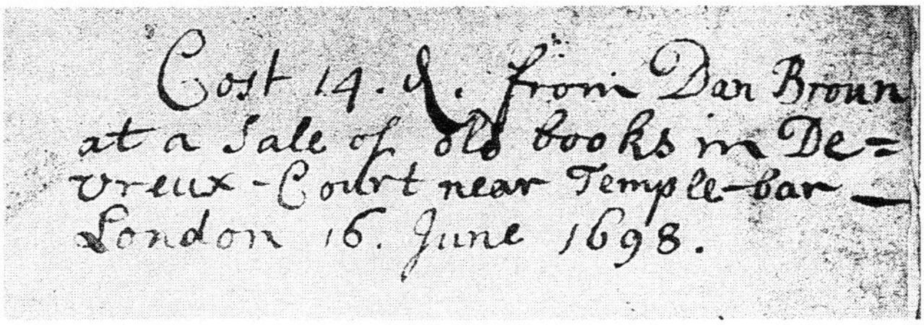

Fig. 2.9 Anonymous note of purchase from a book sale held by Daniel Brown in 1698: J. Bodin, *Artis historicae penus*, 1579, Private collection.

Fig. 2.10 Monogram of Andrew Perne: Peterhouse, Cambridge N.7.24, Q. A. Symmachus, *Epistolarum ad diversos libri decem*, 1580.

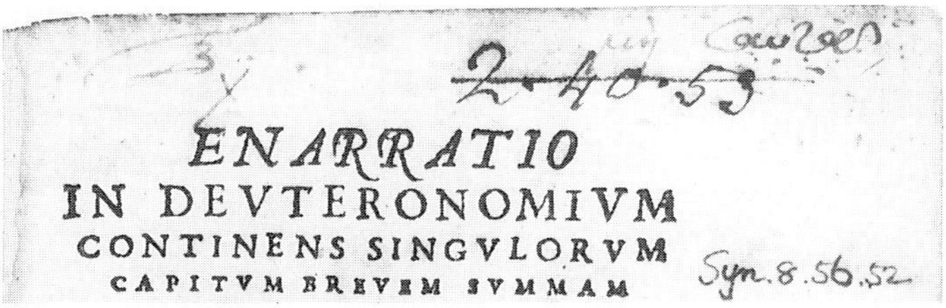

Fig. 2.11 Monogram of Thomas Byng (top left), with his Greek motto μη ταυτα (top right): Cambridge University Library Syn.8.56.52, J. Machabaeus, *Enarratio in Deuteronomium*, 1563.

Fig. 2.12 Monogram of Michael Honywood: Lincoln Cathedral Library, T. May, *The reigne of King Henry the second*, 1633.

18

(1597-1681) used a similar monogram (fig. 2.12). The 'EH' monogram used by Edward, Lord Herbert of Cherbury (1583-1648) is reproduced in Fordyce and Knox's account of Jesus College Library, where many of his books are preserved.[5] Thomas Lorkyn, Regius Professor of Physic at Cambridge (d.1591) used a more complicated monogram incorporating all the letters of his name (fig. 2.13). A later example is C. M. Cracherode (1730-99), benefactor to the British Museum Library, who used a simple monogram of CMC (fig. 2.14). Books which carry a 'W H' monogram followed by a page reference ('p' and a number) in eighteenth-century hand come from the library of William Herbert (1718-95), who amassed a large collection of early English books to enable him to expand Joseph Ames's *Typographical antiquities*; the page number refers to Herbert's augmented edition of 1785-90 (fig. 2.15). A number of monograms and similar devices used by early Scottish book owners are reproduced in *Early Scottish libraries* by J. Durkan and A. Ross (Glasgow, 1961); see their plates XIII (Robert Hindmarsh), XX (unidentified MAE), XXIII (Adam Kinghorn), and XLIII (John Greenlaw).

Other owners have developed codes which indicate their ownership, or show details of acquisition. Philip Bliss (the Oxford antiquary, 1787-1857) marked his ownership of books discreetly by adding a manuscript 'P' before the signature letter 'B', and a 'B' after the signature letter 'P', in the appropriate gatherings (fig. 2.16); a similar system was used by Thomas Jefferson, the American President (1743-1826).[6] John Cosin, Master of Peterhouse and later Bishop of Durham (1594-1672), marked many of his books with the letters 'p m' placed around the imprints, looking very much like a bookseller's code; the significance of these letters has never been worked out (fig. 2.17). Inscriptions in cipher, such as that of Thomas Ma[r?]k (fig. 2.18) may occasionally be met with. Sir Hans Sloane (the physician, 1660-1753, whose library was one of the foundation collections of the British Museum), used a system of alchemical signs to encode price and date of acquisition during the earlier part of his collecting career (fig. 2.19).[7] The Scottish poet William Drummond (1585-1649) occasionally inscribed his name as an anagram; at least one book of his is known which carries the inscription 'Don Murmidumilla'.[8] Sir Edward Sherburne (1618-1702) used to write 'F.S. L.A.' on his title pages, standing for 'Felix Servator Lympidarum aquarum Armiger', a rather tortuous Latinisation of his name: Edward (meaning 'happy guardian', hence 'felix servator') Sherburne (meaning 'bright stream', hence 'lympidarum aquarum').[9]

5 C. J. Fordyce and T. M. Knox, The library of Jesus College, Oxford, *Oxford Bibliographical Society Proceedings and Papers* 5 (1937), 53-115, plate following p. 72.

6 On Jefferson see E. M. Sowerby, *Catalogue of the library of Thomas Jefferson*, Washington, 1952-59, v. 1 p. xiv.

7 See M. A. E. Nickson, Sloane's codes: the solution to a mystery, *Factotum* 7 (1979), 13-18.

8 R. H. MacDonald, *The library of Drummond of Hawthornden*, Edinburgh, 1971, no. 931.

9 See M. D. Reeve, Acidalius on Manilius, *Classical quarterly* ns 41 (1991) 226-239, pp. 235-6.

BASILEAE PER HEN-
RICVM PETRVM.

Fig. 2.13 Monogram of Thomas Lorkyn: Cambridge University Library N*.10.22, A. Benedictus, *Omnium a vertice ad calcem morboru[m] signa*, 1539.

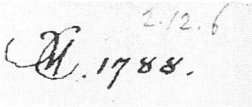

Fig. 2.14 Monogram of C. M. Cracherode: National Art Library Clements HH18, Virgil, [*Opera*], 1545.

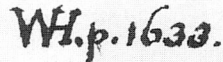

Fig. 2.15 Monogram of William Herbert: Durham University Library SR4.E.19, J. Penry, *A briefe discovery of the untruthes*, 1590.

nature, crooked lines are in some measure reduced to right lines by the definition of quantity, which right lines, *viz.* Sines, Tangents, *P. B. 47.*   and

Fig. 2.16 Characteristic marking of Philip Bliss: Durham University Library ELCY.C45U, T. Urquhart, *The trissotetras*, 1645.

LONDON,
Printed for R. *Dawlman*, at the Signe of the
Bible neere the great Conduit in Fleet-
streete. 1627.

Fig. 2.17 'p m' mark of John Cosin: Cosin's Library, Durham C.III.6, R. Senhouse, *Foure sermons*, 1627.

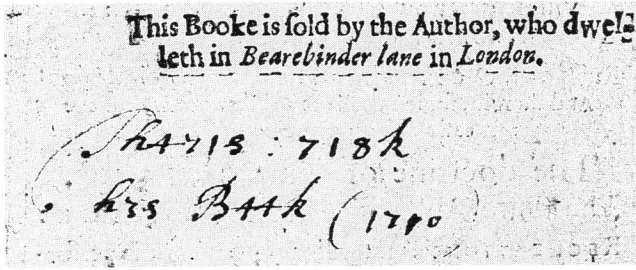

Fig. 2.18 Inscription in cipher of Thomas Ma[r?]k: British Library Ames III/1190, titlepage of W. Webster, *The principles of arithmetick*, 1634.

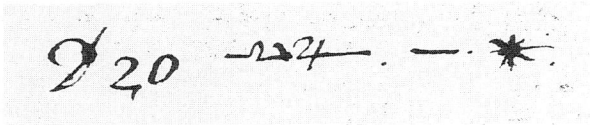

Fig. 2.19 Typical code inscription of Sir Hans Sloane: British Library 545.h.11, H. Mercurialis, *Consultationes*, 1624.

Fig. 2.20 Dating convention used by William Dowsing: British Library Ames III/1679, titlepage of J. Robinson, *The peoples plea*, 1641.

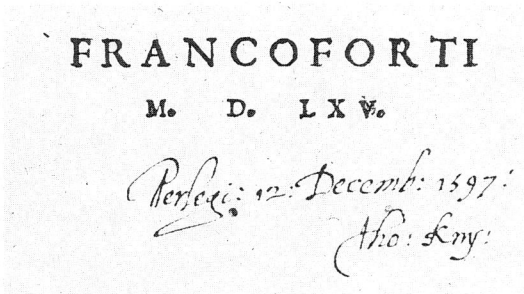

Fig. 2.21 Inscription by Sir Thomas Knyvett, showing the date of reading: Cambridge University Library R.11.18, G. Lily, *Chronicon*, 1565.

It has long been common practice to add the date of acquisition to inscriptions; occasionally, owners have developed unusual and individual ways of expressing the date, such as William Dowsing (1596?-1679?, the iconoclast), who developed a distinctive dating code (fig. 2.20).[10] Less common, but still not infrequently encountered, is the addition of the date of reading; an exponent of this practice was Sir Thomas Knyvett (1539?-1618), who often added a note in the form 'p[er]legi 12 die Decembris 1616' in tiny handwriting at the foot of the title page, or at the end of the book (fig. 2.21). The letters 'C & P', sometimes found on flyleaves, normally stand for 'collated and perfect', to show that the book has been checked as complete. The most celebrated user of this convention is probably Thomas Rawlinson (1681-1725), who regularly wrote 'C & P' on his endleaves, but others have also used it habitually, such as the literary scholar Alexander Dyce (1789-1869), who regularly put 'C. P.' in a small neat hand on his flyleaves (fig. 2.22).[11]

There is a wide variety of other kinds of characteristic marking which owners have developed, and which may be used to establish or confirm provenance identifications. Shelfmarks are more often associated with institutional libraries than private ones, but many individuals with large enough collections have found the need to fix and mark their books in this way. The various pressmarking systems used by John Evelyn (1620-1706) are described and illustrated by Geoffrey Keynes in his bibliography of the diarist.[12] David McKitterick has similarly described the distinctive pressmarks found in the books forming the library of Sir Thomas Knyvett (1539?-1618); in this case the pressmarks were added shortly after the death of the original owner.[13] These were both sizeable libraries, running to well over a thousand volumes, but systematic numbering schemes are also found in more modest collections. The surgeon Joseph Fenton, who was building up his library in the first half of the seventeenth century, regularly marked his title pages not only with his signature and motto, but also with a boxed number (fig. 2.23). Another seventeenth-century example is shown in fig. 2.24, from the collection of an unidentified Thomas Hancox whose library evidently ran to at least 164 books.

Manuscripts previously owned by the Elizabethan scientist John Dee (1527-1608) can sometimes be recognised by a distinctive 'ladder-mark' found in the top right hand corner of a preliminary leaf or the first page of text.[14] The annotations of Gabriel Harvey (1550?-1630) can be recognised not only on the basis of handwriting, but also from his habit of using astrological symbols to denote the subject matter of the text – Mars for military affairs, Mercury for eloquence, and so forth (fig. 2.25).[15] A multiplicity of different marks and signs,

10 See also Maggs catalogue 1156 (1993), no. 105.
11 An example of Rawlinson's 'C. & P.' is reproduced in de Ricci, *English collectors*, p. 46.
12 G. Keynes, *John Evelyn: a study in bibliophily*, Cambridge, 1937, p. 14ff.
13 D. J. McKitterick, *The library of Thomas Knyvett of Ashwellthorpe* c. *1539-1618*, Cambridge, 1978, p. 27 and plate 4.
14 J. Roberts & A. G. Watson, *John Dee's library catalogue*, London, 1990, p. 24.
15 V. Stern, *Gabriel Harvey: his life, marginalia and library*, Oxford, 1979, p. 141.

APHORISMI,

RABI MOY-
SIS MEDICI ANTI-
QVISSIMI AC CELEBERRI-
MI, EX GALENO MEDICORVM
principe collecti: nunc uerò ad ufum
ftudioforum Medicinæ ab interi-
tu uindicati, & iam primùm
in lucem editi.

ITEM,

LOCORVM QVORVNDAM A-
pud Galenum fibijpfis contradicen-
tium caftigatiò & notatio.

DENIQVE,

IOANNIS DAMASCENI A-
phorifmi utiiißimi ad Filium.

Cum INDICE omnium rerum notatu di-
gnarum locupletiffimo.

Cum Gratia & Priuileg. Cæf.Maiefl.

BASILEAE, EX OFFICI-
NA HENRICPETRINA,

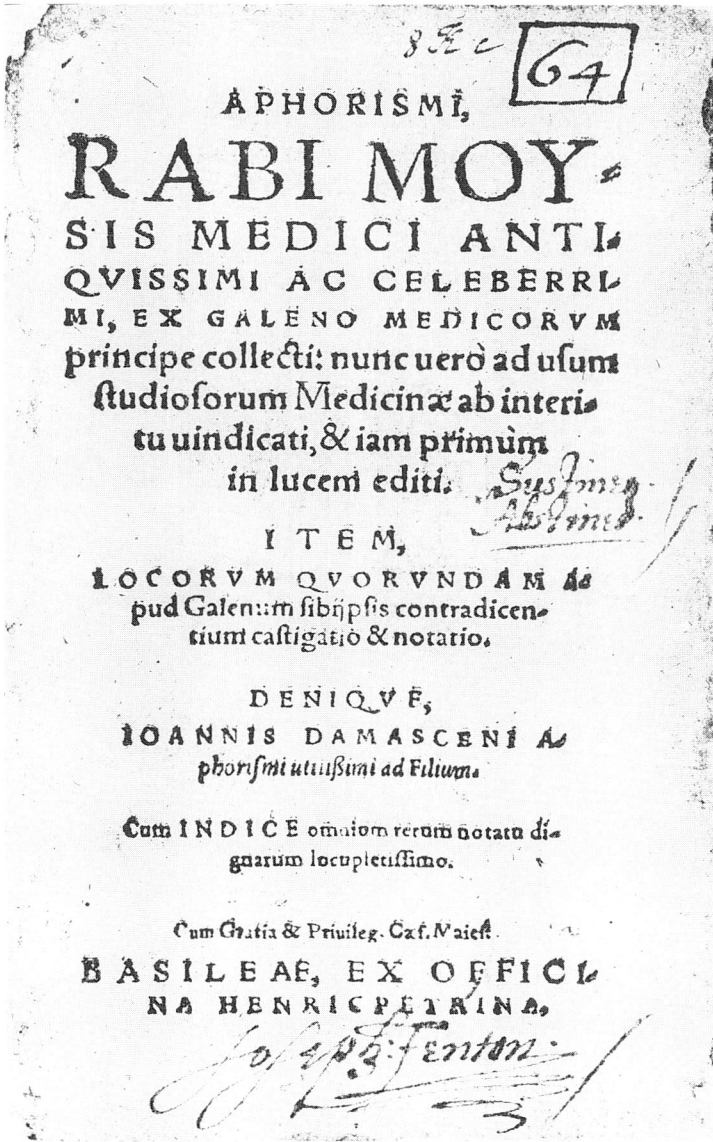

Fig. 2.23 British Library 544.b.22: Moses ben Maimon, *Aphorismi*, 1579, showing the signature, motto and numbering system of Joseph Fenton. '8 K c', to the left of Fenton's number, is the pre-1837 pressmark of the British Museum Library at Montague House. Many of Fenton's books were acquired by Sir Hans Sloane and entered the Museum as part of that foundation collection.

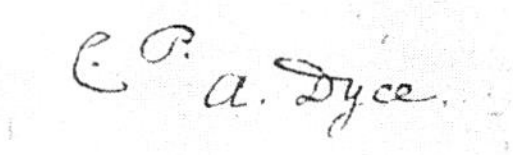

Fig. 2.22 'Collated & perfect' marking of Alexander Dyce: National Art Library Dyce 951, R. Bentley, *The folly and unreasonableness of atheism*, 1693.

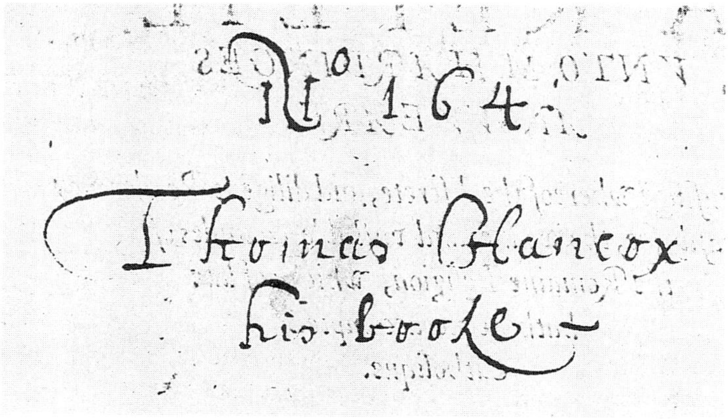

Fig. 2.24 The numbering system of Thomas Hancox: Bamburgh Library, Durham C.IV.11, J. Jewel, *A replie unto M. Hardinges answeare*, 1565.

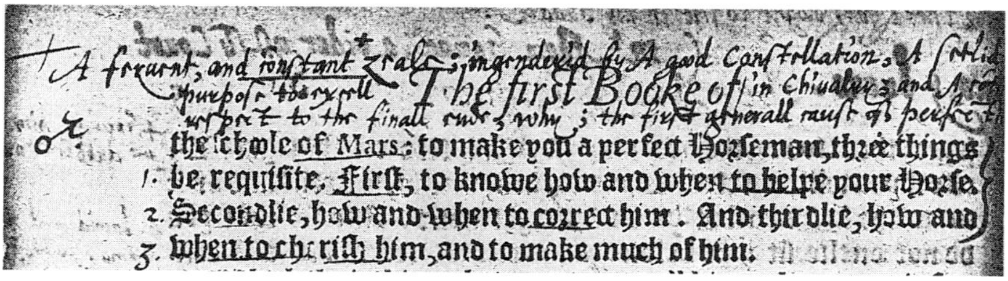

Fig. 2.25 An example of the astrological symbols used by Gabriel Harvey when annotating: British Library C.175.i.4, T. Blundevill, *The foure chiefest offices*, 1580.

which can be used to detect the ownership of John Locke (1632-1704), is described by John Harrison and Peter Laslett in their reconstruction of his library.[16] Distinctive markings may comprise no more than a recognisable handwriting or pattern of inscription, although there is no easy guide to the decipherment of such things; there are odd well-known exceptions such as the

16 J. Harrison & P. Laslett, *The library of John Locke*, 2nd edn, Oxford, 1971, pp. 63-65.

characteristic price and date markings often used by Narcissus Luttrell (1657-1732) on his pamphlets, often the only trace of his ownership.[17]

The tag ... **et amicorum** is often associated with the French collector Jean Grolier (1479-1565), because his celebrated bindings, among the most handsome European bindings of the period, often incorporated the phrase 'Io. Grolierii et amicorum' ('Belonging to Jean Grolier, and his friends').[18] It was however a popular phrase for ownership inscriptions, most particularly in the sixteenth century, and many English and Scottish collectors of the time used it in manuscript inscriptions; examples are John Fox, fellow of Corpus Christi College, Oxford (d. ca. 1530), John Christopherson, Bishop of Chichester (d. 1558), John Greenlaw, of Haddington (d. 1566), and Edward Seymour, Earl of Hertford (1539?-1621), but there are many others. Although the phrase was most commonly used in the sixteenth century, it is also found less frequently among later owners, in the seventeenth century and just occasionally in the eighteenth (e.g. in the books of Joseph Wasse, 1672-1738, the classical scholar). The phrase is also found in variant forms, e.g. 'Liber Frynde et amicorum eius', 'Johannes Gowghe mihi et meis'. A study of the use of 'et amicorum', most particularly its popularity and spread in Europe in the late fifteenth and early sixteenth centuries, was published by G. D. Hobson: 'Et amicorum', *The Library* 5th ser 4 (1949), 87-99.

MOTTOES

During the sixteenth and seventeenth centuries (the habit was at its peak in the second half of the sixteenth century, and the first half of the seventeenth), it became common practice to add mottoes to manuscript ownership inscriptions in books. These mottoes are usually written on the title page, and they may or may not be directly adjacent to the owner's signature; some examples are shown in figs. 2.10, 2.23 and 8.20. A motto is defined in the *Oxford English Dictionary* as (among other things) 'a proverbial or pithy maxim adopted by a person as his rule of conduct'. They are more usually encountered in a heraldic context; the use of mottoes, as distinctive phrases or slogans used by individuals and their descendants, developed during the middle ages as an heraldic extra, and ever since then most families entitled to bear arms have also had a family motto. Although particular mottoes may become firmly identified with particular families and remain unchanged for generations, their use is not regulated by the College of Arms and mottoes are not as a rule specified in grants of arms. Some of the earliest mottoes, e.g. the English royal motto *Dieu et mon droit*, are thought to have originated as war cries, but others clearly developed as puns on family names, e.g. the motto of the Cavendish family, *Cavendo tutus*. Such mottoes are often incorporated in heraldic bookplates.

17 A good example is reproduced as no. 25 in R. E. Stoddard, *Marks in books*, Cambridge, MA, 1985.

18 See H. M. Nixon, *Bookbindings from the library of Jean Grolier*, London, 1965.

The mottoes used in inscriptions in books tend to be rather different in character from heraldic mottoes, which are commonly concerned with such virtues as honour, loyalty or fortitude. The most common type of motto used in books is a pious apothegm on the subject of personal salvation. The popularity of mottoes of this type in the sixteenth and seventeenth centuries can be seen as akin to the contemporary love of emblems and emblem books. There are numerous variations on the theme of Christ's death as our life, or death as gain, e.g. 'Christus mihi vita, et mors lucrum', 'Mihi vita Christus, et mori lucrum', 'Mors Christi vita mea', 'Post tenebras spero lucem', 'Vita Christus mors lucrum', etc. Others incite religious devotion or contemplation in various ways, e.g. 'Cantemus domino gloriose', 'Omnes dies gradus ad mortem', 'Sola salus servire deo'. The more secular themes of Ben Jonson's motto, 'Tanquam explorator', or John Evelyn's 'Omnia explorate: meliora retinente', are less usual. Some are quotations from recognisable sources, such as John Donne's 'Per Rachel ho servito, et non per Lea', a line from Petrarch, which is thought to indicate Donne's reluctant pursuit of a life of action rather than one of contemplation.

Most of these mottoes are in Latin, although it is not uncommon to find ones in English or Greek, less common to find them in Hebrew, French, Italian or Spanish. Some owners adopted one particular motto and used no other (e.g. William Crashawe, who did not deviate from 'Servire deo regnare est'), while others adopted a series of phrases which took their fancy (examples are Thomas Lorkyn, or Sir Thomas Knyvett). Slight variations in wording or word order are sometimes found; Francis Quarles, for example, sometimes wrote 'Frustra fruitur qui non utitur', and sometimes 'Qui hoc non utitur frustra fruitur'. Owners might write several mottoes on the same title page, or vary the language of their motto to suit the language of the book. A few owners used mottoes which reflected their name in some way, as in George Walker's 'He that walkes pure, walkes sure', or the 'Will and walke aright' of William Walker; Matthew Wren always capitalised the letters V in his 'Moriendo ViVam' to show off his initials. One motto in particular, 'Non est mortale quod opto', was especially popular and was used by many people between the end of the sixteenth century and the end of the seventeenth; for a series of notes on this motto and some of its occurrences, see *The Book Collector* 9 (1960), 327-329; 10 (1961), 446; 11 (1962), 211; and 16 (1967), 507-508.

The following is a preliminary attempt to bring together the mottoes used by British book owners. It cannot pretend to be complete, as the practice was very widespread, but it includes the better-known examples and many less-known ones, based on the evidence found in books in a number of libraries. It is always difficult, when confronted with an isolated example, to know whether the motto in question was used as a once-off or as a regular habit; but we cannot sort the categories out until we have tried to construct a systematic record. Brief biographical details are given when it is possible to identify individuals with certainty; in other cases, an approximate date is given. '16/17th c' should be interpreted as 'late sixteenth century or early seventeenth'. I have tried to exclude heraldic mottoes, which owners sometimes added to their books (for example, Edward Seymour, Earl of Hertford, 1539?-1621, sometimes inscribed his books with his family motto 'Foy pour devoir'). Mottoes are worth recording, as a motto without a name may occasionally allow the owner to be identified, although it should not be assumed that particular mottoes listed here were used only by the people named. The finding of 'Non est mortale quod opto' in a book, without a name, will carry the researcher little further forward, but a book with 'Tanquam explorator' in the top right hand corner of the title page is a different matter.

The standard list of heraldic mottoes is *Elvin's handbook of mottoes*, revised by R. Pinches, 2nd revised edition, London, 1971, which lists several thousand mottoes adopted by British families. A number of the mottoes used in books were also used separately as family mottoes, and Elvin is a useful source for translations, which are always included. Another source which may be useful is L. G. Pine, *A dictionary of mottoes*, London, 1983, although this has a greater emphasis on the modern use of mottoes by institutions and military units.

The list below includes references to at least one known example of the occurrence of each motto. In order to keep the list to a manageable size, bibliographical details of the books in question have not been included, but enough information should be given to allow researchers to consult them, if desired; most of the books are uniquely identified by their shelfmarks. The following abbreviations are used within the list:

BC   *The Book Collector*
BL   British Library
Bodl. Bodleian Library
CUL Cambridge University Library
Durkan & Ross *Early Scottish libraries*, 1958
Oates J. C. T. Oates, *A catalogue of the fifteenth-century printed books in the University Library, Cambridge*, 1954

a jamais malheureux
    John Grove 16/17th c; e.g. St. John's, Cambridge Mm.8.54
Adde vel adime
    Edmund Porter early 17th c; e.g. BL 1002.g.1
Age, si quid agis
    Robert Byng, 17th c; e.g. Durham University Library R.XXVII.I.13; Trinity, Cambridge M.16.57, W.11.2
Alterius non sit qui suus essi potest
    Paul Magee 17th c; e.g. BL 1507/1042
Amas victoria curam
    J. Herbord late 16th c; e.g. Emmanuel, Cambridge 311.4.37
Amor vincit omnia
    John Willoughby late 16th c; cited by W. C. Hazlitt, The book-collector, *1904, p. 204*
Ante obitum nemo

J. Gilsom 16/17th c?; see C. Deedes et al, The Old Town Hall Library of Leicester, *1919, p. 65*

Arte non forte
Thomas Moundeford 16/17th c [?the physician, 1550-1630]; e.g. St. John's, Cambridge Ll.4.13

Auspice Christo
Edmund Hastings early 17th c; e.g. Bamburgh Library, Durham O.II.14

Be not dulle
Duckett 16/17th c [possibly Gregory Duckett, d.1624, Cambridge University Librarian, or his brother Lionel, d.1603, fellow of Jesus College, Cambridge]; e.g. Oates 402

Bene qui latuit, bene vixit
Richard Smith 16/17th c; e.g. John Rylands Library R128618; copy of F. Albergati, Trattato del modo di riddure, *1600, in Exeter Cathedral Library*

Cantemus domino gloriose
Stephen Vaughan late 16th c; e.g. BL Ames VII.143

Christus felici tute Christo
Samuel Crooke 17th c [possibly the divine, 1575-1649]; e.g. Emmanuel, Cambridge 333.1.68

Christus mihi vita, et mori lucrum
Alexander Arundell 16/17th c [possibly the Rector of Lapford, Devon, d.1623]; e.g. Pembroke, Cambridge 7.10.22

Christus mihi vita, mors mihi dulce lucrum
Thomas Plumpton 16/17th c; e.g. Peterborough Cathedral B.1.39

Coelum patria Christus via
*William Neale 16/17th c; e.g. BL Ames VII.94; Sidney Sussex, Cambridge M.7.18; Bodl. *4to.B18(1).Art.BS*

Cominus et eminus
Thomas Greensted 16/17th c; e.g. BL Ames I.540

Contemplatio animi pabulum
William Mount, 1545-1602, Master of the Savoy; e.g. CUL Syn.6.56.7

Contentus pace vivere
John Rogers 17th c; e.g. BL Ames I.572

Cor unum via una
William Mount, 1545-1602, Master of the Savoy; e.g. CUL Syn.6.56.7

Crux Christi scala coeli
Edm. Littleton late 16th c; e.g. BL 1008.a.4

Crux Christi vita justi
Henry Wood, 16/17th c; e.g. Winchester Cathedral Library XIX.D.4

Crux veritatis comes
Richard Barnes, 1532-1587, Bishop of Durham, also his son Emmanuel (1561-1614); see M. Raine, A catalogue of the printed books in the Library of the Dean and Chapter of York, *York, 1896, p. vii.*

De juegos el mejor es con la hoja
Rowland Woodward, 1573-1636?, diplomat and friend of John Donne; e.g. BL 568.b.22; Maggs catalogue 1121 (1990), no. 16

De nouveau tout est beau De saison tout est bon
Robert Kemp early 17th c; e.g. BL C.64.e.2

Deum timere est sapere
Thomas Wynne 17th c; e.g. BL Ames III.1965
Deus est via
Richard Webster late 16th c; e.g. Peterhouse, Cambridge K.7.2
Deus providebit
J. Wood 17th c; e.g. Carlisle Cathedral Library Z.5.15
Disce docedus adhuc
Richard Cosin, 1549?-1597, Dean of the Arches; e.g. Westminster Abbey R.2.53
Disce ut doceas
Stephen West, probably the Rector of Barcombe, d.1622; e.g. CUL C.6.21; Winchester Cathedral Library IX.D.4
Disco ut sciam, scio ut doctam
Humfry Byng, 17th c; e.g. Bamburgh Library, Durham A.VI.5
Domat omnia virtus
Robert Langhorne 16/17th c; e.g. CUL F.13.22*
Dominus regent omne: & nihil mihi deerit
Robert Jermyn [probably Sir Robert Jermyn, M.P. for Suffolk and East Looe, d.1614]; e.g. Jesus, Cambridge K.10.27
Dominus regit me et nihil mihi deerit
Joannes Bradford 16th c; e.g. BL 3103.f.1
Δοξα θεω
Alexander Gill, 1565-1635, High-master of St. Paul's School; e.g. Westminster Abbey P.1.63
ἐρχεται νυξ
John Morris, 1595-1648, Regius Professor of Hebrew at Oxford; e.g. BL 978.b.8, CUL Z.3.39, Bodl. 4°.Rawl.597
Esse quod debis esse studeas
William Bagge, d.1657, fellow of Gonville & Caius; e.g. Ushaw College, Durham XVII.F.4.2
Et ad aratram et ad aram
Lancelot Andrewes, 1555-1626, Bishop of Winchester; see D. D. C. Chambers, A catalogue of the library of Bishop Lancelot Andrewes, Transactions of the Cambridge Bibliographical Society *5 (1970) 99-121.*
Et arato et arae
Robert Silby 16/17th c; e.g. CUL H.10.49
Et vitam eternam amen
Robert Ryece 17th c; e.g. CUL B.9.36
Exitus acta probat
*Robert Bowne, early 17th c; e.g. Bodl. *4to.P4(14).Th*
Facta loquantur
Sir Daniel Donne, d.1617, lawyer; e.g. CUL E.12.77
Fato quam voto
Sir Edward Hoby, 1560-1617, courtier; e.g. Christie's sale 21 October 1992, lot 160 (illustrated)
Festina lente
William Haiman 17th c; e.g. St. John's, Cambridge Dd.19.25
William Huett 16th c; e.g. BL 1484.g.8

Fide cui vide
  Edward Michelborne, 1565-1626, Latin poet; e.g. BL 997.i.1
Fide et fortitudine
  Melchior Harvey 16/17th c; e.g. Pembroke, Cambridge 11.1.30
Frugalitas voluntaria quadam paupertas
  Thomas Jermyn 17th c; e.g. BL Ames III.1257
Frustra fruitur qui non utitur
  Francis Quarles, 1592-1644, the poet; e.g. BL 1478.a.25
Fuggire il desio, e fuggire la penitenza
  Robert Kemp early 17th c; e.g. BL C.64.e.2
Futura praeteritis
  Renald Smith late 16th c; e.g. CUL M.5.75*
Gaudet pacientia duris
  Robert Mellish early 17th c; e.g. Pembroke, Cambridge 2.4.15
γηρασκω δ'ἀεὶ πολλὰ διδασκόμενος
  Thomas Skeffington, d.1592, fellow of Trinity College, Cambridge; see P. Gaskell, Trinity College Library: the first 150 years, *Cambridge, 1980, p. 42.* An example outside Trinity College is BL 999.b.5
Gloria vincenti corona
  Thomas Dawson late 16th c [possibly the Rector of Swineshead, d.1639]; e.g. CUL R.12.55*
  G Lawson 16/17th c; e.g. Carlisle Cathedral Library E.5.8
Gratia dei mecum
  W. Ely 16th c; e.g. Hereford Cathedral Library N.5.6
  Robert Hindmarsh, d.ca.1500, canon of St. Andrews; e.g. National Library of Scotland Inc. 309, St. Andrews University Typ.SwBA89AA
Gratia dei sum quod sum
  Anthony Molineux 16th c; e.g. Emmanuel, Cambridge 305.1.27
Habere eripitur habuisse nunquam
  George Sandys, 1578-1644, poet and traveller; see M. A. Rogers, 'Books from the library of George Sandys', BC *28 (1974) 361-370.*
He that walkes pure, walkes sure
  George Walker early 17th c; e.g. Emmanuel, Cambridge 305.4.60
Hebel est omnis Adam
  William Brewster, 1567-1644, pilgrim father; e.g. Sotheby's, New York, 1.11.1993, lot 19
In me vivit qui pro me mortuus est
  Ra. Wright early 17th c; e.g. Hereford Cathedral Library D.8.12
In mundo spes nulla boni
  G. Hauthorn, probably Gilbert Hawthorne, d.1634, Rector of Caundle Bishop, Dorset; e.g. St. Catharine's, Cambridge E.III.61
In silentio et spe erit fortitudo vestra
  John Cameron, mid 16th c, monk of Kinloss; see Durkan & Ross plate XXVIII
In te Jesu spes mea recumbit
  Alexander Anderson, d.1577, Principal of King's College, Aberdeen; e.g. Aberdeen University Inc.50, Inc.95
Introite, nam et hic dii sunt
  James Upton 17th c; e.g. BL 540.a.3, 540.a.7
Inveniam viam
  Robert Sidney, 1st Earl of Leicester, 1563-1626; e.g. BL C.64.i.6

Jesu esto mihi Jesus
Philemon Blethin 16/17th c; e.g. Hereford Cathedral Library G.7.7
Jovis omnia plena
William Camden, 1551-1623, the antiquary; e.g. Bodl. L 23 Art.Seld.
Laus impiorum brevis
James Hill, late 16th c; e.g. Emmanuel, Cambridge S4.5.80
Legendo proficio, proficiendo lego
Samuel Otes 16th c; e.g. CUL 2.25.27
Libenter qui tacet tuto loquitur
James Smith 16/17th c; e.g. CUL P*.1.2-4
Live, love and learn
Robert Bele; e.g. BL 1059.a.5(1)
Live with content
John Marriott 16/17th c; e.g. Peterhouse, Cambridge F.4.44
Lucem spero
Sir Robert Kemp, d.1647; e.g. John Rylands Library SC1863A; King's, Cambridge K.63.46
Mala sperno meliora spero
George Chaworth, Baron & Viscount Chaworth, 1569-1639; e.g. John Rylands Library R17972
μη ταυτα
Thomas Byng, d.1599, Master of Clare College; e.g. Emmanuel, Cambridge 329.7.20; CUL Aa*.3.15, Rel.a.55.4; Bodl. Byw.O.7.2
Mea messis in herba
John Handford 16/17th c; e.g. BL C.64.e.2
Mea portio Christus
Charles Fitzgeffrey, 1575-1638, poet and divine; e.g. BL 1474.aaa.18
Memento mori
William Mount, 1545-1602, Master of the Savoy; e.g. CUL Syn.6.56.7
Mihi vita Christus
George Johnson 17th c; e.g. CUL Syn.8.56.3
Robert Phipps 16th c; e.g. BL Ames VII.62
Mihi vita Christus est, et mori lucrum
Jer. Wright 16/17th c; e.g. CUL L*.16.24
Misericordia dei
Thomas Bradock, d.1608, translator of Jewel; e.g. Westminster Abbey Z.3.34
Moriendo ViVam
Matthew Wren, 1585-1637, Bishop of Ely; e.g. Pembroke, Cambridge 5.2.18, 5.11.15, 9.9.20
Mors Christi vita hominum
Edward Lapworth, 1574-1636, Sedleian Reader of Natural Philosophy at Oxford; see C. J. Fordyce & T. M. Knox, The Library of Jesus College, Oxford, Oxford Bibliographical Society Proceedings and Papers 5 (1937), 53-115, p. 85
Mors Christi vita mea
Myles Bownes, d.1630, Rector of Hampreston, Devon; e.g. BL Ames VIII.518
Mors dat intellectum
Isaac Chorinus 16/17th c; e.g. York Minster Library VII.L.2
Mors mihi lucrum

Samuel Otes 16th c; e.g. CUL 2.25.27
Ry. Wall early 17th c; e.g. CUL O.10.43(2)
Nemo sibi satis est
Hamlet Assheton, late 16th c; e.g. BL Ames I.376
Nescis quid serus vesper vehat
John Day 16/17th c; e.g. CUL M*.11.47
Nihil nisi quod nollem
Edward Fotherby late 16th c; e.g. CUL S.6.68
Nihil virtute deest
John Draycott 16/17th c; e.g. Emmanuel, Cambridge 329.6.62
Nil rectum quod a deo directum
John Ailmer 17th c; e.g. Bamburgh Library, Durham A.IV.35
Non est mortale quod opto
   Henry Bourchier, 5th Earl of Bath, ca.1587-1654; e.g. CUL Q*.11.6; All Souls, Oxford
      SR41.a.5; Marsh's Library, Dublin A.6.32 (see BC 9 (1960) p. 328, 16 (1967) p. 507)
   J. Burton, 17th c; e.g. BL Ames IX.1437
   George Butler mid 17th c; e.g University College, Oxford K.8.1 (see BC 16 (1967) p. 507)
   Fulco Cartwright [probably the scholar of Peterhouse, 1639]; e.g. CUL Q.5.47 (see BC 9
      (1960) p. 327)
   William Dawson 17th c; e.g. St. John's, Oxford HB3/E2 (see BC 16 (1967) p. 507)
   Margaret Draper early 17th c; e.g. CUL TC.54.59 (see BC 9 (1960) p. 327)
   John Gray, 1646-1717, of Haddington; e.g National Library of Scotland Gray 272
   Francis Hall late 17th c; e.g. CUL G.10.35 (see BC 9 (1960) p. 328)
   Ed. Harryson early 17th c; e.g. Sidney Sussex, Cambridge L.6.46
   George Innes mid 17th c; e.g. CUL Syn.8.58.162 (see BC 9 (1960) p. 328)
   Stephen Limiter, fellow of All Souls 1572; e.g. Sotheby's, New York, 1.11.1993, lot 19, and
      see the note by J. Callard, BC 20 (1971), pp. 248-9
   Edward Mainwaring 16/17th c; e.g. Oriel, Oxford X.f.4 (see BC 16 (1967) p. 507)
   Ra. Marshall early 17th c; e.g. Brasenose, Oxford Lath.N.12.1 (see BC 16 (1967) pp.
      507-8)
   Jo. Middleton, 17th c; e.g. John Rylands Library R47447
   William Mount, 1545-1602, Master of the Savoy; e.g. CUL Syn.6.56.7 (see BC 9 (1960),
      p. 328, 'Hownt')
   John Payne early 17th c; e.g. CUL LE.7.79(6) (see BC 9 (1960) p. 328)
   George Ryves, d.1613, Warden of New College, Oxford; e.g. New College MM.12.7,
      MM.13.7, etc. (see BC 16 (1967) p. 508)
   William Spenser 17th c [? the fellow of Trinity College, Cambridge, d.1714]; e.g. CUL
      Ms.Dd.1.24 (see BC 9 (1960) p. 328)
   Richard Stafford early 17th c; e.g. Bamburgh Library, Durham M.III.25
   Thomas Swan early 17th c; e.g. CUL 7.40.11 (see BC 9 (1960) p. 328)
   John Whincop early 17th c [possibly the Rector of Clothall, Herts., d.1647]; e.g. CUL
      Syn.8.61.53 (see BC 9 (1960) p. 328)
   John Young, probably the Master of Pembroke College, Cambridge, 1534?-1605; e.g.
      Westminster Abbey M.2.29
Non mihi sed Christo
   John Field, late 16th c (? fellow of Pembroke, Cambridge, 1593); e.g. Peterborough Cathedral
      D.5.2; Peterhouse, Cambridge D.5.2; Gonville & Caius M.13.3
Non mordet qui moret nec nocet qui docet

John Simson 16/17th c; e.g. St. Catharine's, Cambridge D.III.13
Non omnis moriar
  Samuel Clarke mid 17th c; e.g. Pembroke, Cambridge 3.17.3
Non quaero mihi utile est sed quod utilis
  Thomas James, 1573?-1629, Bodley's Librarian; e.g. Chetham's Library L.7.48; Bodl. 4to.B.3.Th, 8vo.M.6.Art, and numerous others
Nosce teipsum
  Arthur Hildersam, 1563-1632, puritan divine; e.g. Oates 3737
  Thomas Lorkyn, 1528?-1591, Regius Professor of Physic at Cambridge; e.g. BL 547.a.7; CUL N*.12.33
O vita faelici brevis, misero longa
  Thomas Plumpton 16/17th c; e.g. Peterborough Cathedral B.1.39
Omnes dies gradus ad mortem
  William Rogers, 17th c; e.g. Bamburgh Library, Durham H.II.42
Omnia explorate: meliora retinente
  John Evelyn, 1620-1706, the diarist; see G. Keynes, John Evelyn: a study in bibliophily with a bibliography of his writings, *2nd edn, Oxford, 1968, p. 12.*
Omnium daemon viro nato   In }   uno

                            Ab }   } omnium

                            Per } unum }

                            Ad }

  H. Lansell 17th c; e.g. St. John's, Cambridge Kk.2.23
Only sinne is wretchedness
  Katharine Forster 16/17th c; e.g. CUL Syn.8.55.92
οὐδεν γλυκύτερον ἡ πάντα εἰδέναι
  Thomas Skeffington, d.1592, fellow of Trinity College. Cambridge; see P. Gaskell, Trinity College Library: the first 150 years, *Cambridge, 1980, p. 42*
Pacem Jehovah negat impiis
  Thomas Nicolson, d.1625, of Aberdeen; see BC 11 (1962), p. 211
πανταχη την ἀληθειαν
  Narcissus Marsh, 1638-1713, Archbishop of Dublin; see the examples reproduced in M. McCarthy, All graduates and gentlemen, *Dublin, 1980, pp. 48, 123*
Pars mea Cristus
  Thomas Day early 16th c; e.g. CUL Syn.5.51.4
Patiar, ut potiar
  Simon Gunton, 1609-1676, historian of Peterborough; e.g. BL 691.b.6
Per Rachel ho servito, & non per Lea
  John Donne, 1573-1631, the poet; see G. Keynes, A bibliography of Dr. John Donne, *4th edn, Oxford, 1973, pp. 259-60.*
περὶ παντὸς τὴν ἐλευθερίαν
  John Selden, 1584-1654, the lawyer; see W. D. Macray, Annals of the Bodleian Library, *2nd edn, Oxford, 1890, p. 121*
Pervenire ad summum nisi ex principiis non potes
  Robert Bowne, early 17th c; e.g. Bodl. *4to.P4(14).Th
Φιλοτιμεισθε ησυχαζειν
  Thomas Holbech, 17th c; see W. D. Macray, Register of the members of St Mary Magdalen College, *Oxford ns II, 1897, p. 219*
Pietas homini tutissima virtus

John Yerdley late 16th c; e.g. St. Catharine's, Cambridge C.I.16
Pietas magnus questus
    Thomas Horner 17th c; e.g. Canterbury Cathedral Library W/L-6-2
Pietati non patrimonio
    William Pulleyn late 16th c; e.g. University College, Oxford H.31.9
Piu fa tempo che forzza
    Sir Thomas Knyvett, 1539?-1618, of Ashwellthorpe; see D. J. McKitterick, The library of
       Sir Thomas Knyvett, *Cambridge, 1978, p. 7*
Piu pha tempo cha forza. Time doth more than violens
    Henry Wyndham 16th c; e.g. CUL 1.23.23
Plenitudo legis est dilectio
    Richard Cosin, 1549?-1597, Dean of the Arches; e.g. Westminster Abbey T.1.22
πολλὰ μανθανόμενος πλέιο λανθανομένος
    Thomas Skeffington, d.1592, fellow of Trinity College, Cambridge; see P. Gaskell, Trinity
       College Library: the first 150 years, *Cambridge, 1980, p. 42*
Portia meo deus
    Thomas Johe 16/17th c; e.g. BL Ames I.422
Post tenebras spero lucem
    Ra. Downes 16/17th c; e.g. BL Ames I.357
    Humphrey Hyde late 16th c; e,g, Chichester Cathedral 3.D.14
    Renald Smith late 16th c; e.g. CUL M*.5.75
    Richard Taylor 16th c; e.g. Emmanuel, Cambridge 322.6.91
    W. Wickham late 16th c; e.g. St. John's, Cambridge Aa.G.25.23
Potiora spero
    Edward Poyntz early 17th c; e.g. Hereford Cathedral Library S.6.13
Praesentibus feror, spero meliora
    J. Young early 17th c; e.g. CUL C.6.57
Praeter spem bonam nihil
    Melchior Harvey 16/17th c; e.g. Pembroke, Cambridge 11.1.30
Pulchra res est vitam ante mortem consummasse
    Samuel Burton, 1569-1634, Archdeacon of Gloucester; e.g. Gloucester Cathedral O.3.4
Quae nocent docent
    Robert Morely 16th c; e.g. BL IA.39907
Quantum est quod restat
    William Alabaster, 1567-1640, poet; e.g. Bodleian 8vo.S.32.Art.Seld.
Quem fortem videris miserum neges
    Charles Blount 16th c; e.g. Hereford Cathedral Library G.7.3
Qui hoc non utitur frustra fruitur
    Francis Quarles, 1592-1644, the poet; e.g. Sidney Sussex, Cambridge K.4.11
Qui sum sentio Quis ero spero
    Beza Stalham early 17th c; e.g. Sidney Sussex, Cambridge L.6.13
Qui vicerit non ledetur secunda morte
    Edward Maie 16/17th c?; see C. Deedes et al, The Old Town Hall Library of Leicester,
       1919, p. 27
Quod fuit durum pati meminisse dulce est
    Robert Langhorne 16/17th c; e.g. CUL F*.13.22
Quod tibi non vis alteri non fueris
    Thomas Jermyn 17th c; e.g. St. John's, Cambridge N.3.12

Quod veritas voluit, non potest impediri
  Thomas Stevens 16th c; e.g. Peterhouse, Cambridge M.2.1
Quos felices cynthia vidit videt miseros abitura dies
  Henry Briggs 16/17th c; e.g. York Minster Library III.O.4
Res tuas age
  Richard Culverwell, late 16th c, benefactor of Emmanuel College, Cambridge; e.g. Emmanuel 302.3.41
  Henry Molle, c.1597-1658, Public orator at Cambridge; e.g. Sidney Sussex, Cambridge F.3.5
  William Hutchinson, d.1616, Archdeacon of Cornwall; e.g. copy of J. Duns Scotus, Quaestiones, 1580, in Exeter Cathedral Library
Respice finem
  T. Fitzherbert 16th c; e.g CUL A*.7.18
Restat veniam deus sibi praestat
  Thomas Symson 16th c; e.g. Bodl. Auct.1Q4.12(1)
Rosaeus, dominus
  Joannes Luidus 16/17th c; e.g. Peterhouse, Cambridge I.3.18
Ruit hora
  Gilbert Watts, d.1657, fellow of Lincoln College, Oxford; see P. Morgan, Oxford libraries outside the Bodleian, *1980, pp. 63-4*
Rursus post tenebram spero lucem
  William Pulleyn late 16th c; e.g. University College, Oxford H.31.9
Salus mea Christi triscia
  Sir Edward Henden, 1568-1644, Baron of the Exchequer; e.g. Harvard Law School ms.1195
Salus mea ex agno
  Henry Vaughan, 1622-95, poet and physician; see E. Wolf, Some books of early English provenance in the Library Company of Philadelphia, *BC 9 (1960) 275-84, p. 282*
Sapit qui sustinet
  R. Southwell, 16/17th c; e.g. Chetham's Library 2.H.1.51
Sat sito si, sat bene
  Nathaniel Bacon, 1547-1622, sheriff of Norfolk; e.g. BL 1492.ff.18
  Nicholas Felton 17th c [possibly the Bishop of Ely, 1556-1626, or his grandson of the same name, fellow of Pembroke College, Cambridge 1633]; e.g. Pembroke, Cambridge LC.II.5.1
Secreta mea mihi
  J. Holland 16/17th c; e.g. John Rylands Library 6659
Semper infelix nunquam infidus
  John Handford 16/17th c; e.g. BL C.64.e.2
Sero sapere: nihil sapere
  George Chaworth, baron & Viscount Chaworth, 1569-1639; e.g. CUL F.155.e.3.4
Servire deo regnare est
  William Crashawe, 1572-1626, puritan divine; see P. J. Wallis, The library of William Crashawe, *Transactions of the Cambridge Bibliographical Society 2 (1956) 213-228, p. 226*
Servire deo sapere
  H. Mapletoft 17/18th c [?Hugh Mapletoft, Rector of All Saints, Huntingdon, d.1731]; e.g. Pembroke, Cambridge 6.10.3
Si Christum discis, nihil est si cetera nescis

Richard Ferrer 17th c; e.g. CUL Syn.7.61.165
Si Christum discis, sat est si caetera nescis/Si Christum nescis nihil est ci caetera dicis
  Richard Cotes early 17th c; e.g. St. Catharine's, Cambridge L.III.85
Si non ego mihi, quis mihi? et si non hodie quando?
  William Griffith 17th c; e.g. BL Ames VII.1338
Si non hodie quando
  Thomas Payb[ody?] 17th c; e.g. BL IA.40121
  Jo. White 17th c; e.g. Chetham's Library Gall.G.5.58, Oates 3198 etc.
Sic currite ut comprehendatis
  John Walker 16th c; e.g. CUL Aa*.11.54
Sine cruce sine luce
  Matthew Anderton 16/17th c e.g. Guildhall Library, London Bay H.11.5(9)
Sit mens sana in corpore sano
  Nicholas Onley, d.1724, canon of Westminster; his library of ca.630 volumes is preserved in Westminster Abbey Library, to which it was bequeathed
Sola mihi misero, crux tua, Christi, salus
  William Mount, 1545-1602, Master of the Savoy; see M. Raine, A catalogue of the printed books in the Library of the Dean and Chapter of York, *York, 1896, p. xii*
Sola salus servire deo
  William Cottam 16/17th c; e.g. Canterbury Cathedral W/L-6-2
  John Simson 16/17th c; e.g. St. Catharine's, Cambridge D.III.13
Soli deo honor et gloria
  William Irland 16/17th c; e.g. BL Ames I.297, I.301; Peterhouse, Cambridge S.39
Solus deus presidium meum
  John Spottiswood mid 16th c; see Durkan & Ross p. 145
Solus deus protector meus
  Mildmay Fane, 2nd Earl of Westmorland, d.1666; e.g. Oates 2585, 3719; cited by W. C. Hazlitt, The book-collector, *1904, p. 339*
Solus mihi Christus salus et vita
  Sir John Doddridge, 1555-1628, judge; e.g. BL 978.b.8; Marsh's Library, Dublin J.3.32
Sors mea mortalis, sed non mortale quod opto
  Anthony Higgin, d.1624, Dean of Ripon; see J. E. Mortimer, The library catalogue of Anthony Higgin, Proceedings of the Leeds Philosophical and Literary Society 10 (1962) 1-75, p. 4
Spe expecto
  John Steinstoun, d. ca. 1564, precentor of Glasgow; e.g. St. Andrews University Typ.FL.B41PP, National Library of Scotland HF.116, Aberdeen University Inc.88
Sperando spiro operando despero
  Samuel Stallon, d.1613, Rector of North Barsham, Norfolk; e.g. Oates 2793
Spero lucem
  Peter Galbraith, mid 16th c; e.g. National Library of Scotland H.26.e.15
Spes mihi Christi
  John Wall 17th c; e.g. BL Ames III.1461
Spes mea unica Christus
  Ra. Greene 16th c; e.g. Carlisle Cathedral Library E.5.8
Summa religionis initari que colis
  John Gray, 1646-1717, of Haddington; e.g. National Library of Scotland Gray 688
Sustine abstine (or Sustineo abstineo)

Joseph Fenton early 17th c, surgeon; e.g. BL 540.f.30, 540.f.7, 540.c.25, and many others; CUL K.3.24, St. John's, Cambridge Kk.6.43

Sustine et abstine
Henry Cole, ca.1500-80, Dean of St. Paul's; e.g. Bodl. Crynes 770
Hannibal Gamon, b.1582, Rector of St. Mawgan, Cornwall; e.g. CUL Syn.8.59.34; many of Gamon's books are at Lanhydrock, Cornwall
William Hill 17th c; e.g. Emmanuel, Cambridge 335.1.80

Tanquam explorator
Ben Jonson, 1573?-1637, the dramatist; see the introduction and illustrations in D. McPherson, Ben Jonson's library and marginalia, 1974

Timor domini principium sapientiae
John Barnes, son of Richard, Bishop of Durham (d.1587); see M. Raine, A catalogue of the printed books in the Library of the Dean and Chapter of York, *York, 1896, p. vii*

το μελλον ἀόρατον
Robert Baillie, 1599-1662, Principal of Glasgow University; see Durkan & Ross pl. XXXVI

Unum necessarium
Duckett 16/17th c, cf. 'Be not dulle' above; e.g. St. John's, Cambridge N.3.19, O.8.2

Verbi minister es hoc age
George Birkhead early 17th c; e.g. St. John's, Cambridge Ee.12.12

Victoria nostra fides
John Dove, 1561-1618, Rector of St. Mary Aldermary; e.g. CUL P.9.4*

Vincit veritas
Sir Clement Throkmorton, M.P. for Warwickshire 1624-26; e.g. Peterborough Cathedral E.5.59

Vindica te tibi
Sir Kenelm Digby, 1603-1665, diplomat; see W. D. Macray, Annals of the Bodleian Library, *2nd edn, Oxford, 1890, pp. 78-79*

Virescit vulnere virtus
Leighe 16th c; e.g. Oates 3102

Virtus post funera vivit
Edmund Mainwaring 16/17th c; e.g. Oriel, Oxford X.f.4 (see BC 16 (1967) p. 507)

Virtus super omnia vincat
Sir Walter Mildmay, ca.1520-1589, founder of Emmanuel College, Cambridge; e.g. John Rylands Library 4992

Virtus vera nobilitas
Thomas Windsor mid 17th c; e.g. All Souls, Oxford aa.7.10

Virtute non vi
Sir Walter Mildmay, ca.1520-1589, founder of Emmanuel College, Cambridge; e.g. Emmanuel FB7, FB12; John Rylands Library 4992
John Overall, 1560-1619, Bishop of Norwich; e.g. Peterhouse, Cambridge K.7.18

Vita Christus mors lucrum
Toby Matthew, 1546-1628, Archbishop of York; see M. Raine, A catalogue of the printed books in the Library of the Dean and Chapter of York, *York, 1896, p. vii*

Vita via
Alexander Roberts 16/17th c; e.g. Cosin's Library, Durham O.VI.33

Vive memor Lethi
John Fox, d.1530, fellow of Corpus Christi College, Oxford; e.g. Bodl. Vet.F1.e.8

Vive momor lati

Raynold 16th c; see J. Glenn & D. Walsh, Catalogue of the Francis Trigge Chained Library, *1988, no. 311*

Vive ut vivas
   William Holcot late 16th c; e.g. University College, Oxford H.31.11

Vixit redemptor quid desperem
   Richard Neile, 1562-1640, Archbishop of York; e.g. York Minster Library VI.A.10, III.K.19, V.N.7

Voce et odore
   Thomas Lorkyn, 1528?-1591, Regius Professor of Physic at Cambridge; e.g. CUL N*.15.43, N*.7.6, N*.15.12(1)

Vox domini super aquas
   William Atwater, 1440-1521, Bishop of Lincoln; e.g. Oates 1734, Bodl. VI.6.Th.Seld

Will and walke aright
   William Walker, 1570-1642, Vicar of Chiswick; e.g. John Rylands Library 4.e.2; Lambeth Palace Library H2205 (Vicecomes); Peterborough Cathedral Library E.6.48

MANUSCRIPT BOOKPLATES AND CALLIGRAPHIC INSCRIPTIONS

The inscriptions found in books are usually written in everyday hands; just occasionally more painstaking examples are found, such as the black letter inscription of Magdalen Cochran in a copy of *A genealogical history of the ... Stewarts* (Edinburgh, 1710) now in the Grenville Collection in the British Library (fig. 2.26). A handsome early sixteenth century decorated inscription for William Stewart, Bishop of Aberdeen (1479-1545) is illustrated in *Early Scottish libraries* by Durkan and Ross, plate XLVIII. A humbler form of decorative inscription is shown in fig. 2.27, from a book given to someone on his wedding day in 1827. Labels pasted into books to indicate ownership are normally printed as bookplates or book labels (see chapter III), but manuscript labels may sometimes be found, such as that of Sarah Beale, which is pasted into a copy of a 1677 edition of a work by James Ussher, now in the British Library (fig. 2.28). An earlier example is provided by a mid seventeenth-century collector named Henry Feilde (?the fellow of Christ's College, ejected after the Restoration, d.1661 or 62), who appears to have regularly pasted ownership labels written in bold red ink into his books; fig. 2.29 is reproduced from a book in the John Rylands Library, Manchester, but a number of other specimens survive.[19] Manuscript labels like this are not uncommonly found to be the work of women, and they may be quite elaborate exercises in penmanship. For a short article on such labels, illustrated with further examples, see:

B. North Lee: Manuscript ex-libris, *The Bookplate Journal* 7(1) (1989), 18-25.

19 See e.g. Sotheby's, New York, 17 December 1992, lot 95.

Fig. 2.26 Calligraphic inscription of Magdalen Cochran: British Library G.1171, *A genealogical history of the … family of the Stewarts*, 1710.

Fig. 2.27 The drawing and inscription of Christopher Briggs, giving a wedding present to Joseph Higgin in 1827: T. Cotterill, *Family prayers*, 1824, Private collection.

Fig. 2.28 The manuscript ex-libris of Sarah Beale: British Library 1471.k.4, J. Ussher, *A body of divinity*, 1677.

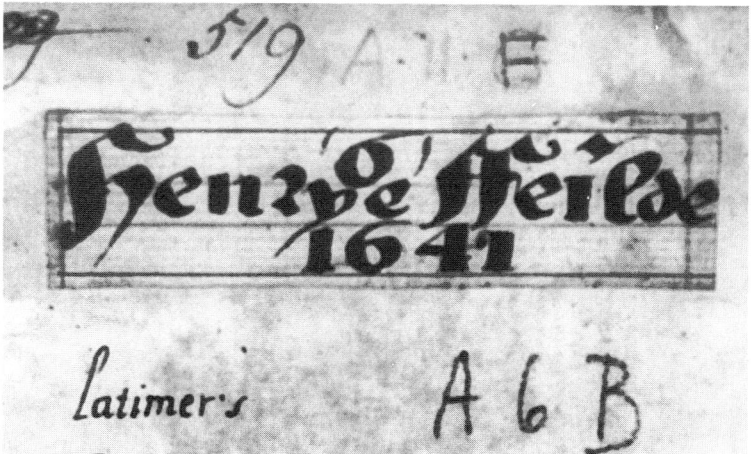

Fig. 2.29 The manuscript ex-libris of Henry Feilde: John Rylands University Library, Manchester 519, H. Latimer, *Fruitfull sermons*, 1607.

PAINTED-IN HERALDIC MARKS OF OWNERSHIP

The ownership of late medieval books can often be detected not from written inscriptions but from heraldic decoration representing the personal coat of arms of the original owner. This practice was widespread throughout Europe in the fourteenth and fifteenth centuries, and many examples survive. The most common location for painted arms is the bottom edge of a decorative border, at the centre of the page, usually on the first significant leaf of text, but there are many possible variations. Arms may also be drawn into decorated initial letters, or incorporated into other pictorial illumination (e.g. in the clothing or accoutrements of figures in miniatures). Fig. 2.30 shows a typical and straightforward example, from an English manuscript written ca.1485 for John Russell, Bishop of Lincoln (d.1494); the decorative border includes his arms in the bottom panel. Just as books from later centuries are found with inscriptions mutilated or scratched out, the subsequent owners of books with heraldic decoration were sometimes concerned to make clear the change in ownership, and painted coats of arms may be found erased or overpainted. The production and decoration of manuscripts in the late middle ages was a well-organised industry, with workshops of scribes and illuminators producing books for a wide market, and it became common practice to leave spaces in borders or initials, in anticipation of the insertion of arms once a book found a buyer. These were not always filled in, and many manuscripts have come down to us today with blank spaces where arms were intended to be drawn. Further examples of the heraldic decoration of manuscripts may be found in any catalogue or descriptive work which illustrates later medieval books; Nigel Thorp's catalogue of manuscripts from Glasgow University Library, *The glory of the page* (1987), might be mentioned as one particularly good example, which illustrates all these points and shows manuscripts from several countries.

The transition from a manuscript-based culture to a print-based one was a gradual process, and most of the characteristic features of manuscript books were deliberately copied by the earliest producers of printed books. It therefore comes as no surprise to observe that the tradition of heraldic decoration continued into the early years of printing. Late fifteenth-century and early sixteenth-century printed books were sometimes illuminated with borders and other features incorporating coats of arms, using the same graphic conventions. The printed decorative borders which were developed by the better continental printing houses relied heavily on this decorative concept, and blank spaces for arms were included just as they were by the producers of manuscript books.

Fig. 2.31 shows an example of the heraldic decoration of a printed book for an English owner; this copy of one of the legal commentaries of Bartolus de Saxoferrato, printed in Venice ca.1471, has the arms of John Morton (1420?-1500, Archbishop of Canterbury from 1486) painted on the first leaf at the head of the text. The decoration also incorporates another favoured device of late medieval book owners, a rebus, which expresses the owner's name in a punning

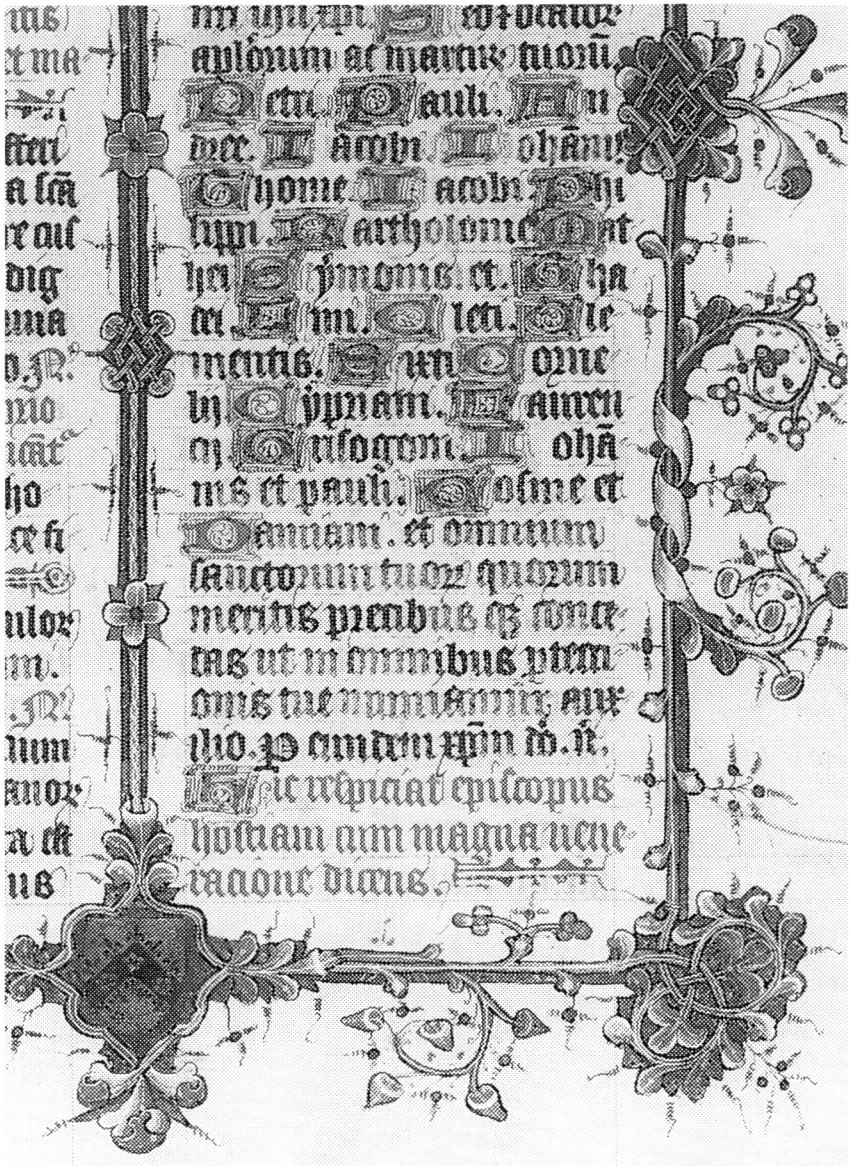

Fig. 2.30 Illuminated border incorporating the arms of John Russell: Cambridge University Library ms.Mm.3.21, *Pontificale*, written between 1480 and 1488.

MOR

VBRICA
ISTA HA
BETVR
diuersimode.
uera Rica e illa
qua dici uobis
legendo & det
dicere costitu-
tio prima alias
liber primus sed no bene stat. ¶Diui-
dit in duas partes per glo. super uerbo
de nouo ¶Tu potes diuidere rubrica
istam i tres partes: primo post queda
rubrica generalissima ad omne opus
faciendum ut inuocatio diuini nomis
Secundo ponitur rubrica generalis ad
totu hunc libru. Tertio post Rubri.
spialis ad hanc costitutione, secuda ibi
Codicis dni iustiani. tertia ibi, de nouo
codice faciendo ¶Item, hec secunda pf
diuidit in tres ptes quia post primo
denotario hui libri cum adiectione
pncipis taq cie efficiens, secudo post
causa materialis. tertio cu formalis. &
lego Rubrici tota ut iuuenes itelligat
secuda ibi, reperite plconis. tertia ibifici

pit costitutio pria ¶In prima pticula
nota. q in principio cuiuslibet operis
debet precedere inuocatio diuini nois
ut habet. j. de epi. et cle. l. deo nobis. &
de offi. pfec. pto. l. in noie dni. & l. i. &
ij. j. de ueteri iur. enuct ¶Ad istud op.
quando nomen xpi inuocatur ab boie
diuerse secte uidet fieri incontemptu
j. de iude. l. iudeos. sed constat q in
boc libro sunt leges diuersoru Impa-
rorum qui fuerunt diuerse secte ergo
ista inuocatio non bene ponit ¶Glo.
dicit super rubrica. ff. q fuit factum
ab expositoribus. qui erant cristiani &
etia Iustinian xpian erat. Et ex boc
haberis q licet notarius cristianus co-
ficiat instrumentu inter duos iudeos
bene potest dicere In nomine dni nri
ibesu xpi non attento qui fuerit cotra-
betes ¶Venio ad sam ptem. & dicit
bic. C. dni iustiniani. Contra qa nome
generis non facit rem esse nomiatam
ut no. j. de rerum pmutac. l super Rica.
sed nomen codicis est nome generis
qui omnis liber potest dici codex ut
l. argentarius § ij. de ede. Rndeo nom

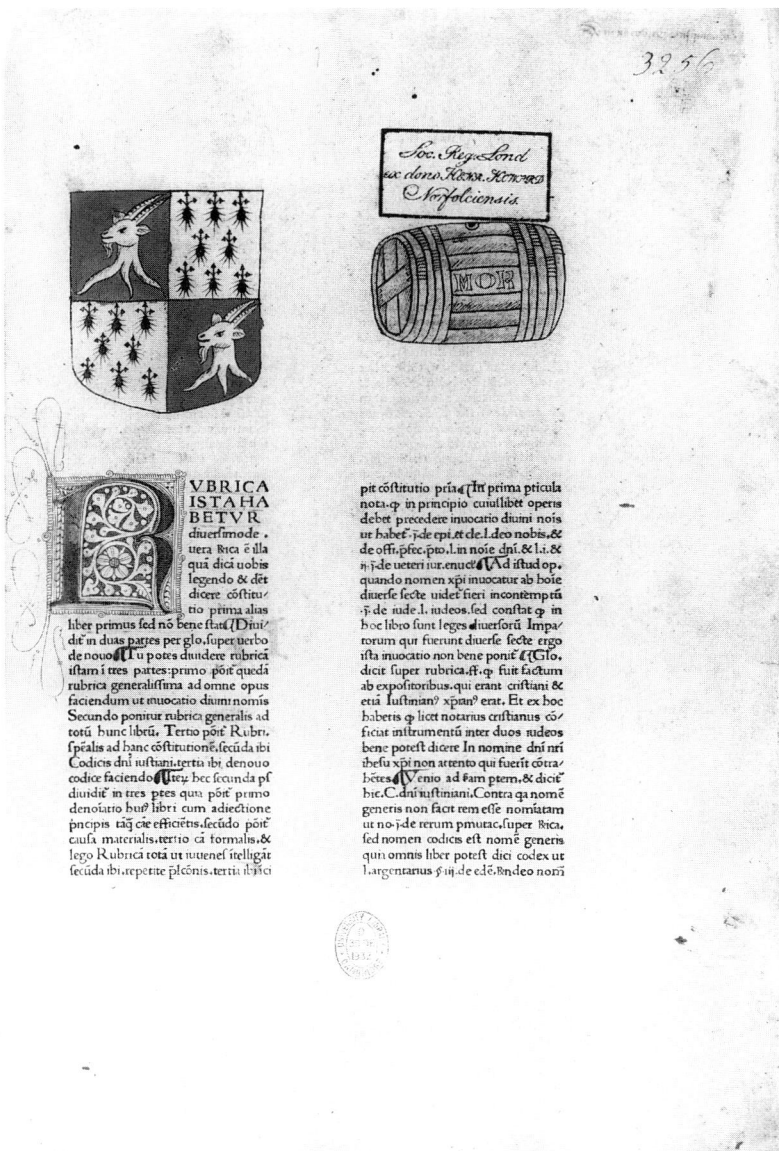

Fig. 2.31 The painted-in arms and rebus of John Morton: Cambridge University Library Inc.1.B.3.1b [3730], Bartolus de Saxoferrato, *Super prime parte codicis*, [1471?].

pictorial fashion. Morton's rebus shows a tun, i.e. a barrel, with 'MOR' written on the side: Mor-tun.[20]

Surviving British examples of the heraldic decoration of printed books are fairly few and far between, and the practice was much more common in continental Europe.

BOOKSELLERS' CODES

Sixteenth-, seventeenth- and (less commonly) eighteenth-century books often carry combinations of letters or symbols, handwritten in ink on their title pages, which are not ownership codes or ciphers but codes used by booksellers to denote the prices of the books. As they can sometimes be confused with owners' marks, especially if they comprise letters which may be mistaken for initials, it may be useful to illustrate some typical examples (see figs. 2.34-2.44). When they appear on the title page, they are often close to the imprint, e.g. as letters or numbers written at either side of the imprint, or as a series of letters at one side. The letters are sometimes in a single line, possibly separated by full stops, or they may be arranged in a vertical sequence; some codes look more like a mathematical fraction, with letters on top of other letters, separated by a short horizontal line. One distinctive form of code is a 'fraction' like this, with a symbol like a large letter 'G' at the left hand side; the letters in the fraction may or may not be accompanied by full stops (fig. 2.41). This code, which was used in the early seventeenth century, always appears on the verso of a rear flyleaf. Another form of code which commonly appears on flyleaves is a combination of letters and short horizontal bars.

It is of course not uncommon for owners to note the price paid for a book in code – the case of Sloane was mentioned above, and figs. 2.32-2.33 show some further examples – but it is usually easy to distinguish an owner's inscription from a bookseller's code. The codes found in the books in Ipswich Town Library have been described and analysed by John Blatchly in an article in *The Book Collector* in 1986, but apart from this the subject has not been seriously studied.[21] The Ipswich codes are largely of the two- or three-letter sort which can be readily related to prices by assigning the letters numerical values, but the examples show that the ciphers are not always so easy to break. The practice was widespread in the British book trade in the seventeenth century and systematic study might make it possible to associate distinctive varieties of code with particular booksellers or locations. The books which belonged to William Chark, for example (the Cambridge puritan who died in 1617) almost invariably

---

20 There is another example of a book with Morton's coat of arms and rebus in Cambridge University Library, G. Boccaccio, *Genealogiae deorum*, 1472 (Oates 1615). For an example of a similar contemporary rebus, used by William Langton (d.1496) and reproduced on some bindings made for him, see N. Barker, A register of writs and the Scales Binder, *The Book Collector* 21 (1972), 356-377, nos. 9 and 10 in the List of bindings.

21 J. Blatchly, Ipswich Town Library, *The Book Collector* 35 (1986), 191-198.

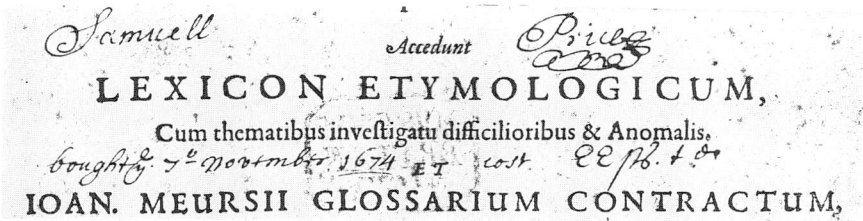

Fig. 2.32 The inscription of Samuel Price, 1674, with coded price: British Library 1505/254, J. Scapula, *Lexicon graeco-latinum*, 1652.

Fig. 2.33 The inscription of John Patrick (1632-95), with coded price: G. J. Vossius, *De vitiis sermonis*, 1666, Private collection.

carry a code of the fig. 2.41 variety, a 'fraction' with a large letter G, although it is also found in books with no Chark connection. If we could identify the bookseller and understand the code we might learn more about the way in which Chark's library was dispersed.

INSTITUTIONAL LIBRARY INSCRIPTIONS

Libraries, like individuals, have long been concerned to indicate their ownership of books in a permanent way, and they have tended to use the same methods. Institutional ownership is most commonly marked nowadays with bookplates or ink stamps (or both – see p. 92 below for library stamps), but from the twelfth century until the beginning of the nineteenth a manuscript note on the title page or flyleaf was the most standard method of recording a book's ownership by a particular library. The conventions for such inscriptions developed early and remained markedly constant over many centuries; the earliest library inscriptions are those used by monastic libraries in the middle ages, and the formulae devised then continued to be used by university, college and cathedral libraries long after the Reformation.

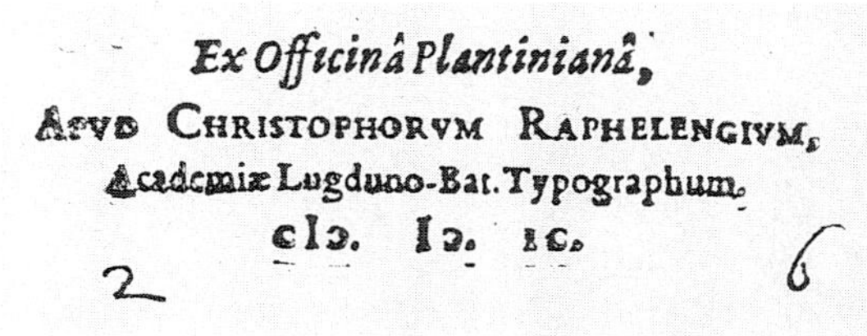

Ex Officinâ Plantinianâ,
Apvd Christophorvm Raphelengivm,
Academiæ Lugduno-Bat. Typographum.
cIↄ. Iↄ. ic.
2 6

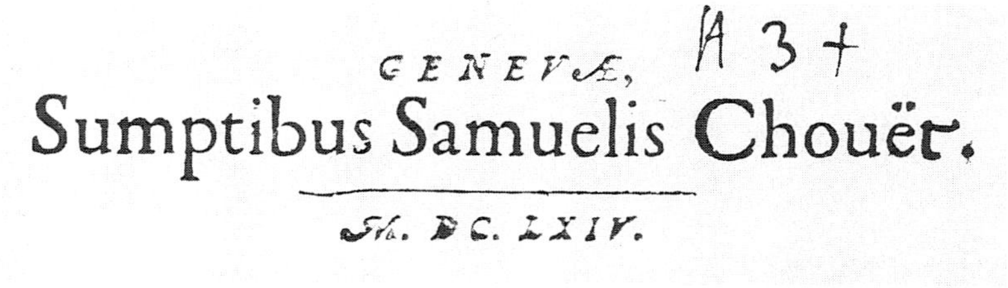

GENEVÆ, A 3 +
Sumptibus Samuelis Chouët.
M. DC. LXIV.

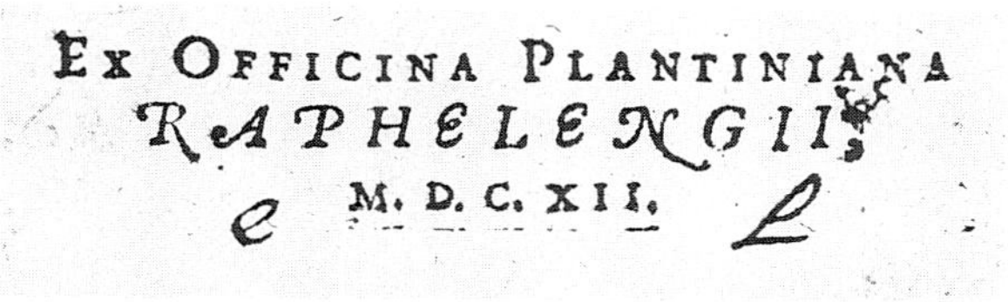

Ex Officina Plantiniana
Raphelengii,
e M. D. C. XII. l

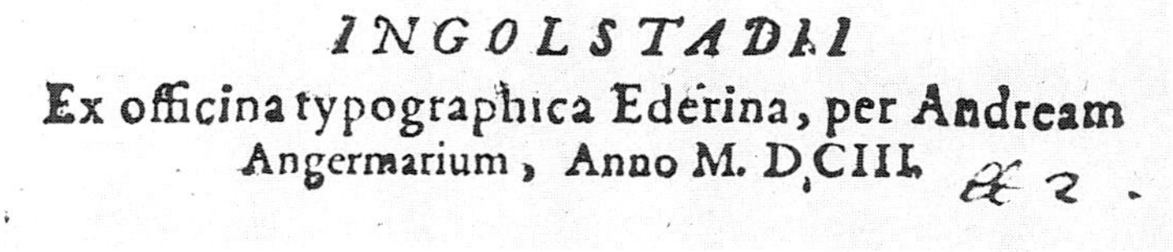

INGOLSTADII
Ex officina typographica Ederina, per Andream
Angermarium, Anno M. D.CIII. &2.

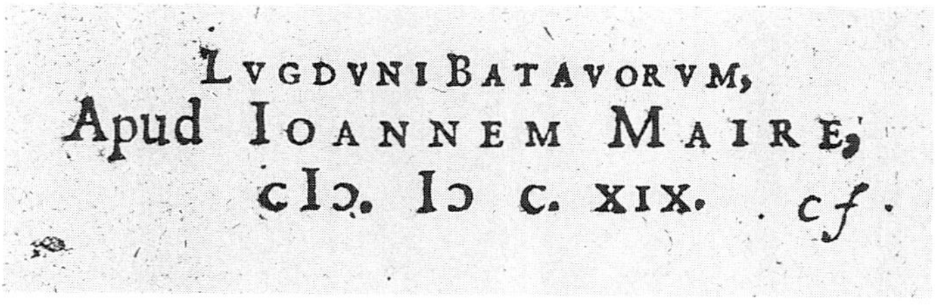

Lvgdvni Batavorvm,
Apud Ioannem Maire,
cIↄ. Iↄ c. xix. . cf.

Figs. 2.34–2.38 Seventeenth-century booksellers' codes, from (from top): Cosin's Library, Durham Y.5.28; Durham University Library R.LXIX.B.5; Durham University Library PJ.4563.M2; Durham University Library R.LXXX.D.3; Durham University Library R.LX.F.33.

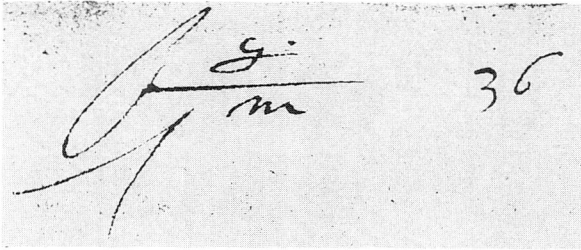

LVGD. BATAVORVM,
Ex Officinâ Elzeviriorum.
Anno cIɔIɔc xxxvii.

Figs. 2.39-2.44 Seventeenth-century booksellers' codes, from (from top): Bamburgh Library, Durham O.I.6; Bamburgh Library G.IV.14; Cosin's Library, Durham K.IV.29; British Library 1492.aa.50; Cosin's Library B.III.12; Durham Cathedral Library G.II.28.

The use of *ex libris* inscriptions for books from the libraries of religious houses became common practice in England during the twelfth and thirteenth centuries. The earliest inscriptions give the name of the patron saint and the place in which the community is based; the introduction of words like *ecclesia*, *libraria* or *monasterium* tends to be a development of the later middle ages. Medieval inscriptions are almost invariably in Latin. At Durham Cathedral Priory, for example, the earliest known inscriptions take the form 'Liber S[an]c[t]i Cuthb[ert]i d[e] Dun[e]lmo', which translates literally as 'The book of St. Cuthbert of Durham'; this phrase began to be used around the beginning of the thirteenth century and remained in use well into the fourteenth. In the early fifteenth century, the phrase 'De co[mmun]i libraria mo[na]chor[um] Dunelm' ('from the common library of the monks of Durham') came into use. At York Minster, the inscription 'Hic est liber S[an]c[t]i Pet[r]i de Eborac[o]' was used in the twelfth century, and 'Liber eccl[es]ie metropolitice b[eat]i Petri Ebor' in the fifteenth.[22] The characteristics of medieval library inscriptions, and their patterns of use, are described in N. R. Ker, *Medieval libraries of Great Britain*, 2nd edition, London, 1964, pp. xvi-xvii, and typical inscriptions of individual libraries are included in some entries in the main body of the work.

Although other forms of ownership marking, such as bookplates and armorial binding stamps, became increasingly common from the seventeenth century onwards, the medieval habit of writing *ex libris* inscriptions on title pages or other preliminary leaves remained common practice for institutional libraries of all kinds from the Reformation until the early years of the nineteenth century. There is no end of examples which may be chosen. Latin remained the preferred language for ownership inscriptions in academic, cathedral and other major libraries. Successive generations of librarians at Durham Cathedral wrote 'Liber Ecclesiae Cathedralis Dunelm' on the title pages of books from the middle of the sixteenth century until at least 1820. Figs. 2.45-2.49 show a variety of examples, from various libraries, from the sixteenth to the eighteenth centuries. A series of sixteenth- and seventeenth-century inscriptions from Glasgow University Library will be found illustrated in John Durkan's article on the history of that Library, published in 1977.[23]

Just as institutions have long marked their books with a statement of ownership, they have also been concerned to insert a shelfmark or pressmark (the terms are interchangeable), for administrative convenience rather than security. The habit of regular pressmarking in English libraries goes back to the thirteenth century at least, and distinctive forms of pressmark devised by different monastic libraries can sometimes be used to trace the origins of

22 On Durham inscriptions, see A. J. Piper, The libraries of the monks of Durham, in M. B. Parkes & A. G. Watson (eds.), *Medieval scribes, manuscripts and libraries*, London, 1978, 213-249; on York inscriptions, see C. B. L. Barr, The Minster Library in G. E. Aylmer & R. Cant (eds.), *A history of York Minster*, Oxford, 1977, 487-539.

23 J. Durkan, The early history of Glasgow University Library: 1475-1710, *The Bibliotheck* 8 (1977), 102-126, plates 1-3.

Fig. 2.45 Mid sixteenth-century library inscription of Durham Cathedral Library: Durham Cathedral Library D.VII.1, St. Jerome, *Opera*, 1516.

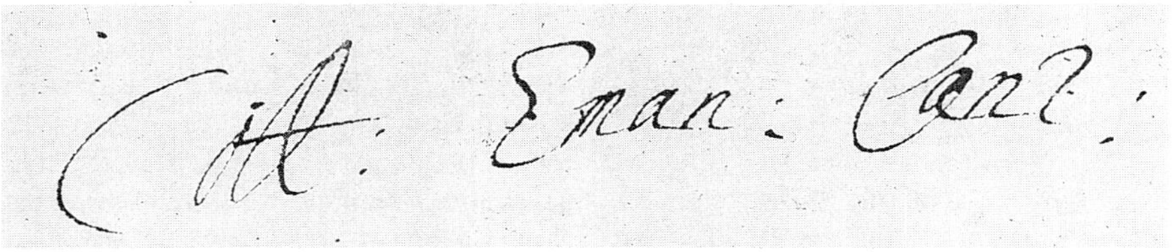

Fig. 2.46 Mid seventeenth-century library inscription of Emmanuel College, Cambridge. Emmanuel K.3.10: T. a Kempis, *Opera*, 1549.

Fig. 2.47 Late seventeenth-century library inscription of Durham Cathedral Library. Durham University Library +ELCB.C76S: J. Speed, *The theatre of … Great-Britain*, 1676.

Fig. 2.48 Early eighteenth-century library inscription of King's College, Aberdeen. Durham University Library +M513.10/EUC: Euclid, *[Opera]*, 1703.

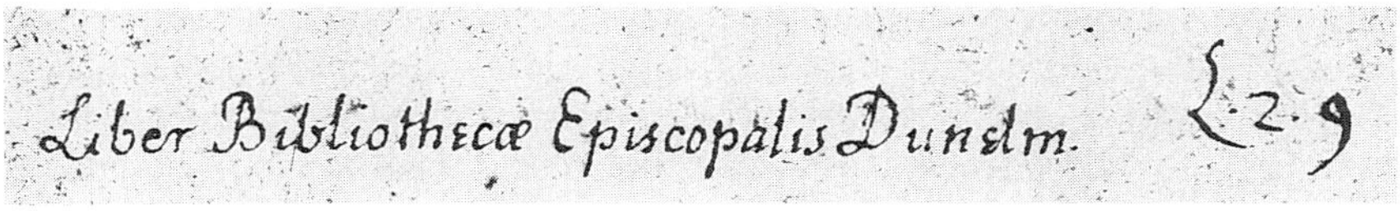

Fig. 2.49 Early eighteenth-century library inscription of Cosin's Library, Durham. Cosin's Library L.2.9: J. Bale, *Scriptorum illustriu[m] maioris Brytanni[a]e*, 1557.

medieval manuscripts.[24] Before the introduction of subject classification schemes like Dewey's, towards the end of the nineteenth century, the great majority of post-Reformation libraries were shelved according to a fixed location system (which usually incorporated some arrangement by subject), so that each book had a permanent definable position on the shelves. The most familiar method of pressmarking relies on three elements: press, shelf, and position on shelf. Each press (i.e. bookcase, however defined) is assigned a number or letter, similarly each shelf within a press, and each book has a numbered position from one end (normally the left-hand end) of the shelf. Shelfmarks therefore take the form A.II.3, B.3.9, 5.7.11, etc. Figs. 2.50-2.52 show some characteristic examples from the seventeenth and eighteenth centuries; see also fig. 2.23, which shows the type of pressmark used by the British Museum Library in the late eighteenth and early nineteenth centuries, and 2.49, which shows an early eighteenth-century pressmark from Cosin's Library, Durham. There are however examples of more elaborate shelving systems which may be found reflected in early pressmarks, where the library space is divided into more than three elements. In Peterhouse, Cambridge, when the new library was erected in the seventeenth century, the division was not only by press and shelf but also by the points of the compass, and left-hand and right-hand, producing shelfmarks such as that shown in fig. 2.53. The likely reading in this case is 'E p[arte] B[orealis] Dext[er] C[lassis] 3 F[igura] 1 L[ocus] 4', i.e. the 4th book on the 1st shelf of the 3rd press on the right-hand side of the northern sector of the Library.

IDENTIFYING MANUSCRIPT INSCRIPTIONS

The most obvious and fundamental requirement for identifying owners is to *read* and *date* their inscriptions. Handwriting can usually be dated within fifty years or so, but hands of all periods can present problems of decipherment; guidance will be found in the books listed in the **Palaeography** section on p. 286. Having read the name, one can then turn to the sources listed in the **Biography** section (p. 297) to try to trace the individual in question. The more common the name, the greater the problem; it is important to remember that several persons with the same name may have been alive simultaneously, who may have owned books. Finding the name 'Francis Bacon' in an early seventeenth century book, for example, one should not immediately conclude that this is the author of the *Advancement of learning*; there were seven people of that name who matriculated at Cambridge between 1570 and 1660.

Establishing precise identification may involve looking at other physical evidence in the book (e.g. the presence of mottoes, or the inscriptions of other

24 See F. Wormald, The monastic library in F. Wormald & C. E. Wright (eds), *The English library before 1700*, London, 1958, 15-31, p. 23; and N. R. Ker, *Medieval libraries of Great Britain*, pp. xviii-xix. A number of characteristic medieval pressmarks are reproduced in *Facsimiles of ancient manuscripts*, New Palaeographical Society, 1st series, 1903-12, pl. 17.

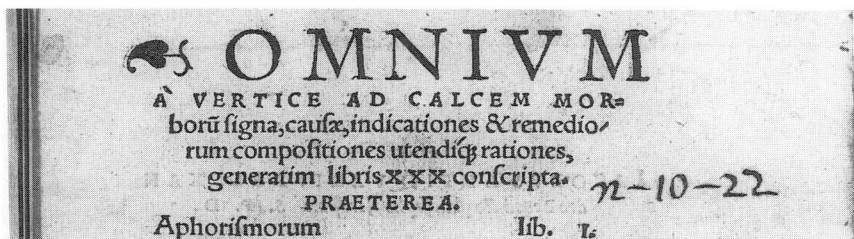

Fig. 2.50 Seventeenth-century pressmark from Cambridge University Library: now N*.10.22.

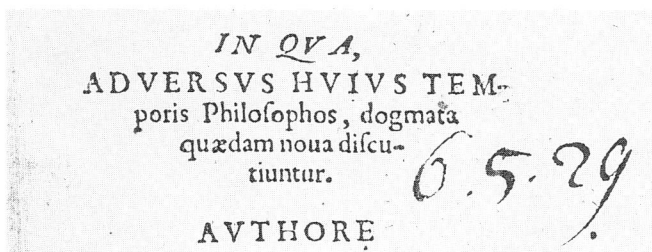

Fig. 2.51 Seventeenth-century pressmark from Emmanuel College, Cambridge.

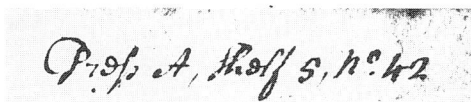

Fig. 2.52 Eighteenth-century pressmark from University College, Oxford; now Durham University Library +ELCP.C75S.

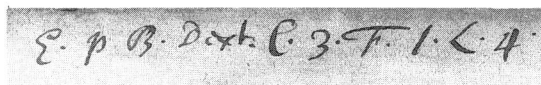

Fig. 2.53 Mid seventeenth-century pressmark from Peterhouse, Cambridge; now Cosin's Library, Durham H.IV.4.

owners), looking for information about the dispersal or other fate of particular collections, or considering geographical evidence like the place of binding (if ascertainable) or the present whereabouts of the book. Common sense must always be brought to bear in the weighing up of alternative probabilities.

A number of collections of facsimile autographs have been published, which may occasionally be helpful in identifying signatures. They have always been assembled with the interests of autograph collectors primarily in mind, and they are usually limited to well-known figures such as royalty, nobility, statesmen or famous writers, but there are several which cover a wide enough range to be worth mentioning in this context. Two books stand out for their bibliographical guidance:

R. Rawlins, *Four hundred years of British autographs: a collector's guide*. London, 1970.
E. Berkeley jr. (ed.), *Autographs and manuscripts: a collector's manual*. New York, 1978.

The first of these comprises an extensive collection of facsimiles covering scientists, medics, and lawyers as well as the more usual royalty, politicians and artists. It also includes a bibliography of other books of facsimiles, and works on autograph collecting. The second, the official handbook of the Manuscript Society (based in the USA), does not include many facsimiles relevant to provenance research, but has useful chapters on the history of autograph collecting and related subjects, and a bibliography covering facsimiles, paper history, literary forgery, collecting theory, etc.

The following list includes some of the principal published collections of facsimiles which may be useful in provenance work. It must be stressed that only the autographs of well-known people will be found here, and the vast majority of inscriptions found in books will not be worth checking against these sources. The list is not exhaustive; fuller lists will be found in the bibliographies of the two books just mentioned.

J. Thane: *British autography. A collection of fac-similes of the handwriting of royal and illustrious personages*. 3v. London, [1793-98?]

> Mostly English statesmen and men of affairs, 16-17th centuries.

J. G. Nichols: *Autographs of royal, noble, learned, and remarkable personages conspicuous in English history, from the reign of Richard the second to that of Charles the second*. London, 1829.

> Includes a number of facsimiles of signatures of scholars and antiquaries of the 16th and 17th centuries.

J. Netherclift: *Autographs of the kings and queens, and eminent men, of Great Britain ... to the present period*. London, 1835.

> Includes a number of statesmen and scholars, as well as monarchs.

L. B. Phillips: *The autographic album. A collection of 470 facsimiles of holographical writings of royal, noble, and distinguished men and women*. London, 1866.

> Includes some continental and American autographs, but mostly British, 16th-19th centuries.

K. Geigy-Hagenbach: *Album von Handschriften berühmter Persönlichkeiten vom Mittelalter bis zur Neuzeit*. Basle, 1925.

> Several hundred autographs with wide ranging coverage by date, occupation, and nationality.

W. W. Greg: *English literary autographs, 1550-1650*. 3v. Oxford, 1925-32.

> A series of 100 high quality facsimiles of dramatists, poets and prose writers of the late Tudor and early Stuart periods, with extensive examples of handwriting in most cases (not just signatures).

R. Rawlins: *The Guinness book of autographs.* Enfield, 1977.

> Includes a wide selection of facsimiles, from many centuries and backgrounds, although intended more for a popular than a scholarly audience.

V. Klinkenborg et at: *British literary manuscripts.*
Series I: from 800 to 1800.
Series II: from 1800 to 1914. 2v. New York, 1981.

> Like Greg's compilation, based largely on extensive reproductions of autograph letters. 259 authors included. Based on mss in the Pierpont Morgan Library.

Beyond this, there are few readily available sources which are geared to the identification of inscriptions and annotations in books. The one standard and important source which is regularly consulted is:

S. de Ricci: *English collectors of books and manuscripts (1530-1930) and their marks of ownership.* Cambridge, 1930.

> De Ricci's book (based on the Sandars lectures for 1929) concentrates specifically on the characteristic forms of inscription, and other physical evidence of ownership, appertaining to many of the most celebrated English collectors from the sixteenth to the twentieth century. It is well illustrated with examples.

Also pertinent (its usefulness is only limited by the necessary selectivity of its examples) is:

R. E. Stoddard: *Marks in books.* Cambridge, Mass., 1985.

> This is the catalogue which accompanied an exhibition at the Houghton Library, Harvard University in 1985 devoted to illustrating and explaining all the different types of marks and physical alterations which may be found in printed books, including printers' and proofreaders' marks as well as a multiplicity of different types of annotation relating to ownership.

The Bibliographical Society is planning a series of publications around the theme of *Marks in books*, envisaged as an open-ended run of fascicules, each concentrating on a particular library, group of owners, or category of physical evidence. Like the Harvard catalogue, this series will cover all kinds of mark (not only those reflecting ownership), but it will greatly expand the range of published illustrations available to students of provenance. It is hoped that fascicules will begin to appear in the mid-1990s.

III

BOOKPLATES, BOOK LABELS
AND BOOK STAMPS

INTRODUCTION

The use of engraved or printed paper labels, carrying an owner's identity, to mark the possession or gift of a book, is almost as old as printing itself, and it is one of the most familiar signs of ownership seen by students of provenance. Many tens of thousands of such labels have been produced in Britain over the last four hundred years, and their study has generated a considerable literature. This chapter aims to list the various sources which can assist in identifying the owner of a particular plate or label, which is one of the commonest problems in provenance research. It is outside its scope to give a detailed history of bookplates (which can be found elsewhere), beyond offering a summary of the major stylistic developments which make it possible to assign approximate dates to individual plates.

A **bookplate** is an ownership label printed from an engraved or etched block, cut in metal or wood. The design is usually armorial or pictorial, and it normally (but by no means always) incorporates the owner's name or initials.

A **book label** is an ownership label created from printers' type and (possibly) type ornaments, and printed by letterpress. A common design comprises an owner's name surrounded by a border of ornaments. Some owners have favoured simple designs like this which are produced by engraving, like bookplates, and these are commonly regarded as labels also. Book labels are typically, but not necessarily, smaller and less ornate than bookplates.

A **book stamp** is here defined as a stamp made of metal or wood used to stamp an owner's name in ink on a title page or other leaf of a book. It is not meant to include any kind of stamp, armorial or otherwise, which may be applied to a binding.

It is not uncommon to find owners using more than one of these devices during their collecting careers, and many collectors had more than one plate, label or stamp. John Gwennap, for example, a Cornish collector who died in 1816, had an engraved bookplate, a printed label and an ink stamp, which can be found in various combinations in the books he owned (figs. 3.1-3.3).

John Gwennap,

Falmouth.

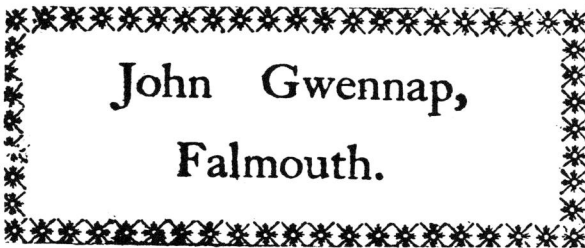

John Gwennap, Falmouth

Figs. 3.1-3.3 The bookplate (Franks 13133), book label (Franks 13132) and ink stamp of John Gwennap.

BOOKPLATES

The use of bookplates began in Germany around 1470, but they are not found in Britain much before the end of the sixteenth century. Some early bookplates were printed to record the gifts of individuals to particular institutions, and the first known British bookplate, recording the gift of books by Sir Nicholas Bacon to Cambridge University Library in 1574, falls into this category.[1] This plate was originally engraved for other purposes – it was an illustration in a book printed six years earlier – and this too is a common characteristic of early bookplates; they were often made to serve a variety of uses. The production of bookplates solely for labelling books is really a seventeenth-century development.

Since the late sixteenth century, bookplates have passed through a variety of recognisable styles, each of which was fashionable for a period, and this makes it possible to date most bookplates, at least approximately, on their design alone. The serious study of bookplates began in the middle of the nineteenth century, and by 1880 terminology was devised which remains in use today, although the names given to some styles are not altogether apposite.

There are hardly enough late sixteenth century bookplates known to define a **Tudoresque** style, but the plate of Sir Thomas Tresham (1543-1605), dated 1585, is typical of those which survive (fig. 3.4). It has a large plain shield bearing the subject's arms, with a helm, crest, and delicate mantling ending in tassels. The characteristics of the **Carolian** period, in the middle decades of the seventeenth century, are a variety of shield shapes encompassed by wreaths, or palms with ribbons. The example shown (fig. 3.5), the plate used by Sir John Marsham of Cuxton (1602-85), is a modest affair, its plain shield surrounded by a wreath. Like Sir Nicholas Bacon's sixteenth-century plate, this engraving was also used in a printed book – it appears on the title page of Marsham's _Diatriba chronologica_ (1649) – and it is very likely that it was originally cut for this purpose.

Bookplates were still an emerging form throughout the middle of the seventeenth century and the identification of characteristic styles is more meaningful once they were better established in their own right. Their use increased considerably after the Restoration and a number were of imposing dimensions, displaying full heraldic achievements. Between about 1695 and 1720 a great number of plates were cut in the **Early Armorial** style, of which Edward Coke's, dated 1701 (fig. 3.6) is typical. A plain shield of squarish proportions, surmounted by a crest and helm, is surrounded by ample mantling, and the owner's name is placed in a panel at the foot. The basic design is a clear descendant of the earlier styles, but these plates are often more modest in their dimensions. The plate of Henry Compton, Bishop of London (1632-1713), is another good example of the style (fig. 3.7). Both plates came from the

1 J. C. T. Oates, _Cambridge University Library: a history_, Cambridge, 1986, p. 111/fig. 9.

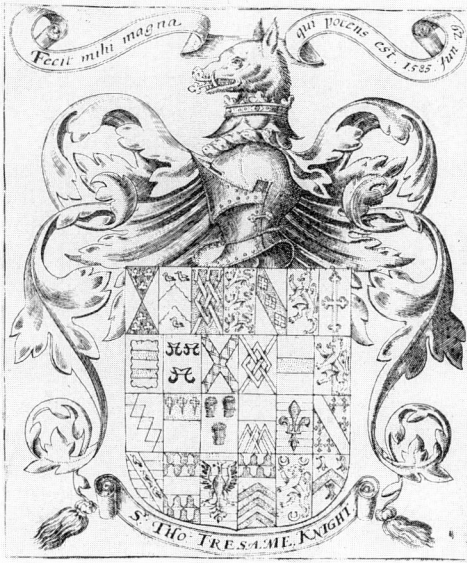

Fig. 3.4 Tudoresque style: the bookplate of Sir Thomas Tresham (Franks 29789).

Fig. 3.5 Carolian style: the bookplate of Sir John Marsham (Franks 19825).

Fig. 3.6 Early armorial style: the bookplate of Edward Coke (Franks 6316).

Fig. 3.7 Early armorial style: the bookplate of Henry Compton (Franks 6576).

58

workshop of the engraver William Jackson, who actively solicited clients for bookplates and who thereby became a major influence in popularising their usage.

The **Jacobean** style was introduced shortly before 1700 and was popular until about 1745; it is so named because its ornamentation is supposedly reminiscent of late seventeenth century woodwork, so the James in question is James II, but it is an unfortunate term as most people automatically associate it with James I. The bookplate of Richard Hopton, M.P. for Herefordshire 1715-22, is an example (fig. 3.8); the basic concept of a mantled shield is still there, but the foliage mantling has become stiffer and less leaf-like, and can almost be pictured as carved wood. The scallop-shell below the shield is a common feature of Jacobean armorials. A finer example, where the mantling has become even stiffer and the scallop is again present, is the plate of Sir Thomas Hare (1688?-1760, fig. 3.9), which incorporates brackets and term figures. The Jacobean style was succeeded by the **Chippendale**, which was in vogue between about 1740 and 1780. The shield loses its symmetry and sometimes appears somewhat at an angle, and its frame becomes fussily elaborate and decorated with natural-looking flowers and foliage. The plate of Robert Clavering, dated 1748, is a relatively restrained example (fig. 3.10); that of John Watson (d.1783, fig. 3.11), shows the excesses to which the style tended, particularly in the latter years of its popularity. The Chippendale period gave way to one of greater simplicity, and between about 1770 and 1800 **Spade shield** armorials became popular; these take their name from the characteristic shape of the shield. The plate of the historian Edward Gibbon (1737-94, fig. 3.12) shows this design in its basic form; that of George Lewis Jones, Bishop of Kilmore (d.1804), shows a slightly more decorated version in a style known as **Wreath and Ribbon** or **Festoon** (fig. 3.13). The late eighteenth-century plate of James Neild (1744-1814, fig. 3.14) shows a spade-shield as part of a pictorial composition; pastoral settings, sometimes incorporating urns, tombs or ancient monuments were popular *motifs* in bookplates of the second half of the eighteenth century.

The spade shield gave way in the nineteenth century to a more four-square shape, often with eared shields, and many plates were cut in what is often called the **Die-sinker** style. An example is the plate of the nineteenth-century Bible collector Lea Wilson (fig. 3.15). The nineteenth century also saw the development of a vogue for circular or otherwise seal-shaped bookplates, such as that of Edward Hailstone, the Yorkshire antiquary (1818-90); this is an example of a plate which was printed gilt-stamped on leather (fig. 3.16), and it was made in two sizes and a variety of colours. The gradual decline in the importance attached to heraldry and the bearing of arms has been matched by a proliferation of purely pictorial styles of bookplate, of which a great variety have been produced in the nineteenth and (particularly) twentieth centuries, which fall outside the scope of the present work.

Although coats of arms have been the predominant feature of most

Fig. 3.8 Jacobean style: the bookplate of Richard Hopton of Can-Frome (Franks 15346).

Fig. 3.9 Jacobean style: the bookplate of Sir Thomas Hare (Franks 13751).

Fig. 3.10 Chippendale style: the bookplate of Robert Clavering (Franks 5995).

Fig. 3.11 Chippendale style: the bookplate of John Watson (Franks 31081).

Fig. 3.12 Spade-shield style: the bookplate of Edward Gibbon (Franks 11808).
Fig. 3.13 Wreath-and-ribbon style: the bookplate of George Lewis Jones (Franks 16665).

Fig. 3.14 Spade-shield in a pictorial setting: the bookplate of James Neild (Franks 21635).
Fig. 3.15 Die-sinker style: the bookplate of Lea Wilson (Franks 32112).

Fig. 3.16 A nineteenth-century circular bookplate, that of Edward Hailstone (Franks 13229).

Fig. 3.17 Bookpile style: the bookplate of William Hewer of Clapham (Franks 14623).

bookplates until almost the end of the nineteenth century, more pictorial *motifs* have also enjoyed popularity at various times. The plate of William Hewer (1642-1715), dated 1699 (fig. 3.17), is an early example of the **Bookpile** style, of which there are numerous eighteenth century examples. A related theme, from the eighteenth century onwards, is the **Library Interior**, such as is found on the plate of Thomas Bolas (fig. 3.18). **Trophy** bookplates, exhibiting the accoutrements and spoils of war, became popular with men with military connections; an example is the mid eighteenth-century Chippendale plate of Sir Charles Frederick (d.1785, fig. 3.19). Bookplates commonly incorporate the name of the owner, but it is not unusual to find plates with initials only, or no name at all. A variation on the use of initials is the fashion for ciphers or monograms, in which initials may be tortuously intertwined. The term **Cipher plates** is normally used to describe these, although technically there is a distinction between monograms and ciphers: a monogram consists of two or more letters superimposed so that letters merge with one another, a cipher has superimposed letters which remain distinct. These devices sometimes incorporate an element of symmetry around a vertical central axis, so that each letter appears twice and the left- and right-hand sides are mirror images of one another.[2] The earliest cipher plates date from the late seventeenth century, but there are many eighteenth century examples, whose owners can be particularly difficult, and sometimes impossible, to identify. Fig. 3.20 shows a relatively straightforward example, the letters 'A H' standing for Andrew Hacket (or Halkett, 1737?-1815), of Moxhull Hall, Warwickshire, sometime High Sheriff of that county. An earlier example can be seen in William Hewer's bookpile plate (fig. 3.17). There are many other themes or styles which feature in bookplates over the last 250 years, and it is impossible to summarise them all in a brief introduction; more detailed analysis will be found in the various histories of bookplates lised at the end of this section.

It has always been common practice to paste bookplates on the inside of the front board (i.e. on the front pastedown), but it is not unusual to find them pasted on the verso of the title leaf. They are sometimes found on rear pastedowns, flyleaves, or even title pages. The wording of bookplates is normally quite simple, incorporating the name of the owner, with the possible addition of address, occupation, or academic degree ('Sir John Smith, Bart: F.R.S. Sydling St. Nicholas, Dorset'; his heraldic motto 'semper fidelis' is also incorporated into the design of his plate, as is commonly found with armorials[3]); the use of the words *ex libris* ('from the library of ...') is a relatively modern habit and is not found much before the nineteenth century. It became popular to include a date on bookplates around 1700, and was particularly so in the first half of the eighteenth century; see for example figs. 3.6, 3.7, 3.9, 3.10, 3.13, and 3.17. Some caution must be exercised in the interpretation of these dates, as

2 See, for example, the late seventeenth-century plate of Jacob Asselin, reproduced in B. N. Lee, *British bookplates*, Newton Abbot, 1979, no. 21.

3 Reproduced in Lee, *British bookplates*, no. 93.

Fig. 3.18 Library interior style: the bookplate of Thomas Bolas (Franks 2962).

Fig. 3.19 Trophy style: the bookplate of Sir Charles Frederick; basically a Chippendale-style plate with decoration to reflect the owner's military achievements (Franks 11308).

plates often continued in use for many years, and sometimes several generations, and the year in which the plate was cut (if this is the date appearing) may
be very different from the year of acquisition of a particular book.

Just occasionally, bookplates were added to books not by pasting them in, but
by printing them directly onto a suitable leaf prior to binding. The practice was
never common and most known instances date from the seventeenth century,
before the trade in purpose-made bookplates took off, at the beginning of the
eighteenth. An example is found among the Ames Collection of title pages in
the British Library; a copy of the title leaf of John Gauden's *Hieraspistes*
(London, 1653), has on the verso an engraved armorial bookplate (the identity
is uncertain, possibly a member of the Nettleton family), printed directly onto
the leaf (fig. 3.21). The plate was clearly printed on the leaf before the book was
bound. The book-production methods of the hand-press era, when books were
commonly sold in sheets to be bound at the specification of the purchaser,
made the creation of such 'personalised' copies perfectly feasible, but the
process was clearly very labour-intensive when compared with the relative ease
of pasting in ready-printed plates. A slightly more common variation is the
printing of bookplates on separate blank leaves of paper, to be bound into
books; there are a number of early gift plates and book labels which were
produced like this.[4] There are also instances of books issued with engraved
frontispieces showing the arms of the dedicatee of the book, and these should
not be confused with bookplates denoting personal ownership.[5]

The great majority of bookplates are printed in black on white, although it is
not uncommon to find nineteenth-century plates printed on coloured paper.
The heraldic colours, whose correct interpretation is important, may be
indicated in one of two ways. Most plates use tinctures, in which the colours are
represented by the slant of the lines used to shade in the background, as shown
in fig. 3.22.

The scheme of tinctures was devised in the first half of the seventeenth
century, but its adoption was gradual and bookplates before 1700 may have the
colours indicated in trick, rather than by tinctures. In this case each part of the
armorial will be labelled with a letter representing the heraldic colour – G for
gules, S for sable, V for vert and so forth. The standard shading conventions
can be seen in use in most of the bookplates reproduced in the illustrations in
this chapter; for example, the background of vertical lines in Richard Hopton's
bookplate (fig. 3.8) shows that the field of the shield is gules (red). It should be
added as a caveat, however, that heraldic inaccuracies and uncertainties
abound, due to engravers' or owners' errors, and small armorials are not always
clear. For further assistance in interpreting coats of arms, see the section on
Heraldry in chapter VIII.

4 For example, the engraved plate of Rachel Bourchier, Dowager Countess of Bath, dated 1671,
which is found on separate leaves bound into books she gave to Emmanuel College, Cambridge.

5 An example is Joshua Sprigg's *Anglia rediviva* (1647), dedicated to Sir Thomas Fairfax, whose
frontispiece displaying Fairfax's arms is sometimes mistaken for a bookplate.

Fig. 3.20 Cipher bookplate of Andrew Hacket of Moxhull Hall (Franks 13280).

Fig. 3.21 A bookplate printed directly onto a title leaf verso: British Library Ames III/2312, the title leaf of J. Gauden, *Hieraspistes*, 1653, with the arms of ?Nettleton.

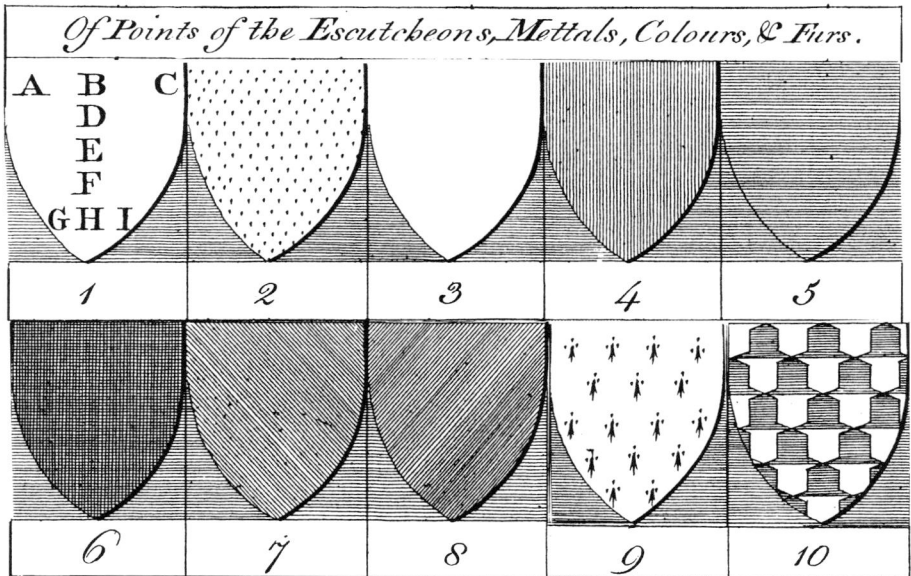

Fig. 3.22 The standard shading scheme used to represent the principal heraldic tinctures and furs, as follows:

2 Or	5 Azure	8 Purpure
3 Argent	6 Sable	9 Ermine
4 Gules	7 Vert	10 Vair

No. 1 shows the different parts and points of an heraldic shield. Further details will be found in the works on heraldry listed in chapter VIII. Adapted from J. Edmondson, *A complete body of heraldry*, London, 1780.

Although the use of bookplates in Britain goes back to the sixteenth century, the term 'bookplate' does not seem to have been used until the end of the eighteenth century, and the first recorded occurrence dates from 1791.[6] The study of bookplates has always been closely allied to bookplate collecting, which was a virtually unknown hobby here before the mid-nineteenth century, but which became popular in the 1880s and has retained a following ever since. The history of bookplate collecting in this country has been chronicled by Brian North Lee:

B. N. Lee: *Bookplate collecting in Britain past and present*. London, 1991.

Bookplate collectors have stimulated much useful work on bookplate history, and the catalogues which exist for some of the major collections provide a starting point for research on the identification of particular plates. It must also be said that they have done immense damage by removing plates from the books

6 W. J. Hardy, *Bookplates*, London, 1893, p. 6.

in which they belong. One of the standard late nineteenth century histories of bookplates, by W. J. Hardy, includes the advice that 'there is, to my mind, no harm in removing, from some perfectly uninteresting or valueless volume, the book-plate of a famous man'. Such sentiments are totally incompatible with the serious study of private libraries, and collectors who remove bookplates should be ranked with autograph hunters who mutilate title pages to cut out owners' inscriptions. It is to be hoped that the steaming-out of bookplates is less common today than it once was, but it is a practice wholly to be discouraged. The great Franks collection of 52,000 bookplates represents tens of thousands of books whose provenance is now lost and cannot be reconstructed.

It should also be pointed out that bookplates have sometimes been pasted into books by people other than the owners, most commonly by members of the book trade. Given that distinguished provenance enhances a book's value, the motive for this practice is easy to see. When the library of Charles Dickens (1812-70) was sold after his death, the auctioneers had a special label printed ('From the library of Charles Dickens, Gadshill Place, June 1870'), which was pasted into books not otherwise bearing one of Dickens's genuine plates.[7] This is fairly acceptable, but more fraudulent cases are recorded; Wilmarth Lewis, describing the library of Horace Walpole (1717-97), wrote that 'older book-sellers have told me that before 1925 when they had a Strawberry Hill book of little value in poor condition they would soak off the book-plate (which was worth half a crown) and sell it separately or stick it into another book'.[8] It is hard to estimate just how prevalent this practice has been, but there can be little doubt that it carries on to this day.

Bookplates can be looked at not only from a bibliographical viewpoint, but also from an art-historical one. Many studies of bookplates deal with their design, or with the artists and engravers who produced them; this is particularly the case with twentieth-century bookplates. This is a line of pursuit which is outside the scope of the present book, and studies of bookplates which concentrate primarily on their design or artistic interest are not included in the list of references.

IDENTIFYING BOOKPLATES

Given a particular bookplate, there are a number of avenues of research which may yield useful information on the owner. There are **biographical** and **heraldic** reference works; **bibliographies** or **lists** of bookplates; major **collections** of bookplates in various institutions; **journals** devoted to the study of bookplates, or likely to contain articles concerning bookplates; published

---

7 See B. N. Lee, The authenticity of bookplates, *The Book Collector* 30 (1981), 62-73, p. 64; this article contains other examples, and a wider discussion, of the kinds of problems mentioned in this paragraph.

8 W. S. Lewis, *Horace Walpole's library*, Cambridge. 1958, pp. 56-7.

catalogues of exhibitions of bookplates; and **books about bookplates** and their history.

The identification of bookplates is often not as simple as it may at first appear. Even a plate with a name and a coat of arms may present problems, as research into the history of the family often reveals several members with the same name within the span of a few generations. Hence it is important to be able to assess roughly when the plate was made. The problems may not stop here, as it is common to find that plates remained in use for many years, and possibly for several generations. An original copper or steel plate may be used to produce several different impressions over a long period of time, with the possibility of slight changes being made between printings. It may therefore be useful to examine the major collections, and the secondary literature, to discover what, if anything, is known of the pattern of use of a particular plate.

The biographical and heraldic reference works often provide the best place to begin when seeking to identify a bookplate and learn more about the owner and his collection. The specialised bookplate literature may then be consulted for supporting information, which may or may not be found, depending on the extent to which that particular plate has been studied. The first thing to do, when looking at a bookplate, is to assign a rough date, based on the decorative style. If it incorporates the owner's name, he or she may be sought through the various biographical sources listed in chapter VIII, using any additional clues which the plate may provide to choose the right place to begin. (If the owner has a degree, for example, he ought to appear in one of the university lists.) With armorial plates, use the heraldic information too: check the arms against Burke's *General armory* if the name is given, or against Papworth's *Ordinary* if it is not. Fairbairn's *Crests* may provide a helpful shortcut through the heraldic maze for bookplates which have a crest or motto. Indications of rank (coronets, helms) should be taken into account. The identification of armorials with no name, or with initials only, must of course rely primarily on the heraldic sources, and fuller details of those just mentioned, and others, will be found in the opening section of chapter VIII.

Several useful articles on heraldic bookplates have been published in *The Bookplate Journal*; for a good introduction to the subject at a basic level, see:

C. R. Lattimore, 'Heraldry and bookplates', *The Bookplate Journal* 2(2) (1984), pp. 61-74.

Two articles by Peter Allpress have dealt with specific heraldic features:

'Augmentations of honour on armorial bookplates', *The Bookplate Journal* 5(2) (1987), pp. 53-89, and 6(2) (1988), pp. 4-93 [the second section is an alphabetical list of bookplates containing augmentations];
'Orders of chivalry and decorations depicted on bookplates', *The Bookplate Journal* 8(1) (1990), pp. 14-40.

Cipher bookplates, in which the owner's initials, or possibly all the letters of his name, are entwined together in an elaborate pattern, present particular problems as the letters forming the design may be difficult, if not impossible, to unravel. There is little guidance to be offered here, beyond pointing out that there are a number of seventeenth and eighteenth century pattern books, which were popular for providing monograms for various uses. Reference to these may at least show how the designers' minds worked, and provide clues for teasing out complicated patterns:

J. Marlow, *A book of cyphers or letters reverst*, London, 1683 (Wing M 698)
B. Rhodes, *A new book of cyphers*, London, [1696?] (Wing R 1326B)
W. Parsons, *A new book of cyphers*, London, 1704 (ESTC t116152)
J. Pigot, *A complete alphabet of cyphers reversed & inverted*, [London, 1705?] (ESTC t125566)
H. Dod, *Book of cyphers*, London, [1710?] (ESTC t95128)
J. Nutting, *A new book of cyphers*, London, [1720?] (ESTC t87042)
S. Sympson, *A new book of cyphers*, London, [1726] (ESTC t145073)
A new book of cyphers, London, for Cartington Bowles and Robert Sayer, [1773?] (ESTC t87386)
J. Lockington, *A new and complete set of cyphers*, [London, 1777] (ESTC t118598)
P. Barraud, *A new book of single cyphers*, [London, 1782] (ESTC t90329)

Standard bibliographies

E. R. J. Gambier Howe: *Franks bequest. Catalogue of British and American book plates bequeathed to the Trustees of the British Museum by Sir Augustus Wollaston Franks*. 3 vols. London, 1903-04.

The catalogue of the Franks collection of bookplates, one of the largest ever assembled before it was bequeathed to the British Museum in 1897, has acquired the status of a standard bibliography of bookplates and it is common to find it cited, by means of the running catalogue numbers ('Franks 12897', etc.) in other works on bookplates. The British and American plates run to over 35,000 (this is the only part of the collection with a published catalogue, but not the sum total of the collection; see the section on *Collections of bookplates* below, p. 73). It is arranged alphabetically by owners' names, with a description of the style in each case ('Jacobean armorial', 'Armorial spade shield', etc.), but is in many ways an unsatisfactory tool as it includes very few illustrations, and biographical information only selectively. It lists different states of particular plates with different reference numbers, but with very little (or no) detail as to the distinguishing features. Despite its disadvantages, it is the most comprehensive list of British bookplates available, and there seems little prospect of its revision or replacement in the forseeable future.

British bookplates printed, or bearing date, before 1641 are listed in A. W. Pollard and G. R. Redgrave, *A short-title catalogue of books printed in England, Scotland, & Ireland ... 1475-1640*, 2nd revised edn, London, 1976-91, in one sequence at the entry point 3368.5 BOOKPLATES (with extensive addenda in volume 3, pp. 267-269). Most of the items listed are strictly printed book labels rather than plates; inked book stamps before 1641 are also included.

Bookplates are excluded from D. Wing, *Short-title catalogue ... 1641-1700*, and from the *Eighteenth-century Short Title Catalogue*.

Collections of bookplates

A number of libraries have collections of bookplates, usually formed by individuals and subsequently acquired by gift or bequest. Such collections, when adequately catalogued, may prove useful for purposes of comparison when trying to identify particular plates. This section lists some of the more significant collections in British libraries. It does not include indexes to bookplates which are still *in situ* in the books to which they belong; such indexes are listed among the provenance indexes in Chapter VII. Fuller details of the addresses and opening arrangements of the libraries concerned can be found in the *Directory of rare book and special collections*, edited by M. I. Williams, London, 1985.

ABERYSTWYTH – NATIONAL LIBRARY OF WALES
The National Library holds a number of discrete collections:
Sir Evan D. Jones collection: about 1700 plates of Welsh interest; a catalogue, *The Welsh book plates in the collection of Sir Evan D. Jones*, was published in 1920 with a *Supplement* in 1928, both by H. M. Vaughan.
Aneurin Williams collection: a miscellaneous collection of about 850 plates, also with a published catalogue by H. M. Vaughan: *National Library of Wales. Catalogue (with notes) of the Aneurin Williams collection of book plates*, Aberystwyth, 1938.
Elenor collection: about 225 miscellaneous plates, presented by H. F. Elenor in 1938; a catalogue is available in the Library.
Arthur Schomberg/H. M. Vaughan collection: ca. 2600 plates; a catalogue made in 1944 is held in the Library.
Hemp collection: about 500 plates, including some Welsh ones, not catalogued.

There are also some smaller collections, and a miscellaneous group of bookplates assembled from various sources. The collections in the National Library, down to 1940, were described by Vaughan in an article on 'Book plates in the National Library of Wales', *The National Library of Wales Journal* 1 (1940), 131-135.

CAMBRIDGE – FITZWILLIAM MUSEUM
Turnbull collection: a collection of ca. 15,000 plates, mostly British but including some European and American ones, 17th-20th centuries. Arranged alphabetically, loose or mounted, in name order; there is no catalogue or index and intending users should apply in writing to the Department of Paintings, Drawings & Prints well in advance of making a visit.

EDINBURGH – NATIONAL LIBRARY OF SCOTLAND
There are a number of separate collections:
Henderson Smith collection: a major collection in 40 volumes, mainly Scottish and English plates 17th-19th centuries, but also including some American and miscellaneous categories.
John A. Lamb collection: another large collection in 23 volumes, mostly foreign bookplates from the middle of the 19th to the beginning of the 20th century. Also includes a collection of labels from Scottish circulating libraries.
Stitt collection: a miscellaneous collection in 3 volumes.
Culley collection: miscellaneous Scottish and English plates, with some American ones, in 5 volumes.
  All these collections are covered by a slip catalogue arranged alphabetically, with unidentified plates arranged by designer, engraver, or type of plate.

HOVE – HOVE CENTRAL LIBRARY
Wolseley collection: A miscellaneous collection of ca. 1500 bookplates, mostly English, 17th-20th centuries, a mixture of personal and institutional owners, assembled by Viscountess Wolseley (1872-1936). There is a manuscript catalogue made by the Viscountess and a separate card index with brief descriptions and biographical notes.

LIVERPOOL – CITY REFERENCE LIBRARY
The Library has extensive holdings of bookplates, the bulk being a collection of ca. 20,000 plates formed by J. F. Smith and incorporating the earlier J. C. Stitt collection, now arranged in an alphabetical sequence, mounted on cards. There are no separate indexes or catalogues.

LONDON – BRITISH LIBRARY
The British Library does not hold any major collections of bookplates, as the Franks and other collections remained with the British Museum when the Library was formed in 1973 (see below). There is a small album of miscellaneous plates and labels, 17th-20th century and largely continental, with shelfmark C.66.f.3.

LONDON – BRITISH MUSEUM
The Department of Prints & Drawings holds the major national collection of bookplates, comprising the Franks bequest and several other important collections:
Franks collection: collected by Sir Augustus Franks, Keeper of British and Medieval Antiquities at the Museum, and bequeathed on his death in 1897. Incorporates the Rozière and Bilco collections of continental bookplates, which Franks acquired *en bloc*. Comprises over 35,000 British and American plates; nearly 5000 German and nearly 9000 French plates; and smaller collections

from other countries. Mounted in albums; the British and American portion (only) has a published catalogue (see p. 71 above).

Rosenheim collection: ca. 11,000 plates, collected by Max Rosenheim and given in 1932. Mostly continental; mounted on cards and arranged in boxes by country of origin. No separate catalogue.

Viner collection: formed by G. H. Viner and given in 1950. Contains over 8000 British plates (ca. 5500 pre-1800), not found in the Franks collection. Arranged in several sequences by owner, engraver or subject; no separate catalogue.

The Department also holds several other miscellaneous sequences of bookplates, mostly modern. For more detailed information on all the collections, and on access to them, see:

A. Griffiths & R. Williams: *The Department of Prints & Drawings in the British Museum: user's guide*, London, 1987, particularly pp. 86-87.

LONDON – CHELSEA REFERENCE LIBRARY

A collection of ca. 3500 bookplates has been acquired through several gifts, miscellaneous in scope and date (16th-20th centuries). There is a card index arranged by names of owners, with a small separate sequence of artists (where known).

LONDON – COLLEGE OF ARMS

Viner collection: given by G. H. Viner between 1935 and 1952; comprises 27 albums of miscellaneous plates, plus a further 13 albums containing a collection of seal-pattern plates, and a sequence of plates belonging to persons mentioned in the *Dictionary of National Biography*. The main series of albums does not include any plates which are not also found in the Franks collection in the British Museum.

Besides the Viner collection, the College has several other small collections of bookplates. There are no catalogues or indexes. All these collections are maintained for the use of the heralds and associated staff of the College, and they are not normally available for direct public consultation. Enquiries relating to armorial identifications should be addressed to the Officer in Waiting in the first instance.

LONDON – GUILDHALL LIBRARY

J. G. Bradford collection: a collection of ca. 5000 miscellaneous plates, mounted in 33 volumes, with a name index.

In addition, the Guildhall Library has a separate un-named collection of ca. 750 miscellaneous plates, mounted on cards and filed alphabetically. These plates are covered by a slip index giving names, brief descriptions and Franks numbers where applicable (this index also includes some references to bookplates found in Guildhall Library books).

LONDON – THE HERALDIC SOCIETY

Porteous collection: ca. 25,000 plates mounted in albums, largely 19th century, both British and foreign. Some thematic arrangement but otherwise rather randomly assembled; no catalogue or index.

Marshall collection: ca. 3000 plates collected by George Marshall, York Herald (d.1905), augmented by a further recent bequest to the Society of a further 3000. Miscellaneous in scope, but largely 19th-20th centuries. This collection is being arranged and indexed.

These collections may be consulted at the Society's Library, 44/45 Museum Street, London, WC1; enquirers must contact the Librarian in advance, preferably in writing.

LONDON – ROYAL COLLEGE OF PHYSICIANS

Barlow collection: a collection of ca. 2700 plates of medics and medical institutions, formed by Horace M. Barlow. A catalogue is available in the Library.

LONDON – ROYAL COLLEGE OF SURGEONS

James collection: ca. 2000 plates of British medical men. 17th-19th centuries, collected by Robert Ruston James (1881-1959). They are arranged by style and mounted in loose leaf binders, interleaved with biographical notes.

The College also has a smaller separate collection of bookplates, mainly 20th century and including foreign and institutional examples; these are mounted on cards and have an accompanying catalogue.

LONDON – SOCIETY OF ANTIQUARIES

Hall Crouch collection: ca. 7000 British bookplates, 17th-20th centuries, arranged alphabetically; given to the Society in 1964.

The Library also houses a few other smaller collections of plates, including the Garroway Rice Collection (mostly 19th century British armorial bookplates, collected by R. Garroway Rice 1880-1900, in 3 volumes, with an index), and the Viner Collection (one volume of Oxford and Cambridge bookplates, 17th-20th centuries, arranged by colleges).

NEWCASTLE-UPON-TYNE – CITY LIBRARY

Hill and Mackay collection: a collection of ca. 1800 bookplates, 17th-20th centuries, appertaining to owners from Northumberland and Durham. Mounted in six loose paper portfolios and arranged alphabetically by owners' names. There is no separate index, but a few plates have annotations or biographical notes.

The Pease Collection of books, drawings, albums and other material relating to the celebrated wood engravers John and Thomas Bewick, formed by J. W. Pease (d.1901) and bequeathed to Newcastle City Library, includes considerable bookplate material. No. 180 in the Collection is a large album of British bookplates and related ephemera, formed by the antiquary John Bell (1823-66) and supplemented by Joseph Crawhall. Many of the plates relate to north country owners. The album is arranged in alphabetical order and is extensively annotated with notes on the collectors. Bell's album contains only a small proportion of Bewick items but Bewick's bookplates are represented in other parts of the Pease Collection (nos. 171, 177; see B. Anderton & W. H. Gibson, *Catalogue of the Bewick Collection (Pease Bequest)*, Newcastle, 1904).

All the above material is available in the Local Studies Department of the Library.

OXFORD – BODLEIAN LIBRARY
The Bodleian possesses two major collections of bookplates, in the John Johnson collection (acquired 1968), and the Harding collection (acquired 1975). Odd collections of loose plates owned by the Library before 1968 have mostly been incorporated into the John Johnson collection.
John Johnson collection: The bookplates fall into two main sequences – a series in sheaf binders in Franks number order, and a separate series mounted on cards and organised in box files in a classified sequence. There are also a few other small sequences within the collection: a binder containing labels from various libraries, classified as *John Johnson Collection Bookplate Labels*, a box of miscellaneous bookplates at *John Johnson Collection Bookplates – Libraries 1*, and three boxes of labels from circulating and lending libraries, at *John Johnson Collection Libraries – Labels*.
Harding collection: the bookplates are mounted on cards and held in a separate alphabetical sequence. There is no separate catalogue.

The combined resources of these collections number many thousands of plates and labels, 17th-20th centuries. They are consulted in Room 132 (Modern manuscripts and John Johnson collection) and it is generally helpful if researchers wishing to use the collections contact the Library in advance of their visit, so that staff responsible for the John Johnson material can give the most effective help.

Collections of bookplates outside the UK

It is not possible, within the scope of this handbook, to provide a detailed guide to collections of bookplates across the world. Naturally, such collections exist in the major libraries of many countries. Two major collections of **Irish** book-plates are held in the Genealogical Office in Dublin (2 Kildare Street), the Chamney collection (ca. 15,000 plates, collected by William Chamney, d.1926) and the Wilkinson collection (ca. 10,000 plates, collected by Sir Nevile Wilkinson, Ulster King of Arms, d.1940). Both these collections are primarily focussed on heraldic plates. Brief details of the most significant collections in **North America** will be found in L. Ash & W. G. Miller, *Subject collections ... in*

the United States and Canada, 5th edition, New York & London, 1978, p. 148.
See also:

C. T. Evans & C. S. Baer, *Census of bookplate collections in public, college and university libraries in the United States*, Washington, 1938.

> Compiled from a postal survey of public, college and university libraries in America; lists many of the major U.S. collections and also a number of smaller ones, but naturally now rather out of date.

Journals

There are a number of past and present journals devoted primarily to the study of bookplates, but articles about bookplates have appeared in many journals, bibliographical and otherwise. There is, fortunately, an extensive index to work about bookplates published in a wide range of journals, down to 1970:

A. S. Arellanes: *Bookplates: a selective annotated bibliography of the periodical literature.* Detroit, 1971.

This covers several hundred periodicals, mainly but not exclusively British or American, and it includes of necessity a detailed analysis of the contents of the specialised bookplate journals (e.g. *The Ex Libris Journal*).

Various societies of bookplate collectors have generated a number of such journals over the last century. Only the most important, for research on historic British plates, are listed below.

Journal of the Ex Libris Society v. 1-18, 1891-1908.

> Contained a wide range of notes and articles on historic and contemporary bookplates, well illustrated. A detailed *General index*, by W. H. K. Wright, was published in 1904, covering vols. 1-12 (1891-1904).

The Bookplate Journal 1983-

> The journal of The Bookplate Society, founded in 1972, which sees itself as a continuation of the Ex Libris Society, although that body ceased to exist as a journal-publishing organisation in 1908. *The Bookplate Journal*, which appears twice a year, carries a range of well-illustrated notes and articles on bookplates and it includes much valuable material on historic plates as well as moden ones. An index is published after every fourth volume. The Society also issues *The Bookplate Society Newsletter* (1972-) which includes short notes on bookplates as well as news of the Society's activities.

Outside the UK, there are numerous journals devoted to bookplates; indeed, every country in which bookplates are seriously collected is likely to have at least one journal. The *American Society of Bookplate Collectors and Designers Yearbook* reached its 50th annual volume in 1989; recent issues have been more concerned with twentieth-century bookplates than historic ones. This Society also produces a newsletter (*Bookplates in the news*) which carries short notes and reviews; its ongoing feature 'From the bookplate literature' provides retrospective and current coverage of a wide range of publications dealing with bookplates.

In France, *L'Ex libris français: bulletin de l'association française pour la conaissance de l'ex libris* is published three times a year. It is a newsletter which carries notes and short articles, and is international in scope.

Exhibition catalogues

Bookplates have been included in numerous exhibitions; some of the more substantial ones have generated published catalogues which form a useful addition to the bookplate literature, especially if they are illustrated. A selection of such catalogues is listed here.

Catalogue of the sixth annual exhibition of the Ex Libris Society held at the Westminster Palace Hotel, London. London, 1897.

> Arranged by exhibitors (Society members), with lists of their exhibits. Includes a chronological list of dated bookplates included in the exhibition.

Catalogue of a loan exhibition of book-plates and super-libros held by the Club of Odd Volumes, at the Museum of Fine Arts, April 25th to June 5th, 1898. Boston, 1898.

> Over 2000 exhibits. Includes some illustrations, a brief historical introduction, a bibliography and an index. The super-libros are a small group of armorial bindings, mostly royal.

A history of bookplates in Britain: catalogue of the Bookplate Society's fourth exhibition. London, 1979.

> Held at the Victoria & Albert Museum. Includes short biographical notes, but not illustrated.

B. N. Lee: *London bookplates. A catalogue of the Bookplate Society's 1984 exhibition at the Guildhall Library.* London, 1985.

> A substantial and very useful catalogue, covering personal and institutional bookplates with a London connection; over 300 plates are described in some detail, with many illustrations.

P. Latcham: *Herefordshire bookplates: an exhibition at Hereford City Museum ... 1988.* Hereford, 1988.

> 100 exhibits, most of them illustrated, 17th-20th centuries, with biographical notes. Useful for Herefordshire plates – the criterion for inclusion was that 'the owner was permanently resident for a period in the county'.

Books about bookplates

The literature on bookplates, written in this country, has reflected the changing popularity of bookplate collecting. The first historical overview was published in 1880 and the next 30 years saw the publication of numerous guides and handbooks, some of which covered much the same ground. This was the period of great activity in bookplate collecting, encompassing the life of the Ex Libris Society (1891-1908). Then for the next 50 years or so, until the formation of the Bookplate Society in 1972, very little work was done, and most of the material published during that time which dealt with bookplates was concerned with the design of contemporary plates, rather than the historical angle. The recent revival of interest has led to the appearance of new studies of the history and development of bookplates, most particularly in the work of Brian North Lee, and in various articles published in *The Bookplate Journal*.

The bibliography below is divided into three parts; the first two parts deal with British bookplates, and are divided in this way so that recent publications are listed first, as they offer the most useful starting point for any research into bookplate history. The older material in Section B is however still useful, particularly if it is well illustrated. Section C offers a highly selective listing of works on foreign bookplates; this is not a field which can be covered systematically in this book, as the literature is very extensive, but it may offer some starting points for tracing non-British bookplates. It should be stressed that all sections are selective rather than comprehensive, and are concerned only with reasonably substantial works which cover a wide field. References to a greater range of material will be found in the **Bibliographies of works on bookplates** listed on p. 82.

A. Recent works

B. N. Lee: *British bookplates: a pictorial history*. Newton Abbot, 1979.

> The best modern introduction to the subject, extensively illustrated to show the chronological development of styles.

B. N. Lee: *British royal bookplates and bookplates of related families*. Aldershot, 1992.

> A detailed and exhaustive study of bookplates and labels connected with British royalty.

B. N. Lee: *Bookpile bookplates*. Birmingham, 1992.

> A detailed and comprehensively illustrated survey of British bookpile plates to 1870, with a briefer examination of post-1870 plates.

B. N. Lee: Pictorial bookplates in Britain. *The Private Library* 3rd ser 5 (1982), 58-116.

> An entire issue of *The Private Library* devoted to a survey of pictorial (as opposed to armorial) bookplates.

B. N. Lee: Gentlemen and their bookplates, in R. Myers & M. Harris (eds.), *Property of a gentleman*, Winchester, 1991, pp. 42-76.

> A well-illustrated survey, concentrating on the late seventeenth and eighteenth centuries.

B. N. Lee: Bookplates and bibliography in R. Myers & M. Harris (eds.), *Bibliophily* (Publishing History Occasional Series 2), Cambridge, 1986, pp. 22-43.

> The text of a lecture giving a summary history of the development of styles, with microfiche illustrations.

A brief history of bookplates in Britain, with reference to examples at the Victoria and Albert Museum. London, 1979.

> A short but well-illustrated essay written to complement an exhibition held by the Bookplate Society at the V & A in 1979.

T. R. Young: *Some Yorkshire bookplates*. Birmingham 1991.

> A listing of 170 plates belonging to men and women with some Yorkshire connection, with many illustrations, and biographical notes.

B. Older material

E. Castle: *English book-plates: an illustrated handbook*. London, 1892; new and enlarged edn, 1893.

> Well illustrated; includes information not available elsewhere on bookplates of the Victorian period.

H. W. Fincham: *Artists and engravers of British and American book plates*. London, 1897.

> An alphabetical list of over 1500 artists and engravers, identified from signed bookplates of the 17th to the 19th centuries, with lists of plates known to be their work. For the purposes of identifying owners, this book is particularly useful for anonymous plates which carry an artist's or engraver's signature.

W. Griggs: *88 examples of armorial bookplates*. London, 1884. *147 examples of armorial bookplates*. London, 1892.

> A series of good quality reproductions of early and rare plates, with biographical notes annexed.

W. Hamilton: *Dated book-plates, with a treatise on their origin and development*. London, 1895.

> An attempt to produce a catalogue of all dated bookplates, English, American, and continental, down to 1895. Includes some illustrations. The arrangement is chronological, but as it has addenda it is advisable to consult the index first.

W. J. Hardy: *Book-plates*. London, 1893.

> One of the best of the early monographs, with many reproductions. There are chapters on European and American plates.

J. J. Howard: *The Wardour Press series of armorial bookplates: Baronets*. London, 1895.

> Reproduces 97 plates, mostly 18th century, with good genealogical notes.

N. Labouchère: *Ladies' book-plates*. London, 1895.

> Principally concerned with British plates, but includes sections on French and German ones. Attempts a catalogue of 'English ladies' book-plates'.

J. P. Rylands: Notes on book-plates (ex-libris), with special reference to Lancashire and Cheshire examples. *Transactions of the Historic Society of Lancashire and Cheshire* 40 (n.s. 4) (1890), pp. 1-54.

J. Leicester Warren (later Baron de Tabley): *A guide to the study of book-plates*. London, 1880, reprinted (unrevised), Manchester, 1900.

> The first major study of bookplates, in which the major stylistic terminologies were stated and defined.

C. Foreign bookplates

Australia: P. N. Barnett: *Australian book-plates and book-plates of interest to Australia.* Sydney, 1950.

> Covers bookplates and labels used in Australia from the end of the eighteenth century to the middle of the twentieth.

Denmark: A. G. Hasso: *Danske exlibris.* Copenhagen, 1942.

> A substantial and well-illustrated survey of the development of Danish bookplates; the great majority of the plates reproduced date from the modern period, but a number of earlier ones are included. There is a short English summary of the text.

France: W. Hamilton: *French book-plates.* London, 1896.

> An attempt to offer an illustrated overview of the history and development of French bookplates.

J. C. Wiggishof: *Dictionnaire des dessinateurs et graveurs d'ex-libris français.* Paris, 1915.

> A dictionary of artists and engravers of historic French plates, with many reproductions of the plates concerned; particularly useful for identifying anonymous plates.

M. Moeder: *Les ex-libris Alsaciens des origines a mil huit cent quatre-vingt-dix.* Strasbourg, 1926.

> Well-illustrated, with biographical details of collectors.

G. Meyer-Noirel: *L'ex-libris: histoire, art, techniques.* Paris, 1989.

> A wide ranging and well illustrated history of the development of the bookplate in France from the sixteenth century to the present day.

Germany: F. Warnecke: *Die deutschen Bücherzeichen (Ex-libris) von ihrem ursprunge bis zur Gegenwort.* Berlin, 1890.

> Lists and describes over 2500 German plates, although only a few are illustrated.

Karl Emich Count zu Leiningen-Westerburg (tr. G. R. Dennis): *German bookplates: an illustrated handbook.* London, 1901.

> A general historical overview.

Ireland: H. F. Burke: *Examples of Irish bookplates from the collections of Sir Bernard Burke.* London, 1894.

> Reproductions of 71 eighteenth-century Irish plates, but no biographical notes.

Italy: A. Bertarelli & D. H. Prior: *Gli ex-libris.* Milan, 1902.

J. Gelli: *3500 ex-libris Italiani.* Milan, 1908.

> The second, enlarged edition of 1930, published as *Gli ex libris Italiani*, has over 1200 illustrations.

Netherlands: F. van Koolwijk & K. Rodel: *Bibliografi over hollandsk exlibrislitteratur 1890-1975.* Frederikshavn, 1977.

> A selective bibliography of material published in Dutch books and periodicals. The numerous illustrations are mostly of modern bookplates.

Poland: E. Chwalewik: *Exlibrisy Polskie: szesnastego i siedemnastego wieku.* Wroclaw, 1955.

> Well-illustrated, with ca. 70 examples of early Polish plates.

Switzerland: A. Wegmann: *Schweizer ex-libris bis zum jahre 1900.* 2v. Zurich, 1933-37.

> The major work on Swiss bookplates and super-libros marks of ownership; many illustrations.

U.S.A.: C. D. Allen: *American bookplates: a guide to their study.* New York, 1895; reprinted (unrevised) New York, 1968.

> Describes the development of bookplates in the U.S.A. down to the end of the nineteenth century, and includes a catalogue of about 1000 U.S. plates, with brief descriptions, and some illustrations.

C. D. Allen: *A classified list of early American bookplates.* New York, 1894.

> Compiled to accompany an exhibition at the Grolier Club. Classified by design, and well illustrated.

Bibliographies of works on bookplates

Interest in bookplates has generated a very considerable literature on the subject, in many languages, although much of it is concerned with the design of contemporary bookplates. The works cited in this chapter form the tip of a very large iceberg, and they have been chosen very selectively as being the most useful starting points for any research on an individual historic plate. There are some bibliographies which list a wider range of material, although there is, unfortunately, no recent guide which is comprehensive in scope.

For periodical articles down to 1970, the most useful bibliography is Audrey Arellanes, *Bookplates: a selective annotated bibliography of the periodical literature,* Detroit, 1971, described in the section on Journals on p. 77 above. Other bibliographies are:

V. J. Brenni: *Bookbinding: a guide to the literature.* London, 1983.

> Chapter 11, pp. 109-116, is devoted to bookplates.

G. W. Fuller: *A bibliography of bookplate literature.* Washington, 1926, reprinted (unrevised), Detroit, 1973.

BOOK LABELS

The definition of book labels, and their distinction from bookplates, is not altogether clear and the standard authorities do not offer satisfactory clarification. John Carter's definition of a book label, in his *ABC for book collectors*, is 'a label of ownership, usually affixed to one of the front endpapers and (whether engraved or printed) simpler in style and smaller than a bookplate', and Philip Beddingham, in *Concerning booklabels*, suggests that a book label 'consists of an inscription only, although in some cases slight decoration is added to the borders and frames'. These definitions might be paraphrased as 'like a bookplate, only simpler', and they rely too much on subjective factors to be truly adequate. Some of the seventeenth century book labels, such as the gift label printed for the books given to St. John's College, Cambridge by Edward Benlowes in 1631, are both larger and verbally more elaborate than most bookplates.[9] Brian North Lee's definition of a bookplate as 'a design conceived as a whole and achieved by engraving, etching or some other reproductive process' offers a more satisfactory basis for distinction and the present writer prefers to define a bookplate as something printed from an engraved plate, of metal or wood, which incorporates the entire design, and a book label as something made up from separate pieces of moveable type and type ornaments. In hand-press terms, bookplates are normally printed on a rolling press, and book labels by letterpress. The exceptions, which do not fit neatly into these rules, are small engraved labels, comprising a name within a simple decorative border, which ought to be bookplates according to the rules just stated but which common sense inclines to call labels. These are not uncommon from the eighteenth century onwards and a number of examples are illustrated at the end of Brian North Lee's *British bookplates* (1979). There is a grey area here which defies neat resolution and a label which is engraved, not letterpress, should be described as an 'engraved book label' to minimise the confusion.

The use of book labels has been, and continues to be, very extensive. The earliest British examples date from the sixteenth century and, until the latter part of the seventeenth century, the production of book labels exceeded that of bookplates (most of the bookplates recorded in *STC* at 3368.5 are strictly labels, according to the definition given above). They are harder to date on the grounds of design, as they have not undergone the same changes of fashion as bookplates, and they must be dated more on their typography. The most commmon pattern for book labels, found in every century from the sixteenth to the present day, is a small rectangular frame, with the long side horizontal, containing the owner's name framed by a simple border of type ornaments. Date, place of residence, or degrees may be added to the name, or a simple phrase indicating ownership ('Elias Ashmole oweth this booke 1635'; 'E libris Rich: Chapman, Coll: Eman: Cantab: 1755'). Many of the early labels are gift labels, recording the donation of books to institutions, and many of the Oxford and Cambridge college libraries have such labels from the late sixteenth and early seventeenth centuries.

The gift labels of Francis Walsingham (1520?-90, fig. 3.23) and Andrew Bendlowes (fig. 3.24), both recording gifts to King's College, Cambridge, are examples of the latter; the Bendlowes label is very simple, without a decorative border. The label of Thomas Henshaw, thought to be ca. 1610, carries only the owner's name (fig. 3.25); the later seventeenth century label of John Milton (fig. 3.26; not the poet, but his nephew, b.1653) shows his college and a precise date (the date of printing? he matriculated the year before). The label of Sheppard

9 Illustrated in B. North Lee, *Early printed book labels*, Pinner, 1876, no. 75.

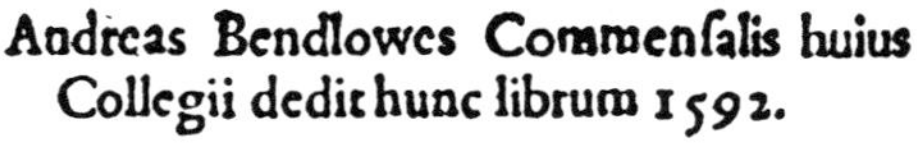

Andreas Bendlowes Commensalis huius
Collegii dedit hunc librum 1592.

Fig. 3.23 Gift-label of Andrew Bendlowes, recording his gift to King's College, Cambridge in 1592.

Ex dono Honoratissimi viri Francisci
Walsingami quondam alumni huius
Collegij. Anno. Domini. 1583.

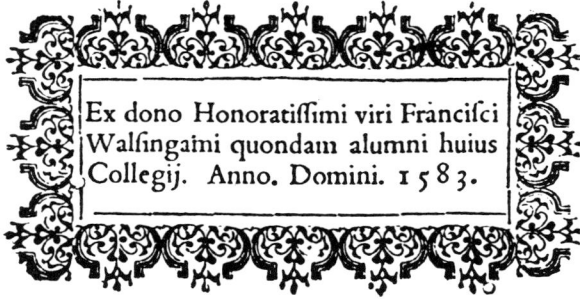

Fig. 3.24 Gift-label of Sir Francis Walsingham, recording his gift to King's College, Cambridge in 1583.

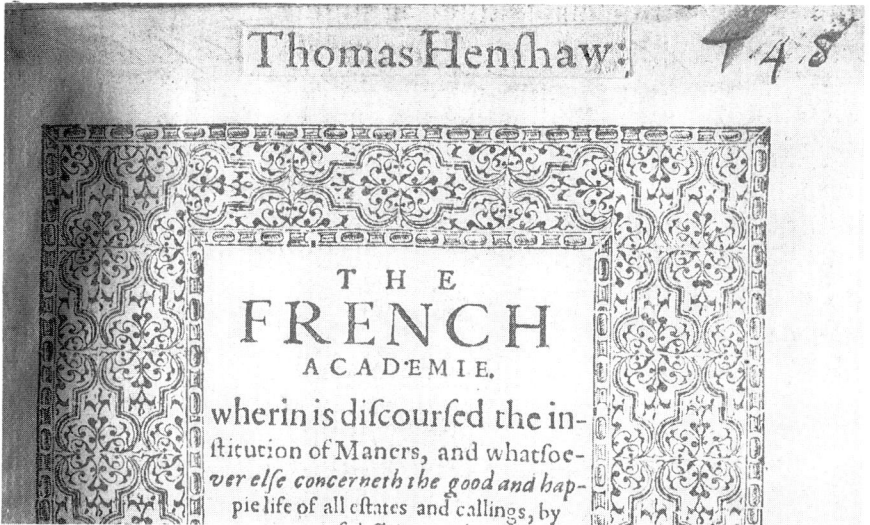

Fig. 3.25 The book label of Thomas Henshaw, ca. 1610, pasted at the head of the title page of P. de la Primaudaye, *The French academie*, 1602: Cosin's Library, Durham T.IV.8.

JOHANNES MILTON,

Aul. *Pembr.* *Cantab.*

Octob. 14. 1659.

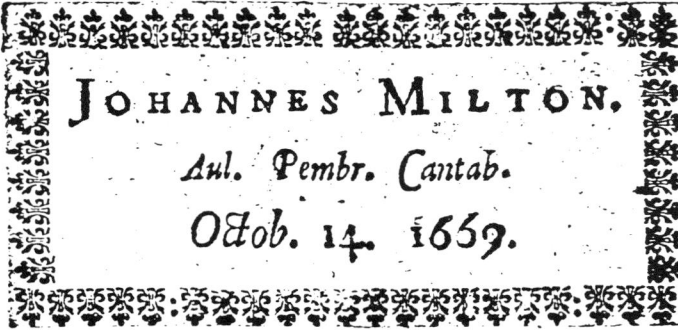

Fig. 3.26 Book label of John Milton, nephew of the poet.

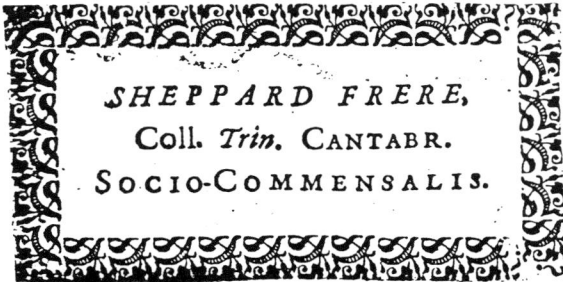

SHEPPARD FRERE,

Coll. *Trin.* CANTABR.

SOCIO-COMMENSALIS.

Fig. 3.27 Book label of Sheppard Frere (Franks 11400).

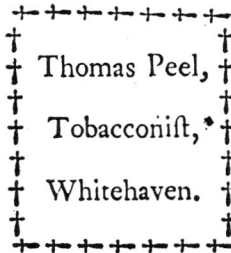

Thomas Peel,

Tobacconist,

Whitehaven.

Fig. 3.28 Book label of Thomas Peel of Whitehaven.

Frere (1714-80, fig. 3.27), who became a fellow-commoner of Trinity College, Cambridge in 1732, shows the same design half a century later, and that of John Gwennap (shown in fig. 3.2) is another example from the second half of the eighteenth century. The label of Thomas Peel of Whitehaven, also from the second half of the eighteenth century, shows a slight variation upon the usual shape (fig. 3.28). Many more examples of book labels are illustrated in Brian North Lee's *Early printed book labels* (see below).

Bookplates are very occasionally found printed directly into books (see p. 66 above) and in much the same way there are odd examples of books with personal ownership 'labels' printed in. Fig. 3.29 shows a nice example; this is a copy of John Stow's *Survay of London* (1599) which belonged to his wife Elizabeth (a gift from John?), and which has 'Elizabeth Stow' printed on the title leaf verso within a frame of type ornaments. It was clearly printed before the book was bound. This is not strictly a book label, as it represents a one-off setting of type and there is no reason to think that it was used to print other labels or inscriptions.

The bibliographical sources which help in the identification of book labels are principally those which relate to bookplates also. Labels are listed in the Franks catalogue and in Pollard and Redgrave's *Short-title catalogue*, and they are represented in the major collections of bookplates. As a genre they are not given much prominence in the secondary works on bookplate history, and they have received little scholarly attention. The one significant exception to this is a major study of dated British book labels down to 1760:

B. N. Lee: *Early printed book labels: a catalogue of dated personal labels and gift labels printed in Britain to the year 1760.* Pinner, 1976.

This attempts to list all known labels which include a printed date; it incorporates much biographical material, and is well illustrated. It is the primary source of reference for dated labels within its period, although its help is more restricted on the many undated labels which exist. Apart from this, there are very few published works devoted specifically to book labels:

Fig. 3.29 British Library G.5972: the title leaf verso of Elizabeth Stow's copy of John Stow's *Survay of London*, 1599, has this 'book label' printed directly into the book.

P. Beddingham, W. Carter, R. Stone: *Concerning booklabels*. London, 1963.

> A short essay on the use of book labels from the earliest times to the present day, illustrated with examples.

A. N. L. Munby: *Donors' labels printed for King's College Library, Cambridge*. [Cambridge, 1950].

> A brief illustrated survey of gift labels printed for King's College, 16th-20th centuries.

BOOK STAMPS

The use of metal, woodcut or rubber stamps, applied to the leaves of books to indicate ownership or gift, is a practice which dates back at least to the sixteenth century and is still widespread today. Rubber did not come into general use in Europe until the nineteenth century, and before then stamps were made by engraving metal or wood, or by piecing together letters of type. Some of the earliest stamps used in Britain are described in Appendix C of Brian North Lee's *Early printed books labels* (pp. 173-175); he mentions three examples dating from the 1560s and 1570s. The earliest ink stamp listed in *STC* is one used by Thomas Layther, Rector of St. Saviour's, York (d.1567). It occurs in a copy of the Works of St. Gregory the Great, printed in 1518 and now in Ushaw College, Durham; a date around 1550-60 seems probable (fig. 3.30).

Even earlier, and unrecorded by *STC*, is a stamp used by Robert Tregonwell, Chancellor of Wells (d.1543), found in an incunable in Aberdeen University Library (fig. 3.31). The British Library has a copy of Erasmus's edition of the

Fig. 3.30 Mid sixteenth-century ink stamp of Thomas Layther, with manuscript inscription above: Ushaw College, Durham, Gregory the Great, *Opera*, 1518.

Disticha de moribus, 1520, with another crude inked stamp in black letter type, 'this is Rychard: Hylles booke' applied on the title page and the final leaf (fig. 3.32); it also carries Hylle's inscription in a mid sixteenth-century hand, and a date roughly contemporary with Layther seems likely. These stamps appear to be made by piecing together black letter type. Another slightly later sixteenth century stamp mentioned by Lee is the one made for the books bequeathed by Clement Litill to the Kirk of Edinburgh in 1580, which was applied to the foot of the title pages of the books concerned.[10] A rather more elegant sixteenth-century stamp is that used by Henry Fitzalan, 12th Earl of Arundel (1511?-80), which occurs many times in the celebrated library which passed from him to John, Lord Lumley (1534-1609) and thence to Prince Henry and the Old Royal Library (fig. 3.33). There are two known examples of the armorial binding stamp of William Stewart, Bishop of Aberdeen (1479-1545) being inked and applied to pages within books, but this is an unusual practice and is essentially different from the other stampings mentioned here, where the stamps were always intended for internal rather than external use.[11]

Although a number of such early stamps are known, their use was not common in Britain in the sixteenth and seventeenth centuries, and more survive from the second half of the sixteenth century than from the whole of the seventeenth. One of the few seventeenth-century examples is the stamp used by the well-known collector Humfrey Dyson (d.1632), dated 1611, which is found in some, but not all, of his books (fig. 3.34). The use of inked stamps became widespread in the second half of the eighteenth century, and there are many late eighteenth and early nineteenth century examples. They often comprise only the owner's name, in upper case or mixed upper and lower case letters, such as the stamps of R. Roe, Mary Ball and John Webb (figs. 3.35-3.37), which all date from ca. 1775-1800. Owners sometimes included dates, or degrees; an example of the latter is shown in the stamp of John Lovat (fig. 3.38; he graduated M.A. in 1777 and died in 1805). Some owners had more than one stamp, such as Thomas Frewen, the Sussex physician who wrote about inoculation (1704-91); in a copy of *The navy-surgeon* by J. Atkins, 1734, now in the British Library, he used the two stamps on successive pages (figs. 3.39-3.40).

Occasionally more elaborate stamps were used, such as the gift-stamp of Lieutenant Higgins (fig. 3.41). It is unusual to find stamps cut as facsimile signatures, but the stamp used by Robert Harley, the founder of the Harleian Library (1661-1724), which is found stamped in gilt on the pastedowns of some of his books, is an example (fig. 3.42). The italic stamp of Sir William Musgrave (d.1799), benefactor to the British Museum Library, is another (fig. 3.43). An earlier example is the Arundel stamp shown in fig. 3.33. Richard Heber (1773-1833), one of the high priests of early nineteenth century bibliomania,

---

10 Reproduced in C. P. Finlayson, *Clement Litill and his library*, Edinburgh, 1980.
11 J. Durkan & A. Ross, *Early Scottish libraries* (*The Innes Review* 9(1), 1958), p. 65.

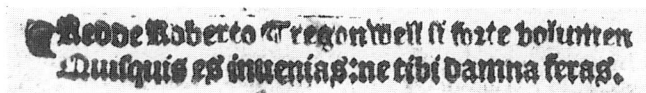

Fig. 3.31 Ink stamp of Robert Tregonwell, before 1543 (the year of his death): Aberdeen University Library Inc. 163, J. de Gaddesden, *Rosa anglica practica medicinae*, 1492.

Fig. 3.32 Mid sixteenth-century ink stamp of Rychard Hylle: British Library 720.f.27, *Disticha de moribus* (falsely attributed to M. P. Cato), 1520.

Fig. 3.33 Ink stamp of Henry Fitzalan, 12th earl of Arundel, next to the manuscript inscription of John, Lord Lumley: British Library C.128.f.12, *Sacrosancti … Concilii Ephesini … acta*, 1576.

Fig. 3.34 Ink stamp of Humfrey Dyson, dated 1611: Cambridge University Library Syn.7.57.51/4, J. Vowel, *The discription of the cittie of Excester*, [1575?].

R.ROE

Fig. 3.35 Late eighteenth-century ink stamp of R. Roe: British Library 1485.aaa.18, Catullus, 1774.

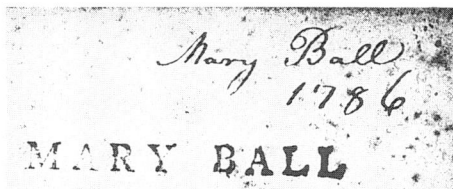

Fig. 3.36 Late eighteenth-century ink stamp of Mary Ball, with her inscription dated 1786: British Library 3052.aa.4, *Bible*, 1732.

I.Webb

Fig. 3.37 Late eighteenth-century ink stamp of John Webb: British Library 1508/1642, W. Saunders, *Elements of the practice of physick*, 1780.

J.S.Lovat A.M

Fig. 3.38 Late eighteenth-century ink stamp of John Lovat: British Library 1607/4237, E. Young, *Works*, 1774.

THO.FREWEN,M.D.   Thomas Frewen, M.D.

Figs. 3.39-3.40 Ink stamps of Thomas Frewen: British Library 1507/1103, J. Atkins, *The navy-surgeon*, 1734.

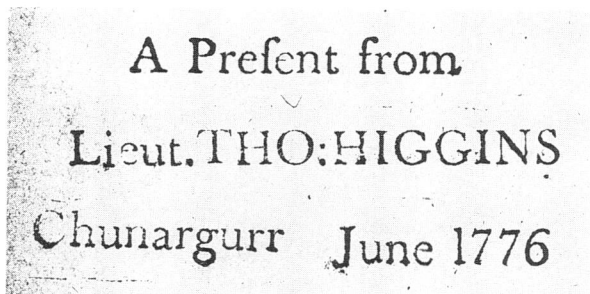

Fig. 3.41 Gift stamp of Thomas Higgins, June 1776: British Library 3006.p.3, *The holy Bible*, 1646.

Fig. 3.42 Facsimile signature stamp of Robert Harley, 1st Earl of Oxford, which was stamped in gilt in his books: British Library 883.e.30, *The acts of the general assemblies*, 1691.

Fig. 3.43 Facsimile signature stamp of Sir William Musgrave: British Library 866.a.5, *Manuale missionariorum regularum*, 1661.

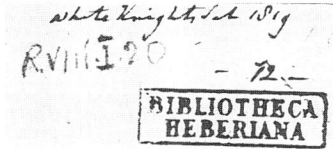

Fig. 3.44 Ink stamp of Richard Heber, with his characteristic inscription noting the method of acquisition ('White Knights Sale 1819'): Durham University Library R.VIII.I.20, C. Curio, *Christianae religionis institutio*, 1549.

Fig. 3.45 Ink stamp of John, 3rd Duke of Roxburghe: National Art Library Dyce 7526, M. Pix, *The double distress*, 1701.

Fig. 3.46 Ink stamp of Stephen Weston: National Art Library Dyce 8907, M. de Sevigné, *Sevigniana*, 1768.

whose celebrated collection of nearly 150,000 volumes was dispersed by auction in 1834-36, used a small rectangular stamp reading 'Bibliotheca Heberiana' (fig. 3.44). The Duke of Roxburghe (1740-1804), another celebrated bibliophile of the same period, had a stamp representing his arms (fig. 3.45). Stephen Weston (1747-1830), a clergyman and antiquary, used a rather funereal-looking stamp incorporating his initials in cipher form, surmounted by a cross (fig. 3.46). An entangled monogram stamp was used by Narcissus Luttrell (1657-1732, fig. 3.47), one of the few ink stamps in use around the end of the seventeenth century and the beginning of the eighteenth.

A variation on the use of ink stamps, producing a similar effect by a different method, was the use of stencils. They are less common than stamps, and are generally found in books from the end of the eighteenth century onwards; the stencil of Mrs. E. Arundell (fig. 3.48) probably dates from ca. 1775-1800. A quainter example is the stencil used by Thomas Clerk in the early nineteenth century (fig. 3.49). Fig. 3.50 shows a stencil of about the same date used by Frederick North, later 5th Earl of Guilford (1766-1827), which reproduces his coat of arms with crest and motto; the design is very similar to a bookplate he was using at the time (Franks 22027/8). The stencil crest stamp used by Sir Thomas Phillipps (1792-1872) may be seen illustrated in plate 119 of Christopher de Hamel's *History of illuminated manuscripts* (London, 1986). The Franks bookplate collection includes a small handful of stencils, e.g. Franks 10, a crest stencil used by Charles Abbot (1832-78), ca. 1850.

British stamps down to 1640 are listed in Pollard and Redgrave's *Short-title catalogue* in the Bookplates section (see p. 71 above), and Brian North Lee's appendix in *Early printed book labels* gives some additional detail on these early stamps. Apart from this, the use of inked stamps is an almost totally unstudied phenomenon, and there are no published lists or guides to help the researcher. They must be dated on typographical grounds, although this is not always easy, and pursued through biographical reference works, using any additional clues which may be provided by the date of the book and other inscriptions.

Library stamps

Until the end of the eighteenth century, institutional ownership of books was indicated mostly by manuscript inscriptions, by bookplates, or by armorial binding stamps. The British Museum appears to have been one of the first institutions in this country to use an ink stamp; the earliest octagonal 'Museum Britannicum' stamps (e.g. fig. 3.51) began to be used in the second half of the eighteenth century (the Museum was founded in 1753). There was a series of these stamps, of differing shapes and sizes, in use from then onwards; fig. 3.52 shows an early nineteenth-century variant, cut to the same pattern. An oval stamp was also used before the turn of the nineteenth century. The early octagonal stamps were colour-coded to indicate the source of the book, according to the following scheme:

Old Royal Library books – blue;
Books from Sir Hans Sloane's collection – black;
Books from the bequest of Arthur Edwards – red;
Books from the bequest of Thomas Birch – green;
Other donations – yellow.[12]

---

12 See F. J. Hill, The shelving and classification of printed books in P. R. Harris (ed.), *The Library of the British Museum*, London, 1991, 1-74, p. 5.

Fig. 3.47 Ink monogram stamp of Narcissus Luttrell: British Library 883.d.21, E. Bohun, *The justice of peace*, 1693.

Fig. 3.48 Late eighteenth-century stencil of Mrs E. Arundell: British Library 1609/1249, W. Shakespeare, [Works], 1774.

Fig. 3.49 Early nineteenth-century stencil of Thomas Clerk: British Library, J. Malcolm, *Sketch of the political history of India*, 1813.

Fig. 3.50 Stencil of Frederick North, later 5th Earl of Guilford: British Library 868.c.8, [*Neon epistolarion*], 1779.

Purchases were stamped in red using an oval stamp. A number of stamps were also cut to be applied to specific collections; fig. 3.53 shows the stamp used for the books purchased from Francis Hargrave in 1813, and fig. 3.54 shows that used for the gift of Lady Banks in 1818.

Other eighteenth-century occurrences of library ink stamps are relatively rare. Sion College Library and Lambeth Palace Library each had octagonal stamps which appear to date from the second half of the century (figs. 3.55-3.56). The Royal Society of London used a series of three rectangular stamps, 'Soc. Reg. Lond.', 'Soc. Reg. Lond ex dono Auctoris', and 'Soc. reg. Lond ex dono Henr. Howard Norfolciensis' (see fig. 2.31), which were certainly in use early in the nineteenth century and probably date from the end of the eighteenth (the Howard stamp is misleading; it refers to the Arundel gift of 1667 but the stamp is much later than that and was used in the nineteenth century for books bought with money from the Arundel Fund). The Faculty of Advocates in Edinburgh began to use a stamp around the beginning of the nineteenth century (fig. 3.57). Once into the nineteenth century, library stamps begin to proliferate and by the middle of the century their use had become common, as has remained the case ever since; figs. 3.58-3.60 show a number of examples from major libraries. Library stamps tend to be simple and non-pictorial in design, but occasional exceptions are met with, such as the nineteenth-century stamp used by the Royal Asiatic Society (fig. 3.61), with its elegant representation of banyan trees. Perforating stamps, such as that shown in fig. 3.62, are generally twentieth-century in date. Library ink stamps sometimes incorporate the date of acquisition, and this may provide useful evidence for associating a book with a particular sale catalogue, and thereby establishing another link in the chain of provenance.

Many collectors of prints, drawings, and other artworks have marked their items in characteristic ways, using stamps or inscriptions which may feature initials, monograms, ciphers, or full names. Several published guides to such marks have been compiled, most importantly *Les marques de collections de dessins et d'estampes* by Frits Lugt (Amsterdam, 1921, with a substantial supplement published in The Hague in 1956). Lugt reproduces many hundreds of marks, of both institutional and private collectors, with historical and biographical details. The remit did not include book collectors who were not also collectors of artworks, so its relevance in this context is very limited, but it is worth mentioning as it illustrates a number of library stamps which were used in books as well as on prints and drawings.

Fig. 3.51 Ink stamp used by the British Museum Library ca. 1760.

Fig. 3.52 Ink stamp used by the British Museum Library ca. 1820.

Fig. 3.53 Ink stamp used by the British Museum Library for books from the collection of Francis Hargrave, purchased 1813.

Fig. 3.54 Ink stamp used by the British Museum Library for books from the gift of Lady Sarah Sophia Banks, 1818.

Fig. 3.55 Late eighteenth-century ink stamp of Sion College Library.

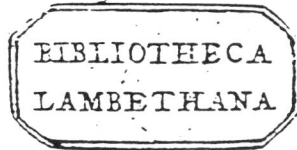

Fig. 3.56 Late eighteenth-century ink stamp of Lambeth Palace Library.

Fig. 3.57 Early nineteenth-century ink stamp of the Faculty of Advocates in Edinburgh.

Figs. 3.58-3.60 Late nineteenth-century ink stamps from institutional libraries: Cambridge University Library; The National Art Library; Durham University Library (used for books bequeathed by M. J. Routh in 1855).

Fig. 3.61 Nineteenth-century ink stamp of the Royal Asiatic Society.

Fig. 3.62 Perforating stamp used by Westminster City Library in the twentieth century.

EDITORI

ALFIERI & LACROIX - MILANO

WESTMINSTER
PUBLIC LIBRARY

IV
ARMORIALS, OTHER BINDING
STAMPS & EXTERNAL FEATURES

This chapter deals with the evidence which may be found on the outer covers of books, which reveals their previous ownership. It takes various forms; an armorial binding stamp is a frequently encountered one, but there are numerous other possibilities – names or initials tooled onto bindings, distinctive binding styles, inscriptions and other marks on the edges of leaves, or labels attached to boards. Ownership stamps applied to bindings are sometimes called *super-libros*.

ARMORIALS

Bookbindings stamped with coats of arms and other heraldic insignia began to appear in Europe in the fifteenth century. Louis XII of France (reigned 1498-1515) had a series of armorial bookstamps which were used on his bindings, and there are a number of other French examples from the first half of the sixteenth century.[1] The first English armorial bindings are royal ones, and there are a number of surviving bindings from the personal libraries of the early Tudors, decorated with their arms. The practice did not become common in England until the latter half of the sixteenth century, when the nobility and gentry began to have stamps of their arms made to decorate their bindings. The earliest non-royal English armorial identified to date is one made for the Earl of Arundel ca. 1555.[2] There are a number of mid-sixteenth century armorial stamps used by Scottish collectors, but it is likely that most if not all of these were made in France.[3] From about 1570 onwards the habit grew in popularity with English book-owners, and since then many hundreds of armorial stamps have been used.

The essential characteristic of an armorial binding stamp is that it reproduces the coat of arms, crest, or other unique heraldic identifying device of the owner of the book. The most common design for an armorial binding is a plain one with the armorial stamp placed at the centres of the boards, and the remaining decoration on the boards limited to fillets or other simple features. Fig. 4.1

1 J. P. Harthan, Armorial bookbindings from the Clements Collection, *Apollo* 71 (1960) 179-183, p. 180.
2 H. M. Nixon, *Five centuries of English bookbinding*, London, 1978, no. 15.
3 See W. S. Mitchell, *A history of Scottish bookbinding 1432 to 1650*, Edinburgh, 1955, ch. III.

Fig. 4.2 Armorial binding of C. M. Cracherode: National Art Library Clements HH18, Virgil, [Opera], 1545. (Reduced from 17 × 11 cm.)

Fig. 4.1 Armorial binding of George Wilmer: National Art Library Clements TT2, A. Boetius de Boodt, *Gemmarum et lapidum historia*, 1609. (Reduced from 23 × 17 cm.)

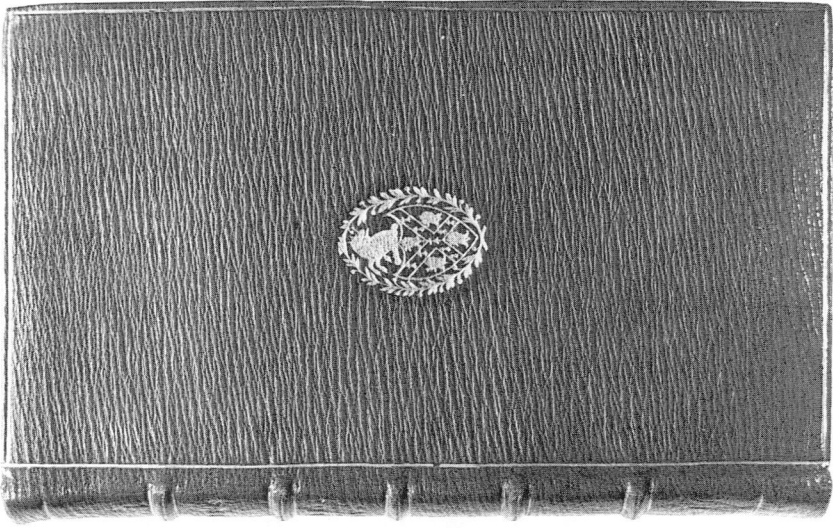

Fig. 4.4 Armorial binding of Sir Edward Hungerford: National Art Library Clements DD4, Eusebius, *The auncient ecclesiastical histories*, 1609. (Reduced from 29 × 20 cm.)

Fig. 4.3 Armorial binding of Richard Towneley: National Art Library Clements Dr.7, [*Acts of Parliament*], 1597–1606. (Reduced from 29.5 × 20 cm.)

shows an example from the beginning of the seventeenth century, a binding for George Wilmer (1582-1626); fig. 4.2 shows one made perhaps 150 years later, for C. M. Cracherode (1730-99). The armorial tools are usually stamped in gilt, although they are sometimes found blind-stamped or stamped in silver, such as the example of Richard Towneley (fl. ca. 1580-1640) shown in fig. 4.3. Unlike bookplates, armorial stamps rarely represent the correct heraldic tinctures, although some use patterns of hatching or dots to try to indicate the appropriate colours. Occasionally, armorials on bindings were painted with the correct colours, a habit favoured by, for example, Sir George Carew, Earl of Totnes (1555-1629).[4] Another way of coping with this problem, but also uncommon in practice, was the use of coloured leather onlays; bindings made for Henry Hare, Baron Coleraine (1636-1708) had a red leather patch onlaid at the centres of the boards on which his armorial stamp was applied in gilt, thus reproducing his correct heraldic tinctures of red and gold (gules two bars and a chief indented or). More elaborate armorial bindings may have various kinds of additional decoration; fig. 4.4 shows a handsome binding for Sir Edward Hungerford (1596-1648), made ca. 1630. Armorial tools may occasionally be found fitted inside other larger tools; this is particularly applicable to the large centrepieces used in the late sixteenth and early seventeenth centuries.[5]

Armorial tools are normally single stamps, engraved in brass like any other binding tool, and a few early stamps survive today. The British Museum, for example, preserves one of the armorial binding stamps used by Christopher Hatton, 1st Baron Hatton (1605?-70) in the early seventeenth century.[6] Some of the earliest English armorial bindings, made for Tudor royalty in the first half of the sixteenth century, made use of a series of small individual tools to build up a coat of arms, but this practice was soon superseded by the use of single stamps.[7] An unusual and very early variation on this theme is manifested in a London binding made about 1480 by the 'Scales binder', reproduced as plate VIII in G. D. Hobson's *Bindings in Cambridge libraries* (Cambridge, 1930); in this case a series of small tools is arranged to form a coat of arms. Although the great majority of armorial bindings are made of stamped leather, it should be added that a number of needlework armorial bindings were made when needlework bindings were in vogue (in Britain, in the late sixteenth and early seventeenth centuries).[8]

Armorial tools may comprise a full coat of arms, with or without crest and motto, or a crest alone; they may be large and impressive, or small and modest. The armorial of Thomas Coke, Earl of Leicester (1697-1759), fig. 4.5, has his

4 See the illustration in Maggs catalogue 1075 (1987), no. 25.
5 See, for example, the binding for Matthew Parker reproduced in *Fine bindings 1500-1700 from Oxford libraries*, Oxford, 1968, no. 120, or the binding for Sir Robert Berkeley shown in the J. R. Abbey sale catalogue, part I, Sotheby's, 21-23 June 1965, lot 131.
6 British Museum 1913/7-10/7 (Dept. of Medieval and Later Antiquities).
7 See for example the bindings for Henry VIII reproduced in Nixon, *Five centuries*, nos. 10-11.
8 See for example M. Foot, *The Henry Davis Gift*, vol. II, London, 1983, nos. 59, 66.

Fig. 4.5 Armorial binding stamp of Sir Thomas Coke, Earl of Leicester: British Library 1492.c.6, P. de Marca, *Dissertationum de concordia ... libri octo*, 1704. (Reproduced actual size.)

Fig. 4.6 Armorial binding stamp of Sir Thomas Shirley: National Art Library Clements Dr.8, J. Selden, *Titles of honor*, 1631. (Slightly enlarged from 8.5 × 8 cm.)

Fig. 4.8 Armorial binding of John Fleming: National Art Library Clements KK10, C. Tacitus, *The annales*, 1604. (Reduced from 28 × 20 cm.)

Fig. 4.7 Armorial binding stamp of Sir Peter Venables: National Art Library Clements Dr.4, [*He palaia diatheke*], 1653. (Reproduced actual size, 6 × 5 cm.)

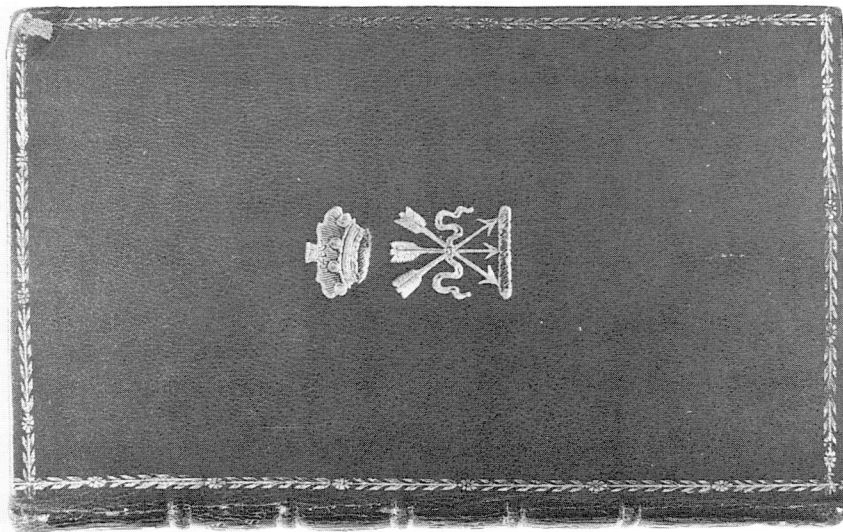

Fig. 4.10 Armorial binding with the crest of Sir John Rivers: National Art Library Clements U49, [*Vita Christi*, ca. 1607]. (Reduced from 21 × 13.5 cm.)

Fig. 4.9 Armorial binding with the crest of Sir Thomas Egerton, Earl of Wilton: National Art Library Clements LL.24, J. Walton, *Toxophilus*, 1788. (Reduced from 16.5 × 10.5 cm.)

coat of arms, complete with crest, mantling, and motto. In the armorial stamp of Sir Thomas Shirley (ca. 1590-1654), fig. 4.6, the shield is rather dwarfed by the mantling and the two crests of the Shirleys and the Harpurs (his wife's family), a Saracen's head and a boar passant. The majority of armorials do not incorporate the name of the owner, but there are exceptions, such as the stamp of Sir Peter Venables (1603-69), shown in fig. 4.7 (he had three similar stamps, this is the largest). Alternatively, armorial bindings are occasionally decorated with initials, such as the binding for John Fleming (1575-1643) shown in fig. 4.8.

Many armorial binding tools make use of the owner's crest alone, rather than his full coat of arms (for a definition of a crest and its place in an heraldic achievement, see p. 281 below). Fig. 4.9 shows a binding made for Sir Thomas Egerton, Earl of Wilton (1749-1814), with the family crest of three arrows[9], accompanied by a baron's coronet. This is quite discreet in its dimensions but crest-based tools are not always so modest, as can be seen from fig. 4.10, which shows a binding from the library of Sir John Rivers (ca. 1579-ca. 1651). The large oval tool is based on the Rivers crest of a bull statant ducally crowned and ringed. Small tools based on crests were often used in the eighteenth and nineteenth centuries to decorate spines, and fig. 4.11 shows three examples. The book on the left, with the crest placed once only at the head of the spine, comes from the collection of Henry Fox (b.ca. 1755), a younger son of Henry, 1st Baron Holland, and shows the family crest: on a chapeau azure turned up ermine a fox sejant or. The middle example, with the crest at head and foot, is the book from Sir Thomas Egerton's library whose front board is shown in fig. 4.9. The book on the right, with the crest in every spine compartment (except for the title compartment), belonged ca. 1730 to Robert Lovett, of Liscombe, Buckinghamshire, and uses a rather eccentric interpretation of the Lovett crest of a wolf passant (it should have three legs on the ground). Books with armorial spine decoration may or may not employ armorial stamps on the boards also.

Another kind of heraldic device which was sometimes used as the basis of armorial tools is the badge. Badges, in heraldry, are distinctive insignia, not connected with a shield or helm, associated with particular families.[10] They are usually quite simple and their graphic vocabulary is akin to that of crests; in some cases, the device used on a crest is also used as a badge, but the two can be distinguished because a crest should normally rest on a torse (which represents wreaths of cloth wound round a helmet). Fig. 4.12 shows an early example of the use of a badge as an armorial stamp; this is an early sixteenth-century binding with the slightly later stamp of Augustine Steward (d.1597) impressed in blind at the centres of the boards, representing his badge of a ragged branch with a broken sword at the base. Fig. 4.13 shows another binding which makes rather bolder use of a badge; the dog, technically a talbot

9 Technically three arrows argent headed and feathered sable banded or, but the armorial tool does not show the heraldic tinctures.
10 For a fuller definition, see J. P. Brooke-Little (ed.), *Boutell's heraldry*, London, 1983, ch. xiv.

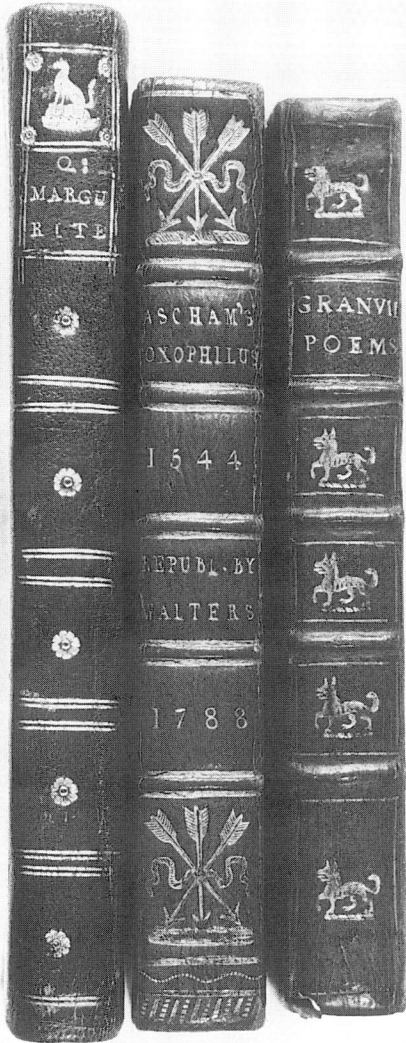

Fig. 4.11 Examples of spines decorated with crests: (from left to right) National Art Library Clements AA15, *Les mémoires de la Roine Marguerite*, 1629; Clements LL24, J. Walters, *Toxophilus*, 1788; Clements NN20, G. Granville, *Poems*, 1726.

Fig. 4.12 Binding with the blind-stamped badge of Augustine Steward: National Art Library Clements Dr.3, *Biblia sacra*, 1527. (Reduced from 34 × 22 cm.)

Fig. 4.14 Armorial binding of the Dean and Chapter of Durham: Durham Cathedral Library ms.A.IV.32, Donors' book, begun in 1628 or shortly thereafter. (Reduced from 29 × 19.5 cm.)

Fig. 4.13 Armorial binding with the badge of Elizabeth Grey, Countess of Kent: National Art Library Clements CC15, Ovid, *Le metamorfosi*, 1584. (Reduced from 23.5 × 18 cm.)

passant, is the badge of the Talbot family and the initials 'E G' stand for Elizabeth Grey, née Talbot, Countess of Kent (d.1651).

A coat of arms on a binding may not always indicate personal ownership; many libraries and institutions have had armorial tools cut. Fig. 4.14 shows an armorial used for Durham Cathedral Library in the 1630s, the first of a series of armorial tools cut for the Dean and Chapter there between the seventeenth century and the nineteenth. It is also worth remembering that gifts to institutions were sometimes marked by decorating the bindings of the books involved with the arms of the donor. When Thomas Morton (1564-1659) gave several hundred pounds to St. John's College, Cambridge in the 1620s and 1630s, the books bought with the money had Morton's arms gilt-tooled on the covers, although these were not books ever owned by Morton. The use of an armorial as a kind of gift-plate was a not uncommon practice in the seventeenth and eighteenth centuries. A variation on this theme is the use of armorial stamps to decorate special presentation copies of an author's works. Fig. 4.15 shows a binding decorated with the crest of Francis Bacon (a boar passant ermine armed and hoofed or a crescent for difference), covering a copy of his *Instauratio magna* presented to Cambridge University in 1620, the year in which the book was published. There are a number of other copies known in bindings like this (the Cambridge one is bound in velvet, others are bound in vellum), which were evidently bound for presentation.[11] The crest was also used on books from Bacon's personal collection.[12] There are, similarly, a number of surviving copies of Edward, Lord Herbert of Cherbury's work *De veritate* (1648) in presentation bindings, which incorporate Herbert's crest (six arrows in saltire one in pale banded).[13]

One anomalous phenomenon which should be mentioned in this context is the output of Elkanah Settle, who generated a series of armorial bindings in the early years of the eighteenth century. Settle (1648-1724) was a poet who presented copies of his works to wealthy patrons in the hope of financial reward, and who gilded these lilies by having them covered in morocco bindings carrying the arms of the intended recipients. He produced over 80 bindings like this between 1703 and 1724. They are fairly recognisable, as they all come from the same (unidentified) workshop, and the coats of arms are built up from small tools, rather than being single stamps; this latter fact differentiates them clearly from other, 'genuine', armorial bindings of the time. Settle sent his poems unsolicited, and they were often returned unwanted; in these instances, he had a leather onlay pasted over the original coat of arms, and a new set of arms was substituted. A Settle binding, therefore, does not necessarily imply that the person whose arms are on the cover really owned the book. Settle's activities are

11 See F. A. Bearman et al, *Fine and historic bookbindings from the Folger Shakespeare Library*, Washington, 1992, no. 7:9.

12 e.g. National Art Library Clements RR19, *Book of common prayer*, 1618.

13 See M. Foot, *The Henry Davis Gift*, vol. I, London, 1978, pp. 51-52.

quite well documented and there are several references which can be followed up.[14]

It is not uncommon to find English bindings decorated with the coat of arms of the reigning sovereign and it is important to stress that a royal coat of arms does not necessarily imply royal ownership of the book. There is a long tradition of using royal armorials as a decorative feature, either as a statement of respect or because the contents of the book have some appropriate link (e.g. official texts, books dedicated to the monarch). Two examples of the latter sort from the beginning of the eighteenth century may be seen in the Henry Davis collection at the British Library: *A sermon preach'd before the Queen,* and *A collection of ... statutes,* both decorated with the arms of Queen Anne.[15] The habit goes back a lot earlier than this, though, and panel stamps incorporating the royal arms were popular in the second quarter of the sixteenth century.[16] A very early and rather puzzling royal arms stamp, used by a binder associated with Caxton and his successors at the end of the fifteenth century, is known today from two surviving examples.[17] Having said this, it should be added that royal arms were regularly applied to genuine royal library books, and there is a changing succession of armorial tools appertaining to different sovereigns. Mirjam Foot has published a study of the armorial stamps of James I and Charles I, and illustrations of royal bindings from the early Tudor period onwards may be found in many of the standard works on bookbindings.[18] It will be clear from these sources that these armorial tools were not exclusively reserved for use on royal books, and that royal bindings are not always elaborate. On balance, therefore, one should never assume that a binding with a royal armorial was once in royal ownership on the basis of the tool alone, without further careful investigation and the presence of other evidence.

As with bookplates, it is not unusual to find that particular owners used more than one armorial tool in the course of their collecting career. Some owners had tools of different sizes to suit different-sized books – Sir Peter Venables, mentioned above, is a case in point – and some used a mixture of stamps based on a full coat of arms or a crest alone. Sir Christopher Hatton (1540-91) used three armorial stamps, one displaying his full achievement (a shield with helm, mantling and crest), one showing his coat of arms within a circular frame

14 See H. M. Nixon & M. Foot, *The history of decorated bookbinding in England,* Oxford, 1992, pp. 80-81, and the references given there.

15 Foot, *Henry Davis* v. 2, nos. 157-158.

16 Nixon & Foot, pp. 16-17.

17 See H. M. Nixon, Caxton and bookbinding, *Journal of the Printing Historical Society* 11 (1976/7), 92-113 and his comments on bindings 19 and 35, tool 241.

18 For example: Nixon, *Five centuries,* nos. 10, 11 (Henry VIII), 13, 14 (Edward VI), 28 (James I); Nixon & Foot, *The history* pls. 22, 24, 25 (Henry VIII), 21, 23 (Edward VI), 34 (Elizabeth), 49, 50, 51 (Charles I); Foot, *Henry Davis* v. 2 nos. 35 (Edward VI), 38 (Mary). On James I and Charles I see M. Foot, Some bindings for Charles I in G. A. M. Janssens & F. G. A. M. Aarts (eds.), *Studies in seventeenth century English literature, history and bibliography,* Amsterdam, 1984, 95-106 (reprinted in her *Studies in the history of bookbinding,* Aldershot, 1993, 340-351).

Fig. 4.16 Early 17th-century binding with the 19th-century armorial binding stamp of the Earl of Scarborough added: National Art Library Clements F26, D. Person, *Varieties*, 1635. (Reduced from 19 × 14 cm.)

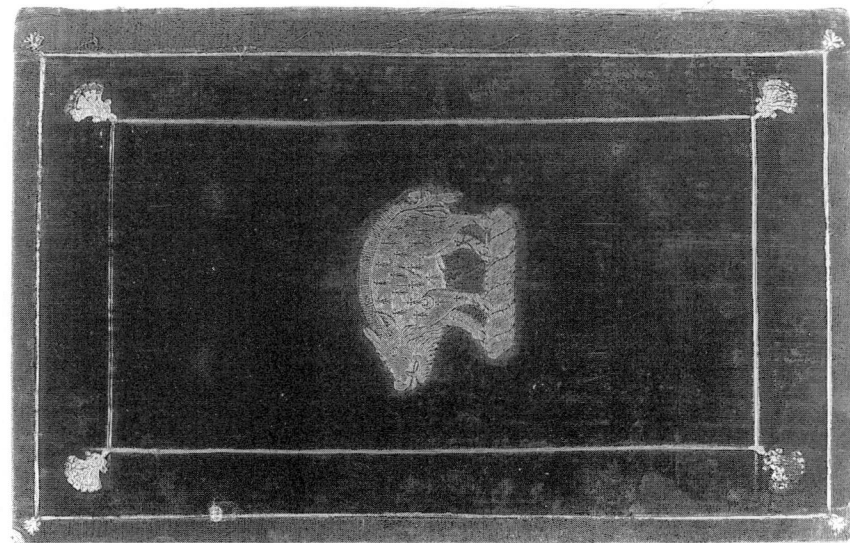

Fig. 4.15 Armorial presentation binding of Francis Bacon: Cambridge University Library Sel.2.85, F. Bacon, *Instauratio magna*, 1620. (Reduced from 25 × 22.5 cm.)

representing a garter and carrying the motto of the Order of the Garter, and one comprising only his crest of a hind statant.[19] There are many other examples which could be chosen.

A point to bear in mind, when looking at armorials, is the fact that armorial stamps are not necessarily contemporary with the bindings to which they are applied; they may post-date their bindings by several centuries. Fig. 4.16 shows a simple example, where the nineteenth-century armorial of the Earl of Scarborough (? the 8th Earl, 1788-1856) has been added to an early seventeenth-century binding. A number of more striking examples of this practice are illustrated in Howard Nixon's catalogue of Grolier bindings, where several cases of aesthetically questionable later armorial additions to sixteenth-century bindings are reproduced.[20]

Identifying armorials

The most obvious way to decipher an armorial binding stamp is to identify the arms in question, through heraldic reference sources. For guidance, see the section on **Heraldry** on pp. 274-286. There are however a number of other avenues of pursuit, which may prove to be short cuts or which may provide useful information supplementary to the basic identification. Many of the more commonly encountered armorials have been reproduced in print, and some work has been done on pinpointing the particular family members who used particular stamps. Armorials can present the same kinds of problems as anonymous heraldic bookplates; they may have remained in use over more than one generation, and identifying the family does not necessarily identify the individual. The date of the binding will obviously be a factor in assessing the period of currency of a stamp, but the point made above about the addition of stamps to earlier bindings should always be remembered.

Collections of armorials

There are a number of collections of armorials, or rubbings of armorials, which have been assembled by individuals and may now be consulted in libraries to which they were given. The most important of these is the **Clements Collection** in the **National Art Library, Victoria & Albert Museum, London**. H. J. B. Clements (d.1940) put together a collection of about 1150 armorials which he bequeathed to the Museum. They are almost all British ones, and this collection comprises the most complete assemblage of British

19 Examples of the three Hatton stamps will be found on Cambridge University Library L*.2.3 (Krantz, *Saxonia*, 1575), British Library G.12228 (*Bible*, 1588), and Durham University Library Cosin K.I.8 (Beza, *Vignon*, 1582), respectively. On the three Venables stamps, see G. Smith & F. Benger, *A collection of armorial bookbindings*, London, 1927 (Ellis sale catalogue), p. 50.

20 H. M. Nixon, *Bookbindings from the library of Jean Grolier*, London, 1965; see e.g. nos. 36, 111.

armorials available in any one place. The bindings have been preserved intact on the books which they cover. A listing was published in 1958:

D. Woodfield: *An ordinary of British armorial bookbindings in the Clements Collection, Victoria and Albert Museum*, London, 1958.

This is arranged as an heraldic ordinary, i.e. the stamps are listed according to their heraldic descriptions. It includes an index of mottoes and legends, and one of names (although the name index does not include page references to the ordinary). There are unfortunately no illustrations. In addition to this, a handlist of the collection is available in the Library, in which the names of the owners (as identified from the armorials) are interfiled with the names of the authors of the books in one alphabetical sequence. The collection includes Clements' own extensively annotated copy of Davenport's *English armorial bookbindings*, and a large assemblage of notes made by Clements, which are now stored in ca. 35 binders. All this material is available on request. The notes mostly comprise annotated rubbings of armorials, arranged alphabetically by owner, with some references to further examples of particular armorials which Clements traced outside his own collection. A thorough cataloguing operation on the Clements Collection was begun in 1991, and full records, searchable by owner, will be found on the Library's on-line catalogue for all books which have so far been catalogued. A well-illustrated description of the collection, which also serves as a good historical introduction to the use of armorials in Britain, was published in 1960-61:

J. P. Harthan: Armorial bookbindings from the Clements Collection. *Apollo* December 1960, 179-183; June 1961, 186-191; December 1961, 165-171.

Other collections of armorials include:

CAMBRIDGE – UNIVERSITY LIBRARY   There is a large collection of assorted rubbings of, and notes on, armorial bindings in Cambridge University Library; it has no shelfmark but is available on request in the Rare Books Room. Most of the material relates to books in Cambridge libraries, including the college libraries as well as the University Library. There is a collection of rubbings and associated notes made by E. G. Duff, and also material collected by C. Sayle. Sayle's rubbings are only partly sorted. The most accessible and recent element is a set of rubbings made by John Morris, ca. 1965, now held in one alphabetical sequence in five small box files; the notes include locations of armorial stamps found in Cambridge University Library, and also some copies of the earlier rubbings made by Duff. Duff's annotated copy of Davenport's *English heraldic book-stamps* is available as Adv.b.104.9.

LONDON – BRITISH LIBRARY   A collection of ca. 400 armorial book stamps, 16th-19th centuries, was assembled by Sir Augustus Franks and bequeathed to the British Museum in 1897. The stamps are cut from bindings and mounted in two albums (there is no record of the books from which they came), with an index at the front. About two thirds are French, and there are only about 35 English ones. The collection is now in the British Library with shelfmark L.R.406.i.9. It was described by A. W. Pollard in 'The Franks Collection of armorial bookstamps', *The Library* 2 ser 3 (1902), 115-34.

OXFORD – BODLEIAN LIBRARY The Special Collections Department holds a card index of British armorials (2 drawers of large cards, with rubbings mounted on the cards). It was begun by F. S. Ferguson and has been extended by Bodleian staff; it covers material from Sotheby's sales and from booksellers' catalogues, since ca. 1920, as well as books in the Bodleian and other Oxford libraries. Its coverage of the Bodleian's holdings is far from comprehensive. It includes small separate sections on English royal armorials, and on continental armorials. In addition, the John Johnson collection includes a box of 'armorial bindings', containing rubbings and photographs of miscellaneous armorials in the Bodleian, both British and continental. This also contains a small collection of gilt stamps cut from the covers of (unidentified) books, mostly eighteenth-century or later.

Other sources

The 'standard' published work on British armorials, apart from Woodfield's ordinary of the Clements collection, is:

C. Davenport: *English armorial bookbindings*. London, 1909.

This lists and illustrates about 250 armorials, with biographical notes on the collectors. It is still widely used, but is very selective in its coverage, and incorporates a substantial number of errors. E. G. Duff's annotated copy, preserved in Cambridge University Library (Adv.b.104.9), carries his tart note, 'About the most worthless book ever compiled', which is just a shade strong but conveys the frustration which he was not alone in feeling. Davenport should be consulted in conjunction with the list of corrections given by Henry Clements at the end of his article which serves as a summary introduction to the subject of armorial bindings:

H. J. B. Clements, Armorial book-stamps and their owners, *The Library* 4 ser 20 (1939), 121-135.

Clements also produced an alphabetical list of all personal armorial stamps known to him, which was published in *The Book Collector's Quarterly*:

H. J. B. Clements, Check list of English armorial book stamps, *The Book Collector's Quarterly* 14 (1934), 64-72; 15 (1934), 68-78; 16 (1935), 64-72; 17 (1935), 36-46. A separately published supplement to this series was issued in 1938, entitled *Check-list of English armorial book-stamps*.

This provides only a list of names and dates without any descriptions of the armorials themselves. Apart from these, there are only a few other published articles which deal with armorials in a general sense:

W. Y. Fletcher, English armorial bookstamps and their owners, *Bibliographica* 3 (1897), 303-343.

W. Y. Fletcher, English armorial stamps on bindings, *Journal of the Ex-Libris Society* 9 (1899-1900), 31-34, 48-52.

Details of some sixteenth and seventeenth century armorial stamps used by Scottish collectors will be found in:

W. S. Mitchell, *A history of Scottish bookbinding 1432 to 1650*. (Aberdeen University Studies, 134.) Edinburgh, 1955: see pp. 27-51, 88-93, and the further references given there.

A number of exhibitions on the subject of armorial bindings have generated catalogues:

A guide to an exhibition of armorial and related bookbindings 1500-1800. New York, Pierpont Morgan Library, 1935.

> 149 items, British and continental; no illustrations.

R. A. Rye & M. S. Quinn: *University of London: historical and armorial bookbindings exhibited in the University Library*. London, 1937.

> 83 items, not all armorials; some illustrations.

In addition to the sources above which are specifically focussed on armorial bindings, it should be remembered that many of the standard works on bookbindings, and exhibition catalogues devoted to fine bindings, include some documentation on armorials. Armorial bindings have long been a collectible commodity and many examples have surfaced in booksellers' and auctioneers' catalogues. A number of catalogues have appeared over the last century or so which have been primarily devoted to armorials, and such catalogues can offer an important additional source of reference, particularly if they are illustrated. A major example is the Ellis catalogue of 1927, *A collection of armorial bookbindings of the Tudor, Stuart, and Hanoverian periods. Described by George Smith and Frank Benger*, which contained about 600 armorials, most of which are illustrated (albeit not very well, the pictures are very small). The section on 'Major booksellers' in chapter V below includes a number of references to specific catalogues which may prove useful – see particularly the entries for Ellis, Leighton, Pearson, Quaritch and Sawyer.

Non-British armorials

The works cited above are primarily concerned with British armorial bindings. There are a number of standard sources to help with the identification of continental armorials, of which the following are among the best known:

J. Guigard: *Nouvel armorial du bibliophile*. 2v. Paris, 1890.

> Divided into separate sections, on sovereigns, ecclesiastical collectors, women, etc. Predominantly but not exclusively French in coverage.

E. Olivier, G. Hermal & R. de Roton: *Manuel de l'amateur de reliures armoriées françaises.* 29pts + index. Paris, 1924-38.

> Comprises reproductions of armorials and monograms, with biographical notes on owners.

Le Vicomte de Jonghe d'Ardoye, J. Havenith & G. Dansaert: *Armorial Belge du bibliophile.* 3v. Brussels, 1930.

> A major reference source for armorial bindings from Belgium and the Low Countries, covering both private and institutional owners. Well illustrated with drawings of armorial stamps, and pictures of bindings.

Further references

The list of printed sources given above is very selective and includes only the most commonly-cited works on armorial stamps. The fullest bibliography, covering both monographs and periodical articles on an international basis, will be found in:

F. A. Schmidt-Künsemüller: *Bibliographie zur Geschichte der Einbandkunst von den Anfängen bis 1985,* Wiesbaden, 1987.

> This is a major bibliography on the literature of bookbinding and includes in section 9 ('Bibliophilie') a sequence on 'Supralibros' (pp. 88-95), listing about 100 references to published works on armorial bindings.

NAMES, INITIALS, MONOGRAMS AND CIPHERS

The use of armorial tools to decorate bindings is clearly restricted to owners who are armigerous – those who are, or consider themselves to be, entitled to bear arms. A simpler – and more immediately comprehensible – method of marking ownership on the outside of a book is to stamp it with letters making up the owner's name. This was a common practice for many centuries; it has been used on bindings of all kinds, from the finest to the simplest, and by collectors from all points on the social scale.

Names

As with armorials, the practice of tooling names on English bindings is essentially one which begins in the middle of the sixteenth century, following a slightly earlier continental lead. The celebrated French collector Jean Grolier (1479-1565) began to have his name added to his bindings in the late 1530s.[21] Fig. 4.17 shows an early English example, with the name 'Thomas Lonnard' tooled on a binding of the late 1540s. It was about this time that the well-known English collector Thomas Wotton (1521-87), who has been called 'the English Grolier', began to have the legend 'Thomae Wottoni et amicorum' added to his

21 Nixon, *Grolier*, p. xv.

bindings, but it has been demonstrated that these bindings were produced in France.[22] There are however a number of other genuinely English examples known from the middle of the sixteenth century, and from that time onwards it is not uncommon to find bindings which incorporate the name of the owner on the covers.[23] Numerous examples survive from the second half of the century.[24] Examples before that date are exceptional but not unknown; the Scales Binder, who worked in London in the second half of the fifteenth century, produced at least one binding with the name of the owner cut into the leather.[25]

Names on boards are commonly stamped in gilt using a series of individual letters, and the results often display the crudeness or unevenness which is inherent in that method. Names will be found on both plain and finely decorated bindings. One of the better-known enthusiasts for this form of ownership mark is Edward Gwynn (d.ca. 1645), from whose library many volumes have survived looking like the example shown in fig. 4.18.[26] This very plain early seventeenth-century binding is typical of many from his collection, but his name is also found on more elaborately-decorated bindings.[27] Fig. 4.19 shows a later example; here, the name of 'Tho: Granger Gent' has been added to an early eighteenth-century binding, somewhat later in that century. As with armorials, it is important to be alert to the possibility that names tooled on bindings may be later than the date of the original binding. The examples thus far have shown the names of living owners added to books from their own collections; fig. 4.20 shows an intriguing variation, in which the binding is intended to act as a memento of someone deceased. Susanna, wife of Sir John Dormer, died in 1673. Bindings incorporating owners' names sometimes include a date as well as a name, but this is generally the exception rather than the rule in English practice.

Initials

Many owners have had the covers of their books stamped not with their full name, but with their initials only. This clearly offers a simpler and cheaper way

22 M. Foot, Thomas Wotton and his binders, in *Henry Davis Gift* I, p. 140ff.

23 See, for example, an early binding for William Cecil with the name of himself and his second wife Mildred on the covers (H. M. Nixon, Early English gold-tooled bookbindings, in *Studia in bibliografia ... in onore di Tammaro de Marinis*, Verona, 1964, v. 3, 283-308, p. 303); or the binding for Lord Cobham, ca. 1550 (H. M. Nixon, *English bindings in the library of J. R. Abbey*, London, 1940, no. 10).

24 See, for example, the William Alyn binding of 1571 and the Lady Russell binding of ca. 1580 reproduced in the first sale catalogue of J. R. Abbey (Sotheby's, 21-23 June 1965, lots 211, 526), and the binding of similar date for Sir John Savile in Bearman, *Folger*, 7:2.

25 Now in the Guildhall Library, London. See N. Barker, A register of writs and the Scales Binder, part II, *The Book Collector* 21 (1972), 356-377, no. 13 in the List of bindings.

26 See W. A. Jackson, Edward Gwynn, in *Records of a bibliographer*, Cambridge, Mass., 1967, 115-119.

27 A handsome example will be found in the Clements Collection in the National Art Library, Clements N9, *Medulla Parliamentalis*, ms., ca. 1622.

Fig. 4.18 Early seventeenth-century binding with the name of
Edward Gwynn: Durham University Library SR4.A.15, *The primer*,
1546. (Reduced from 19.5 × 14.5 cm.)

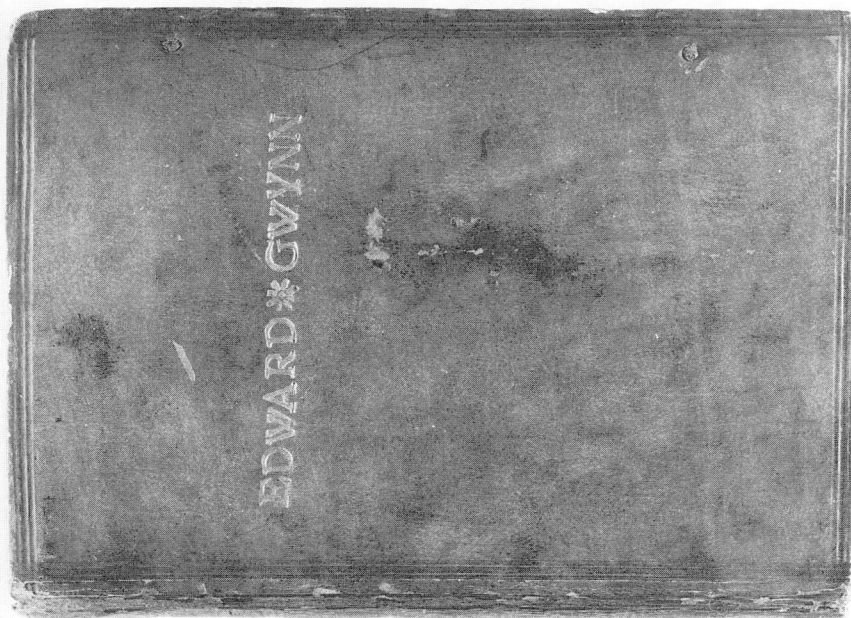

Fig. 4.17 Mid sixteenth-century binding with the name of Thomas
Lonnard: British Library C.66.b.14, J. Bekinsau, *De supremo et
absoluto regis imperio*, 1547. (Reduced from 14.5 × 10 cm.)

Fig. 4.20 Late seventeenth-century binding with a memorial inscription for Susanna, Lady Dormer: Durham University Library SR6.D.12, J. Welles, *The soules progresse*, 1639. (Reduced from 18.5 × 14 cm.)

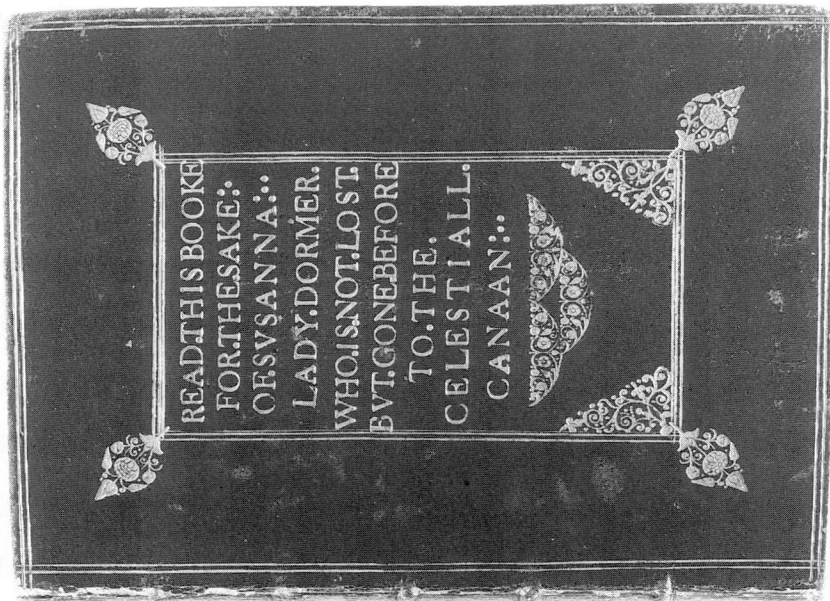

Fig. 4.19 Early eighteenth-century binding with the name of Tho. Granger added: National Art Library Dr.36, *Book of common prayer*, 1704. (Reduced from 41 × 26 cm.)

of personalising a binding, although it is considerably more frustrating for the researcher, as the initials often elude identification unless an inscription or other evidence within the book offers further clues. Like the addition of names to bindings, the addition of initials begins to be seen around the middle of the sixteenth century and numerous examples can be traced.[28] Fig. 4.21 shows a binding of ca. 1582 with the initials of Edward Coke (1552-1634, subsequently Lord Chief Justice) placed around a centrepiece; the placing of initials round centrepieces like this was a popular device while centrepieces were in vogue, around the late sixteenth and early seventeenth centuries.[29] Fig. 4.22 shows an example two centuries later; the initials 'J. H.', placed within a central decorative frame, stand for John Holmes, who acquired the book in 1773 from a Mrs. Sutton. Henry Yelverton, 1st Viscount Longueville (1664-1704), who assembled a sizeable library at the end of the seventeenth century, had his books stamped with the initials 'H L' surmounted with a viscount's coronet (fig. 4.23). Initials may be found on both boards, or on the upper board only; another possibility which is sometimes encountered is the stamping of different single initials on upper and lower boards, which should be read together.[30] The binding shown in fig. 4.22 has 'J. H.' on the lower board, but 'J. E. S.' on the upper board, so in this case the two sets of initials represent a donor (Mrs. Sutton) and a recipient.

Monograms and ciphers

A more personalised, if more cryptic, variation on the use of initials was the use of binding stamps comprising monograms or ciphers (for the distinction between the two, see p. 64 above). There are a few early instances – the Henry Davis Gift includes a mid-sixteenth century binding decorated with the monogram of Thomas Goodrich, Bishop of Ely (d.1554)[31] – but the practice was uncommon in England before the second half of the seventeenth century, and it was never as popular in this country as it was on the continent. Fig. 4.24 shows a binding with the cipher of James II, used before 1685 when he was Duke of York – the interpretation of the letters has been variously postulated, but the reading 'Jacobus Dux' (the J is upside-down) seems most likely.[32] Several members of the royal family favoured monograms or ciphers on their bindings around this time; the bindings made for Charles II, with a cipher of two interlocking Cs back-to-back, are the best known, but several others can be

28 See, for example, the London binding of ca. 1550, for William Bill, with W B on the boards, in Foot, *Henry Davis* II, no. 36, or the two bindings of 1562-63 by the Initial Binder in Nixon, *Five centuries*, nos. 19-20.

29 Other examples can be seen illustrated in Foot, *Henry Davis* II, no. 43; Bearman, *Folger*, 8:3.

30 For example, Bearman, *Folger*, 5:6; H. M. Nixon, *Broxbourne Library: styles and designs of bookbindings*, London, 1956, no. 65.

31 M. Foot, *Studies in the history of bookbinding*, Aldershot, 1993, no. 56.

32 See Maggs catalogue 1075 (1987), no. 59.

Fig. 4.22 Mid-eighteenth century binding with the initials of John Holmes: National Art Library Dr.61, J. Barrow, *A new and universal dictionary*, 1754. (Reduced from 41 × 26 cm.)

Fig. 4.21 Late sixteenth-century binding with the initials of Edward Coke: Cosin's Library, Durham P.IV.9, R. Dinoth, *De bello civili Gallico*, 1582. (Reduced from 22 × 16 cm.)

Fig. 4.24 Late seventeenth-century binding with the cipher stamp of James II, when Duke of York: National Art Library Clements Dr.7, H. Robinson, *Annalium mundi universalium … tomus primus*, 1677. (Reduced from 32 × 20.5 cm.)

Fig. 4.23 Late seventeenth-century binding with the initials of Henry Yelverton, Viscount de Longueville: Durham University Library SR4.A.25, *The ordre of the communion*, 1548. (Reduced from 19.5 × 14 cm.)

found.[33] As with royal coats of arms on bindings, it must not be assumed that the presence of royal ciphers automatically indicates royal ownership. A non-royal owner whose cipher bindings are well known is John Evelyn (1620-1706) – the tools were originally designed in France but later used in England – and the Evelyn sale catalogues include plentiful illustrations of both the Evelyn ciphers, and the monogram used by his father-in-law Sir Richard Browne (1605-83).[34] Monograms and ciphers designed as binding tools are generally less convoluted than the examples often found on bookplates, but fig. 4.25 shows an exception to this rule in the monogram tool of Sir George Hungerford (1630-1712), which incorporates all the letters of his name.

MOTTOES ON BOARDS

Armorial tools sometimes include the owner's heraldic motto; examples are the tools of Richard Towneley and Thomas Coke shown in figs. 4.3 and 4.6. Just occasionally, ownership may be deduced from the presence of a motto tooled onto a binding in a non-heraldic context. An example may be seen on a mid-sixteenth century binding covering a slightly earlier manuscript of Boccaccio, now in the British Library; the placing of the Seymour motto, 'foy pour devoir', at the centre of the boards supports the belief that the binding was made for Edward Seymour, Duke of Somerset (1506?-52).[35] Examples like this are rare in English practice.

ENGRAVED METAL PLATES

Engraved metal plates attached to bindings, inscribed with names, initials, or monograms, offer an alternative method of indicating ownership on the outsides of books. This was not uncommon in the seventeenth and eighteenth centuries, and is particularly associated with Bibles, prayer books, or other devotional works. Fig. 4.26 shows a late seventeenth-century example, with the initials 'I B 1675' engraved on a silver plate attached to the centre of the front board. An inscription within the book makes it possible to identify I B as John Boucher. Silver is the metal most commonly used (brass is a cheaper alternative), and such bindings usually have metal cornerpieces, and possibly also clasps, as well as the central plate.[36]

33 See e.g. Nixon & Foot, *The history of decorated bookbinding*, plates 51 and following (Charles II), plate 55 (William and Mary); Maggs catalogue 1121 (1990), no. 42 (William Duke of Gloucester).

34 Christie's, 22-23 June 1977, 30 November-1 December 1977, 15-16 March 1978, 12-13 July 1978.

35 Illustrated and described in Nixon, *Five centuries*, no. 12.

36 Other examples may be seen in Foot, *Henry Davis* II no. 156, and in Bearman, *Folger* nos. 10:13 and 10:17; these range in date from 1690-1747 and show the several possibilities of a name, a monogram, or initials engraved on the central plate.

Fig. 4.25 Monogram binding stamp of George Hungerford: National Art Library Clements M7, P. Leycester, *Historical antiquities*, 1673. (Reduced from 4 × 4 cm.)

Fig. 4.26 Late seventeenth-century binding with an engraved silver plate marked 'I B 1675': National Art Library Dr.1, *The Holy Bible*, 1658. (Reduced from 12 × 7 cm.)

LABELS ON BOARDS

Before the development of book-cases (in which books are shelved upright with spines vertical), which began to emerge at the end of the sixteenth century, books in libraries were generally stored on lecterns or in chests, in which they rested on their sides on a flat or sloping surface. Library users saw rows of boards, rather than the rows of spines with which we are familiar today, and it was therefore sensible to fix labels to the boards as a means of identifying the contents. Such labels, written on paper or parchment, could be pasted onto the surface, or fixed by placing them beneath a kind of miniature picture frame comprising a layer of transparent horn and thin strips of brass. The brass surrounds were attached to the boards with small nails, suitable for the wooden boards which were commonly used for the bindings of larger books until the middle of the sixteenth century.

Fig. 4.27 Late sixteenth-century paper label under a horn and brass frame: Magdalen
College, Oxford, *Biblia sacra*, 1573. (Outer dimensions of frame: 13 × 7 cm.)

As an extension of this principle, institutional libraries sometimes employed this method to mark donations, using labels carrying the donor's name and perhaps the date of gift. An early example is described and illustrated in the catalogue of the Bodleian Library's Lyell manuscripts; Lyell ms.8, a collection of sermons written in the first half of the thirteenth century and given to Fountains Abbey by Gilbert Scot not long afterwards, has a near-contemporary parchment label under horn reading 'Collectaneu[m] ex dono Frat[ri]s Gilb[er-]ti Scot'.[37] Neil Ker names a number of institutions from which bindings with labels like this survive, in the preface to *Medieval libraries of Great Britain*.[38] The practice continued well into the era of printing, and some of the earliest printed book labels, recording gifts by individuals to institutional libraries, were fixed to the boards using brass and horn frames, rather than being pasted inside.[39] Fig. 4.27 shows a handsome late sixteenth-century example from Magdalen College, Oxford; the printed label, recording the gift of the book by Nicholas Bonde in 1595, is decorated with Bonde's arms and is fixed to the front board with a brass and horn frame.

The labelling of boards in this way gradually died out, for two reasons: books ceased to be shelved flat, and wooden boards increasingly gave way to pasteboards, which were not suitable for nailing. By the beginning of the

37 See A. de la Mare, *Catalogue of the collection of medieval manuscripts bequeathed to the Bodleian Library, Oxford, by James P. R. Lyell*, Oxford, 1971.
38 2nd edn (1964), p. xxii.
39 See B. N. Lee, *Early printed book labels*, Pinner, 1976, nos. 9, 16, 17, 18, 24, 34, 47, and p. xvi.

seventeenth century, wooden boards were only rarely used by English binders. The catalogue of the library at Guildford Grammar School includes a good illustration of a paper label under horn, dated 1604; they are not found much later than this.[40]

EDGES

Although indications of provenance which occur on the outsides of books are normally found on the boards or the spine, the edges of the leaves offer an additional external possibility. Edges are not normally visible in libraries shelved spine outwards, in the orthodox modern way, but it must be remembered that it was common practice to shelve books fore-edge outwards before the middle of the seventeenth century, and, as stated in the preceding section, late medieval libraries often stored books using a lectern-system in which they rested on their sides rather than the bottom edge. It is therefore very common to find sixteenth- and seventeenth-century books from private or institutional ownership which have titles or pressmarks written on the leaf edges, to aid identification.[41] Although one might therefore expect to find owners' names written on edges also, this was never a common habit and examples are not often found. Fig. 4.28 shows a very late example, a school text book of 1682 on which a contemporary user has written 'William Morgan his' up the fore edge. Fig. 4.29 shows an even more unusual instance of the use of leaf edges to indicate provenance; when William Herris gave a number of books to Pembroke College, Cambridge in 1622, each volume had the letters 'W H' stamped in gilt in the middle of the fore edge (as well as Herris's arms on the boards). A grander way of indicating ownership using leaf edges is to decorate them with the collector's coat of arms; this, too, is not often encountered but an example is shown in fig. 4.30. This is a book from the library of Archbishop Richard Bancroft (1544-1610), with elaborate fore edge decoration incorporating his arms at the centre. The bulk of Bancroft's large collection survives today in Lambeth Palace Library and although there is a small handful of other books with fancy edge decoration like this, they are very few and far between in his collection as a whole.[42]

DISTINCTIVE BINDINGS

Before the introduction of mechanised binding processes early in the nineteenth century, all books were individually bound and finished by hand.

---

40 G. Woodward & R. A. Christophers, *The chained library of the Royal Grammar School, Guildford: catalogue*, Guildford, 1972, pl. IV.

41 See, for example, plate 8 in P. Gaskell, *Trinity College Library: the first 150 years*, Cambridge, 1980.

42 For other examples of fore edges decorated with coats of arms, or owners' initials, see G. D. Hobson, *English bindings 1490-1940 in the library of J. R. Abbey*, London, 1940, nos. 42, 62. For an instance of the even more uncommon practice of gauffered edge decoration incorporating an owner's name, see D. Burke, Quintuplex psalter, Paris, 1509 in C. de Hamel & R. A. Linenthal (eds.), *Fine books and book collecting*, Leamington Spa, 1981, pp. 44-46.

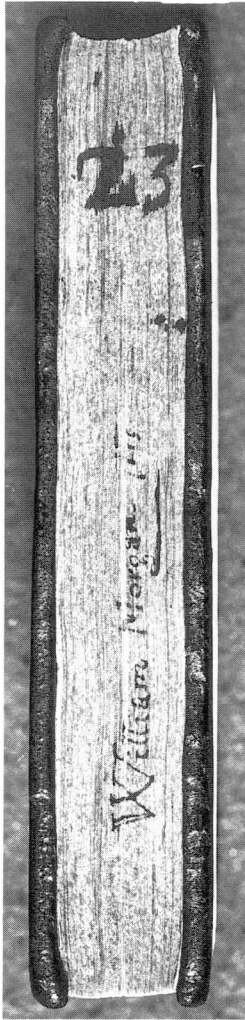

Fig. 4.28 'William Morgan his' written up the fore edge: British Library 1489.m.64, H. Robinson, *Scholae Wintoniensis phrases Latinae*, 1682.

Fig. 4.29 Gilt initials stamped on the fore edge: Pembroke College, Cambridge 3.2.8, Synesius, [*Opera*], 1612.

Fig. 4.30 Early seventeenth-century binding with decorated edges, incorporating the arms of Richard Bancroft, Archbishop of Canterbury: Lambeth Palace Library *H890.T4V, G. Vasquez, *Commentariorum ... in primam partem S. Thomae*, 1598.

Although there was always a market for ready-bound books, many purchasers relied on the system of buying their books before they were bound, and therefore having the opportunity to dictate the style and sophistication of the bindings. The tools which were used to decorate bindings were also, on the whole, individual and unique, although each generation had prevailing styles and patterns which were extensively copied.[43] Different binders working at the same time were always likely to have collections of tools which were similar, but not identical.

It has always therefore been possible for individual collectors to own suites of binding tools and to insist that books bound for them should be personalised through the use of these tools, which would then be found on their books alone. In practice, this has never been a feature of our bibliophilic culture. Owners who have wished to have their bindings marked with an identifiable sign of ownership have relied on armorials, names, initials, monograms, or ciphers, but not on decorative tools which do not incorporate any of these features. They have often been concerned about the quality or the overall level of decoration, and they have sometimes been concerned about the type or colour of the leather, but not with the tools chosen for finishing. Similarly, in the hand-press era, owners have not dictated particular patterns or layouts for binding designs; they have generally accepted the prevailing fashions of the time. The great early eighteenth-century collector Edward Harley, 2nd Earl of Oxford (1689-1741) has posthumously given his name to 'Harleian bindings' – bindings with a gilt roll round the perimeter and a large lozenge-shaped central decoration made up from small tools – but although he did indeed have many books bound like this, the style was not unique to him and the binders who bound for him used the same tools on other bindings for other people.[44]

There are a few exceptions to these general rules, and they are on the whole well known. Fig. 4.31 shows a typical binding made for Thomas Hollis (1720-74), an independent philanthropist who endeavoured to disseminate his passionate beliefs in political liberty by giving away specially-bound copies of suitable texts. He designed a series of binding tools (a liberty-cap, the goddess Libertas, a palm-branch, etc.) which he had cut and which were reserved for use on his chosen gift-books by several binders who worked for him.[45]. His contemporary Jonas Hanway (1712-86) indulged in similar practices, but with a

---

43 The long-held assumption that *all* binders' tools were unique, because they were individually engraved in brass, was challenged by Staffan Fogelmark in his book on *Flemish and related panel-stamped bindings*, New York, 1990, one of the most important books on binding research of recent years. He has demonstrated that many fifteenth- and early sixteenth-century panel-stamps were cast, not engraved, so that identical tools could be used by several binders in different places. His arguments are confined to large tools of that period and there is no reason to doubt that the majority of smaller tools used in subsequent centuries were engraved and not cast.

44 The best overall account is H. M. Nixon, Harleian bindings in *Studies in the book trade in honour of Graham Pollard*, Oxford, 1975, 153-194.

45 See W. H. Bond, *Thomas Hollis of Lincoln's Inn*, Cambridge, 1990, especially ch. 2.

Fig. 4.31 Binding for Thomas Hollis: National Art Library Dr.60, J. Toland, *The life of John Milton*, 1761. (Reduced from 21 × 14 cm.)

more restricted range of tools specific to himself.[46] There are instances of large collections being more or less uniformly bound and being thus possible to identify, and a number of examples are cited by Seymour de Ricci in *English collectors of books and manuscripts*[47], but on the whole the use which can be made of distinctive bindings to identify owners is limited.

Having said this, it should be added that binding evidence often plays an important part in establishing provenance, if not in so direct a way as to pinpoint a particular owner. Because bindings before the early nineteenth century are of necessity unique, and because decorative fashions have been constantly evolving and changing, individual bindings can be dated, at least approximately, and sometimes localised. A book's binding will always reveal something about its history, just as inscriptions and bookplates do, although the information may not relate to the earliest stages of its life if it has been rebound. If the binding is more or less contemporary with the book, it will reflect the choice of an early owner, and if the place of binding can be determined, information may be deduced about that owner's movements or likely place of residence. All such evidence must be weighed with caution and common sense but, to suggest a simple example, given a late sixteenth-century book with a contemporary Oxford binding and a contemporary inscription on the title page, Foster's *Alumni Oxonienses* is a sensible place to begin in order to identify the owner. If the inscription was a century later than the book, Foster would still be a reasonable starting point, as books often circulated within the same locality for several generations. But there are no rules in this area, and alternative possibilities should always be investigated.

When assessing or determining provenance, therefore, any evidence which the binding has to offer should be taken into account. When looking at books printed abroad, one should try to assess whether the binding is British or foreign. The importation of bound books was prohibited in 1534, and although the British book trade handled huge quanitites of books printed on the continent, most of those sold in this country during the sixteenth and seventeenth centuries were brought in as unbound sheets and bound here. It follows from this that a sixteenth-century continental book in a contemporary continental binding, now in an English collection, is more likely to have crossed the Channel some time after it was printed, than during the first few generations of ownership. This is not a rule, more an historical observation, and there are of course many exceptions.

INITIALS ON BINDERS' TOOLS

A caveat to mention in the context of identifying names and initials on bindings is the point that a number of sixteenth-century binders used tools which

---

46 See Nixon, *Five centuries*, no. 78; Nixon, *Broxbourne*, no. 92.
47 Cambridge, 1930; see for example his plate I (Earl of Pembroke) and plate VII (J. B. Inglis).

incorporate their initials or a similar device. The binding shown in fig. 4.12, from the workshop of the London binder John Reynes (fl. 1510-44), is decorated with a roll which incorporates Reynes's trademark, an R surmounted by a crossed zigzag like an N on its side. A number of binders of this period used signed rolls like this – the Cambridge binders Garret Godfrey and Nicholas Spierinck are well-known examples – and some panels and single tools were signed also. The possibility of confusing the initials in a roll with those of an owner may be slight, but some of the single tools may be more confusing.[48] The practice began in the late fifteenth century but had more or less ceased by the end of the sixteenth, except for cases where old tools were re-used long after they were originally cut. The continued use of rolls in Oxford meant that one signed roll of the 1550s was still being applied 60 years later,[49] and other signed rolls were in use in Oxford in the 1620s, but once roll binding of this type petered out, the use of signed tools became extremely uncommon.

48 See, for example, the Martin Dature tool reproduced in Foot, *Henry Davis* II no. 31, or the W G tool shown in no. 4. The early section of the Henry Davis Gift shows numerous examples of signed tools of this period.
49 See N. R. Ker, *Pastedowns in Oxford bindings*, Oxford, 1954, p. 205, 212-214 (roll XII).

V

SALE CATALOGUES

The study of provenance is concerned with the ownership of books, and with detecting how and when books pass from one owner to another. The book trade, and in particular the trade in second-hand books, provides a framework to facilitate the movement of books from owner to owner, down the generations, and its records, in the form of booksellers' and auctioneers' catalogues, are of prime importance for provenance research. Sale catalogues can provide a record of the books which were in demand and passing from hand to hand at any particular period, and as such they may offer a more useful index to changing interests in readership than bibliographies of books being printed. The trade in books is as old as books themselves, and for many centuries booksellers have been purchasing books from one owner and selling them on to the next. The vast majority of these transactions have taken place without any surviving record, so the steps cannot be retraced. Neither should it be forgotten that many books pass from owner to owner without any involvement from the trade, by gift, bequest, sale, or theft. But for the last 350 years or so, an appreciable proportion of the traffic in books in Britain has been documented, in the form of printed catalogues produced by a bookseller or auctioneer, and the survival of many of these catalogues preserves vital evidence of previous ownership.

Sale catalogues offer provenance information in three ways:
i) sales of entire libraries of named collectors, or parts of libraries, provide a record of that collector's books at the time of the sale;
ii) the descriptions of books being sold may include information on bookplates, inscriptions, or other evidence of previous ownership in particular books.
iii) marked-up copies of sale catalogues, compiled by auctioneers or by others in attendance, reveal the names of purchasers.

The first sort is more commonly associated with auction catalogues than booksellers' catalogues, although this distinction is less applicable in the seventeenth and eighteenth centuries. This category of information is fairly readily available, through lists and indexes of sales. The second category applies to both auctioneers' and booksellers' catalogues, and is not at all easy to access.

The sale catalogues of the auction houses and the major antiquarian book-sellers, particularly during the last century or so, contain vast amounts of information on the provenance of books passing through the firms' hands, but it is almost completely unindexed and the only way to get at this information is to read through the catalogues. As the more substantial catalogues are often illustrated with reproductions of title pages or bindings, their value to provenance researchers is further enhanced. An index to twentieth century book sale catalogues, covering the items within the catalogues, would be an indispensable aid to provenance research, but the enormity of the task would be extremely daunting.

The third category, like the first, is particularly associated with auction catalogues, but there are instances where marked-up master sets of booksellers' catalogues survive, as for example with the run of Ellis catalogues in Cambridge University Library (see p. 159 below). Many auctioneers kept interleaved catalogues in which hammer prices and buyers' names were recorded, and many important runs like this are preserved in the British Library. Auction houses now issue printed price lists after each sale, carrying the same information. It must be remembered, of course, that buyers at auction sales are often dealers rather than private collectors, and that the names recorded are sometimes fictitious (see the example shown in fig. 2.6; this practice has a long history and continues to the present day).

Sale catalogues may be categorised in various ways; they can be divided up into auctioneers' catalogues and booksellers' catalogues, or into sales of particular collections and sales of miscellaneous stock from no one named source. The first method of subdivision was employed in one of the earliest studies of sale catalogues and their use to appear in print, Richard Gough's 'The progress of selling books by catalogue', published in the *Gentleman's Magazine* for 1788; he stated that sale catalogues 'are of two sorts; by *auction* and by *hand*'. As has already been mentioned, sales of named libraries are generally associated with sale by auction, and this has commonly been the case for the last 200 years. There are however many seventeenth and eighteenth century catalogues of named collections, sold by booksellers at pre-determined prices, and the practice has continued right up to the present day. Booksellers have always been interested in buying entire libraries, but such books are often likely to be merged with existing stock when listed in a catalogue.

The most obvious time at which to expect a private library to be dispersed is shortly after the death of its owner, and many sale catalogues of particular collections follow this pattern – the sales of Lazarus Seaman (1676), Samuel Johnson (1785), Robert Southey (1845), or John Sparrow (1992) are just a few examples. Many libraries have however been sold, sometimes in part and sometimes in their entirety, during their owners' lifetimes, for a variety of reasons including financial impecunity, shortage of space, or boredom. Francis White (1564?-1638), appointed Bishop of Carlisle in 1628, is reputed to have sold all his books then, on account of the expense involved in transporting them to the north of England; malicious tongues suggested that he needed the money to bribe the patrons who had secured his preferment.[1] John Bellingham Inglis (1780-1870), who assembled a strong collection of early English literature, incunabula, and other desirable material early in his career, chose to sell much of it at auction in 1826, although he continued to collect books, and later sales were held after his death, in 1871 and 1900.[2] Oscar Wilde's library (together with the rest of his belongings) was hastily auctioned in 1895, shortly before his imprisonment and bankruptcy, to satisfy the demands of his creditors.[3] T. F. Dibdin (1776-1847) sold his bibliographical reference collection in 1817, apparently for reasons of financial necessity.[4] It should also be remembered that many libraries have been more or less kept together and subsequently sold many years after their owners' decease. This applies particularly to collections which have been bequeathed down several generations, sometimes accruing fresh material and sometimes not, before coming to the sale room because the family dies out or because the latest in a line of owners decides to sell. Many of the books and manuscripts of William Cecil, Lord Burghley (1520-97) were auctioned in London, nearly a century after his death, in 1687. The library of Michael Wodhull (1740-1816), one of the celebrated English bibliophiles of the second half of the eighteenth century, was not sold until 1886; the bulk of John Evelyn's library (the diarist, 1620-1706) reached the sale room in 1977, mixed up with books bought by later members of the family. The list of examples could be carried on indefinitely.

The earliest British printed booksellers' catalogues are lists of new books for sale; the first known example is Andrew Maunsell's *Catalogue of English printed bookes* of 1595, and there are a number of such catalogues from the first half of the seventeenth century. Between 1617 and 1628, versions of the Frankfurt Book Fair catalogue were printed in London. Catalogues issued by the London bookseller Robert Martin, which include second-hand material, have survived from the 1630s.[5] The earliest British booksellers' catalogue of second-hand stock from a named collector is that issued by John Martin and James Allestree in 1655, when they imported the library of the French medic Jean Riolan and offered it for sale in London. There is then a gap until 1677, when Robert Scott issued a catalogue of Humphrey Henchman's library, but from the end of the seventeenth century onwards a steady stream of booksellers' catalogues of

1 See D. Pearson, The libraries of English bishops, 1600-40, *The Library* 6th ser 14 (1992), 221-257, p. 255.

2 S. de Ricci, *English collectors of books and manuscripts*, Cambridge, 1930, pp. 97-98.

3 The catalogue is reproduced in facsimile in A. N. L. Munby (ed.), *Sale catalogues of libraries of eminent persons*, vol. I: *Poets and men of letters*, London, 1971, 371-388.

4 See A. N. L. Munby, Dibdin's reference library: the sale of 26-28 June 1817, in R. W. Hunt et al (eds.), *Studies in the book trade in honour of Graham Pollard*, Oxford Bibliographical Society Publications ns 18, 1975, 279-314.

5 The catalogues of imported books issued by Robert Martin, Henry Fetherstone and George Thomason around this period are described in D. E. Rhodes, Some notes on the import of books from Italy to England 1628-1650, *Studi secenteschi* 7 (1966) 131-138.

second-hand stock survives. The earliest examples have no prices printed in, but it became normal practice to include prices from about 1730 onwards. Before the end of the seventeenth century, evidence of the operation of the second-hand book trade is scanty and hard to come by; there is no doubt that it was going on, and that whole libraries and smaller collections were bought and sold just as they were (and are) in the era of printed catalogues, but the picture can only be reconstructed from traces which survive here and there. The relative scarcity of books during the medieval period, and the cost and labour involved in producing them, ensured that second-hand manuscripts could usually find a ready purchaser, and indeed it has been asserted that 'the trade in books throughout the Middle Ages was largely a second-hand business'.[6] In the middle of the fifteenth century, the provosts of Henry VI's new foundations at Eton and Cambridge petitioned the King to allow a particular London stationer (John Pye) special rights in the second-hand market, in order to benefit their respective libraries.[7] John Bale, in the middle of the sixteenth century, reported finding 'many notable antiquitees' in the shops of stationers and bookbinders.[8] Moving on a century, a well-known document survives in the State Papers for 1628, listing the 'names of such booke sellers, as deale in old libraryes', although it is no more than a series of names and addresses, all in London.[9] In addition to such occasional documentation, some evidence on the early second-hand trade is scattered in inscriptions in books; a copy of Curio's *Pro uera & antiqua ecclesiae Christi autoritate*, [1550?], in the British Library (1020.kk.17) has the inscription 'Tho. Montforte empt. 11° Maij 1610 a Martino Clar[kio?] ex reliquijs bibliothecae Dris. Wood'. This seems to imply that the London bookseller Martin Clark, who is known to have been in business 1606-11, sold the library of Robert Wood (Canon of Westminster, d.1609) after his death, and that this particular book was purchased by Thomas Moundeford (?the man of that name who was Vicar of St. Martin in the Fields, d.1633, or possibly his namesake who was President of the Royal College of Physicians, d.1630). The manuscript notes of seventeenth-century booksellers which are sometimes found on rear flyleaves, promising fixed cash or part-exchange prices should the books be brought back to the shop, offer further glimpses of the operation of the second-hand trade.[10] These are only random examples of categories of evidence which have never been systematically examined, and a great deal of work remains to be done on the workings of the early second-hand trade.

6 C. Buhler, *The fifteenth-century book*, Philadelphia, 1960, p. 33.

7 A. N. L. Munby, Notes on King's College Library in the fifteenth century, *Transactions of the Cambridge Bibliographical Society* 1 (1951), 280-286, p. 281. See also G. Pollard, The English market for printed books, *Publishing History* 4 (1977), 7-48, pp. 10-11.

8 Quoted in M. McKisack, *Medieval history in the Tudor age*, Oxford, 1971, p. 17.

9 Reprinted in W. W. Greg, *A companion to Arber*, Oxford, 1967, pp. 240-1.

10 See J. C. T. Oates, Booksellers' guarantees, *The Library* 5th ser 6 (1951), 212-3, and 5th ser 10 (1955), 125-6.

It is well known that the first English book auction was held in London in 1676, when the library of Lazarus Seaman (d.1675) was sold by William Cooper, and numerous copies of the printed catalogue survive. The practice came to England from Holland, where book auction sales with printed books had been going on since at least 1593. It soon became accepted as a popular method of selling collections of books, and by the end of the seventeenth century auction sales, with printed catalogues, were being held at the rate of at least ten a year, and were taking place both in London and in a wide range of provincial locations. The earliest auctioneers were usually booksellers whose entrepreneurial skills led them to diversify their methods of selling, but the eighteenth century saw the beginning of specialised firms who made auctioneering their main or sole business, and some of these eighteenth century firms (e.g. Christie's, Sotheby's) continue in business today.

Sale by public auction was quickly established as a suitable method of disposing of entire libraries, often after the death of a particular collector, and many thousands of such sales have been held since 1676. The printed catalogue which generally accompanies a sale usually states the owner's name on the titlepage, and the student of provenance is thus furnished with a ready-made list of the contents of a particular collection. Judgment must of course be exercised in assessing whether a sale represents the entire contents of a library, or only a part of it. Difficulties arise when several collections were sold together at one sale, a common practice, when the books were often listed in one sequence without any distinction as to which collector owned what. For example, when the library of the astronomer Edmund Halley was auctioned in 1742, his books were mixed in with those of 'a late eminent serjeant at law', and whereas it is possible to guess that the scientific books in the sale were probably Halley's, there is no trustworthy way of separating out the books in other disciplines. It should also be added that the sale of named collections only constitutes a fraction of the total auction trade in books, at all periods; anonymous sales of 'choice and valuable books' (or words to that effect) have always been a major element in the trade, often used by booksellers as a vehicle for shifting slow-moving stock. Auctions have also played a major part in the internal workings of the book trade, through various kinds of 'trade sales' which have been used as a regular system of sharing out publishing rights or stock remainders. Printed catalogues survive from these sales too, but they are concerned with new books and the trade amongst publishers and booksellers, so they are not directly relevant in the context of provenance studies.[11]

It should always be remembered that a great number of early sale catalogues have not survived, and that some sales were held without a printed catalogue to accompany them. This applies both to auction sales and to booksellers' sales, and to sales of particular libraries as well as more general sales of anonymous stock. Several studies have been published which demonstrate, by analysing

11 See J. Feather, *A history of British publishing*, London, 1988, pp. 72-73, and the references given there.

early newspaper advertisements, that many sales were held in the eighteenth century, of which no other record survives today (see the articles by MacDonald and Swaim cited at the end of this chapter). A great quantity of otherwise unrecoverable information on the dispersal of eighteenth-century collections is buried in newspaper announcements, although there are no short-cuts to its access. Sale catalogues have always suffered from their ephemeral nature, despite a long and continuing tradition which respects their worth as bibliographical evidence, and their survival has often been a matter of chance.

The conventions followed when describing books in sale catalogues have developed over the centuries, and, as a rough rule of thumb, it may be said that they have tended to become fuller as time has progressed. Seventeenth- and eighteenth-century catalogues usually have very basic entries with author, brief title, date, and occasionally selective information about binding or condition. When Richard Heber's copy of Ringhieri's *Cento giuochi liberali et d'ingegno* (1551) was sold at his sale on 19 January 1835 (lot 3648), it merited only the briefest of one-line entries in the catalogue. When the same book was sold at the Holford sale at Sotheby's in 1927 (9 December, lot 707), it was given an 11-line entry; when it reappeared in the Abbey sale (Sotheby's, 23 June 1965, lot 584), it received 17 lines and an illustration. The earliest auction catalogues are normally arranged by format (folios first, followed by smaller formats) and language, and this convention continued until the middle of the twentieth century. Early booksellers' catalogues look very much like auction catalogues, but they gradually developed a greater emphasis on a subject approach, being more convenient for booksellers and customers alike. For the student of provenance, the important point to note is an increasing tendency, over time, to include information on the previous ownership of particular books within a catalogue.

The recording of provenance in sale catalogues is allied to fashions in collecting and the interest which will be aroused in prospective purchasers. Sale catalogues exist primarily to sell books, not to further bibliographical scholarship – this is a side benefit, which is not to deny that many catalogues involve considerable scholarship in their compilation, or that some catalogues do advance scholarship – and booksellers and auctioneers include details which will make their books more attractive. The cult of the association copy is probably as old as books themselves, and books which have previously belonged to famous people and celebrated bibliophiles have always been collectible. From around the beginning of the nineteenth century onwards, distinguished provenances are increasingly noted in sale catalogues. The William Beckford sale of 1817, for example, has numerous notes along the lines of 'from Dr. Chauncy's collection', 'the royal arms on the sides', or 'De Thou's copy'. The 1823 sale catalogue of David Garrick's library is liberally sprinkled with notes about presentation copies, or evidence of noteworthy previous ownership: 'The autograph of T. Hearne the antiquary is on a fly-leaf' (lot 1002), 'It is presumed this once belonged to a Dauphin of France' (lot 1560). Another kind of provenance which has long been cherished is that of the celebrated scholar who has enriched his books with manuscript notes and adversaria, and the tradition for advertising such material is perhaps older than that for advertising royal and aristocratic provenance. The preface to *Bibliotheca Hookiana*, the 1703 sale catalogue of Robert Hooke's library, makes the point that Hooke 'hath left behind him many curious notes on some [books], considerable mss. improvements to others, not unworthy the view and perusal of the virtuosi of the age: for whose advantage, and better information, he unquestionably at first design'd them'. Later in the century, the sale of the manuscripts of the celebrated collector Anthony Askew (1722-74) included an extensive section of printed books with valuable adversaria. The title page advertised 'auctores classici, in quorum marginibus scriptae sunt, suis ipsorum manibus, doctissimum virorum notae atque observationes', and the preface outlined the importance of the collection:

> 'The manuscript marginal notes and observations which these books exhibit, are the production of several most eminent scholars. Among them, the curious observer will trace the hand writing of Gale, Bentley, Needham, Wasse, Chishull, Chandler, Waterland, Harris of Salisbury, Askew, Isaac Casaubon, Henry Stephens, and others.'

There were 312 lots (from a total sale of 633) comprising 'printed books, with manuscript notes', and copies of the catalogue which are marked up with buyers' names show that the spoils were divided out between some of the most famous bibliophiles of the late eighteenth century, such as Richard Farmer, Isaac Gossett, Michael Lort, P. H. Maty and Michael Wodhull.[12]

It has to be added that less noteworthy provenances have received less attention, and indeed the preference of earlier generations for discarding contemporary bindings, washing out inscriptions and removing bookplates did not create an encouraging climate for noting the presence of ownership marks when selling books. Tastes have changed, and most people buying a seventeenth century book today would prefer one in a contemporary binding with the scribbles of earlier owners, to one which was washed clean in the nineteenth century and rebound in morocco. Catalogue descriptions have reflected this steady shift in attitudes as interest in previous ownership – not just 'association copies' – has grown. As a general rule of thumb, it may be said that catalogues are worth examining for provenance information attached to individual entries from the early nineteenth century onwards, and by the end of the century the major antiquarian dealers were regularly including notes about previous ownership, particularly when the owners were identifiable and of some fame. The threshold of noteworthiness needed to qualify for such mention has gradually gone down, and there are now a number of booksellers who regularly note in their catalogues all inscriptions and bookplates which occur in their

---

12 See, for example, the copy in Cambridge University Library, Adv.c.75.8.

books, whether or not the owners can be identified. It has to be said that such booksellers remain a minority, and they do not include any of the major firms or auction houses, whose policy as regards the noting of provenance in catalogue entries is still selective.

IDENTIFYING AND LOCATING SALE CATALOGUES

The remainder of this chapter is devoted to ways of identifying and finding auction catalogues and booksellers' catalogues. The first section below deals with various kinds of lists and indexes of catalogues; this is followed by a section on the locations of major collections of catalogues, and one on catalogues which have been published in facsimile. The final section, detailing works on the history of bookselling and catalogue production, is preceded by two sections which offer brief details of the major auctioneering and bookselling firms whose catalogues are likely to be sought by students of provenance.

Lists and indexes

Sale catalogues have received a considerable amount of bibliographical attention and there are a number of lists and indexes, as well as secondary works and studies, which help in tracing particular catalogues, or in establishing whether or not a sale catalogue of a particular collection is known. They are nevertheless not always easy things to track down, and the more recent they are the more difficult the task can become. Bibliographical control of British sale catalogues is good down to 1800, but much less good for the nineteenth and twentieth centuries. The problem with the pre-1801 material lies not so much with existing documentation, as with the fact that so many catalogues from this period have not survived.

There are two major listings of British sale catalogues before 1901:

A. N. L. Munby & L. Coral: *British book sale catalogues, 1676-1800.* London, 1977.
List of catalogues of English book sales 1676-1900 now in the British Museum. London, 1915.

The first of these is a union catalogue, taking in the major collections in Great Britain, parts of Europe and America, and covering all kinds of book sale catalogues (retail or auction), except trade sales. It is not exhaustive and there are a number of sales and locations which slipped the net, but it is the best list available and is well established as the standard reference work within its defined scope. It was based on the British Museum *List*, which it supersedes for the period down to 1801. Sales are listed in chronological order, with separate indexes of consignors and auctioneers/booksellers.

The second list covers the holdings of only one library, the British Museum Library as it stood in 1915 (now the British Library), but it remains important for its coverage of the nineteenth century. Its scope is more restricted than

Munby and Coral as, for the nineteenth century, it only includes auction catalogues and not booksellers' catalogues, and it omits many anonymous sales. It includes an index of consignors of collections, but not of auctioneers or booksellers.

A. N. L. Munby's extensively annotated copy of the British Museum *List*, whose pre-1801 section formed the basis for Munby & Coral, is now in Cambridge University Library (shelfmark Munby.c.532). It includes many notes and additions relating to nineteenth-century sales, with references to locations of catalogues outside the British Library, and to additional sales not in the printed *List*. A xerox reproduction of Munby's copy is available in the British Library (N.L. 2a), in the British Library Department of Manuscripts, and in the Bodleian Library (X.3.25 in Room 132).

In addition to these two major reference sources, there are a number of other lists and indexes which may be useful:

Catalogus der bibliotheek van de vereeniging ter bevordering van de belangen des boekhandels te Amsterdam. 8 vols. The Hague, 1920-79.

> This library, now held in Amsterdam University Library, holds a very large collection of book sale catalogues from all over the world, both auction catalogues and dealers' catalogues, including long runs of British sale catalogues from the nineteenth and twentieth centuries. The *Catalogus* contains lists of these, with each catalogue briefly and separately described; these lists are useful as a record of the output of particular firms, as well as providing locations for those able to make direct use of the Library. The first set of lists in volume 4, 1934 (Antiquariaats-en magazijncatalogi, pp. 65-214, Catalogi van boeken-, prenten-en teekeningen veilingen, Groot-Britannie en Ierland, pp. 366-407) is supplemented by similar lists in volume 8, 1979 (*Supplement-catalogus 1932-1973*), pp. 113-380 and 432-479. The sale catalogues form only one part of this very large and wide-ranging collection, and the *Catalogus* as a whole comprises a major international bibliography of books and articles about the book trade, and book collecting.

J. Blogie: *Répertoire des catalogues de ventes de livres imprimés*. Brussels, 1982-

v. 1 (1982): *Catalogues belges appartenant à la Bibliothèque royale Albert Ier*

v. 2 (1985): *Catalogues français appartenant à la Bibliothèque royale Albert Ier*

v. 3 (1988): *Catalogues anglais appartenant à la Bibliothèque royale Albert Ier*

v. 4 (1992): *Catalogues neerlandois appartenant à la Bibliothèque royale Albert Ier*

v. 5 (forthcoming): *Catalogues allemands et autrichiens appartenant à la Bibliothèque royale Albert Ier*

> The volumes in this series list the sale catalogue holdings of the Royal Library in Brussels, divided by country of origin. Volume 3 contains a list of English book auctions and booksellers' catalogues, in separate sections, the first arranged chronologically, the second arranged alphabetically by booksellers. The entries in each section give dates, subjects, and names of owners of collections, where these are identified in the catalogue. Owners' names are included in the index. The holdings of both kinds of catalogues are extensive, including auction catalogues 1694-1980, and runs of nineteenth and twentieth century booksellers' catalogues.

G. Loh: *Bibliographie der Antiquariats- Auktions- und Kunstkataloge*. Leipzig, 1975-

> An attempt to compile a detailed listing of all the catalogues issued by major European booksellers and book auctioneers. Issued in parts (part 11, 1992); each part deals with a number of firms, listing all their catalogues within a given period, with details of catalogue

contents and previous owners (when named on the title pages of the catalogues). The series includes indexes of owners. The only English firms covered to date are Christies', 1960-72, and Sotheby's, 1960-70.

F. Lugt: *Répertoire des catalogues de ventes publiques intéressant l'art ou la curiosité.* 3v. The Hague, 1938-64.

> A chronological listing of ca. 59,000 auction sale catalogues of works of art, antiquities, coins, and other colllectibles, 1600-1900. Gives brief details of the sales (place, date, consignor, auctioneer, main contents, number of lots) and locations of surviving copies. International in coverage (Europe and America), both as regards sales and copies. Does not cover sales which only included books, but includes many references to mixed sales, in which books were sold alo:ng with other objects.

J. M. Chalmers-Hunt: *Natural history auctions 1700-1972: a register of sales in the British Isles.* London, 1976.

> A catalogue of surviving sale catalogues of collections of zoological, botanical or geological specimens, birds, butterflies, shells, etc. Arranged by date with details of consignors, contents, auctioneers, and locations of copies. Mostly concerned with non-book sales, therefore, but a number of sales of specimens did include books, and these are included in the catalogue and the presence of books in the sales is noted.

S. H. Folter: *Private libraries of musicians and musicologists: a bibliography of catalogs.* Buren, 1987.

> An annotated list of catalogues (largely but not exclusively sale catalogues) of the collections of musicians, 1649-1983; locations of known copies are included. International in coverage; 392 catalogues listed.

There are a couple of works devoted specifically to Irish sales:

F. O'Kelley: *Irish book-sale catalogues before 1801. Publications of the Bibliographical Society of Ireland* 6 (1953), 35-55.

> A short essay on early Irish book-sale catalogues, with a list of 63 surviving catalogues, with locations, 1698-1800.

W. G. Wheeler: *Check-list of auction-sale catalogues in Ireland* [Typescript: copy in Cambridge University Library at Munby.a.15].

> This formed the second part of a dissertation on *Libraries in Ireland before 1855* submitted in part requirement of the University College, London Diploma in Librarianship in 1957. Comprises a chronologically-arranged list of Irish book auction catalogues, with locations, between 1698 and 1935.

Some older listings of sale catalogues should also be mentioned:

J. Nichols: *Literary anecdotes of the eighteenth century.* 6v. London, 1812.

> Volume III, pp. 608-693, contains an expanded and annotated version of Richard Gough's 'Progress of selling books by catalogue', first printed in the *Gentleman's Magazine*, 1788. This includes a useful list of auctioneers in the eighteenth century (particularly the second half), with some biographical notes, and lists of major sales.

S. L. Sotheby: *A list of the original catalogues of the principal libraries which have been sold by auction, by Mr. Samuel Baker, from 1744.* London, 1818.

> An early attempt to compile a list of all the sales held by the firm which became Sotheby's, from 1744 to 1818, assembled by one of the nineteenth-century partners. An expanded, revised version was published in 1828; a copy in the British Library (shelfmark 011899.b.73) has manuscript additions down to 1843.

The emphasis in this section has been on British sales, and it is beyond the scope of this Handbook to attempt the same level of coverage for sales held abroad. It should however be added that there are two major bibliographies of American sale catalogues:

G. L. McKay: *American book auction catalogues 1713-1934: a union list.* New York, 1937.

> Locates catalogues held in 11 major U.S. libraries. Includes a list of American auction houses, with their trading dates, and an introductory essay on the history of book auctions in America by C. S. Brigham. Two supplementary lists were printed by McKay in the *Bulletin of the New York Public Library* for March 1946 and August 1948.

R. B. Winans: *A descriptive checklist of book catalogues separately printed in America 1693-1800.* Worcester (Massachusetts), 1983.

> This is a descriptive catalogue of all known American printed book catalogues, both sale catalogues and library catalogues (private and institutional), which includes locations of surviving copies. Most of the locations given are in the U.S.A.; the only British location cited is the British Library. Names of owners of collections consigned for sale are included in the general index.

For continental book sales, in addition to the sources listed above (e.g. Blogie, Loh, Lugt), it should be added that Pollard & Ehrman, *The distribution of books by catalogue* (see p. 169 below) includes two lists of early catalogues: table XXVII, pp. 222-228, comprises a list of Dutch book auction catalogues to 1700, with the names of owners and locations of surviving copies, and table XXIX, pp. 230-233, is a similar list of book auctions held in Germany and Scandinavia before 1721. H. D. Gebauer's *Bücherauktionen in Deutschland im 17. Jahrhundert* (Bonn, 1981) comprises a list of known German book auctions before 1701, with an extensive historical introduction. There is a detailed bibliography of French book sale catalogues down to 1750: F. Bléchet: *Les ventes publiques de livres en France 1630-1750.* Oxford, 1992. This is based on the collections of the Bibliotheque Nationale in Paris, and includes an extensive historical introduction.

Unpublished indexes

In addition to the published resources listed above, a number of libraries maintain unpublished indexes to sale catalogues, which are available for consultation:

BODLEIAN LIBRARY, OXFORD   A card index held in Room 132 (16 drawers) indexes all named consignors of books in Sotheby's catalogues from ca. 1900 to the present day.

NATIONAL ART LIBRARY, VICTORIA & ALBERT MUSEUM, LONDON   The Library built up a card index to auction catalogues of all types, including book sales, which indexes named consignors to the major auction houses since the late nineteenth century (including Sotheby's, Christie's, Phillips, and Bloomsbury Book Auctions). This index (36 drawers) is openly available in the Library and covers the period down to 1986. Sale catalogues from 1 January 1987 have been individually catalogued, with access points for named owners, and the records are searchable through the on-line catalogue.

NATIONAL LIBRARY OF SCOTLAND, EDINBURGH The Library has an extensive consignors' index covering book auction sales (Sotheby's, Christie's, Phillips, Parke-Bernet, Puttick & Simpson, Bloomsbury Books Auctions, and several smaller firms). It is held in sheaf binders and indexes consignors named in catalogues, on title pages or within the text, from ca. 1900.

Lists of catalogues in journals

A number of journals have published regular lists of contemporary booksellers' and auctioneers' catalogues, which may occasionally be useful for revealing the existence of catalogues, or dating catalogues which are numbered but not dated (a common problem with booksellers rather than auctioneers):

Between 1903 and 1946 *Notes and Queries* ran a regular column on 'Booksellers catalogues', often mentioning the highlights of particular catalogues. These columns are not covered by the annual indexes.

The *Book-Collectors' Quarterly*, which ran to 17 issues between 1930 and 1935, included in each number a list of recent second-hand and antiquarian booksellers' catalogues, arranged alphabetically by bookseller, in a section entitled 'The booksellers' register'.

Since 1966, *The Book Collector* has included in its 'News and comment' section a regular summary of noteworthy antiquarian catalogues, and of auction sales.

The *Antiquarian Book Review* (previously *Antiquarian Book Monthly Review*) has since 1975 included in each issue a listing of 'New catalogues', with brief details of new and forthcoming booksellers' catalogues from all over the English-speaking world.

Facsimiles of sale catalogues

Some early sale catalogues have been published in modern facsimile form:

A. N. L. Munby (gen. ed.): *Sale catalogues of libraries of eminent persons.* 12v. London, 1971-75.

> This series reproduces the sale catalogues of 64 noteworthy people from the early eighteenth century to the end of the nineteenth. There are seven volumes devoted to poets and men of letters, and one each devoted to actors, antiquaries, architects, politicians, and scientists.

A. Hyatt King (ed.): *Auction catalogues of music.* Buren, 1973-

> A series devoted specifically to reproductions of the sale catalogues of musicians or music collectors. Six volumes have been published to date; the London sales covered are those of Charles Burney (1814, no. 2 in the series), Vincent Novello (1852-62, no. 5), and E. F. Rimbault (1877, no. 6).

All Sotheby catalogues, 1733-1970, have been reproduced on microfilm by Xerox University Microfilms (see the notes on Sotheby's below, p. 152). Many eighteenth-century sale catalogues, listed by the *Eighteenth Century Short-Title Catalogue*, have been microfilmed as part of the series *The eighteenth century*, issued by Research Publications; details will be found on the ESTC file, or in the published guide which accompanies the microfilms, *The Eighteenth Century: guide to the microfilm collections* (Woodbridge, 1984-). The series *The nineteenth century*, published by Chadwyck-Healey, comprises extensive full-text microfilm facsimiles of nineteenth century British books, issued in large subject groupings. The module on *Publishing, the book trade and the diffusion of knowledge* includes a number of booksellers' and auctioneers' catalogues (e.g. Ellis & Elvey, Hodgson, Quaritch, Sotheby); titles and reel numbers are given in the printed guide to the module.

Collections of sale catalogues

The collecting of book sale catalogues has a rather chequered history. On the one hand, their value as bibliographical tools has long been recognised by private collectors, and major catalogues have been a marketable commodity for many centuries.[13] On the other, they have always been a vulnerable category of material, likely to be treated as ephemeral and disposable once they have served their immediate purpose, and the survival rate of catalogues which are not of the first rank is generally low. This applies particularly to libraries and institutions, where sale catalogues tend to be acquired as part of the working process of buying books, rather than as material deliberately purchased for stock, and the extent to which they are retained and catalogued in their own right is very variable. Libraries which have extensive holdings of early sale catalogues often owe this fact to the acquisition of collections of individual bibliophiles, who have recognised their importance. Durham University Library, for example, derives its holdings of nineteenth-century catalogues from the bequest of Martin Routh (1755-1854), although many of his catalogues did not survive the transfer from Oxford to Durham.[14] The Bodleian Library's holdings of sale catalogues are drawn from many sources, but the collection which came with the bequest of Francis Douce's library in 1834, comprising Douce's own marked-up copies of auctioneers' and booksellers' catalogues, is one of the foundation stones of those holdings. It is worth remembering that catalogues produced by firms outside London may sometimes survive in

---

13 The collecting of sale catalogues for bibliographical purposes, from the sixteenth century onwards, is extensively studied by Archer Taylor in his *Book catalogues: their varieties and uses* (2nd edn, revised by W. P. Barlow, jr, Winchester, 1986), most particularly in ch. II, 'The uses of catalogues'. He makes the point that the value of sale catalogues as bibliographical tools has declined as the study of bibliography has increased, because specialised bibliographies supersede lists of individual collections; he dates the turning point as early as 1750 (p. 116).

14 See A. I. Doyle, Sale catalogues, *The Durham Philobiblon* 1 (1951), 30-36, p. 30.

libraries in the region; Glasgow University Library, for example, has significant holdings of Scottish catalogues, and of Glasgow catalogues in particular (a separate index of sale catalogues, held in the Special Collections Reading Room, lists all catalogues down to 1920).

The sections which follow below, on **auctioneers** and **booksellers**, include notes on runs of catalogues in particular places, but this section offers brief summaries of some of the major repositories of British sale catalogues.

THE BRITISH LIBRARY, LONDON **Printed Books** The British Library has extensive holdings of sale catalogues, although it is not always possible to determine precisely what is available from the Catalogue. The chief strengths of the collection lie in the unique runs of marked-up auctioneers' copies from many of the major sale rooms, but most of the major booksellers are represented to some extent. Most sale catalogues are held at pressmarks beginning S-C, although a number of individual pre-twentieth-century catalogues will be found scattered elsewhere in the collections. They will normally be entered in the General Catalogue under the name of the auction firm or bookseller. Individual auction catalogues down to 1900 can be traced through the printed *List* (see p. 139 above), but for many bookselling firms the General Catalogue gives only a summary entry which does not show in any detail which catalogues are and are not held.

Department of Manuscripts It should be noted that the British Library Department of Manuscripts has extensive holdings of booksellers' catalogues, acquired as working tools as they have been used for selection. These include many nineteenth-century dealers' catalogues which are not held elsewhere in the Library. They are not included in the main British Library catalogue, but a separate *List of English book-sellers' and dealers' catalogues in the Department of Manuscripts, 1801-1900, not included in the British Museum List* is available for consultation in the Department (on microfilm, shelfmark M981). A microfilm copy of the British Museum *List*, annotated with shelfmarks of Department of Manuscripts copies, and details of catalogues down to 1800 which are not included in the *List*, is available as M980.

CAMBRIDGE UNIVERSITY LIBRARY **The Munby Collection** A. N. L. Munby (1913-75), probably the most celebrated twentieth-century bibliographer for the study of sale catalogues, built up a major personal library of auction and booksellers' catalogues, most of which was sold to Cambridge University Library after his death. The collection includes many thousands of catalogues, with many highlights such as annotated catalogues from the library of Sir Thomas Phillipps, and many items which are rare or unique. The collection also includes some private and institutional library catalogues, early prospectuses, material relating to circulating libraries, and miscellaneous other items concerning the book trade. A separate handlist, shelfmark Munby.a.16, contains a detailed breakdown of the contents. The collection is described in:

D. J. McKitterick: The Munby Collection in the University Library. *Transactions of the Cambridge Bibliographical Society* 6 (1975), 265-270.

Outside the Munby Collection, the University Library has appreciable holdings of sale catalogues; older material is well listed in the catalogue, but twentieth-century holdings are not fully catalogued. Particularly noteworthy is the major collection of Ellis catalogues (see p. 159 below). A copy of the 1915 British Museum *List*, marked up to show the Library's holdings, is kept on the open shelves in the Rare Books Room (B885.1).

THE BODLEIAN LIBRARY, OXFORD   The importance of sale catalogues has long been recognised at the Bodleian, where systematic efforts to create a sale catalogue collection began in the mid-nineteenth century, and this enlightened tradition, together with a number of major benefactions which have included blocks of historic catalogues, has fostered the development of extensive holdings of both British and foreign material. The donation of the Broxbourne Collection, in 1978, brought many rare or unique early sale catalogues, being the material on which Pollard and Ehrman's *The distribution of books by catalogue* was based (see p. 169 below). There are many long runs of booksellers' and auctioneers' catalogues; some of the earlier catalogues are kept at shelfmarks beginning Mus.Bibl.III. It is the Library's general policy to catalogue and add to the collections all antiquarian and second-hand booksellers' catalogues which it receives. Sale catalogues will normally be found entered in the Bodleian catalogues under the name of the bookseller or auctioneer. A card index (2 drawers, 'Booksellers index') kept in Room 132 lists many individual catalogues, or runs of catalogues, dating from the nineteenth and twentieth centuries. Several other special finding aids in Room 132 relate to sale catalogues, including a photocopy of Munby's interleaved British Museum *List*, marked up with Bodleian shelfmarks (X.3.25), and a handlist of Sotheby's catalogues, 1745-1899, in the Mus.Bibl. collection (X.3.27).

THE NATIONAL ART LIBRARY at the Victoria and Albert Museum, London, has major holdings of sale catalogues, and although the primary collecting emphasis has been focussed on the fine and decorative arts, many book sale catalogues are held also. The Library's runs of Christie's and Sotheby's catalogues extend back to the eighteenth century. **Manchester Central Library** has one of the country's largest provincial collections of early sale catalogues, covering books, pictures and house contents, with over 550 pre-1900 catalogues. A. N. L. Munby, in his lecture on 'The libraries of English men of letters' (printed in his *Essays and papers*, London, 1977, pp. 101-120) briefly described a number of other significant collections of sale catalogues, including **Durham University Library**, **Trinity College, Cambridge** (these catalogues are currently deposited in Cambridge University Library, and should be requested through the Rare Books Room there), and **Worcester College, Oxford**.

AUCTIONEERS

This section gives brief details of the major auction firms which have been involved with selling books since the beginning of the nineteenth century. The starting date is chosen because bibliographical control of British sale catalogues is much less good for the nineteenth and twentieth centuries than it is for the seventeenth and eighteenth. Locations of significant holdings of each firms' catalogues are indicated where possible.

Bloomsbury Book Auctions

Bloomsbury Book Auctions 1983-

Bloomsbury Book Auctions was set up in 1983. Its birth was brought about by the closure of Hodgson's Rooms, and changes at Sotheby's, which left a gap in the market for a London-based auction firm, devoted to books, which could handle a regular throughput of mid-priced material as well as more spectacular items. Since 1983, the business has flourished, and it now has a well-established niche in the book trade; its 200th sale was held in 1993. A pamphlet issued in 1993 (*Bloomsbury Book Auctions 10th anniversary: a celebration*) provides a brief history of the firm.

Location of catalogues: Many libraries have subscribed to Bloomsbury Book Auction catalogues from the firm's foundation, and runs are generally not hard to find.

Christie's

James Christie 1766-77
Christie & Ansell 1777-84
Christie 1785-1831
Christie & Manson 1831-59
Christie, Manson & Woods 1859-

James Christie (1730-1803) began his auctioneering career as an assistant to another auctioneer named Annesley, and set up in business on his own in Pall Mall in 1766, when his first known sale was held. This comprised household goods and furniture, but Christie soon began holding the sales of pictures and works of art for which the firm subsequently became pre-eminent. Book sales have always formed a significant feature of the business, and the first Christie auction to include books was held in 1770. Since then many noteworthy collections have passed through Christie's rooms, including for example the libraries of Samuel Johnson (1785), Cox Macro (the manuscripts, 1820), Samuel Rogers (1856), C. Fairfax Murray (1917-18), the Evelyn family (1977), and A. A. Houghton, jnr. (1979-80).

Christie was in partnership with Robert Ansell between 1777 and 1784, and very briefly with the firm of Sharpe and Harper in 1797. After his death in 1803 the business was taken over by his eldest son James (1773-1831), and it was under his direction that it moved to the King Street address which it has occupied ever since. In 1831 James's sons James Stirling Christie (d.1834) and George Henry Christie (retired 1863, d.1887) took over, and at this time also William Manson became a partner. The last member of the Christie family to be involved with the running of the firm was George's son James H. B. Christie, who retired in 1889. The business became Christie, Manson & Woods in 1859, when Thomas Woods (retired 1903, d.1906) was taken into partnership.

For an account of the history of the firm down to 1925, see:

H. C. Marillier: *'Christie's' 1766 to 1925*. London, 1926.

This book includes a chronological list of the most important sales, 1794-1925, although they are mostly picture auctions. A 'List of Christie's sales containing books, mostly 1801-37', compiled by Lenore Coral, is kept with the Munby Collection in Cambridge University Library, at Munby.b.138[4].

Location of catalogues: Christie's, unlike many of the other major London auction houses, retains its archives on the premises. The firm holds the only known complete run of catalogues, from 1766 to the present day, with only occasional gaps. The catalogues down to 1941 are marked up with prices, buyers, and vendors; after 1941, vendor information is not available (unless declared in the printed text of the catalogue), only prices and buyers. A separate index of vendors, as printed in the catalogues, was maintained down to 1980 in a series of 'green books'. The catalogues are available for public consultation, at Christie's headquarters, during normal working hours, and intending users should contact the Archivist, Christie, Manson & Woods Ltd., 8 King Street, St. James's, London SW1Y 6QT, to arrange appointments.

The British Library has more or less complete holdings of Christie's catalogues from 1880, has patchy holdings for the 1860s and 1870s, and has only sporadic holdings before 1860. The Bodleian Library's series begins in 1885, with some catalogues before that date, and the set in Cambridge University Library is continuous only from 1973, but includes a number of other catalogues back to 1776. The National Library of Scotland has a continuous run from 1948, and a number of earlier catalogues. The National Art Library has 24 pre-1800 catalogues, extensive holdings of nineteenth- and early twentieth-century catalogues (particularly strong for the period 1850-75), and a complete set of catalogues from 1921.

Evans

R. H. Evans 1812-46

Evans began life as a bookseller, and took over the flourishing bookselling business of James Edwards in 1804. He began his career as an auctioneer with the famous Roxburghe sale of 1812, and during the first half of the nineteenth century he established himself as one of the leading book auctioneers of London, handling many celebrated sales (e.g. Hibbert, Valpy, the Duke of Sussex, and part of Heber's collection) and a number of lesser ones. He went bankrupt in 1846 and his stock and business were purchased by Sotheby's, although he continued as a bookseller until his death in 1857.

Location of catalogues: Evans's own set of his sale catalogues, 1812-45, interleaved with prices and buyers' names, is in the British Library. It is accompanied by a rough manuscript index of consignors' names. Evans is well represented in the Munby Collection at Cambridge.

Fletcher

See the section on **Stewart** below, p. 154.

Hodgsons

Robert Saunders 1807-25
Saunders & Hodgson 1825-28
Edmund Hodgson 1828-67
B. B. & H. H. Hodgson 1867-71
H. H. Hodgson & Co. 1871-1900
Hodgson & Co. 1901-67

The founder of the firm, Robert Saunders, held his first sale in Reading in 1807, but moved to London the following year. The business was taken over by Saunders's partner Edmund Hodgson in 1828, and the firm remained in the control of the Hodgson family for several generations. Hodgson's always concentrated their business in sales of books and literary property, and they are the only auctioneers to have done so over such a long period. During the nineteenth century they also ran trade sales at which publishers passed on their remainder stock to the booksellers, and the extensive run of printed catalogues from these sales constitutes an important resource for the history of the nineteenth century book trade. During the twentieth century, Hodgson's tended to deal with the cheaper and more general end of the market, while major sales were more the preserve of Sotheby's. The firm was bought by Sotheby's in 1967, although sales continued to be held at Hodgson's Rooms, under the aegis of Sotheby's, until 1981. For notes on the first century of the firm's history, see:

One hundred years of book auctions, 1807-1907. Being a brief record of the firm of Hodgson and Co., London, 1908.

A more recent, and more informal, account of the firm will be found in *Rare books and rarer people*, by O. F. Snelling, London, 1982.

Location of catalogues: The British Library holds a more or less complete set of Hodgson's catalogues, 1807-1967; some catalogues are marked up with prices and buyers' names. The Library also has an extensive set of Hodgson's trade and remainder sales throughout the nineteenth century. The Bodleian Library has a substantial but incomplete run of catalogues, 1883-1967 (2591.d.2). The National Library of Scotland has a continuous set 1943-67.

The firm's archives were given to the British Library and are available in the Department of Manuscripts there as Add.Mss.54580-54723 (dating from 1825-1964) and 58128-58148 (some supplementary material, and the records for 1964-67). The Munby Collection in Cambridge University Library includes a typescript list of owners of libraries sold at Hodgson's between 1807 and 1900.

King

> T. King 1785-1806
> King & Lochée 1806-15
> T. King 1816
> T. King, junior 1781-1815

Thomas King began his career as a bookseller in London ca. 1768, and subsequently turned to auctioneering; Munby and Coral record 35 of his sale catalogues 1785-1800. He continued into the nineteenth century and was in partnership with his son-in-law John Lochée (d.1815) from 1806. He was noted by Nichols as being one of the major figures on the London auctioneering scene at the turn of the nineteenth century, and libraries sold by him included the celebrated collections of Richard Farmer (1798), and Isaac Reed (1807). He was based at King Street, Covent Garden.

His son Thomas King, junior, established a separate auctioneering business, apparently as early as 1781; his catalogues are readily distinguishable from those of his father by the different address (mostly Tavistock Street, Covent Garden), and the appellation 'junior' which he regularly used.

Location of catalogues: Surviving catalogues before 1801 are listed in Munby and Coral. The British Library has 45 nineteenth-century catalogues of the elder King, and a similar number of his son's. The Munby Collection at Cambridge has 9 King & Lochée catalogues, 1806-13.

Lewis

> L. A. Lewis 1825-77

A general auctioneer who sold furniture, prints, and miscellaneous items, but books formed a major part of his business. Book sales were largely anonymous but some named libraries were auctioned by Lewis.

Location of catalogues: The British Library has the auctioneer's set, interleaved with prices and buyers' names, covering the period 1825-52 only, with a gap for 1845. A few other Lewis catalogues from the 1850s are separately listed in the British Library catalogue. There is a small handful of Lewis catalogues for the 1850s in the Munby Collection at Cambridge.

Phillips

Phillips 1796-1879
Phillips & Son 1879-82
Phillips, Son & Neale 1882-1971
Phillips 1971-

Harry Phillips, the founder of the firm, was clerk to the auctioneer James Christie before setting up in business on his own in 1796. He quickly became established as a fashionable auctioneer and held numerous noteworthy sales in the early years of the nineteenth century, such as the effects of Queen Caroline (1822) and the books, pictures and other effects from Fonthill (1823). When Phillips died in 1840 his son William Augustus (d.1887) took over, taking his son into partnership in 1879, and his son-in-law Frederick Neale in 1881. The firm acquired the business of Puttick & Simpson in 1954. Phillips has always been a general auctioneering house, dealing with a wide range of artistic and household objects, including books.

Location of catalogues: The British Library holds the auctioneers' set of catalogues, interleaved with prices and buyers' names, 1850-1975, with a continuous run of unmarked catalogues thereafter. The Bodleian Library has a complete set of Phillips catalogues only since 1974. The National Art Library holds book sale catalogues from 1969, and a complete set of all sale types from 1976. A typescript list of Phillips' sales including books will be found in the Munby Collection at Cambridge (Munby.b.138/5).

Puttick & Simpson

Puttick & Simpson 1846-1971

The general auctioneering business which was founded by William Stewart in 1794 (see section on **Stewart** below), and which eventually became the property of James Fletcher, was sold to the partnership of Thomas Puttick and William Simpson in 1846, and the firm was then re-named. Their descendants continued to be involved in the running of the business until the early years of the twentieth century, but in 1937 it was sold to Victor Jones, from whom it passed to Robert Clarkson (1942), who sold it to the auctioneering firm of Phillips, Son & Neale in 1954. Puttick & Simpson continued to have a separate identity until 1971, when a reorganisation at Phillips brought an end to the Puttick & Simpson series.

Puttick & Simpson were always general auctioneers and they sold a wide range of material, including books and prints, but also furniture, antiquities, wine, works of art, coins, stamps, and other collectibles. During the second half of the nineteenth century they acquired a dominant position for the sale of music and musical instruments, and in this period they also occupied a significant position in the book trade. They handled a number of major book sales, such as those of Dawson Turner (1859-60), Thomas Moore (1853-74), Sir Charles Isham (1874), part of the Dering library (1858-65), and the Earl of Sunderland (1881-83), and also a great many more minor ones. The sale of books continued, in a diminishing way, well into the twentieth century.

The best account of the history of the firm will be found in:

J. Coover: *Music at auction: Puttick and Simpson (of London) 1794-1971*. (Detroit Studies in Music Bibliography, 60). Detroit, 1988.

Although this is primarily concerned with the music materials sold by Puttick & Simpson, the introductory section includes much information about the general history of the firm's activities.

Location of catalogues: The British Library holds the auctioneers' set, 1846-1967, interleaved with prices and buyers' names, together with a run of un-annotated catalogues 1958-71. This set has a few gaps here and there. The Bodleian Library has an apparently complete set of Puttick & Simpson book or manuscript sales (with a few other sales interspersed), 1846-1950 (2591.d.3). Non-book sales, 1889-1949, are held separately at 175003.d.113. Cambridge University Library has an imperfect set, 1849-1941. An index of consignors of books, containing information which was not always included in the printed catalogues and covering sales 1846-70, was compiled in 1871 and a typescript transcript of this index is available in the British Library (shelfmark C.131.k.15), and in the Bodleian Library (Room 132, shelfmark X.3.28). This index was not used when the *List of English book sales 1676-1900 now in the British Museum* was drawn up, and in some cases it will provide provenance information not found in the *List*.

Sotheby's

Samuel Baker 1745-66
Baker & Leigh 1767-78
G. Leigh 1778
Leigh & Sotheby 1778-1800
Leigh, Sotheby & Son 1800-04
Leigh & S. Sotheby 1804-16
S. Sotheby 1816-28
Sotheby & Son 1828-36
S. Leigh Sotheby 1837-43
S. Leigh Sotheby & Co. 1843-50
S. Leigh Sotheby & John Wilkinson 1850-63
Sotheby, Wilkinson & Hodge 1864-1924
Sotheby & Co. 1924-75

Sotheby Parke Bernet & Co. 1975-84
Sotheby's 1984-

The oldest-established British book auctioneering firm still in existence today, whose position as one of the leading auction houses for books was won in the nineteenth century, and has been retained ever since. The founding father, Samuel Baker, began to issue fixed-price catalogues some years before his first auction catalogue in 1745. Although books formed the major part of Sotheby's business during the eighteenth and nineteenth centuries, diversification into sales of prints, coins and antiquities had begun by the beginning of the nineteenth century, and the business expanded during the twentieth century to cover a wide spectrum of fine art and collectibles. For a substantial and very readable history of the firm, see:

F. Herrmann: *Sotheby's: portrait of an auction house*. London, 1980.

Since the mid-1980s, it has been common practice to provide indexes to the more important book sales, but provenances noted in the descriptions of the lots are not usually listed in these indexes. However, a number of major sales have had catalogues which included separate provenance indexes, e.g.:

Dyson Perrins, 9.12.1958, 1.12.1959, 29.11.1960 (combined index in part III)
J. R. Abbey, parts I-III, 21-23.6.1965, 14-16.11.1966, 19-21.6.1967
Harrison D. Horblit, 10-11.6.1974, 11.11.1974
Broxbourne Library, 14-15.11.1977, 8-9.5.1978 (combined index in part II)

Location of catalogues: The auctioneers' set of sale catalogues, interleaved with prices and buyers' names, 1739-1961, is in the British Library (S.C.Sotheby). Copies of more recent catalogues, down to the present time, are also available there. Many libraries have twentieth-century runs of Sotheby catalogues.

The British Library's interleaved master set of catalogues was microfilmed and published in this form by Xerox University Microfilms in 1973. A printed guide (*Sotheby & Co.: catalogues of sales. A guide to the microfilm collection*) accompanies the films. Both the Bodleian Library and Cambridge University Library have sets of these microfilms.

Southgate

J. W. Southgate 1825-30
Southgate, Grimston & Wells 1830-33
Southgate, Son & Grimston 1834
Southgate & Son 1835-37
J. W. Southgate 1838-40
Southgate & Son 1840-42
H. Southgate & Co. 1842-43
H. Southgate 1844-45
Southgate & Barrett 1845-64
Southgate & Co. 1865-71

Books formed a major part of the business throughout the life of this firm, although they also sold prints, paintings, furniture and other miscellaneous material. Book sales included the libraries of named collectors (e.g. James Nasmith, 1825, H. F. Lyte 1843-51), as well as anonymous sales; they also sold off a number of circulating libraries.

Location of catalogues: The British Library holds the auctioneer's set, interleaved with prices and buyers' names, covering the period from 1825-68, with a small gap in 1856, and lacking the last three years' sales 1868-71. It also has a second set, with prices and buyers' names written in, almost complete for 1825-71. The Bodleian Library has a run of 124 Southgate catalogues, 1825-50 (2591.d.119).

Stewart

W. Stewart 1794-1825
Stewart & Wheatley 1825
Stewart, Wheatley & Adlard 1826-28
Wheatley & Adlard 1829-31
Wheatley 1831-37
Fletcher & Wheatley 1837-40
J. Fletcher 1841-46

The business was founded by William Stewart, who is first known of as a bookseller in 1791. In 1825 he took Benjamin Wheatley into partnership, and the following year a further partner, Adlard, was brought in. The firm's name underwent several changes as partners subsequently left; Wheatley died in 1837, and the business was bought by James Fletcher. The Wheatley in Fletcher & Wheatley, 1837-40, is Benjamin's son B. R. Wheatley. Fletcher ran the business on his own from 1841 till 1846, when it was sold to Thomas Puttick and William Simpson (see the section on **Puttick & Simpson** above). Noteworthy named collections which passed through the firm's hands included those of Reginald Heber, Bishop of Calcutta (1827), William Disney, Hebrew Professor at Cambridge (1829), and William van Mildert, Bishop of Durham (1836).

Location of catalogues: The British Library has about 25 Stewart/Wheatley/Fletcher catalogues, 1800-45. The Munby Collection at Cambridge has an important collection of catalogues from this firm, with ca. 140 catalogues between 1822 and 1846, and particularly good holdings of Fletcher catalogues of the 1840s. The Bodleian Library has an apparently complete run of Fletcher catalogues from January 1842 to June 1846 (2591.d.3*), and a run of 18 Wheatley & Adlard/Wheatley sales, 1830-34 (2591.d.118).

BOOKSELLERS

This selective listing attempts to cover some of the most significant retail firms, founded before 1930, whose catalogues have regularly included provenance data. Some are still in existence today, others are defunct. The catalogues issued by these booksellers are likely to prove good hunting ground for anyone interested in the libraries of collectors of some identifiable standing – people who used armorial stamps or bookplates, or who occupy some definable place in history. They are less likely to record details of humble or obscure collectors. As a rough rule of thumb, the earlier the catalogue, the less comprehensive its treatment of provenance information is likely to be. Some attempt has been made to mention catalogues which are particularly noteworthy for the student of provenance. The list, and the information on holdings, is far from exhaustive, and more firms deserve to be included, but it should give some guidance in largely uncharted territory. It is restricted exclusively to British firms.

John Gray Bell

Began business as a bookseller in London in 1848; moved to Manchester in 1854 and continued in trade there until his death in 1866. Published various antiquarian and genealogical works (see *DNB*). Bell issued a monthly series of catalogues entitled *The bibliographer's manual, and collector's assistant*, of miscellaneous antiquarian books, manuscripts, and prints; he also issued separate catalogues of autograph letters and 'clearance catalogues', mostly devoted to antiquarian stock. In 1862 he produced a *Catalogue of ... early printed books, with autograph annotations by the great reformers Luther and Melancthon, carefully selected from the ... library of S. Leigh Sotheby*.

The British Library Department of Manuscripts has 63 John Gray Bell catalogues, 1849-65. The Bodleian Library has 61 catalogues, 1852-65 (shelfmark 2593.e.118).

Blackwell's

Founded in Oxford in 1879 by B. H. Blackwell, whose father (d.1855) had earlier been a second-hand bookseller in Oxford. The business flourished and has not only become synonymous with bookselling in Oxford, but has branches and subsidiaries all over the world. Although principally known today for its trade in new books, B. H. Blackwell began his career selling second-hand and antiquarian material, and the firm has always maintained this side of its activities. The first catalogue was issued in 1879 and many hundreds have appeared since. Blackwell's have always had a ready supply of stock from the libraries of Oxford academics, and many of their catalogues, particularly down to about 1950, have been named collections (e.g. Mark Pattison, catalogue 16, 1886; Lewis Carroll, catalogue 62, 1898; Ingram Bywater, catalogue 163, 1916). A list of all Blackwell catalogues, 1879-1978, which have included antiquarian material, is appended to the *Centenary catalogue of antiquarian and rare modern books*, catalogue A-1, 1979. For a full history of the firm, see:

A. L. P. Norrington: *Blackwell's 1879-1979*. Oxford, 1983.

An extensive set of Blackwell's catalogues is preserved by the firm today, containing all the catalogues of second-hand and antiquarian material issued between 1879 and the late 1960s. Coverage is then patchy for about a decade, but complete from 1979 onwards. The firm has no archivist or formal facilities for consulting these catalogues, but they will normally be happy to make them available in response to reasonable requests. Enquiries should be directed to Blackwell's Rare Books in Oxford. The Bodleian Library also has a complete set of Blackwell's catalogues from no. 1 (1879) onwards (2593.e.183). The British Library has a fairly complete set from no. 252 (1929) onwards, and less complete holdings between no. 88 (1903) and 248 (1929), particularly patchy in the earlier part of that period.

Bohn

Henry George Bohn (1796-1884), the most famous member of the Bohn family, set up on his own as a bookseller in Covent Garden in 1831, when he issued his first catalogue of *A very select collection of books*. He amassed a huge stock of second-hand and antiquarian material and his 1841 catalogue, containing 23,208 items, is the largest single catalogue ever issued by a British bookseller. His attention turned increasingly to the remainder market and to publishing, and he is probably best known today for his series of popular and useful texts, issued in uniform cheap formats in the 1840s and 1850s, as Bohn's Standard Library. He continued to issue catalogues of early printed books and manuscripts during the 1840s, 1850s and 1860s, and his *General catalogue. Part the second. Fourth and concluding section* appeared in 1867. Much of his antiquarian stock was dispersed by auction between 1865 and 1875.

His father John Henry Bohn (1757-1843) also issued catalogues of antiquarian material; he began business in England in 1795, primarily as a bookbinder, but he gave up binding to concentrate on bookselling in 1815. His business continued to operate in parallel with that of his son Henry, and he issued catalogues up to the time of his death in 1843.

A third separate Bohn bookselling business was run by James Bohn (1803-80), John's younger son and Henry's brother, who began trading in the Strand in 1834. He did not prosper, and abandoned the venture shortly after 1840, when he issued a substantial *Catalogue of ancient and modern books*. He set up again as a bookseller in 1845, but gave up once more in 1847.

The major catalogues of the Bohn family are relatively easy to find, and are preserved in many collections. The Bodleian Library has a number of H. G. Bohn's smaller and later catalogues of ca. 1845-67 (2593.e.97).

John Cochran

Worked as a junior partner in the firm of Ogles, Duncan & Cochran from ca. 1814, and subsequently in the firm of Rivingtons & Cochran, before setting up on his own in business as a bookseller in 1826. He issued a number of substantial and well-annotated catalogues of manuscripts, dating from the middle ages to the eighteenth century, as well as catalogues of antiquarian and second-hand printed books. He continued in business until ca. 1844.

The British Library has 6 Cochran catalogues, 1826-37; also, 3 are held by the Department of Manuscripts there (1826-37). Cambridge University Library holds 5 catalogues, 1826-37, including 3 in the Munby Collection. The Bodleian Library has 4 catalogues, 1829-37.

James Coleman

A London bookseller who specialised in genealogy, history and topography, whose first catalogue was issued in 1859 and who continued in business until at least 1897. His main numbered series of catalogues offered miscellaneous antiquarian material, and often included related manuscript items such as deeds, wills, autograph letters and court-rolls. He also issued a few catalogues outside the numbered sequence, of e.g. old wills or royal deeds. He was briefly in partnership with John Pearson in 1860.

The British Library has an almost complete run of Coleman catalogues, 1859-97, nos. 1-231 (S.C.1098). The Bodleian Library has a nearly complete set of catalogues 1-86 (1859-72) (Sir Thomas Phillipps's copies, 2593.d.105).

Davis & Orioli

A partnership which traded for many years from both London and Florence; the first Florence catalogue was issued in 1911, and in 1913 a new series was begun from the London office, separately numbered. The firm handled high quality antiquarian material; they continued to issue catalogues until the 1960s, which regularly contained provenance information. Orioli's autobiography (*Adventures of a bookseller*, London, 1938) is a colourful account of his career which includes, rather buried amongst wide-ranging reminiscences and observations, some first-hand descriptions of his contemporaries in the anti-quarian book trade.

The British Library has a fairly complete set of both series of catalogues from no. 5 (1913) to no. 170 (1967). The Bodleian Library has an almost complete run of both series from the foundation of the firm in 1911 to the late 1930s, and a number of catalogues from the 1960s (all at 2593.e.169).

Dobell

Bertram Dobell (1842-1914) opened a stationery shop in north London in 1869 and developed his business into bookselling, issuing his first catalogue in 1876. His business flourished, moving to Charing Cross Road in 1887, and he issued many catalogues of general antiquarian material. After his death the firm continued under the direction of his sons P. J. and A. E. Dobell; in 1934 P. J. Dobell moved to Tunbridge Wells, while his brother Arthur maintained the London shop. The partnership between the two brothers continued until 1945; in 1949 Percy Dobell took his son Robert into partnership, and he continued to run the business from Tunbridge Wells after Percy's death in 1956. During the 1930s both P. J. and A. E. Dobell were partners in the firm of Colbeck Radford & Co., which issued a series of catalogues of autograph letters and manuscripts, under the title *The Ingatherer* (an almost complete file of these catalogues, nos. 1-82, 1929-39, is held in the Bodleian Library at 2593.e.182; Cambridge University Library has a partial run of nos. 1-63).

Both Bertram Dobell and his son Percy were particularly noted for their literary scholarship, and some of their catalogues were highly respected as contributions to the bibliography of seventeenth- and eighteenth-century literature. Father and son also published numerous contributions to literary studies, most notably the editions of Traherne's works, issued by Bertram Dobell in 1903-08.

The British Library has only a small handful of Bertram Dobell's catalogues, ca. 1911-14, and a run of P. J. & A. E. Dobell catalogues from no. 290 (1920) to no. 329 (1925). It also has a run of Tunbridge Wells catalogues from new series no. 45 (1939) to no. 185 (1971), and a run of catalogues issued by Arthur Dobell alone in London, new series no. 2 (1946) to no. 15 (1953). The Bodleian Library has an apparently continuous run of all the Dobell catalogues between 1885 and 1971 (2593.e.125-128); it also has a copy of Bertram Dobell's first catalogue of 1876 (2593.c.1). Surviving archives from the firm constitute the prime source material for the study of the early twentieth-century antiquarian book trade published by A. and J. I. Freeman as *Anatomy of an auction* (London, 1990; see their Appendix I). Many of Bertram Dobell's letters and other papers, relating to both his commercial and his literary endeavours, are preserved in the Bodleian Library as Mss.Dobell (mss.38445-38624 in the *Summary catalogue*).

Francis Edwards

One of the major names in English antiquarian bookselling throughout the twentieth century, the firm was founded by Francis Edwards I in 1855 and carried on by his son of the same name. The business was based in London until 1989, when it changed hands and moved its base to Hay-on-Wye. Catalogues covering many fields have been produced since the firm began, although travel, topography and history have traditionally been major interests. Provenance information is increasingly, but sporadically, noted in catalogues of fine and rare material from about 1920 onwards.

The British Library holds a run of Edwards catalogues from no. 194 (1892) onwards, with gaps in the earlier period. The Bodleian Library has an apparently complete run from no. 156 (1887) onwards (2593.e.150). The National Library of Scotland holds catalogues from 1928.

Ellis

F. S. Ellis (1830-1901) was one of the major English booksellers of the latter half of the nineteenth century, official buyer for the British Museum, editor of the catalogue of the Huth Library, friend of Morris, Rossetti, Swinburne and Ruskin, and one of Bernard Quaritch's greatest rivals in the sale rooms. He began his bookselling career as apprentice to Edward Lumley in 1846, and first opened a bookshop on his own account in Covent Garden in 1860, where he soon developed a flourishing business in antiquarian books. He was trading in partnership with C. M. Green, as Ellis & Green, 1871-72, and with David White, as Ellis & White, 1872-84. Ellis retired in 1885, following a heart attack, and although his stock was sold at Sotheby's the business was carried on by his nephew Gilbert Ellis, working in partnership with James Scrutton as Ellis & Scrutton. Robert Elvey took the place of Scrutton on the latter's death in 1886, and the firm traded as Ellis & Elvey 1887-1905, although Elvey retired in 1897 and Gilbert Ellis died in 1902, when the business was taken over by James Holdsworth and George Smith. The firm's name reverted to Ellis in 1905; Holdsworth retired in 1929, and the business was then carried on by George Smith, into the 1940s.

Many of the twentieth-century Ellis catalogues advertise the business as 'established 1728', a reference to the fact that F. S. Ellis acquired the much older Boone firm in 1872. The business did indeed have a continuous history back to 1728, when it was founded by John Brindley (d.1758). It then passed through the hands of James Robson (d.1806), William Fell and John Nornaville (till 1839), and Thomas and William Boone. The history of the firm was published by G. Smith and F. Benger, *The oldest London bookshop*, London, 1928, and Ellis catalogues 100 and 150 also have prefaces describing the firm's development.

The first Ellis catalogue was issued in 1860 and the regular production of catalogues of high quality rare books and manuscripts continued until the business ceased trading. The very first catalogue included a book from the collection of John Dryden and much provenance information is found throughout the series. Noteworthy catalogues include no. 165 (1916), *Rare and interesting books … including an unique collection of British armorial bindings*, and no. 335 (1936), *Old books in bindings upon which … owners have had stamped arms, crests, or devices … with an index to owners*, but fine and armorial bindings feature in many Ellis catalogues. Some catalogues were produced outside the main numbered series, such as the *Catalogue of British and American book-plates collected by the late Sir Augustus Wollaston Franks*, issued in three parts in 1905, and the *Collection of armorial bookbindings of the Tudor, Stuart and Hanoverian periods. Described by George Smith and Frank Benger* of 1927; a substantial catalogue was issued in boards, outside the numbered series, in 1894.

The major collection of Ellis catalogues is that held by Cambridge University Library, to whom George Smith gave the firm's marked-up set of catalogues

1-259 (1860-1928). These are bound up in 33 volumes with shelfmark 8880.d.47-79. Smith also gave the Library his own manuscript 'Index to the more important works in catalogues 20-55 [1867-85]', which is now Add.ms.7479 there, although this only covers authors and titles, not previous owners or the people who bought the books. The British Library has a very poor collection of Ellis catalogues, with a few Ellis & Green catalogues of 1871-72 and a handful of later catalogues, mostly from around 1900-05. The Bodleian Library has a fairly complete run from catalogue 30 (1872) to no. 354 (1946) (2593.e.142; also a collection of ca. 30 catalogues, ca. 1930, at 2593.f.17).

E. P. Goldschmidt

A London-based firm whose first catalogue was issued in 1923, and which remained in business until 1993, when the stock was dispersed at Christie's (8-9 July). Over 170 catalogues were issued. The founder, Goldschmidt, died in 1954; he was born in Vienna in 1887, worked for some years on the *Gesamtkatalog der Wiegendrucke* and ran a bookshop in Vienna before moving permanently to London. He specialised in fine and rare early printed books from the outset of his career and many high quality catalogues were produced, which contained extensive provenance information. As well as the main sequence of catalogues, a separately numbered series of lists was issued.

The British Library and the Bodleian Library both have complete sets of Goldschmidt catalogues, from 1923 onwards. Cambridge University Library has a set of catalogues 1-100, from the collection of Robert Dougan (a cataloguer for the firm), as well as later catalogues. The National Art Library has an incomplete run of catalogues 3-51.

Thomas Kerslake

Second-hand and antiquarian bookseller in Bristol, 1828-70 (in partnership with his brother-in-law Samuel Cornish 1830-39, and on his own thereafter). After his retirement he pursued various historical and archaeological interests until his death in 1891 (see *DNB*). Issued general catalogues of books and manuscripts, and some catalogues of named collections (e.g. Books from Daylesford House, 1854; The library of Prior Park, 1857). Kerslake's catalogues came in various sizes, covering several hundred items or several thousand, and, by the standards of the mid-nineteenth century, they are rich in provenance information.

The British Library Department of Manuscripts has 49 Kerslake catalogues, 1845-62. The Bodleian Library has 38 catalogues, 1844-70 (2593.d.108, some duplicates at 2593.e.112).

J. J. Leighton

A London firm dating back to the late eighteenth century when Archibald Leighton and his descendants established a bookbinding business, which branched out into publishing and bookselling during the nineteenth century. The antiquarian side of the business was developed by Walter J. Leighton (d.1917) and around the beginning of the twentieth century the firm issued a number of substantial illustrated catalogues of high-quality material. A *Catalogue of early printed and other interesting books* was issued in nine parts, 1902-05, with six supplementary parts (numbered X-XV) issued 1906-11; part XI included 'a selection of fine decorated bindings from royal and other libraries', and an index of other bindings then in stock, with sections on arms and devices of collectors. A new series of catalogues was begun ca. 1920, continuing until the firm ceased to trade in 1937; the first twelve catalogues in this series continue the earlier tradition of major illustrated compilations which are rich in provenance material. The index to catalogue 4 (new series), *A selection of notable books … for their subject, typography, decoration, binding, or association*, has an index with a section on 'Owners, armorial bindings, autographs, etc.', and other catalogues in this series have indexes which include provenance entries.

The catalogues from the first decade of the century will be found in the British Library, the Bodleian Library, and Cambridge University Library. The British Library has a complete run of the new series of catalogues, nos. 1-31 (11915.bb.1).

Joseph Lilly

Born in Birmingham in 1804, Lilly began working for Lackington & Co. of Finsbury Circus in 1820, and set up an independent business as a bookseller in London in 1829; he remained active until his death in 1870. He built up a major trade in antiquarian material, issued general catalogues, and also many catalogues of named collections, e.g. that of Warren Hastings (1853), William Conybeare (1858). In 1862 he issued a *Catalogue of … old books, chiefly selected from the libraries of … Sir Henry Savile and Sir John Savile … Archbishop Tenison, Dr. S. Knight … Sir Edward Dering … and other sources*. He was particularly instrumental in supplying material to Henry Huth (1815-78), who is reputed to have favoured Lilly with over £40,000 worth of business. Lilly's stock was dispersed at Sotheby's after his death.

The British Library Department of Manuscripts has 64 Lilly catalogues, 1843-65, and there are about 60 catalogues listed in the *General catalogue of printed books*, 1831-70. The Munby Collection at Cambridge includes 7 Lilly catalogues, 1863-66, and the University Library's other holdings include 5 catalogues, 1867-69. The best collection will be found in the Bodleian Library, which holds about 180 Lilly catalogues, 1829-70 (2593.d.77); many of these were previously Sir Thomas Phillipps's copies.

Maggs Bros.

Founded by Uriah Maggs, who began trading in books in 1853 and opened his first bookshop in London in 1855. The firm became Maggs Bros. after Uriah's retirement in 1894, when control passed to his sons, and subsequent members of the family continued to foster the business which became, as it remains today, one of the major London bookshops for fine and rare books and manuscripts. Catalogues began to be issued in the nineteenth century and the many hundreds which have appeared since (catalogue 1000 was issued in 1980) have included a great deal of provenance information. A short history of the firm was prefixed to the centenary catalogue 812, published in 1953. There is a useful bibliography of all the catalogues produced 1918-68:

H. C. Maggs: *A catalogue of Maggs catalogues 1918-1968*. London (Maggs Bros.), 1969.

This covers the catalogues numbered 365-914, as well as some subsidiary series, and it includes an index with a section on former owners who featured prominently in particular catalogues (for example, Maggs catalogue 837 (1956) comprised *Books from the library of Edward First Lord Herbert of Cherbury*).

The British Library holds a complete run of Maggs catalogues from no. 226 (1907) onwards, with fragmentary holdings from no. 53 (1884) – 225 (1906). It also has a complete set of the series of smaller catalogues entitled *Mercurius Britannicus* which began in 1933. The Bodleian Library has an apparently complete set from no. 46 (1883) to the present day (2593.e.135; there is a second, incomplete set from no. 475 (1926) at 2593.d.25). The National Art Library has a long run, with some gaps, from no. 244 (1909) to the present day. The holdings of the National Library of Scotland begin in 1921.

The firm's archives are being deposited in the British Library.

Payne & Foss

One of the most important London firms dealing in antiquarian books and manuscripts in the first half of the nineteenth century. The business originated in the eighteenth century under Thomas Payne I (1719-99), who began his career as an assistant to his brother Oliver, whose bookselling business failed in 1739. He retired in 1790 in favour of his son Thomas II (1752-1831), who took Henry Foss into partnership in 1813. John Payne, nephew of Thomas II, succeeded him around 1825, and the Payne & Foss partnership continued until 1850 when they retired from business. Their stock was sold at auction the same year. Payne & Foss issued numerous substantial catalogues of high quality antiquarian material, including large sections of incunabula, books printed on vellum, Aldine Press books and other similar material which was eagerly sought after by early nineteenth-century collectors. They also produced catalogues of the libraries of named collectors, e.g. that of Sir George Nayler, sold 1837-43.

The British Library *General catalogue* lists 13 Payne & Foss catalogues, 1815-48, and the Department of Manuscripts there holds 20 catalogues, 1830-48. The Munby Collection at Cambridge has 27 catalogues, 1815-48, including some annotated by Sir Thomas Phillipps (who was a major customer). The Bodleian Library holds 16 catalogues, 1818-48 (2593.e.7, 2593.f.21). The National Library of Scotland has 8 catalogues, 1824-30. Many of the firm's archives survive in the Grolier Club in New York.

J. Pearson & Co.

A London business begun in the middle of the nineteenth century by John Pearson (d.1919), and continued after his retirement, ca. 1890 by C. E. Shepheard and F. A. Wheeler, whose partnership was dissolved in 1924. The firm's stock was then sold at Sotheby's, but Wheeler continued to trade as J. Pearson & Co. (London) Ltd. until the mid-1930s. Pearson's first catalogue was issued in 1860. The firm specialised in high quality antiquarian material, including bookbindings and significant association copies, and many of their catalogues contain extensive provenance information. Noteworthy catalogues include *Two hundred books from the libraries of the world's greatest book collectors* (1909) and the *Catalogue of ... English and foreign armorial and contemporary bindings of four centuries ... with an addenda of association books* (ca. 1920), but many other Pearson catalogues repay study.

Despite the importance of these catalogues, they are not easy to trace. The British Library has only 7 (most at shelfmark S.C.1105). The Bodleian Library has a good collection of nineteenth-century catalogues, including about 20 early catalogues 1860-ca. 1880, and a bound set of catalogues 54-83, 1883-1900 (shelfmark 2593.e.131). The Bodleian also has five boxes of twentieth-century catalogues (2593.d.29), containing 20 separate catalogues. The National Library of Scotland has about 15 catalogues, ca. 1900-16. A partial bibliography of Pearson catalogues was published in 1991:

L. Navari: *The bookseller's art: catalogues issued by the firm of J. Pearson & Co. Ltd.*, London (Maggs Bros.), 1991.

This is mostly concerned with the firm's twentieth-century history, and describes a collection of 76 catalogues, post-1900, which was offered for sale in Maggs catalogue 1118 (Bibliography). This Maggs catalogue also included 19 separate catalogues, which are described in some detail.

Pickering & Chatto

The fame of William Pickering (1796-1854) as a bookseller is overshadowed by his more celebrated printing and publishing activities, but when he first set himself up in business on his own in London in 1820, it was his intention to be an antiquarian bookseller. He soon began to publish his Diamond Classics and this side of the business grew steadily, but he also functioned as a bookseller, and a catalogue of rare books and manuscripts issued in 1834 contained 4326 entries. After his death, his son Basil Montagu Pickering refounded the bookselling business in 1858, and following his death in 1878 it was taken over by Thomas Chatto (d.1929). Charles Massey (d.1928) was taken into partnership in 1880, although the name of the firm remained Pickering & Chatto, as it has continued to the present day.

The British Library has an extensive run of catalogues from 1893 to the present day, with a few earlier holdings. The main catalogue series was entitled *The book-lover's leaflet*, which began in 1886. The Bodleian Library has an apparently complete set of this from no. 151 (ca. 1905) – no. 362 (1962), with some earlier issues and other catalogues (2593.e.121). The firm itself has a big collection of its catalogues from the late nineteenth century onwards, kept at its premises in Pall Mall, London, and these can be made available by appointment.

Bernard Quaritch

Bernard Quaritch, born in Saxony in 1819, spent some years in the German book trade before coming to London in 1842 to work for Henry Bohn. In 1847 he set up in business on his own and he quickly established himself as a major figure in the English antiquarian book trade. He became the dominant purchaser in the British book-auction rooms in the last quarter of the nineteenth century, and vast quantities of high quality material passed through his hands. By the time of his death in 1899 he had developed 'the most extensive trade in old books in the world' (*DNB*), and his business was carried on after his death under the direction of his son Bernard Alfred Quaritch (d.1913). The firm has never lost its position as one of the senior and most prestigious British businesses dealing in antiquarian books and manuscripts and it continues to flourish today.

The first Quaritch catalogue was issued in 1847 and since then many hundreds of catalogues have been produced. Quaritch began issuing huge catalogues of his entire stock in 1858 (ca. 5000 items) and continued to produce ever larger catalogues at intervals thereafter; *A general catalogue of books, arranged in classes* (1868) has 12,866 items in its main sequence, *A general catalogue* of 1874 has 18,803 items and the *Supplement* of 1875-77 adds a further 15,315. These catalogues include some provenance data on particular items; the catalogues have indexes, but provenances are not covered. In addition to these very large catalogues, smaller monthly catalogues have been produced in various numbered series; the current series, which reached catalogue 1000 in 1979, originated as 'rough lists' which ran in parallel with a separate numbered sequence which reached no. 370 in 1886, and was dropped shortly thereafter. The 'rough list' nomenclature was discontinued at the end of the nineteenth century. The smaller catalogues tend to cover particular subject areas; a number of catalogues of the late nineteenth and early twentieth centuries comprise books from named collections (e.g. no. 248, 1869, *Catalogue of European manuscripts, chiefly from the libraries of the late Marquis of Hastings, and the late Dr. Wellesley*; rough list 75, 1886, *The choicest portion of the Wodhull Library*; no. 343, 1916, *Catalogue … including … selections from the renowned library of Thomas Herbert, 8th Earl of Pembroke (1656-1733)*). Catalogue 1099 (1988) was devoted to *Books from the library of Michael Wodhull*. Provenance information is found in the general run of catalogues; some catalogues are particularly noteworthy, e.g. rough list 93 (1888), *Bookbinding: a catalogue of 1500 books remarkable for the beauty or the age of their bindings or as bearing indications of former ownership by great book-collectors*; catalogue 166 (1897), *Examples of the art of book-binding and volumes bearing marks of distinguished ownership*. Catalogue 175 (1897), *Monuments of printing*, appears to be the first Quaritch catalogue to contain an index which includes provenance entries; catalogue 367 (1921), *English and foreign bookbindings*, has an index of arms, badges and provenances. Catalogues which have included sections of 'association books' have included no. 281 (1909), 316 (1912), 328 (1914), 362 (1921), 435 (1930), 436 (1930), and 525 (1936).

The British Library has a patchy run of Quaritch catalogues from 1864 onwards, increasingly complete from about 1880. The Department of Manuscripts there has extensive holdings from catalogue 13 (1850). The Bodleian Library's holdings begin in 1855. The National Art Library has a good run of Quaritch's monthly catalogues, 1852-1869, and extensive holdings of catalogues between 1880 and 1910. The National Library of Scotland has broken holdings from 1859 onwards.

The firm's business archives, 1885-1974, were given to the British Library in 1985, where they are catalogued as Add.Mss.64132-64415. Day books, ledgers and customer lists are included; some material is restricted and will not be available for use until after the year 2000, or later.

W. H. Robinson

Established in Newcastle-upon-Tyne in 1881, moved to London in 1930. The business was begun by W. H. Robinson, and continued by his sons Lionel and Philip until 1956, when they retired from business. The Robinson firm is best known for the purchase of the residue of the collection of Sir Thomas Phillipps (1792-1872) in 1945, and for the outstanding catalogues of rare books and manuscripts which ensued (catalogues 78-84, 1949-54), but they issued many other catalogues of high quality antiquarian material, which include provennce information. Particularly noteworthy catalogues are no. 14 (1926), *The library of Mrs. Elizabeth Vesey, 1715-91*, 53 (1935), *Rare books including volumes from the library of Edward Gibbon*, and 71 (1940), *Catalogue of rare books … from the library of Sir Roger Twysden, 1597-1672*, but many other more general catalogues are rich in provenance data.

The later Robinson catalogues are generally easy to find as they have been preserved in a number of libraries. The British Library has an almost complete run from no. 9 (1923) onwards.

Thomas Rodd

Two booksellers of this name, father and son, were in business in London, ca. 1804-22 (the father), and 1822-49 (the son). Both men issued catalogues, but those of Rodd the younger are the more noteworthy for size and range. The elder Rodd (1763-1822) was also an author of poems and sermons. His son (1796-1849) was a major figure in the trade in manuscripts and rare books in the second quarter of the nineteenth century, and was well known to the institutional and private collectors of the time. His remaining stock was sold at Sotheby's after his death.

The best collection of Rodd catalogues is that held in the Munby Collection in Cambridge University Library, where there are over 150 catalogues, 1810-49; many of these belonged originally to Sir Thomas Phillipps. The British Library *General catalogue* lists 5 catalogues of Rodd the elder, and about 20 of his son; the Department of Manuscripts there has 38 catalogues, 1815-34. The Bodleian Library has only a small handful of catalogues, 1815-34. The National Library of Scotland holds 3 catalogues of Rodd the younger, 1837-47.

A six-part catalogue issued by the elder Rodd in 1819-22 has been reprinted in facsimile (*Catalogue of twelve thousand tracts, pamphlets, and unbound books, in all branches of literature*, containing 19,058 items, reissued as *Thomas Rodd's booksellers catalogue of tracts and pamphlets*, Doncaster, 1975).

Sawyer

A London-based business founded in 1894 by Charles James Sawyer, whose first catalogue was issued in 1906. After his death in 1931, the firm was taken over by his sons J. E. S. and C. R. Sawyer, and subsequently by his grandson R. E. B. Sawyer. They dealt in good quality antiquarian material in all subjects, and issued many illustrated catalogues. Noteworthy examples, from the provenance point of view, include no. 91 (1928), *Books and manuscripts including a collection … from the library of David Garrick*, no. 144 (1938), *Recent purchases, including fine English and French armorial bindings*, nos. 193 (1949) and 255 (1960), *Bibliopegy: association bindings, and others of artistic beauty*, and no. 202 (1950), *Fine bindings of association interest*. A number of catalogues of fine bindings issued in the 1950s include provenance indexes.

The British Library has a more or less complete run of catalogues from no. 127 (1935) onwards, and patchy holdings back to no. 73 (1924). The Bodleian Library has an almost complete set from 1906 onwards, with a few gaps in the early years (2593.d.23). The National Library of Scotland has a continuous run from 1949.

John Russell Smith

In business in London as a bookseller and publisher of antiquarian reprints, 1834-88; he died in 1894, aged 84. Smith issued many catalogues of general antiquarian material, including a series entitled the *Old book circular*, which began in 1837. A number of his more noteworthy catalogues of second-hand material are mentioned in his *DNB* article.

The British Library Department of Manuscripts has 25 Smith catalogues, 1839-54. The Munby Collection at Cambridge has 16 catalogues, 1863-67, and 5 other catalogues, 1856-78, are held in the University Library's general collections. The Bodleian Library has extensive holdings of catalogues, 1834-88, at shelfmark 2593.e.107; many of the catalogues from the 1830s were unopened in 1992.

Sotheran

Thomas Sotheran, who came from a York bookselling family, opened a shop in London in 1812; he was joined in business by his son Henry in 1842. They became established during the nineteenth century as one of the major firms dealing in antiquarian material and they handled the sale of the Althorp Library of Earl Spencer to Mrs. Rylands in 1892. The firm remained in the hands of a member of the Sotheran family until the death of Henry Cecil Sotheran in 1928, after which it continued as a limited company retaining the Sotheran name. Between 1856 and 1866 the firm was operating as Willis and Sotheran, in partnership with George Willis (1813-95).

A series of monthly catalogues, the *Price current of literature*, began in 1845; this nomenclature continued until 1958. The series included a wide range of specialised and general catalogues of antiquarian and second-hand material. A number of other separate series of catalogues have also been issued, e.g. *Piccadilly notes*, nos. 1-20, which appeared in 1933-37.

The British Library has a set of the *Price current*, and other Sotheran catalogues, from no. 154 (1860) onwards, with some gaps. The Bodleian Library has a run from no. 46 (1851) to no. 153 (1859), and from no.4 (1882) to the present day (2593.e.129). The National Library of Scotland has a run of catalogues between 1871 and 1884, and a few individual catalogues 1877-1907.

Thomas Thorpe

Began business as a bookseller in London ca. 1818, after an initial career as a baker, and continued until his death in 1851. Despite long-running financial difficulties (he almost went bankrupt at least once), he handled great numbers of early printed books and manuscripts, making a speciality of historical and topographical manuscripts. He issued numerous catalogues, including many named collections.

British Library Add.mss.19438-19444 comprise an index to Thorpe's catalogues of manuscripts and printed books, 1842-48. The Department of Manuscripts has 102 Thorpe catalogues, 1820-51. The Munby Collection at Cambridge includes 44 catalogues, 1824-51. The Bodleian Library has extensive holdings, covering Thorpe's entire career, 1819-51 (2593.e.81). The National Library of Scotland has a major run of over 100 catalogues, 1822-48.

Tregaskis

A major firm of the late nineteenth and early twentieth century, issuing many catalogues of high quality antiquarian material, often illustrated and including extensive provenance information. The business was run by James Tregaskis (1850-1926) from the Caxton Head Bookshop, originally opened in Birmingham by Robert Wilde and taken over by W. P. Bennett in 1881, who moved the shop to London in 1885. Tregaskis married Bennett's widow and the first Caxton Head catalogue to carry his name appeared in 1890. Catalogue 1000 (1931) includes a brief history of the firm.

The British Library has a few catalogues 1895-1914, and a fairly complete run of catalogues 758-1027 (1914-ca. 1936). The Bodleian Library holds a set from 1889-1937 (catalogues 186-1037, including the *Caxton Head Bulletin* nos. 1-22; shelfmarks 2593.e.154, 2593.d.17).

Voynich

Wilfrid Voynich was born in Lithuania in 1865, and his early career was more than usually colourful for a member of the book trade; following involvement with the Polish revolutionary movement, he was imprisoned, first in Warsaw and later in the Siberian salt mines, from which he escaped in 1890. He made his way to England, where he established an antiquarian book business, based in London but eventually with offices in Paris, Florence, Venice and Warsaw. He spent his later years largely in the United States, and he died in New York in 1930. A fuller and more personal account of Voynich, by one of his employees, will be found in *Rare people and rare books* by E. M. Sowerby, London, 1967, pp. 7-33.

Voynich specialised in incunabula and early printing, and he issued a series of highly scholarly and detailed catalogues, which are particularly noteworthy for the quality of bibliographical description, but which also include much provenance information. He began with a series of *Lists*, numbered 1-9, issued between 1898 and 1902; he changed the format in 1903, and began a sequence of *Short catalogues* which ran from 1 to 34 (the term 'Short' was dropped for nos. 22-34). The first *Short catalogues* were indeed shorter than the *Lists*, but they became more substantial as the series progressed. In 1902 Voynich offered a 'Collection of unknown or lost books, lately discovered in different monastic libraries', on sale for 4000 guineas. He did a lot of book buying in Italy, where he unearthed many rare treasures.

The British Library has a run of the nine *Lists*, and patchy holdings between catalogues 15 and 34 (S.C.1097, S.C.1529). The Bodleian Library and Cambridge University Library both have complete sets of Voynich lists and catalogues. The National Art Library has lists 4-5 and 7-9, and 7 catalogues between nos. 26 and 34.

WORKS ON THE HISTORY OF SALE CATALOGUES

Sale catalogues have generated a considerable literature beyond the lists and indexes described above, and there are numerous works which deal with the history of sales in general, with individual sales, and with the importance of sale catalogues as a field of study. This section offers a selective list of material on the subject in general, excluding studies of specific sales or auctioneers; further references will be found in the bibliographies and footnotes appended to many of these works. One book in particular is of outstanding importance in this context:

G. Pollard & A. Ehrman: *The distribution of books by catalogue from the invention of printing to A.D. 1800. Based on material in the Broxbourne Library*. Cambridge, for the Roxburghe Club, 1965.

This traces the development of the catalogue as an aid to bookselling, from the first printed broadsides of the fifteenth century to the beginning of the nineteenth century, thus embracing the rise of both retail and auction catalogues. Coverage is detailed, and international in scope. It is regrettable that such an important work as this was produced in a very limited edition, which is only publicly available in a few major libraries, and the production of a less expensive reprint would be a great benefit. Other useful works are:

J. Lawler: *Book auctions in England in the seventeenth century*. London, 1898.

> Lawler's text is largely built around a chronological list of seventeenth-century book auctions, and although the comprehensiveness of this list is superseded by the work of Munby and others, he gives many details of books included in sales, and prices realised, which are not readily available elsewhere without returning to the original catalogues.

A. Taylor: *Book catalogues: their varieties and uses*. 2nd edn, revised by W. P. Barlow, Jr. Winchester, 1986.

> A study of the rise, development, and use of book catalogues of all kinds, including library catalogues as well as sale catalogues. Includes an historical treatment of the use of sale catalogues by bibliographers; his list of 'Catalogues of private libraries recommended by bibliographers' (pp. 229-266) includes many sale catalogues. See also his section on 'Dealers' catalogues' (pp. 70-81) and 'Bibliographies of dealers' catalogues' (pp. 214-219).

G. Walters: Early sale catalogues: problems and perspectives in R. Myers & M. Harris (eds.): *Sale and distribution of books from 1700*, Oxford, 1982, pp. 106-125.

> A useful essay on the importance of sale catalogues, on the difficulties of tracing them, and
> on some of the earlier bibliographical attention which was given to them.

T. F. Dibdin: *The bibliographical decameron*. London, 1817.

> The first section of volume 3 ('The ninth day', pp. 3-181) is devoted to book auctions, and
> is largely taken up with a detailed account of noteworthy book auctions held between 1811
> and 1817.

W. R. MacDonald: Book auctions and book sales in the Aberdeen area 1749-1800,
   Aberdeen University Review 42 (1967), 114-132.
E. A. Swaim: The auction as a means of book distribution in eighteenth-century
   Yorkshire, *Publishing History* 1 (1977), 49-91.

> These two articles are case-studies of the importance of using provincial newspaper
> advertisements as a record of early bookselling activity in the provinces, which demons-
> trate that the number of catalogues which have survived offer a very fragmentary glimpse
> of the total picture.

Although many aspects of the history of the book trade have been written about
in extenso, there are relatively few works which look in detail at the operations of
the second-hand trade, or which chronicle the histories of particular firms.
Katherine Swift's article 'Bibliotheca Sunderlandiana: the making of an
eighteenth-century library' (in R. Myers & M. Harris (eds.), *Bibliophily*,
Cambridge, 1986, 63-89) is particularly useful for its analysis of book trade
methods at the turn of the eighteenth century. Another important source
relating to this period is *The diary of Humfrey Wanley*, ed. C. E. & R. C. Wright,
London, 1966, which affords primary documentation on the dealers in antiquarian material who supplied books to the Harleian Library. The workings of the
trade two centuries later are well documented by Arthur and Janet Ing Freeman
in their book *Anatomy of an auction: rare books at Ruxley Lodge, 1919* (London,
1990), which includes much biographical and historical detail on the major
antiquarian businesses of the period. Another good source for the history of
firms which were operating during the first half of the twentieth century is
Andrew Block's *Short history of the principal London antiquarian booksellers and
book auctioneers*, London, 1933. For information on the major nineteenth-
century booksellers, one of the primary printed sources is the series of *Phillipps
studies* by A. N. L. Munby (5v., Cambridge, 1951-60); Sir Thomas Phillipps
(1792-1872) dealt with most of the significant tradesmen of the time in building
up his library and Munby's analysis includes details of the businesses as well as
Phillipps's purchases (volume 3, *The formation of the Phillipps Library up to the
year 1840*, 1954, is particularly important in this respect). Nicolas Barker's
Bibliotheca Lindesiana (London, 1977), a study of the development of another
great nineteenth-century collection, is similarly significant as a quarry for
information on many of the major antiquarian dealers of the time.

VI

CATALOGUES AND
LISTS OF PRIVATE LIBRARIES

INTRODUCTION

Catalogues of private libraries have an obvious relevance for provenance research. They offer a record of collections which may be long dispersed, and their existence allows us to assess the scope and importance of particular libraries within their contemporary context. They may be sought by people seeking to identify an owner from an inscription or bookplate, or they may be a starting point for those wishing to trace the whereabouts of collections which are no longer together. Many catalogues and lists have been made over the centuries, covering libraries large and small; they have been made for a variety of purposes, and some were printed while others remained in manuscript. Some have been reprinted and studied in the recent past, a part of the burgeoning tide of interest in the history of the book; others have lain unconsulted for centuries. That tide has included a number of important works which facilitate access to those catalogues, or promote knowledge of their whereabouts. It is the aim of this chapter to describe these within a systematic discussion of the different kinds of private library catalogues which exist.

There are two seminal works on the history and development of such catalogues to which researchers should be directed:

Archer Taylor: *Book catalogues: their varieties and uses*. 2nd edn, revised by W. P. Barlow, jr. Winchester, 1986.

G. Pollard & A. Ehrman: *The distribution of books by catalogue from the invention of printing to A.D. 1800. Based on material in the Broxbourne Library*. Cambridge, for the Roxburghe Club, 1965.

Archer Taylor's book is a detailed historical survey of the use, development, and bibliography of catalogues of all kinds. It is pan-European in scope and includes (pp. 175-207) a section on 'bibliographies of catalogues of private libraries'. Chapter IV, 'A list of catalogues of private libraries that have been recommended for reference use', provides details and locations for many early printed catalogues. The main thrust of Pollard and Ehrman's book rests with sale catalogues, but chapters X, XIII and XIV (Inventories, The private library open to scholars, and The personal library) are concerned with private library catalogues, and include several listings of important catalogues printed before 1800.

Both these works subdivide private library catalogues into various categories, reflecting the different reasons which lie behind their compilation. Archer Taylor breaks them down into three basic types: inventories, owners' catalogues, and sale catalogues. This chapter is concerned with the first two types; sale catalogues are dealt with in chapter V. To Taylor's list we might add one additional category, which will also be dealt with here: union catalogues, and similar listings, which include private libraries. It should be added that private library catalogues, like sale catalogues, may be useful to students of provenance not only because they offer a list of one particular collection, but also because some catalogues may include within individual entries information on earlier ownership. For example, the catalogue of Lord Leicester's manuscripts which Seymour de Ricci published in 1932 is valuable because it includes the provenance of the manuscripts (where determinable) prior to their arrival at Holkham Hall, as well as providing a record of a collection which is now partly dispersed. On the whole, this point applies to certain private library catalogues published within the last century or so, and relevant catalogues are listed among the provenance indexes in chapter VII. This chapter is concerned only with **catalogues** or **lists** of libraries. **Studies** of private libraries, including general histories of book collecting or narrative accounts of particular collections, are dealt with in chapter VIII in the section devoted to works on book collecting and library history.

PRINTED LISTS AND CATALOGUES

The tradition of producing printed editions of personal library catalogues goes back to the seventeenth century. The earliest known example is Sir James Ware's *Librorum manuscriptorum in bibliotheca Iacobi Waraei ... catalogus*, printed in Dublin in 1648, which lists manuscripts brought together by Ware to further his studies in Irish history. There are a number of other examples from the seventeenth and eighteenth centuries – there are many more continental ones than British ones in this period – and the habit became more popular after the turn of the nineteenth century, since when a steady stream of catalogues has been printed. The earliest English example is the *Catalogus bibliothecae Kingstonianae*, printed for Evelyn Pierrepont, Duke of Kingston (1711-73) in 1726, to record the contents of his library. There are several possible motives for printing such catalogues – vanity or pride, a wish to create a lasting memorial, the desire to further bibliographical or other studies, preparation for a sale – and some or all of them are likely to have played a part in most endeavours of this kind. Pollard makes a distinction between catalogues produced by those wishing to make their collections available to scholars, and those seeking only to record their personal achievement, but these categories are rarely likely to be exclusive.

MANUSCRIPT LISTS AND INVENTORIES

Before 1800, printed catalogues of British private libraries, other than sale catalogues, are few and far between; there are very many more manuscript lists. Numerous owners had catalogues of their collections written out, for private use; one example among many may be seen in the catalogue of the library of Edward Gibbon (1737-94), drawn up ca. 1777 in a large folio blank book which now survives in the British Library (Additional ms.46141), which records 1920 titles in about 3300 volumes. A more unusual manuscript catalogue is a slightly later one recording Gibbon's library at Lausanne, written on the backs of 1676 playing cards, which are also now preserved in the British Library (Additional ms.34716A-B).[1] There are also simpler or less formal lists such as the 'Note of all the bookes of chyrurgerye that I haue in my studye' which Joseph Fenton wrote on the flyleaf of one of his books early in the seventeenth century, running to 37 titles.[2] The corpus of manuscript lists is greatly swelled by the existence of probate or other inventories.

Probate inventories

The practice of drawing up detailed lists of the property of deceased persons is very ancient, and it has been established in law in one form or another since the Middle Ages. Such lists clearly play an important part in establishing title to property when it changes hands. In 1521 the law governing such matters was strengthened and it became obligatory to draw up an inventory of the goods left by all people immediately upon their death, whether or not they had made a will. The statute (12 Henry VIII ch. 5) called on executors to make 'a true and perfect inventory of all the goods, cattels, wares, marchandizes, aswell moveable as not moveable whatsoever' of the deceased person. For the rest of the sixteenth century, this was generally interpreted as a requirement to include in the inventories of those who died owning books a full list of all the titles on their shelves. The thoroughness of the practice gradually lapsed, and after the turn of the seventeenth century probate inventories often included books only as a one-line consolidated valuation.[3] Another problem about probate inventories is their survival rate. Although, in principle, wills and inventories were both filed in perpetuity in the various ecclesiastical courts which administered probate matters, in practice the wills have survived much more extensively than the inventories, which were often separated out and looked after in a more cursory way. Many inventories, therefore, have perished.

---

1 See G. Keynes, *The library of Edward Gibbon*, 2nd edn, Winchester, 1980, 20-23, for further details. The playing card catalogue is illustrated in N. Barker, *Treasures of the British Library*, London, 1988, p. 140.

2 In Fenton's copy of E. Rudius, *De affectib. externarum corporis humani partium libri septem*, Venice, 1606, British Library 548.l.3.

3 The pattern, and survival rates, of probate inventories listing books are discussed in detail in Sears Jayne, *Library catalogues of the English renaissance*, 2nd edn, Winchester, 1983, 9-17.

Despite these caveats, inventories are an important source of information on private book ownership, particularly when they are full enough to comprise catalogues of entire collections. As a class of material, they have received some attention from bibliographers and library historians, but much more could be done.[4] Much of the work which has been done on probate inventories has concentrated on those which survive from Oxford and Cambridge, which is understandable because the universities, which had their own probate jurisdictions, were obvious centres of book ownership. An important series of sixteenth- and early seventeenth-century inventories survives in both places. The Cambridge inventories have been comprehensively transcribed and edited:

E. S. Leedham-Green: *Books in Cambridge inventories: book-lists from Vice-Chancellor's court probate inventories in the Tudor and Stuart periods.* 2v. Cambridge, 1986.

This substantial and important publication lists in full 200 book lists from probate inventories, dated between 1536 and 1760, and identifies the books concerned. A. B. Emden, in his *Biographical register of the University of Oxford A.D. 1501 to 1540* (Oxford, 1974, Appendix B) drew on the Oxford series for the early sixteenth century to print a number of lists of books owned by university men of that period, and the Oxford inventories are being further edited for publication by *PLRE* (see p. 177 below), but otherwise there is no detailed or comprehensive corpus of probate inventory book lists in published form.

There is, however, an extensive and scattered body of published work which makes use of probate inventories; many of these books and articles deal primarily with social or economic history, and they may or may not touch upon books. The following bibliography covers a wide range of such material:

M. Overton: *A bibliography of British probate inventories.* Newcastle-upon-Tyne, 1983.

> This lists: i) published books and articles which are concerned with, or make use of, probate inventories; ii) published transcripts of probate inventories; and iii) published indexes to probate inventories held in particular repositories.

An international conference on the importance and study of probate inventories was held at Leeuwenborch in 1980 and its proceedings include a number of useful papers on the subject (although they are not specifically concerned with books):

A. van der Woude & A. Schuurman (eds.): *Probate inventories: a new source for the historical study of wealth, material culture and agricultural development.* (Hes studia historica, 3). Utrecht, 1980.

The extensive footnotes to Rachel Garrard's paper on 'English probate inventories and their use in studying the significance of the domestic interior, 1570-1700' provide many references to the wider use of probate inventories.

---

4 Examples of studies based on probate inventories are C. Cross, A medieval Yorkshire library, *Northern History* 25 (1989), 281-290; M. H. Smith, Some humanist libraries in Tudor Cambridge, *Sixteenth-Century Journal* 5 (1974), 15-34.

Local historical societies, which focus on particular counties or groups of counties, have traditionally taken an interest in probate documents and a great deal of valuable work on wills and inventories has been published in this way. This work may comprise transcripts, calendars or abstracts of wills and inventories, or indexes to the wills and inventories held in particular record offices. The Yorkshire Archaeological Society, for example, has published an extensive series of indexes to the probate documents in the York Registry, as well as a volume of transcripts of sixteenth- and seventeenth-century probate inventories.[5] The relevant volumes can most conveniently be traced using the following bibliographies, which give details of all the monograph publications of the local record societies in England, Scotland and Wales:

E. L. C. Mullins: *Texts and calendars: an analytical guide to serial publications.* (Royal Historical Society, Guides and Handbooks, 7). London, 1958.

E. L. C. Mullins: *Texts and calendars II: an analytical guide to serial publications 1957-1982.* (Royal Historical Society, Guides and Handbooks, 12). London, 1983.

D. & W. B. Stevenson: *Scottish texts and calendars: an analytical guide to serial publications.* (Royal Historical Society, Guides and Handbooks, 14). London, 1987.

Mullins has also published *A guide to the historical and archaeological publications of societies in England and Wales, 1901-1933* (London, 1968) which lists all the individual articles published in a wide range of historical society journals between the given dates; the index, under wills, identifies many additional references to transcripts.

Whether published or not, the original inventories themselves will now be found in the many record offices all over the country which are designated repositories for probate documents. Before 1858, wills were proved in ecclesiastical courts, which operated at various hierarchical levels; the court in which a particular will was proved, and the documents subsequently filed, depended on the value and extent of the deceased's property. Many probate documents are now deposited in county record offices – for example, wills proved in the Consistory Court of the Archdeaconry of Cornwall will now be found in the Cornwall Record Office at Truro – but there are all kinds of exceptions. Fortunately, there are a number of guides which clarify the situation, of which the following may be mentioned:

A. J. Camp: *Wills and their whereabouts.* London, 1963.

J. S. W. Gibson: *Wills and where to find them.* London, 1974.

J. S. W. Gibson: *A simplified guide to probate jurisdictions: where to look for wills.* Banbury, 1980.

The first two books offer a detailed county-by-county breakdown of the whereabouts of wills and associated documents of all periods, with lists of the published and unpublished indexes which are available. (It must be remembered that many inventories have no published indexes, and can be traced only

---

5 Yorkshire Archaeological Society, Record Series, vols. 4, 6, 11, 14, 19, 22, 24, 26, 28, 32, 35, 49, 60, 68, 89, 93, 134; see *Texts and calendars* for full details.

through the indexes of the record office in which they are deposited.) The third book is an abridged version of the second, omitting information on pre-sixteenth-century wills, but including most of the essential details for post-Reformation material.

Wills

The emphasis in the foregoing section was on probate inventories as sources of provenance information, but it should be added that wills themselves often include details of books owned, which may be listed as specific bequests. They also have a wider significance for provenance research, as they offer evidence of the importance which was attached to books by testators. When Richard Cliff, chaplain of Christ Church, Oxford died in 1566 he wished his memorial within the College, 'a monument and token of my there beinge to thencrease of learninge, and furtherance of Godes glorie', to be a book, his 'greate Tigurine Bible'; to one of his friends he left a Geneva Bible, 'the verie treasure of trewe Christianitie'.[6] Cliff's will is quite short and the disposition of particular books takes up a significant part of it. A study of the wills of early seventeenth-century bishops revealed a frequent concern for the the disposal of libraries, through major gifts to institutions, particular gifts to friends, and bequests to children fenced round with conditions to ensure that the recipients remained worthy of the bequests.[7] Susan Cavanaugh carried out an extensive survey of medieval wills as the foundation for her *Study of books privately owned in England 1300-1450*[8]; for the post-Reformation period, a few studies have appeared which make use of wills, but much more work remains to be done.[9] The sources listed above for tracing published details of probate inventories, and for locating unpublished inventories and indexes, should also be used for wills.

Other manuscript lists

Although probate inventories form a large and recognisable category of manuscript book lists, many other kinds of list exist. Library catalogues and lists, drawn up by owners for their own use during their lifetimes, were mentioned earlier and they may be either large or small. Lists of libraries were often made because the books were about to be moved or sold, because they were to be given to an institution, or because ownership was disputed, and examples from all these categories will be found in the bibliographies listed below. It should also be remembered that bills and vouchers from booksellers

6 Oxford, Chancellor's register GG. fo.207b.

7 D. Pearson, The libraries of English bishops, 1600-40, *The Library* 6th series 14 (1992), 221-257, pp. 230-1.

8 Ph.D. thesis, University of Pennsylvania, 1980; see p. 308 below.

9 See, for example, J. Barnard, A puritan controversialist and his books: the will of Alexander Cooke (1564-1632), *Publications of the Bibliographical Society of America* 86 (1992), 82-86.

or bookbinders may constitute lists of books owned; for example, the archives of the Duke of Bedford at Woburn Abbey include book-bills whose lists of titles reflect the book-collecting concerns of the First Duke.[10]

Bibliographies of manuscript lists and catalogues

One bibliography is of outstanding importance in this context:

Sears Jayne: *Library catalogues of the English renaissance*. 2nd edn, Godalming, 1983.

This book, first issued in 1956 (the revised edition adds only a new preface with some additional references), lists 848 separate book lists from the period 1500-1640 which survive in various manuscript sources. It covers both institutional and private libraries, and relies heavily on donors' registers, probate inventories from Oxford and Cambridge, as well as a range of other sources. Each entry gives details of the number of books involved. Although it could be expanded in several ways, it is an indispensable and invaluable reference book.

For the period after 1640, there is no equivalent to Sears Jayne, which brings together manuscript lists from a range of places. There is, however, a very useful handlist which covers all kinds of manuscript book-lists and catalogues in the British Library:

R. C. Alston: *Handlist of library catalogues and lists of books and manuscripts in the British Library Department of Manuscripts*. (Occasional Papers of the Bibliographical Society, 6). London, 1991.

The following work lists early manuscript inventories of all kinds, which have been transcribed and printed. It is divided into countries and arranged chronologically within countries; the English section (pp. 136-335 in volume 1) lists 2900 inventories dated between the tenth century and 1794. Its main limitation lies in its early date; there is no comparable bibliography of inventories printed this century:

F. de Mély & E. Bishop: *Bibliographie générale des inventaires imprimés*. 3v. Paris, 1892-95.

Private Libraries in Renaissance England

An important project which should be mentioned in this context is *Private Libraries in Renaissance England* (often abbreviated to *PLRE*), which brings together edited book lists of the Tudor and Stuart periods in a unified and standardised format. The project, which began in 1988 under the general editorship of Robert Fehrenbach with Elisabeth Leedham-Green serving as editor in the United Kingdom, is a collaborative one which involves many

---

10 Some of these are transcribed in G. S. Thomson, *Life in a noble household 1641-1700*, London, 1937, ch. XIV, 'The Library'.

scholars in the USA, Canada, Britain, and the continent. Hitherto unpublished book lists are being edited, according to an agreed set of rules, for publication in an open-ended series of volumes. The information is all held in an automated database, which will be published in CD-ROM format (expected in 1995). The first volume, published in 1992, contains four large library lists of the late sixteenth and early seventeenth centuries (Richard Cox, Sir Edward Stanhope, Sir Roger Townshend, and Sir Edward Dering); volumes 2-7 will contain book lists from the Oxford University probate inventories, 1507-1653. The database is also being enriched with details of library catalogues which have already been published elsewhere. Published volumes to date are:

R. J. Fehrenbach & E. S. Leedham-Green (eds.): *Private libraries in renaissance England: a collection and catalogue of Tudor and early Stuart book lists.*
vol. 1: (PLRE 1-4). New York and Marlborough, 1992.
vol. 2: (PLRE 5-66, Oxford probate inventories, 1507-44). New York and Marlborough, 1993.
vol. 3: (PLRE 67-86, Oxford probate inventories, 1558-70). New York and Marlborough, 1994.
vol. 4: (PLRE 87-112, Oxford probate inventories, 1570-76). New York and Marlborough, 1994.

EARLY UNION CATALOGUES

A union catalogue is one which lists the holdings of more than one library. It is an ancient and worthy device, and one whose usefulness continues to the present day. Union catalogues are almost invariably concerned first and foremost with texts; their *raison d'etre* is to allow scholars to find bibliographical details and physical locations for the items they seek, without needing to work through numerous separate library catalogues. In line with the general trends in cataloguing practice, union catalogues which have been compiled during the last few decades are quite likely to include copy-specific information about the books they list, and they therefore have a direct importance for the provenance researcher. Union catalogues like this fall within the scope of the following chapter of this book, which lists library catalogues which include provenance information, and the appropriate sequence will be found at p. 242 below. The focus of this section is different. A number of union catalogues and lists have been compiled over the centuries which now have a value as a record of collections which once existed, but which are now dispersed; they are like any of the other printed or manuscript lists which form the subject of this chapter. They are therefore listed here, in chronological order. The list encompasses both manuscript and printed items, and it is mostly restricted to those which include at least some information on private libraries as well as institutional ones.

The earliest British union catalogue is a medieval one, compiled by the Oxford Franciscans in the first half of the fifteenth century. It lists the holdings of the libraries of many British monasteries, and several medieval copies of the catalogue survive; one version of it was printed in Thomas Tanner's *Bibliotheca Britannico-Hibernica* (London, 1748). It is of course concerned solely with institutional, rather than personal, ownership. A scholarly modern edition of this catalogue, with an extensive historical introduction, has been published in the series *A corpus of British medieval library catalogues*: R. H. & M. A. Rouse (eds.), *Registrum Angliae de libris doctorum et auctorum vivorum*, London, 1991.

R. L. Poole (ed.): *Index Britanniae scriptorum quos ex variis bibliothecis ... collegit Ioannes Baleus*. Oxford, 1902, reprinted Cambridge, 1990. This is an annotated edition of a notebook by John Bale (now ms.Selden supra 64 in the Bodleian Library) which formed the basis of his bibliography of early British authors, first published in 1546 (*Illustrium maioris Britanniae scriptorum summarium*). The notebook contains an alphabetical list of authors and their works, with sources of reference, which may be printed works or manuscripts seen by Bale in institutional or private collections. It is not strictly a union catalogue, therefore, but it includes numerous references to specific manuscripts in sixteenth-century collections. The 1990 reprint, edited by C. Brett and J. P. Carley, has a new introduction with biographical notes on the collectors mentioned by Bale.

J. Joscelyn: *Nomina eorum, qui scripserunt historiarum gentis Anglorum, & ubi extant*, printed by Thomas Hearne in his edition of *Roberti de Avesbury de mirabilibus gestis Edwardi III*, Oxford, 1720, pp. 269-98. A list of medieval British historians, with the whereabouts of surviving manuscripts, drawn up by Matthew Parker's secretary John Joscelyn ca. 1566. It is extensively, but not exclusively, derived from Bale; the relationship between the two is examined by C. E. Wright in The dispersal of the monastic libraries and the beginnings of Anglo-Saxon studies, *Transactions of the Cambridge Bibliographical Society* 1 (1951) 208-237, pp. 214-16. Joscelyn also compiled a short list of Anglo-Saxon manuscripts known to him, with their owners, printed on pp. 267-8 of Hearne's Avesbury.

T. James: *Ecloga Oxonio-Cantabrigiensis, tributa in libros duos: quorum prior continet catalogum confusum librorum manuscriptorum in ... bibliothecis ... Oxoniae & Cantabrigiae ...* London, 1600. The first part comprises a list of manuscripts in the college libraries of Oxford and Cambridge, and in Cambridge University Library, arranged in separate sequences by institution; it does not cover any private collections.

[The lists of Scipio le Squyer, ca. 1620-30]: Scipio le Squyer (1579-1659), civil servant and antiquary, compiled two lists of medieval monastic cartularies known by him to be in the hands of contemporary collectors. The lists survive in manuscripts in the John Rylands University Library, Manchester, and an edited transcript has been published: R. Ovenden, Scipio le Squyer and monastic cartularies, *The Library* 6th ser 13 (1991), 323-337.

Bodleian Library MS. Dugdale 48: A manuscript compiled by Sir William Dugdale, ca. 1649, containing lists of books owned by several contemporary collectors. It includes a 'Catalogus registrorum omnium modo existentium per totam Angliam (domibus religiosis quondam spectantium) et in quorum manibus', listing monastic cartularies traced by Dugdale, with information on their owners. A number of later lists based on this original are listed in G. R. C. Davis, *Medieval cartularies of Great Britain: a short catalogue*, London, 1958, pp. xvi-xvii.

E. Bernard: *Catalogi librorum manuscriptorum Angliae et Hiberniae in unum collecti*. Oxford, 1697. A major early attempt at a union catalogue of manuscripts in British and Irish libraries, both institutional and private, which lists over 20,000 manuscripts. It is arranged by collection, and includes university, college and cathedral libraries, as well as the manuscript holdings of about 30 private collectors of the second half of the seventeenth century. The private libraries include big collections like those of John Moore, Hans Sloane and Thomas Gale, and lesser known ones such as those of Edward Tyson, William Bromley and Hugh Todd.

H. Wanley: *Antiquae literaturae septentrionalis liber alter. Seu ... librorum vett. septentrionalium, qui in Angliae bibliothecis extant ... catalogus*. This comprises volume II of G. Hickes, *Linguarum vett. septentrionalium thesaurus grammatico-criticus et archaeologicum*, Oxford, 1705. It is an attempt by Wanley to compile a union catalogue of surviving Anglo-Saxon manuscripts in British libraries. Largely devoted to the institutional libraries of Oxford, Cambridge and London, but includes a number of private libraries as well (e.g. John Moore, Robert Burscough).

G. Haenel: *Catalogi librorum manuscriptorum qui in bibliothecis Galliae, Helveticae, Belgii, Britanniae M., Hispaniae, Lusitaniae asseverantur*. Leipzig, 1830. This is an attempt to produce a union catalogue of manuscripts in the major libraries of Europe. The listing of British private libraries is limited to a series of brief summaries on cols. 908-910, except for an extensive list of the contents of Sir Thomas Phillipps's collection at Middle Hill as it stood in the late 1820s.

SUBSCRIPTION LISTS

A different kind of list which might usefully be mentioned in the context of this chapter is the subscription list which may be found in printed books from the seventeenth century onwards. Cash flow is one of the perennial problems of book production; a publisher has to lay out a substantial sum of money to have an edition of a book printed, and although he may ultimately make a profit through retail sales, the return may be slow. Subscriptions offer a way round this; when a book is first planned, a prospectus is issued inviting people to support its production by paying a deposit in advance, of part or all of the purchase price, on condition that they receive a copy as soon as it appears. Subscribers may receive a discount on the full purchase price by paying in advance. It is normal practice to include a printed list of subscribers in the preliminary pages of books whose production has been supported in this way. The first British book to include such a list was John Minsheu's polyglot dictionary, published in 1617; there are a number of other seventeenth-century examples, but the practice did not become widespread until the eighteenth century, and it has continued to the present day.

Such lists have an obvious relevance for provenance research, as they provide evidence of book ownership by named individuals, even though the copies concerned may no longer be traceable. The presence of a name on a subscription list is not *certain* proof that the man in question once owned the book – for one reason or another, he may never have received his subscriber's copy – but it is a reliable guide in most cases, and is at least an indication of intent. Subscription lists have not hitherto been extensively exploited by students of provenance – systematic work on such lists is a dauntingly large task – but they should be borne in mind as a potentially important source of information. Much of the work that has been done on subscription lists has been carried out at Newcastle by the team responsible for the Project for Historical Bio-Bibliography (PHIBB). They have published a listing:

F. J. G. Robinson & P. J. Wallis: *Book subscription lists: a revised guide.* Newcastle-on-Tyne, 1975.

This describes about 5000 books, published between 1617 and 1973, which contain subscription lists. Supplements were produced in 1976 (compiled by C. Wadham) and 1980 (compiled by L. Menhennet). The *Eighteenth-Century Short Title Catalogue* (ESTC) systematically records the presence of subscription lists; *A check-list of eighteenth-century books containing lists of subscribers*, by R. C. Alston, F. J. G. Robinson and C. Wadham (Newcastle-on-Tyne, 1983) lists all ESTC books in the British Library which have subscription lists, although the expansion of the ESTC file since 1983 means that many more titles can now be identified. An article by P. J. Wallis on 'Book subscription lists' (*The Library* 5th ser 29 (1974), 255-286) considers the history and possible application of these lists; the bibliography in Robinson and Wallis's *Revised guide* provides further references.

VII
PROVENANCE INDEXES

INTRODUCTION

Lists and indexes of the previous owners of books in particular collections are naturally of prime importance for provenance research. They offer a starting point for anyone wishing to trace the books of a particular individual, and they reveal a wealth of information for the historian of private or institutional libraries. This chapter brings together the resources which are currently available for British, American and Canadian libraries. There are four categories covered:

i) *published catalogues:* many published catalogues of whole libraries or parts of libraries, both public and private, include details of the previous ownership of the books; these are described here, whether or not the provenance information is covered by an index. The regular provision of an index, where provenance data is included in the text of a catalogue, is an inconveniently recent development.

ii) *unpublished catalogues:* increasingly, libraries with historic collections tend to include provenance data in their catalogue entries, and to build provenance indexes which are available for consultation in person, or by correspondence. These indexes rarely cover collections comprehensively, but they are being steadily augmented.

iii) *exhibition catalogues:* catalogues of major library exhibitions often contain provenance information, and these are selectively included.

iv) *donors' registers:* old-established institutional libraries, whose growth depended on gifts (there often being no funds for the purchase of books), frequently have donors' registers, listing the names of benefactors and the titles of the books they gave. It may be necessary to treat them with caution, as evidence of books owned by particular individuals, as people often bought books specifically to give away, or gave money which was silently translated in the registers into titles of books bought. It should also be remembered that members of cathedrals and colleges were sometimes obliged to give books on installation, matriculation or graduation.[1] These caveats notwithstanding,

---

[1] The interpretation of early donors' registers is discussed at some length by Sears Jayne in his *Library catalogues of the English renaissance*, Godalming, 1983, pp. 18-21.

donors' registers contain a great deal of information on the previous ownership of books which may no longer be traceable. Many donors' registers include substantial lists of collections bequeathed in their entirety to a particular institution, which are as useful as sale catalogues for reconstructing individual collections. Details of surviving donors' registers are given here for British libraries founded before 1750. The only exception to this chronological cut-off criterion is the British Library, which is too important to miss out. It should be noted that these details do not include isolated lists or catalogues of individual collections given or bequeathed, and they are restricted to post-medieval donation registers. Donors' books for medieval libraries, and catalogues of such libraries which include material on donations, are comprehensively listed in N. R. Ker, *Medieval libraries of Great Britain*, 2nd edition, London, 1964, in the sections at the head of each entry, and there seems little point in attempting to duplicate this information here. Ker's indispensable handbook, and the supplement by A. G. Watson (London, 1987), should be consulted for details of donation registers before 1540.[2]

The information in this chapter is derived partly from personal visits to the libraries concerned, but largely from correspondence. It was not possible to visit all the libraries, and the list is therefore subject to the problems of comprehensiveness and consistency which beset all directories compiled in this way. This applies particularly to the American and Canadian sections, where the details of unpublished indexes are based entirely on written enquiries. Without in any way implying criticism of the many librarians who responded helpfully and sometimes at length to these enquiries, there can be no doubt that the coverage of North American libraries is less thorough than that for British libraries. There is scope for a separate survey of American resources, addressing more rigorously the interests of historians of American libraries and collectors, but it should be compiled in America. As stated in the Introduction, this *Handbook* focusses primarily on British book ownership and the coverage of American libraries is attempted in recognition of the fact that very many books from British collections have migrated across the Atlantic. It will be pointed out, quite rightly, that books from British collections have moved all over the world, and this chapter should therefore cover libraries in Europe, Australia, Japan and possibly elsewhere. But comprehensive international coverage would be a very ambitious target, and the wider the net is opened, the greater the omissions become. It seemed pragmatic to limit the listing to Britain and North America, and although it is not therefore an all-embracing bibliography, it is hoped that it will prove useful in bringing together information which has not been so conveniently available before.

The arrangement of entries is primarily geographical, beginning with Great Britain, with an alphabetical sequence which should be self-explanatory. In

2 I have broken this rule only for A. B. Emden's work on St. Augustine's Abbey, Canterbury, which is specifically about donors and is not listed in Ker/Watson.

each case, details of donors' registers, and unpublished indexes, precede those for published indexes. When the only information given relates to published catalogues, it can be assumed that enquiries have established that there are no other indexes available in that library. There are no 'negative' entries for libraries which have neither published nor unpublished indexes. For each country, the sequence of institutional libraries is followed by one for union catalogues or catalogues with national coverage, and one for catalogues of private libraries. The latter category includes only catalogues which were not drawn up as sale catalogues (for which see chapter V), although it does include some collections which have subsequently been dispersed. Catalogues of private libraries are included only if they carry details of ownership prior to that of the collector in question. This criterion has not always been easy to apply, and the dividing line between inclusion and exclusion is rather grey. The late nineteenth and early twentieth centuries saw the publication of numerous private library catalogues by aristocratic or wealthy collectors, in which provenances were not noted systematically, but 'association copies' were indicated to some extent. If there are appreciable numbers of such entries, the catalogues have been listed, but others have been omitted where the treatment of provenance seems too scanty to merit inclusion. In more recent times, a number of studies of the libraries of eminent men have been published, in which surviving books from their collections have been identified. These are included if a fairly full provenance history for at least some of the books is given, but excluded if they describe only the inscriptions of the owner who is the subject of the study. Collections which consist entirely of oriental material, or other material in non-Roman scripts, are not covered.

The two main subdivisions (Great Britain and North America) are preceded by short sections devoted to directories which list whole collections. These are distinct from the 'catalogues with national coverage' because they describe libraries rather than individual books within libraries, but they are important for identifying whole collections or parts of collections which have been absorbed by institutions. They should be consulted at the outset of any search for the books of a named individual, although it should be borne in mind that the existence of a major block of material from a particular private library in one place will not preclude the discovery of other books from the same source in other places. Books often stray during an owner's lifetime, and many gifts or bequests have been alienated in whole or in part as libraries lost books over the centuries, through sale, exchange, or theft. It is unfortunate that the major directories are not indexed with the needs of the provenance researcher in mind, and information about individual collections cannot easily be retrieved.

The lists include catalogues of manuscripts, excluding those of an archival nature. The separation of manuscripts from printed books, which is today accepted automatically, following the practice of the major libraries, has not always been observed. Many collectors from earlier centuries had a mixture of manuscript and printed material on their library shelves, and anyone attempting to reconstruct those collections must look for both. The importance of provenance has been recognised by manuscript cataloguers for many years, and most modern published descriptions of western manuscripts will include information on previous ownership as a matter of course. On the printed books side, it might be added that incunabulists have often been the most prominent in recording provenance data systematically, as incunabula have long been singled out for special (if not disproportionate) attention, and the early establishment of a high degree of bibliographical control for fifteenth-century printing has allowed cataloguers to concentrate more on the individual features of particular copies.

Further details on the libraries listed, including addresses, telephone numbers, and information about access to the collections, will be found in the main national directories listed at the beginning of each section.

GREAT BRITAIN AND IRELAND

Directories listing whole collections

M. I. Williams (ed.), *A directory of rare book and special collections in the United Kingdom and the Republic of Ireland.* London, 1985.

> This is the major directory of rare book collections in the British Isles; a revised edition is due to appear ca. 1995. It contains entries for about 1300 publicly accessible libraries of all kinds, with summary descriptions of their holdings and catalogues. Much information is included about private libraries which have been acquired by gift or purchase, whether those collections have been kept separate or absorbed into general stock. The index is, unfortunately, patchy in its coverage of personal names and a number of libraries were inadvertently left out (both these problems are to be addressed in the revised version).

The parochial libraries of the Church of England: report of a Committee appointed by the Central Council for the Care of Churches. London, 1959.

> This, the major publication on the history and extent of English and Welsh parish libraries, includes (pp. 63-107) a list of all such libraries known to contain, or have contained, at least a dozen books printed before 1800, whether or not the collections are still in existence. The description of each library includes details of its origin, often a gift or bequest from a particular incumbent. The index has a separate sequence of 'Donors of books or money'. A revised and expanded edition of this directory is in preparation, to be compiled by Michael Perkin.

P. Morgan: *Oxford libraries outside the Bodleian: a guide.* 2nd edn. Oxford, 1980.

> An invaluable directory of the college and departmental libraries of Oxford, giving brief histories of the collections, with notes on major donors and other sources.

A. N. L. Munby: *Cambridge college libraries.* Cambridge, 1960.

> Similar in arrangement to Paul Morgan's Oxford guide, but limited to college libraries and much briefer in its level of detail. Only the most substantial gifts are mentioned.

Aberdeen – University Library

Donors' book: The University archives include a Catalogue of books presented to King's College, 1684-1860 (K114-115), a Catalogue of books presented to Marischal College, 1669-1713 (M71), and a series of later donation registers for the University Library, 1860-1985 (U461-462/2).

The Library maintains provenance indexes to its older collections, held partly in ledger and partly in sheaf form, although these do not cover the collections comprehensively. Provenance data is now added to records created in the Library's automated catalogue, but it is not yet possible to retrieve it.

M. R. James: *A catalogue of the medieval manuscripts in the University Library, Aberdeen.* Cambridge, 1932.

> Provenances noted in the text; separate provenance index.

W. S. Mitchell: *Catalogue of the incunabula in Aberdeen University Library.* (Aberdeen University Studies, 150). Edinburgh, 1968.

> Provenances noted in the text; separate provenance index.

H. J. H. Drummond: *A short-title catalogue of books printed on the continent of Europe, 1501-1600, in Aberdeen University Library.* Oxford, 1979.

> Provenances are noted in the text, extensively but not exhaustively; separate provenance index, with dates and brief biographical information.

W. P. D. Wightman: *Science and the Renaissance: an annotated bibliography of the sixteenth-century books relating to the sciences in the Library of the University of Aberdeen.* (Aberdeen University Studies, 144). Edinburgh, 1962.

> Many provenances noted in the text, but not indexed.

Aberystwyth – National Library of Wales

The Library has provenance indexes, held on cards, covering i) incunabula; ii) sixteenth-century foreign books; iii) STC and Wing books (about 6000 entries, very incomplete; also includes a few entries for eighteenth century books). For books catalogued since January 1986, provenance information has been input to the automated cataloguing system which is now in use.

The Department of Manuscripts has no separate provenance indexes, but references to previous ownership are included in the general manuscript indexes.

Some of the major collections which helped to form the Library are described in W. Ll. Davies, *The National Library of Wales: a survey of its history, its contents, and its activities,* Aberystwyth, 1937, ch. 8-9.

V. Scholderer: *Handlist of incunabula in the National Library of Wales.* (*National Library of Wales Journal, supplement series* 1 no. 1). Aberystwyth, 1940.

> Provenances noted in the text; separate provenance index.

Exhibition catalogue: *The National Library of Wales. Catalogue of the manuscripts and rare books exhibited in the Great Hall of the Library 1916*. Aberystwyth, 1916.

> A miscellaneous exhibition (269 exhibits), strong in Welsh material. A few provenances noted in the text, but not indexed.

Birmingham – University Library

A provenance index covering most of the Library's special collections is held on cards (currently 12 drawers), and is available on request in the Heslop Room. The index has been maintained since the 1950s and new entries are added as material is acquired or recatalogued. It includes some entries for books in Worcester Cathedral Library.

I. Fenlon: *Catalogue of the printed music and music manuscripts before 1801 in the Music Library of the University of Birmingham Barber Institute of Fine Arts*. London, 1976.

> Provenances noted in the text; separate index of previous owners.

P. Morgan: St. Mary's Library, Warwick. *Transactions of the Birmingham Archaeological Society* 79 (1964), 36-60.

> Includes at end (pp. 44-60) a list of 'former owners and donors of books, and persons connected with the Library'. The collection is now part of Birmingham University Library.

B. S. Benedikz and S. Raine: *University of Birmingham Library: catalogue of the Little Malvern Devotional Collection, deposited in the University Library by T. M. Berington*. Birmingham, 1986.

> Provenances noted in the text, but not indexed.

Blackburn – Public Library

J. B. Darbyshire: *The Hart collection of early printed books 1450-1700*. Thesis submitted for the Fellowship of the Library Association, 1967.

> A catalogue of the collection, now held in Blackburn Public Library. Provenances noted in the text, but not indexed.

Bracknell – National Meteorological Library

A microfiche union catalogue of the rare book holdings of the National Meteorological Library and the Royal Meteorological Society Library was completed in 1982. Provenances are noted in the text of this catalogue, but not indexed.

Brighton – Public Library

Catalogue of manuscripts and printed books before 1500. Brighton, 1962.

> Provenances noted in the text; no index.

Brighton – University of Sussex

J. M. Potter: *Catalogue of the Travers Collection in the University of Sussex Library.* Brighton, 1990.

> 335 items, 15th-20th centuries (but the majority 16th or 17th century), collected by Michael Travers (d.1977); wide-ranging in subject. Provenances noted in the text; separate provenance index, with biographical information and notes on collections and their dispersal.

Bristol – Bristol City Library

Donors' book: Bristol City Library was founded in 1613 and the surviving early collections are now housed in the Central Library (Avon County Reference Library). A list of donations, 1773-1829, is now available there as B26972.SR70; two nineteenth-century donation registers are now B26785.SR70 (1822-62) and B7407.6I1 (1856-92). Several lists of particular eighteenth- and nineteenth-century donations also survive.

Cambridge

A. N. L. Munby's guide to *Cambridge college libraries* (see p. 185 above) mentions the major benefactions.

P. R. Robinson: *Catalogue of dated and datable manuscripts c.737-1600 in Cambridge libraries.* Cambridge, 1988.

> Covers manuscripts in the University Library and the college libraries. Provenances noted in the text, and included in index 5 of 'people and places connected with the manuscripts'.

G. D. Hobson: *Bindings in Cambridge libraries.* Cambridge, 1929.

> Detailed descriptions of fine or interesting bindings selected from the college libraries and the University Library. Some provenances noted in the text; separate index of owners.

Cambridge – Christ's College

Donors' book: A Library benefactors' book (ms.22) was begun in 1623, with retrospective coverage back to the re-foundation of the College in 1505. Continued in use until ca. 1660, listing donors' names and titles of books given. A photocopy of the original, with a typescript index of donors' names, is available in the Library. Some lists of particular donations are also available there.

The Old Library was recatalogued ca. 1990, on cards. Donors' names, and bookplates, are noted on the cards, but not indexed.

M. R. James: *A descriptive catalogue of the western manuscripts in the Library of Christ's College, Cambridge.* Cambridge, 1905.

> Provenances noted in the text; no index.

Cambridge – Clare College

Donors' book: A register of benefactors (Clare Archives Safe C: 7/1) was begun ca. 1700; includes some retrospective coverage back to ca. 1620, and continued in use into the 19th century. Includes gifts of all kinds to the College, not just books. Lists donors' names and monetary values of their gifts, but not details of books, although benefactors to the Library are listed as such. A draft version of this book (Safe A: 5/6) also survives. A detailed register of gifts of books to the Library was kept between ca. 1680 and ca. 1715 by Nathaniel Vincent (now Acc.1988/17:4/1), listing donors' names and titles of books given. A few other lists of individual benefactions survive in the archives.

See also *Foundress, by-founders and benefactors of the House or College of Clare in Cambridge*, Cambridge, 1888, section V (pp. 16-18): 'The Library: gifts of books to the College Library', which lists major benefactors, with a brief summary of their gifts, from the fourteenth century down to 1886.

M. R. James: *A descriptive catalogue of the western manuscripts in the Library of Clare College, Cambridge.* Cambridge, 1905.

> Provenances noted in the text; no index.

Early printed books to the year 1500 in the Library of Clare College, Cambridge. Cambridge, 1919.

> Provenances noted in the text; no index.

Cambridge – Corpus Christi College

Donors' book: A catalogue of the Library begun in 1613 (ms.490) is substantially a register of gifts subsequent to the Parker benefaction, and lists donors' names and titles of books given from ca. 1590 to 1660. At the other end of the book is a series of coats of arms of donors of money or plate, 1590-1743. A second Library benefactors' register (W-18) was begun ca. 1673, arranged alphabetically by surnames, with retrospective coverage back to the early seventeenth century. Continued in use until 1781, listing donors' names and titles of books given.

M. R. James: *A descriptive catalogue of the manuscripts in the Library of Corpus Christi College, Cambridge.* 2v. Cambridge, 1912.

> Provenances noted in the text, and included in the general index. See also the addenda by R. Vaughan and J. Fines, in *Transactions of the Cambridge Bibliographical Society*, 3 (1960), 113-123.

S. Gaselee: *The early printed books in the Library of Corpus Christi College, Cambridge.* Cambridge, 1921.

> Covers books printed before 1521. Provenances noted in the text; no index.

Cambridge – Emmanuel College

Donors' book: No early donors' register survives, but *The Library of Emmanuel College* by Bush & Rasmussen (full reference below) includes on pp. 209-212 a table of donors, 1584-1637.

The Library archives include at Lib 4.1 a notebook, compiled earlier this century, which mostly comprises a list of ownership inscriptions found in the books, arranged in pressmark order, but not indexed by name. The Library also has a notebook, compiled by Isobel Keith and Oliver W. Rottmann in 1938, containing a series of special indexes to the Library; these include a list of bookplates (pp. 3-6) and of signatures in books (pp. 39-83). Arrangement is alphabetical by name, and pressmarks are given (but not author/title details of the books concerned).

M. R. James: *The western manuscripts in the Library of Emmanuel College.* Cambridge, 1904.

> Provenances noted in the text; separate indexes of owners and donors.

S. Bush & C. J. Rasmussen: *The Library of Emmanuel College, Cambridge, 1584-1637.* Cambridge, 1986.

> An edited transcript of the 1637 inventory of Emmanuel College Library, identifying books which survive today. Owners and donors noted in the text, and included in the index.

Cambridge – Fitzwilliam Museum

Most of the Library's printed books are now included in the on-line catalogue, which is accessible within the Museum Library, or from any terminal with access to the on-line cataloguing system of Cambridge University Library (e.g. those within the University Library; the system is also available over JANET). Provenances are included in the entries, and are indexed and searchable.

M. R. James: *A descriptive catalogue of the manuscripts in the Fitzwilliam Museum.* Cambridge, 1895.

> Provenances noted in the text and included in the index of names.

M. R. James: *A descriptive catalogue of the McLean collection of manuscripts in the Fitzwilliam Museum.* Cambridge, 1912.

> Provenances noted in the text; separate index of 'names of owners, scribes, places, etc.'

F. Wormald & P. M. Giles: *A descriptive catalogue of the additional illuminated manuscripts in the Fitzwilliam Museum acquired between 1895 and 1979 (excluding the McLean collection).* 2v. Cambridge, 1982.

> The description of each manuscript includes a provenance section; provenances included in the general index.

P. M. Giles: A handlist of the Bradfer-Lawrence manuscripts deposited on loan at the Fitzwilliam Museum. *Transactions of the Cambridge Bibliographical Society* 6 (1973), pp. 86-99.

Provenances noted in the text, and included in the name index at the end.

C. E. Sayle: *Fitzwilliam Museum McClean bequest: catalogue of the early printed books.* Cambridge, 1916.

> Largely comprises incunabula, but also includes sixteenth- and seventeenth-century material. The description of each item includes a provenance section; provenances included in the general index.

Exhibition catalogue: D. Scrase and P. Croft: *Maynard Keynes: collector of pictures, books and manuscripts. Catalogue of an exhibition held at the Fitzwilliam Museum, 5 July - 29 August 1983.*

> 183 books included, 16th-20th centuries. Some provenances noted in the text, but not indexed. The books are from Keynes's bequest to King's College, Cambridge.

Cambridge – Gonville and Caius College

Donors' book: There is no early donors' register, but see:

J. Venn: *Biographical history of Gonville and Caius College.* 3v. Cambridge, 1897-1901.

Vol. 3 includes (pp. 281-284) a list of benefactors to the Library, with brief details of books presented; fuller details are available, in some cases, in Venn's edition of the College Annals (Cambridge Antiquarian Society Publications, Octavo series, 40, 1904), although books are not precisely identified and pressmarks of surviving items are not given.

M. R. James: *A descriptive catalogue of the manuscripts in the Library of Gonville and Caius College.* 2v. + supplement. Cambridge, 1907-14.

> Provenances noted in the text and included in the general index.

W. R. Collett: *A list of the early printed books in the Library of Gonville and Caius College, Cambridge.* Cambridge, 1850.

> Includes books printed before 1521 (and therefore largely superseded by Schneider's catalogue, see below). Some provenances noted in the text, but not included in the general index. Separate index of donors (only; does not list owners who were not donors).

G. A. Schneider: *A descriptive catalogue of the incunabula in the Library of Gonville & Caius College, Cambridge.* Cambridge, 1928.

> Owners and donors noted in the text. Separate donors' index, but owners who were not donors are not indexed.

E. S. Leedham-Green: A catalogue of Caius College Library, 1569. *Transactions of the Cambridge Bibliographical Society* 8 (1981), 29-41.

> A transcript of the early catalogue of the library which survives in the College matriculation register. Books surviving today are identified, with their provenance if known.

Cambridge – Jesus College

Donors' book: A Library benefactors register (R.2.25) was begun ca. 1633, at the expense of Lionel Gatford, fellow of the College 1625-38. Lists donors' names and titles of books given, with retrospective coverage back to 1556; continued in use until 1715.

M. R. James: *A descriptive catalogue of the manuscripts in the Library of Jesus College, Cambridge*. London, 1895.

   Provenances noted in the text; separate indexes of owners and donors.

Cambridge – King's College

Donors' book: A Library benefactors register (now Archives Lib.2) was begun in the first half of the seventeenth century, with retrospective coverage back to the middle of the sixteenth. It continued in use until ca. 1710, listing donors' names and titles of books given. Arranged by categories of donors, in a hierarchical system – fellows who were doctors, fellows who were masters of arts, outside donors, etc. The catalogue of the Library which was begun ca. 1612, and continued in use, with additions, throughout the seventeenth century (now Lib.1), also includes at the end a list of donors; this was used as the basis for the separate donors' register when this was begun. A later register of books given to the Library, 1740-1887, also survives (Lib.24).

A comprehensive index of donors to the Library, 1527-1850, was compiled by F. L. Clarke at the beginning of the twentieth century and is now arranged in two albums, in chronological order (Lib.13-14). There is an alphabetical index at the front of each album. Clarke's entries, which are very thorough, are based on Library muniments and other College archives, and on the books themselves; his slips include biographical information, titles, shelfmarks, and transcriptions of the donation inscriptions for all surviving books. A separate alphabetical index of Library donors, compiled by Clarke in a notebook, is now Lib.13A; this includes some entries for former owners who were not donors.

The Library also has an index of armorial binding stamps, compiled by R. A. N. Petrie, mid-twentieth-century. This includes about 40 entries, with rubbings and notes, mostly British. An extensive, but not complete, index of bookplates in the Library has been compiled, with photocopies and notes, mounted in a series of albums; these are available in the Library on request.

M. R. James: *A descriptive catalogue of the manuscripts other than oriental in the Library of King's College, Cambridge*. Cambridge, 1895.

   Provenances noted in the text and included in the general index.

A list of the incunabula in the Library of King's College, Cambridge. Cambridge, 1908.

   Provenance index, and index of donors, with brief biographies.

A. N. L. Munby: *A catalogue of the manuscripts and printed books in the Sir Isaac Newton collection forming part of the library bequeathed by John Maynard, Baron Keynes ... to King's College*. [Cambridge, 1936-49].

   The manuscripts section is an annotated copy of the sale catalogue of Newton papers held at Sotheby's, 13 July 1936; the section on printed books, in typescript, includes provenances in the text, but is not indexed. There is a copy in Cambridge University Library at A122.7 K25.

P. Bicknell: *The picturesque scenery of the Lake District 1752-1855: a bibliographical study.* Winchester, 1990.

> Based primarily on the library of King's College, Cambridge; the provenances of copies held at King's are noted in the text, but not indexed.

Cambridge – Magdalene College

Donors' book: A Library donors' register (now F.4.33, described as ms.33 in M. R. James's catalogue below) was begun in 1629. Lists donations retrospectively back to the gift of Thomas Neville (Master 1582-93, d.1615), and continued in use until ca. 1700, listing donors' names and titles of books given.

M. R. James: *A descriptive catalogue of the manuscripts in the College Library of Magdalene College, Cambridge.* Cambridge, 1909.

> Provenances noted in the text; no index.

N. A. Smith: *Catalogue of the Pepys Library at Magdalene College, Cambridge. Vol. 1: Printed books.* Cambridge, 1978.

> One or two provenances prior to Pepys are noted in the text; no index.

R. McKitterick & R. Beadle: *Catalogue of the Pepys Library at Magdalene College, Cambridge. Vol. 5: Manuscripts. Part i: Medieval.* Cambridge, 1992.

> The description of each manuscript includes a provenance section; provenances are included in the 'index of persons and places'.

Cambridge – Pembroke College

Donors' book: The Library donors' register (ms.LC.II.77) was begun in 1617, with retrospective coverage back to the fourteenth century; continued in use until the beginning of the eighteenth century. Lists donors' names, and titles of books given. A list of early benefactors to the College Library ('copied from an old register'), covering ca. 1380-1570, was printed by G. E. Corrie, 'A list of books presented to Pembroke College, Cambridge, by different donors, during the 14th and 15th centuries', *Communications made to the Cambridge Antiquarian Society* 2 (1860), 11-23.

M. R. James: *A descriptive catalogue of the manuscripts in the Library of Pembroke College, Cambridge.* Cambridge, 1905.

> Provenances noted in the text and included in the general index.

Cambridge – Peterhouse

Donors' book: There is no donors' book as such. The catalogue of the Library made ca. 1675 (now ms.410) is arranged alphabetically by authors, with donors' names added to each entry; additions were made down to ca. 1700. There are two other manuscript catalogues, organised in the same way, one of which appears to be a close copy of ms.410, begun not long afterwards and similarly continued down to the beginning of the eighteenth century (this is now ms.408), and one which was begun in 1708 and continued down to the latter half of the eighteenth century (ms.409). A separate list of books given by Isaac Barrow in 1674 survives in an early borrowers' book (ms.406).

A comprehensive provenance index to the Perne Library (i.e. the old library), on cards, was completed in 1992 and is available for consultation there.

M. R. James: *A descriptive catalogue of the manuscripts in the Library of Peterhouse.* Cambridge, 1899.

> Former owners and donors are noted in the text. Separate provenance indexes.

Early printed books to the year 1500 in the Library of Peterhouse, Cambridge. Cambridge, 1914.

> Some provenances noted in the text, but not indexed.

Cambridge – Queens' College

Donors' book: A donors' register (ms.F.IV.22) was begun, retrospectively, ca. 1632; covers the period 1562-1820. Lists names of donors and titles of books given.

Work is in progress on a provenance index for the Old Library.

M. R. James: *A descriptive catalogue of the western manuscripts in the Library of Queens' College, Cambridge.* Cambridge, 1905.

> Provenances noted in the text; no index.

F. G. Plaistowe: *Early printed books to the year 1500 in the Library of Queens' College, Cambridge.* Cambridge, 1910.

> Provenances noted in the text; no index.

Cambridge – Saint Catharine's College

Donors' book: There is no donors' book as such. The oldest College register, begun in the fifteenth century (now College Muniments XL/8), includes at the end (pp. 134-6) an early sixteenth-century catalogue of the Library, including lists of several donations from Robert Woodlark, the founder, onwards. These lists were printed by G. E. Corrie in the *Publications of the Cambridge Antiquarian Society* 1 (1840) and reprinted by M. R. James on pp. 4-7 of his catalogue of the College manuscripts (see below), and also by W. H. S. Jones on pp. 376-385 of his *History of St. Catharine's College* (Cambridge, 1936), where Corrie's notes are also reproduced. All the books included in these lists were lost during the sixteenth century. A series of notes on donations to the Library, 1673-1730, was made by Henry Philpott (Master of the College, 1845-61), and these are preserved in the Muniments at XL/17/10.

M. R. James: *A descriptive catalogue of the manuscripts in the library of St. Catharine's College, Cambridge*. Cambridge, 1925.

> Provenances noted in the text; no index.

J. B. Bilderbeck: *Early printed books in the Library of St. Catharine's College, Cambridge*. Cambridge, 1911.

> Provenances noted in the text; separate index of inscribed names and donors, with biographical details.

Cambridge – Saint John's College

Donors' book: The Library's *Liber memorialis*, begun in 1628, gives the names and coats of arms of major donors to the Library 1628-1718, but has very few details of books given. Lists of several seventeenth-century benefactions can be found in two ms. catalogues of the Library, begun in the 1630s but added to down to ca. 1700, mss. U.2 and U.3. The College Commemoration Book of 1683 (College archives C11.4) is a general list of benefactors, including gifts to the Library; it gives some details of titles of books given, but is mostly confined to donors' names and numbers of books given. A later catalogue of benefactors (C11.6), drawn up by Robert Lambert ca. 1725, has some references to gifts of books, but it general it does not distinguish Library benefactors separately.

Benefactions of all kinds to the College, from its foundation down to the end of the ninteenth century, are summarised in A. F. Torry, *Founders and benefactors of St. John's College, Cambridge*, Cambridge, 1888, which includes much useful biographical information.

A provenance index on cards (one and a half drawers) was compiled earlier this century, but its coverage is not comprehensive.

M. R. James: *A descriptive catalogue of the manuscripts in the Library of St. John's College, Cambridge*. Cambridge, 1913.

> Provenances noted in the text and included in the general index.

M. Cowie: *A descriptive catalogue of the manuscripts and scarce books in the Library of St. John's College, Cambridge*. Cambridge, 1843.

> Mostly lists manuscripts – and therefore superseded by the work of M. R. James – but also lists some printed books, particularly continental, sixteenth-century. Some provenances noted in the text, but not included in the index.

F. Korsten: *A catalogue of the library of Thomas Baker*. Cambridge, 1990.

> A significant part of the large library of Thomas Baker (1656-1740) – Frans Korsten traces over 4000 volumes – was acquired by St. John's College after his death, but many books were sold or otherwise dispersed. This catalogue endeavours to reconstruct the whole collection from a range of sources. Provenances previous to, and later than Baker noted in the text; separate provenance index (appendix III).

Cambridge – Selwyn College

C. W. Philips: *List of incunabula, Selwyn College, Cambridge*. Cambridge, 1934.

> Provenances noted in the text; no index.

Cambridge – Sidney Sussex College

Donors' book: A Library benefactors' book (ms.91) was begun in 1611 and records gifts from the foundation of the College in 1596, down to 1798. A few larger collections are not included (James Montagu, 1618, Francis Combe, 1641, and Thomas Goodlad, 1707).

The shelf-catalogue of the Library compiled in the 1920s includes occasional notes of provenance, added by C. B. Hurry. The Library is currently being recatalogued in automated format and provenances are indexed and searchable. The records are held in the Departmental file of the Cambridge University On-Line Catalogue System, which can be accessed through the OPAC of Cambridge University Library, either on-site or via JANET.

M. R. James: *A descriptive catalogue of the manuscripts in the Library of Sidney Sussex College, Cambridge.* Cambridge, 1895.

> Provenances noted in the text; separate indexes of owners and donors.

Early printed books to the year 1500 in the Library of Sidney Sussex College, Cambridge. Cambridge, 1922.

> Provenances noted in the text; no index.

Cambridge – Trinity College

Donors' book: The *Memoriale* (ms.R.17.8) was begun in 1614; it lists benefactions of all kinds to the College, summarising major gifts back to the time of the foundation under Edward III. Gifts to the Library are listed on pp. 85-133, covering the period 1549-1673; summarises benefactions 1549-1604, from 1604 onwards lists donors' names, and titles of books given.

Philip Gaskell's *Trinity College Library: the first 150 years* (Cambridge, 1980) includes as Appendices F and G lists of donors of mss. and printed books (showing the number of volumes given, but not individual titles), and as Appendix H a catalogue of scientific books in the Library in 1645, in which donors' names (but not other provenances) are noted. The *Memoriale* is described and illustrated on pp. 34-36.

A provenance index to the printed books is available in the Wren Library. It was begun by H. M. Adams and although it includes several hundred entries in his hand, it is very far from complete; it has been added to a little since Adams's time.

M. R. James: *The western manuscripts in the Library of Trinity College, Cambridge: a descriptive catalogue.* 4v. Cambridge, 1900-04.

> Provenances noted in the text; some, but not all, included in the general index in vol. 4. Lists of major donations at the beginning of vol. 2.

R. Sinker: *A catalogue of the fifteenth-century printed books in the Library of Trinity College, Cambridge.* Cambridge, 1876.

A few provenances noted in the text, but not indexed. Separate index of donors at the end, with brief biographical details, although the information on donation is not usually included in the descriptions of the books.

R. Sinker: *A catalogue of the English books printed before MDCI. Now in the Library of Trinity College, Cambridge.* Cambridge, 1885.

Some provenances noted in the text, but not indexed. Separate index of donors at the end, with brief biographical details, although the information on donation is not always included in the descriptions of the books.

J. Hayward: *The Rothschild library: a catalogue of the collection of eighteenth-century printed books and manuscripts formed by Lord Rothschild.* 2v. Cambridge, 1954.

The description of each book includes a provenance section; there is one general index which includes provenances thus noted.

D. Pearson: The books of Peter Shaw in Trinity College, Cambridge. *Transactions of the Cambridge Bibliographical Society* 9 (1986), 76-89.

A list of ca. 140 volumes given to the Library by Peter Shaw in 1601. Surviving volumes are identified where possible, with provenances other than Shaw noted in the text, but not indexed.

Cambridge – Trinity Hall

Donors' book: There is no early donors' register as such. A manuscript catalogue begun in 1804 to record books given by Sir William Wynne (Master 1803-15) was continued as a general Library donors' book until 1841, recording several other benefactions.

William Warren (1683-1744), Vice-Master of Trinity Hall 1723-43, compiled a series of manuscript collections on the history of the College, drawing on a variety of sources, including early College records now lost. A complete edited transcript of Warren's original (now in the College archives) by A. W. W. Dale was published by Cambridge University Press in 1911 as *Warren's book.* This includes (chapters X-XIII, pp. 223-328) a complete list of benefactors to the College, 1350-1740; a number of these were donors to the Library, and lists of titles are given where possible.

Typescript lists of certain particular donations are available in the Library.

M. R. James: *A descriptive catalogue of the manuscripts in the Library of Trinity Hall.* Cambridge, 1907.

Provenances noted in the text; no index.

Early printed books to the year 1500 in the Library of Trinity Hall, Cambridge. Cambridge, 1909.

Provenances noted in the text; no index.

Cambridge – University Library

Donors' book: The Catalogue of the Library begun ca. 1650 by Jonathan Pindar, now Ms. Oo.7.52, is generally described as the Library's principal donors' book. The first 61 pages comprise a catalogue of the Library down to 1658, written by Pindar, arranged chronologically by donors, with retrospective coverage back to the fifteenth century. The catalogue was continued by other hands down to ca. 1680, and then sporadically down to 1718, listing further donations. For the early period, it is neither reliable nor comprehensive (see the entries under 'Donor's book' in the index of J. C. T. Oates's *History*, full reference below). A transcript of Pindar's Catalogue, made by Thomas Baker, survives in the British Library as Harleian Ms. 7029, fo. 103-107 (a further transcript of the transcript is now Cambridge University Library Ms. Mm.2.22 fo. 1-4).

The Rare Books Room has two card indexes which relate to provenance:
i) bookplates (3 drawers of cards; covers a very small proportion of the bookstock);
ii) adversaria (covered also by vol. 6 of the published catalogue of manuscripts, see below).
A provenance index to printed books in the Library was begun by Charles Sayle in 1894; he noted inscriptions and mottoes which he found in the books in a large notebook which is now available in the Manuscripts Room as Add. Ms. 6450. It contains many hundreds of entries, including a few for manuscripts; unfortunately, only a very few additions have been made since Sayle's death in 1924. No other provenance indexes exist for the printed books. It should however be noted that the index to western manuscripts (on cards, in the Manuscripts Reading Room) includes some entries for signatures found in printed books, as well as manuscripts. It does not cover the collections comprehensively or systematically, but it is always worth checking. There is also a separate card index (2 drawers) of Owners and donors of manuscripts. In addition, an index of 'Owners and donors' of manuscripts, handwritten on paper slips and shelved in the Manuscripts Reading Room (on the shelves after A236.22), includes some information not found in the card catalogue, or the printed catalogues.

A great deal of provenance information will be found in the two-volume history of the Library: J. C. T. Oates, *Cambridge University Library: a history. From the beginnings to the copyright act of Queen Anne* (Cambridge, 1986); David McKitterick, *Cambridge University Library: a history. The eighteenth and nineteenth centuries* (Cambridge, 1986). Both authors are concerned to describe the way in which the Library was built up, and the sources from which the books came; Oates, in his preface, explains that one of his targets was to write a history describing 'when, why, whence and in what manner every important manuscript or printed book' was added to the collections. The indexes to these two volumes therefore include the names of many previous owners of University Library books.

A catalogue of the manuscripts preserved in the Library of the University of Cambridge. 6v.
    Cambridge, 1866-74.

Some provenances are noted in the text, but these are not on the whole included in the index (in vol. 6). Vol. 6 includes a Catalogue of adversaria and printed books containing ms. notes, with its own separate index.

J. C. T. Oates: *A catalogue of the fifteenth-century printed books in the University Library, Cambridge*. Cambridge, 1954.

Provenances noted in the text; separate provenance index, with dates and brief biographical information. The interleaved copy of this catalogue, available in the Rare Books Room of Cambridge University Library, is marked up with additions since 1954, including additions to the provenance index.

D. J. McKitterick: *The library of Thomas Knyvett of Ashwellthorpe* c. *1539-1618*. Cambridge, 1978.

Knyvett, a Norfolk landowner and country gentleman, assembled a collection of about 70 mss. and 1400 printed books, most of which were subsequently acquired by John Moore and hence became part of George I's gift to Cambridge University Library in 1715. David McKitterick's catalogue (an edited transcript of a ms. catalogue of Knyvett's collection made in 1618, now CUL ms. Ff.2.30), identifies items which are now in the UL and (where possible) those which have strayed elsewhere. Provenances previous to, and later than, Knyvett are noted in the text, and included in the index in one alphabetical sequence at the heading 'Owners'.

C. Sayle: The library of Thomas Lorkyn. *Annals of Medical History* 3 (1921), 310-323.

A list of the 272 volumes bequeathed to Cambridge University Library by Lorkyn, who was Regius Professor of Physic at Cambridge from 1564 until his death in 1591. Most of the books survive today and their pressmarks are given. Provenances previous to Lorkyn are noted in the text, but not indexed.

A. T. Bartholomew & C. Gordon: The library at King Edward VI School, Bury St. Edmunds. *The Library* 3rd series 1 (1910), 2-27.

Includes at end an appendix of selected books in the library; provenances noted in the text, but not separately indexed. The library is now in Cambridge University Library.

G. Keynes: *Bibliotheca bibliographici: a catalogue of the library formed by Geoffrey Keynes*. London, 1964.

Provenances noted in the text; separate index of owners and donors. The collection is now in Cambridge University Library.

J. C. T. Oates: 'Non est mortale quod opto'. *The Book Collector* 9 (1960), 327-329.

A list of books in Cambridge University Library with seventeenth century ownership inscriptions accompanied by the motto 'Non est mortale quod opto'; the information is derived from Charles Sayle's notebook mentioned above. See also the follow-up notes (by Oates and Paul Morgan), listing books from other libraries in which the motto is found, in *The Book Collector* 10 (1961), 446; 11 (1962), 211; and 16 (1967), 507-8.

Canterbury – St. Augustine's Abbey

The Abbey was dissolved in 1538 and surviving books, now widely scattered, are listed in N. R. Ker's *Medieval libraries of Great Britain* (1964) and its *Supplement* by A. G. Watson (1987).

Donors' book:. The late fifteenth century library catalogue (now Trinity

College Dublin ms.D.1.19) includes much information on donors, which has been extracted and published as a alphabetical list with biographical details: A. B. Emden: *Donors of books to S. Augustine's Abbey Canterbury*, Oxford, 1968 (Oxford Bibliographical Society occasional publication 4).

Canterbury – Cathedral Library

Donors' book: A register of donations (now Canterbury Cathedral Archives Literary Ms.E.40) was begun in 1628 and covers the period from then until ca. 1725, listing donors' names and sometimes the titles of books given. A transcript is available in the Library. A few loose lists of eighteenth-century donations also survive.

All the printed books pre-1901 were recatalogued (using an automated system) between 1978 and 1983 and provenances were recorded. Copies of the catalogue, printed out, are held in the Library and in the Library of the University of Kent at Canterbury; separate provenance indexes are available in the Cathedral Library. Cataloguing of the Mendham Collection (deposited by the Law Society) is in progress.

C. E. Woodruff: *A catalogue of the manuscript books in the Library of Christ Church, Canterbury*. Canterbury, 1911.

> Provenances noted in the text; separate provenance index.

Cartmel – Cartmel Priory Library

D. Ramage & S. Taylor: *The ancient library in Cartmel Priory Church ... catalogue.* 2nd edn. Durham, 1959.

> Provenances not noted in the text, but the appendix on 'Names in books' is a comprehensive provenance index.

Cashel – GPA-Bolton Library (formerly Cashel Diocesan Library)

In the printed catalogue of 1973 (*Catalogue of the Cashel Diocesan Library*, Boston, 1973), a system of asterisks is used to denote the pressmarks of books known to have belonged to Narcissus Marsh, or William King.

Chichester – Cathedral Library

Donors' book: The manuscript catalogue of the Library compiled in 1753 includes at the end lists of donors to the Library, divided into members and non-members of the Cathedral body, listing the names of donors and titles of books given, from the late seventeenth century onwards. The lists were added to during the second half of the eighteenth century, and in 1775 a separate catalogue of benefactions was drawn up by Richard Shenton, arranged alphabetically by donors. An earlier eighteenth-century catalogue of the Library (pre-1735) also includes a list of books given.

The card indexes available in the Library include sequences of donors (1 drawer), and other former owners (1 drawer).

Colchester – Harsnett Library

G. Goodwin: *A catalogue of the Harsnett Library at Colchester.* London, 1888.

> Some provenances noted in the text; no index. The Library is now housed in the Central Library, Trinity Square, Colchester.

Coleraine – University of Ulster

B. S. Benedikz: *The Ulster gift: books presented to the University of Ulster.* Coleraine, 1990.

> A catalogue of books given by Henry Davis. Provenances noted in the text; separate provenance index.

Coventry – Coventry Grammar School

The School was founded in 1546 and in 1602 the corporation of Coventry established a library there, intended to serve as a public library for the general use of the town (see T. Kelly, *Early public libraries*, 1966, p. 74). It was dispersed by auction at Hodgson's on 11 November 1908.

Donors' book: Begun early in the seventeenth century, and continued in use down to the early eighteenth century. Arranged alphabetically by surnames, listing donors' names, and titles of books given. It was lot 292 in the sale of 1908 and is now Add.Ms.4467 in Cambridge University Library, kept alongside a 1697 catalogue of the Library (Add.Ms.4468), which has no donor information other than a list of 23 books 'ex dono Mri Humfredi Wanley' on the penultimate page.

Dublin – Chester Beatty Library

E. G. Millar: *The Library of A. Chester Beatty: a descriptive catalogue of the western manuscripts.* 4v. Oxford, 1927.

> The description of each manuscript includes a provenance section; immediate previous provenances and monastic provenances are noted in the contents list at the beginning of each volume.

Dublin – Marsh's Library

Muriel McCarthy's book on the history of the library, *All graduates and gentlemen*, Dublin, 1980, pays particular attention to noteworthy former owners of books now in the collections (see especially pp. 38-47).

N. J. D. White: *An account of Archbishop Marsh's Library, Dublin*. Dublin, 1926.

> Includes at end (pp. 31-43) a section by N. B. White, 'Autographs in Marsh's Library', which lists noteworthy provenances, arranged alphabetically by owners. Pressmarks are given, but not full author/title details of the books concerned. An expanded version of this list is available in the Library.

R. Charteris: *A catalogue of the printed books on music, printed music and music manuscripts in Archbishop Marsh's Library, Dublin*. Clarabrichen, 1982.

> Provenances noted in the text, although often only in the form 'Bishop Stillingfleet collection'; provenances included in the general index.

Dublin – Milltown Park (Jesuit Fathers)

P. Grosjean & D. O'Connell: *A catalogue of incunabula in the library at Milltown Park, Dublin*. Dublin, 1932.

> The books comprise part of the bequest of Judge William O'Brien (1832-99). Provenances noted in the text; separate provenance index.

Dublin – Trinity College

Donors' book: A list of presentations to the Library, 1837-1968, is now kept in the Manuscripts Department (MUN/LIB/1/32-356). A catalogue of the manuscripts in the Library made ca. 1745 by John Lyon (now MUN/LIB/1/53) includes information on donors, and a list of 'benefactorum nomina', although it is neither comprehensive nor reliable. Apart from this, there are no general donors' registers.

A provenance index on cards was begun in 1970 and covers all material acquired since then, with a little earlier material included. Significant collections covered are the Burgage Collection of eighteenth century broadsides, the College Historical Society Library, the Pollard School Book Collection, and the Townley Hall Collection. It presently occupies 70 catalogue drawers.

T. K. Abbott: *Catalogue of the manuscripts in the Library of Trinity College, Dublin*. Dublin, 1900.

> Some provenances noted in the text, but not included in the general index.

M. L. Colker: *Trinity College Library Dublin: descriptive catalogue of the medieval and renaissance Latin manuscripts*. 2v. Aldershot, 1991.

> Provenances noted in the text, and included in the general index (owners are denoted in the index with asterisks).

T. K. Abbott: *Catalogue of the fifteenth-century books in the Library of Trinity College, Dublin*. Dublin, 1905.

> Provenances noted in the text; separate provenance index.

Durham – Cathedral Library

Donor's book: A Library donors' register (ms. A.IV.32) was begun in 1628 to mark the re-foundation of the Library; it continued in use only until 1642, and has a couple of entries for the 1670s. Lists donors' names and monetary values of their gifts (mostly in fact installation and sealing fees). It was re-commenced ca. 1715 by Thomas Rud, and then continued in use, to record donors' names and titles of books given, until the beginning of the 19th cenury. Benefactions between 1636 and 1679 were also recorded in the ms. catalogue of the Library (ms.B.IV.47) begun ca. 1633; these entries were transcribed by Rud into the Donor's Book.

The pre-1801 books were recatalogued in 1978-82 and there is a comprehensive provenance index available in the Library, in sheaf binders.

Durham – University Library

A provenance index in sheaf binders was begun in the 1940s and provenances of all newly acquired or recatalogued material have been systematically incorporated since then; the index probably runs to about 10,000 entries at present, in 29 binders. The Routh Library is partially covered by this index, the Bamburgh Library less so. Cosin's Library was recatalogued in 1984-86 and all provenances are recorded in a computerised database. A printout of the Cosin Catalogue is available in the Special Reading Room, with provenances noted in the text, and a separate index will eventually be available.

Durham – Ushaw College

A provenance index on paper slips was begun some years ago, but it has not been possible to complete it, and it is not at present being continued; it covers about five of the presses in the Big Library.

Edinburgh

Lists of fifteenth century books in Edinburgh libraries. Edinburgh, 1913.

> A series of short-title lists compiled by various members of the Edinburgh Bibliographical Society (and published by them). Covers the University Library, the Advocates' Library (now the National Library of Scotland), the Signet Library, and a number of smaller libraries. Provenances noted in the text in some cases – not the Advocates' Library – but not indexed.

G. D. Hargreaves: *A catalogue of medical incunabula in Edinburgh libraries.* Edinburgh, 1976.

> Provenances noted in the text; separate provenance index.

D. T. Bird: *A catalogue of sixteenth-century medical books in Edinburgh libraries.* Edinburgh, 1982.

> Provenances noted in the text; separate provenance index, with dates and brief biographical details.

Edinburgh – National Library of Scotland

The National Library of Scotland was established in 1925 by transferring to national ownership the non-legal books of the Faculty of Advocates of Edinburgh, whose Library was founded in 1682.

Donors' book: The earliest donors' register for the Advocates' Library was begun in 1683 and is now ms.F.R.116b in the NLS. It continued in use until 1701 (although the book was subsequently filled up with other catalogues and lists), recording donors' names and titles of books given. A new donors' book was begun in 1703 (ms.F.R.139). It was continued only until 1709, although there are a few additional entries for 1716 and 1760-74. Later donation registers cover the period 1800-1926 (ms.F.R.140, F.R.140a-c, F.R.140g-j). It should be added that Brian Hillyard's article on 'The formation of the Library, 1682-1728', in P. Cadell & A. Matheson (eds.), *For the encouragement of learning*, Edinburgh, 1989, 23-66, contains extensive analysis of the early donations, and on private collections purchased at that time.

A number of special indexes are available on request in the Library's South Reading Room. A file of provenance information on printed books has been maintained since the 1960s, arranged by pressmark, with an index of names, institutions, and places. The main file is held in four large sheaf binders and the entries include transcriptions of, and notes on, the inscriptions found in the books. Coverage is rather haphazard, and the majority of entries relate to pre-1800 Scottish inscriptions. The index of names currently runs to eight sheaf binders. Provenances of items acquired by the Library since this index was begun have been included. The Library's cataloguing is now automated and it is hoped that provenance information will be included, and searchable, in the on-line public catalogue sometime during the 1990s.

A separate index of bookplates found in NLS books is also maintained (eight sheaf binders). There is an extensive collection of rubbings of noteworthy bindings, which includes indexes to names recorded on the covers, and names found in the books. Separate indexes, in sheaf binders, are also held for inscriptions and bookplates found in the library of Blairs College, which was deposited in the NLS in 1974. There is also a separate index of school prize books (bookplates, prize bindings, etc.), arranged alphabetically by names of schools.

Dr. Brian Hillyard is developing a file on Scottish book collectors; access is available on request in the South Reading Room. The file is based on sale catalogues, inventories, and references to private libraries in other sources, and is attempting to bring together in one alphabetical sequence notes on appreciable private collections which are known to have existed once, whether or not they are now dispersed.

Typescript indexes for manuscripts which are not fully described in published catalogues (e.g. the Advocates' mss., for which only a handlist has been published), which include provenance information, are available in the South Reading Room.

National Library of Scotland: catalogue of manuscripts acquired since 1925. 8v. Edinburgh, 1938-92.

> Provenances noted in the text, and usually, but not always, included in the general indexes found at the end of each volume.

I. C. Cunningham: Latin classical manuscripts in the National Library of Scotland. *Scriptorium* 27 (1973), 64-90.

> A detailed catalogue of 37 medieval and renaissance manuscripts containing Latin classical texts, all but one from the Advocates' Library collection. Provenances noted in the text, but not indexed.

W. Beattie: *Supplement to the hand-list of incunabula in the National Library of Scotland*. Edinburgh, 1944.

W. Beattie: *Second supplement to the hand-list of incunabula in the National Library of Scotland*. Edinburgh, 1946.

> These supplement the amalgamated volume of hand-lists for Edinburgh libraries published in 1913. Provenances noted in the text, but not indexed. A third supplement, by Michael Pegg, covering the period 1946-66 and published in the *Sonderdruck aus Beitrage zur Inkunabelkunde* 3 (1966), does not include provenances.

M. Townley: *The best and fynest lawers and other raire bookes*. Edinburgh, 1990.

> A facsimile and transcript of the earliest surviving catalogue of the Advocates' Library, drawn up in 1683, listing 433 items. Donors are identified, using the separate donors' register, and other ownership inscriptions are included in the text; both are covered by the index of donors.

W. A. Kelly: Catalogue of James Sutherland's library. *The Bibliotheck* 14 (1987), 30-106.

> Lists ca. 300 items bought for the Advocates' Library in 1707 from James Sutherland (1638?-1719), Professor of Botany at Edinburgh. There is a small separate index of former owners on p. 106, although provenances are not noted in the text.

Edinburgh – Royal College of Physicians of Edinburgh

Donors' book: Three early donation registers survive, covering gifts to the Library 1681-1724 (ms.19), 1699-1826 (ms.20), and 1850-1888 (ms.21).

Edinburgh – University Library

Donors' book: A register of donations was begun in 1667 by William Henderson (librarian 1667-84), with some retrospective coverage. Lists donors' names, and titles of books given, 1667-1755, with a later sequence of entries 1764-1824. This is now Edinburgh University Library ms.Da.1.31. Ms.Da.1.29 comprises a collection of 27 lists of books donated, or purchased, 1619-44, some of which are printed. Mss.Da.1.32-33 contain details of donations made by matriculating students and graduates, usually monetary sums used to buy books, between 1627 and 1696. Mss.Da.1.46 and Da.1.55-61 are a series of accession and donation registers covering the periods 1762-92, 1864-92, and 1894-1928. The University manuscript collections also include a number of early lists of particular donations to the Library.

New College Library, now the Divinity Section of Edinburgh University Library, was founded in 1843 but includes the originally separate Edinburgh Theological Library, which was created by divinity students in 1698. Its donors' book survives, now New College AA 2.2.20; it was begun in 1698, continued until 1729, then maintained patchily between 1744 and 1847 (particularly detailed for the period 1829-47). It was maintained again as a New College Library donation book, 1947-65, following the merger of the Theological Library with New College Library in the mid-1930s. Lists donors' names and titles of books given, or the values of monetary gifts.

A provenance index for the Library's printed books currently occupies nine sheaf binders, arranged in four alphabetical sequences covering different chronological periods. There is also a separate index, in the same format, for provenances of manuscripts.

Separate provenance indexes have also been compiled for two of the Library's special collections, the libraries of C. M. Grieve (Hugh McDiarmid) and Arthur Koestler; the former is not yet complete.

The Library now operates an automated cataloguing system, using a Geac computer and software. Since 1985, acquisitions for the Library's special collections (including the library of New College, Edinburgh) have been catalogued in this way, and it is hoped that retrospective cataloguing of earlier acquisitions may eventually be possible, with provenance data included in the records.

C. R. Borland: *A descriptive catalogue of the western manuscripts in Edinburgh University Library*. Edinburgh, 1916.

> The description of each manuscript includes a provenance section; provenances included in the general index.

Catalogue of the printed books in the Library of Edinburgh University. 3v. Edinburgh, 1918.

> Books which were presented to the Library often have the donor's name printed in italics at the end of the title. No other provenances are noted, and there is no index to the donors' names.

C. P. Finlayson: *Clement Litill and his library: the origins of Edinburgh University Library*. Edinburgh, 1980.

> Includes (pp. 29-59) an inventory of Litill's bequest, the foundation collection of Edinburgh University Library, with surviving books (over 200) identified. Provenances previous to Litill are noted in the text, and included in the general index.

M. C. T. Simpson: *A catalogue of the library of the Revd. James Nairn (1629-1678) bequeathed by him to Edinburgh University Library*. Edinburgh, 1990.

> Ca. 1700 items listed. Provenances noted in the text; separate provenance index.

Exhibition catalogues: Benefactors of the Library in five centuries: an exhibition of books and manuscripts selected from donations to the Library from the 16th to the 20th century. Edinburgh, 1963.

> 137 exhibits. A particularly useful catalogue of items selected specifically to illustrate major and minor donations to the Library, 1580-1958.

William Drummond of Hawthornden (1585-1649): book collector and benefactor. An exhibition of books and manuscripts from the Drummond Collection held in ... Edinburgh University Library ... November 1985-March 1986. Edinburgh, 1985.

> 88 exhibits; some provenances prior to Drummond noted in the text, but not indexed.

There to remain: treasures of Edinburgh University Library. Edinburgh, 1989.

> 70 exhibits, illustrating the growth of the Library over four centuries. Provenances noted in the text, but not indexed.

Eton – College Library

There are no provenance indexes to the printed books available at present, beyond some notebooks compiled by Robert Birley and now kept in the Library. Much information on major donations to the Library will be found in Birley's *History of College Library*, Eton, 1970.

M. R. James: *A descriptive catalogue of the manuscripts in the Library of Eton College.* Cambridge, 1895.

> Some provenances noted in the text, but not included in the index.

R. Birley: *Eton College Library: one hundred books.* Eton, 1969.

> 'One hundred interesting books in Eton College Library'. Some provenances noted in the text; index of donors.

Exhibition catalogues: P. Quarrie: *International League of Antiquarian Booksellers: an exhibition of manuscripts & printed books.* Eton, 1984.

> Donors, and some other provenances, noted in the text.

P. Quarrie: *Treasures of Eton College Library: 550 years of collecting.* New York, 1990.

> 237 exhibits, including some prints and watercolours. The catalogue of an exhibition held at the Pierpont Morgan Library in 1990. Provenances noted in the text, but not indexed.

Exeter

M. P. Crighton: *A catalogue of the medical books and manuscripts including a selection of the scientific works in Exeter Cathedral Library.* Exeter, 1934.

> Some provenances noted in the text; no index.

R. L. Bruni & D. Wyn Evans: *A catalogue of Italian books, 1471-1600, in the libraries of Exeter University, Exeter Cathedral, and the Devon and Exeter Institution.* Exeter, 1978.

> Provenances noted in the text, and included in the index.

R. L. Bruni & D. Wyn Evans: *A catalogue of Italian books, 1601-1700, in Exeter libraries.* Exeter, 1982.

> Some provenances noted in the text; no index.

Exeter – Cathedral Library

Donors' book: A donors' register for the Library (Dean & Chapter Archives, ms.3733) was begun ca. 1670, and covers gifts 1670-1709, 1760-1825. Lists donors' names, and titles of books given, or monetary sums (except for the big donation of Edward Cotton in 1676, when only the number of volumes is stated). Many of the gifts from 1770 onwards are installation fees. The register notes one more unusual gift – on 26 December 1677, 'Mr Basill Wood of this Citty gave a skeleton'.

There is not at present any comprehensive provenance index to the Library, although catalogue records created since 1978 (using the automated system at Exeter University) include details of inscriptions found in the books. A separate provenance index, on cards, is being created in the Library, which provides some coverage of material not included in the automated catalogue, but it is not likely to be complete for some years to come.

Finedon – Parish Library

J. L. H. Bailey: *A catalogue of books in the Monk's Cell Library in St. Mary's Church Finedon, Northants.* Finedon, 1979.

> Provenances noted in the text (mostly members of the Dolben family; the Library was founded by Sir J. E. Dolben in 1788). No provenance index.

Glamorgan – Fonmon Castle

M. Evans: *A catalogue of the Library at Fonmon Castle.* Cardiff, 1969.

> Separate index of 'association marks', i.e. provenance, although the inscriptions are not recorded in the text.

Glasgow – Mitchell Library

A. G. Hepburn: *Catalogue of incunables and STC books in the Mitchell Library, Glasgow.* Glasgow, 1964.

> Provenances noted in the text; separate provenance index.

Glasgow – University Library

Donors' book: All the surviving records relating to gifts to the Library down to 1727 will be found transcribed in *Munimenta Alme Universitatis Glasguensis*, Glasgow, 1854, mostly in the section 'Bibliotheca', vol. 3, pp. 403-464. The records transcribed in this section are also described in the introductory table to that volume, pp. xxvi-xxxvi. The earliest gifts recorded date from 1475. A catalogue of the Library begun in 1578 and continued into the seventeenth century is largely arranged as a series of donations (beginning with that of

Andrew Hay, 1577); this is transcribed in *Munimenta* vol. 3 p. 407 ff. The original records survive in the University Archives.

A separate donors' book was begun in 1692, and continued until ca. 1714, listing donors' names and titles of books given (or monetary sums). The original is kept in the Library as ms.Gen.1110; the contents are transcribed entire (apart from one stray later entry of 1797) in *Munimenta* vol. 3 pp. 437-451.

A later register of donations to the Library, 1845-63, is preserved as ms.Gen.1089.

It should be added that gifts to the Library down to 1710 are described in some detail in John Durkan's article, 'The early history of Glasgow University Library: 1475-1710', in *The Bibliotheck* 8 (1977), 102-126.

Several separate provenance indexes are available in the Special Collections Reading Room, mostly held in sheaf binders:

i) to printed books, outside the Hunterian Collection (23 binders, about 6600 entries, mostly covering material catalogued since 1968 but with some entries for material catalogued before then);

ii) to printed books in the Hunterian Collection (3 binders, about 950 entries);

iii) to manuscripts, including the Hunterian and other collections (2 binders, about 550 entries);

There is also a sheaf binder of rubbings of armorial bindings found in the Library, identified where possible. A separate binder indexing 'purchase details' for the Hunterian mss. gives references to the sales of particular collections at which items were acquired by Hunter.

Since 1986, all new cataloguing has been done on-line to the Library's computer; provenance information has been recorded (by extending the standard format to cope with this) but on-line retrieval of these details is not yet possible.

A typescript collection of *Notes on bindings in the Hunterian and general libraries in Glasgow University*, made by J. B. Oldham in 1938, now kept as ms.Gen.759, includes many references to provenances.

J. Young & P. H. Aitken: *A catalogue of the manuscripts in the Library of the Hunterian Museum in the University of Glasgow*. Glasgow, 1908.

> Provenances are noted in the text, but not indexed.

Exhibition catalogues: Three Glasgow book collectors. William Ewing, 1788-1874, John Ferguson, 1837-1916, David Murray, 1842-1928. An exhibition of books and manuscripts held in the Hunterian Library, University of Glasgow, November 1969. Glasgow, 1969.

> 116 exhibits; some provenances prior to Ewing, Ferguson and Murray noted in the text, but not indexed.

British bookbindings 16th-19th century. An exhibition held in the Hunterian Library. Glasgow, 1970.

> 108 items. Some provenances noted in the text, but not indexed.

J. Baldwin: *William Hunter, 1718-1783: book collector. Catalogue of an exhibition … Glasgow University Library 14 April-30 September 1983.* Glasgow, 1983.

> 76 exhibits; some provenances noted in the text, but not indexed.

N. Thorp: *The glory of the page: medieval & renaissance illuminated manuscripts from Glasgow University Library*. London, 1987.

> 143 items. The entry for each manuscript includes a separate provenance section; separate indexes (V and VI) cover private and corporate owners.

Gloucester – Cathedral Library

Donors' book: A benefactors' books (Cathedral Library ms.71) was begun in 1658, shortly after the Library's refoundation during the Commonwealth period, and continued in use until 1740. Lists donors' names, and titles of books given.

S. M. Eward: *Catalogue of Gloucester Cathedral Library*. Gloucester, 1972.

> Donors (only) noted in the text; not indexed.

Grantham – Trigge Library

J. Glenn & D. Walsh: *Catalogue of the Francis Trigge chained library, St. Wulfram's Church, Grantham*. Cambridge, 1988.

> Provenances noted in the text; separate provenance index.

Guildford – Grammar School Library

Donors' book: A list of names of donors to the Library, 1574-1745, is given in the footnotes on pp. 76-77 of O. Manning & W. Bray, *The history and antiquities of the county of Surrey*, vol. 1, London, 1804; the information found there is incorporated in the donors' index of the Woodward & Christophers catalogue below.

G. Woodward & R. A. Christophers: *The chained library of the Royal Grammar School, Guildford: catalogue*. Guildford, 1972.

> Provenances recorded in the text; separate provenance index.

Hatfield, Essex – Parish Library

B. S. Pugh: *St. Mary's Church Library, Hatfield Broad Oak: catalogue*. Hatfield Broad Oak, 1984.

> Donors recorded where known.

Hereford – All Saints' Church

F. C. Morgan: *Catalogue of the books in All Saints' Church, Hereford bequeathed by Dr. William Brewster (1655-1715)*. 1963. Typescript copy available in Hereford, and in the British Library at Cup.504.f.8.

> Provenances noted in the text; separate index at the beginning of 'names of donors and owners of books before William Brewster'.

Hereford – Cathedral Library

Donors' book: A register of donors was begun in 1611 and continued in use to the end of the nineteenth century. Arranged alphabetically by surnames; lists donors' names, and titles of books given. Coverage is retrospective back to the medieval period, although information on gifts before 1611 is not wholly reliable. The Vicars Choral Library, now amalgamated with the Cathedral Library, has its own donors' book, begun ca. 1620 and continued down to 1767, listing donors' names and titles of books given. This is partly transcribed in F. C. Morgan's pamphlet (see below).

A donors' index on cards (one box) covers all the Library's early printed books. Penelope Morgan compiled a complete list of all the printed books in the Library, arranged in order of accession, from 1475 to 1980, in two large notebooks – donors' names are included. There is not at present any index covering owners who were not donors.

A. T. Bannister: *A descriptive catalogue of the manuscripts in the Hereford Cathedral Library*. Hereford, 1927.

> Provenances noted in the text; separate indexes of owners and donors.

F. C. Morgan: *Hereford Cathedral: the Vicars Choral Library*. Hereford, 1958.

> As well as describing the history of the Library (now part of Hereford Cathedral Library), this pamphlet includes a transcript of the donors' book, ca. 1660-1767, giving the present shelfmarks of items still in the collection today, and biographical details of the donors.

Ipswich – Town Library

Donors' book: Begun in 1615 and continued in use to 1767; includes retrospective coverage back to the foundation of the Library in 1599. Lists donors' names and titles of books given, or values of monetary gifts. John Blatchly's account of the Library (see below) includes extensive analysis of the Benefactors' Book.

J. Blatchly: *The Town Library of Ipswich: a history and catalogue*. Woodbridge, 1989.

> Provenances noted in the text; separate indexes of donors and of former owners of the books.

King's Lynn – St. Margaret's Church Library

Donors' book: The Library was founded ca. 1619 and a benefactors' register was begun in 1641, listing gifts retrospectively back to 1631. Includes donors' names, and titles of books given; continued in use until 1835. The register is described and illustrated in T. E. Maw, 'The church libraries of King's Lynn', *The Antiquary* 40 (1904), 235-40; it is now kept, together with the surviving books from the Library, in King's Lynn Central Library.

Knutsford – Tatton Park

S. Pargeter: *A catalogue of the Library at Tatton Park, Knutsford, Cheshire*. Chester, 1977.

> Some provenances noted in the text; no index. The Library was built up by the Egerton family, 1598-1958, and is now administered by the National Trust.

Lampeter – St. David's College (University of Wales)

B. L. James: *A catalogue of the tract collection of St. David's University College, Lampeter*. London, 1975.

> Some provenances noted in the text; no provenance index.

Langley – The Kederminster Library

F. C. Heward: *Catalogue of the Kederminster Library adjoining the church of St. Mary the Virgin, Langley Marish, Buckinghamshire*. 1953. Typescript copy in the British Library at 11918.m.19.

> Some provenances noted in the text, but not indexed.

Leeds – University Library

A provenance index on cards is maintained for pre-1801 English books in the Brotherton Collection; this covers all material acquired since October 1952, but only a small number of items received before then. The index currently includes about 2000 names, found in about 3000 books.

A provenance index has been started for the Special Collections, but it is a fairly recent development and coverage is very incomplete.

An index to verse in the Brotherton Collection's seventeenth- and eighteenth-century manuscripts is currently being compiled, and provenance details are being recorded; this information is held on an automated database.

It should be added that the Library staff will often be able to supply information on the previous ownership of many of the printed books and manuscripts which do not have formal entries in the provenance index.

Leicester – Town Library

Donors' book: An account of the Library was printed in J. Nichols, *The history and antiquities of the county of Leicester*, London, 1815, vol. I pt. 2, pp. 505-10. This includes extensive extracts from a donors' register, now lost, covering gifts from the foundation of the Library down to 1743, listing donors' names and titles of books given.

C. Deedes et al: *The Old Town Hall Library at Leicester: a catalogue*. Oxford, 1919.

> Provenances noted in the text, but not indexed.

Lichfield – Cathedral Library

A provenance index for the printed books is currently being prepared by Dr. B. S. Benedikz and the Revd. Dr. E. C. C. Hill. The project has been delayed by Dr. Hill's death, but it is hoped that it will be completed by 1994. (Enquiries to Dr. Benedikz, at Birmingham University Library.)

B. S. Benedikz: *Lichfield Cathedral Library: a catalogue of the Cathedral Library manuscripts.* 3rd edn. Birmingham, 1986.

> The description of each manuscript includes a provenance section. No provenance index.

Lincoln – Cathedral Library

R. M. Thomson: *Catalogue of the manuscripts of Lincoln Cathedral Chapter Library.* Woodbridge, 1989.

> Provenances noted in the text; separate index of 'Manuscripts, owners, donors, scribes, and annotators'. This supersedes the earlier catalogue of Lincoln manuscripts by R. M. Woolley (1927).

C. Hurst: *Catalogue of the Wren Library of Lincoln Cathedral: books printed before 1801.* Cambridge, 1982.

> Only books bearing Michael Honywood's ownership monogram are noted.

Liverpool – Cathedral Library

D. F. Cook: *Liverpool Cathedral – Radcliffe Library. Short title catalogue of books printed before 1801.* Liverpool, 1968.

> A few provenances noted in the text; no provenance index.

Liverpool – University Library

A provenance index on cards was begun in the early 1970s, and includes printed books and manuscripts acquired since then, with some coverage of earlier acquisitions. The index presently covers about a third of the Library's Special Collections, and occupies 6 catalogue drawers.

London – British Architectural Library (Royal Institute of British Architects)

A provenance index on cards, covering about half the stock of pre-1841 printed books, is available in the Library. A computerised cataloguing project is presently under way, which will cover all pre-1841 material. All inscriptions, bookplates, etc. are being recorded in the copy notes and this information will eventually be available through a published catalogue; it is hoped that this will include a provenance index. The catalogue is being issued in parts and the first instalment (*Early printed books 1478-1840: a catalogue of the British Architectural Library's early imprints collection*, vol. 1 (A-D)) is scheduled for 1994.

London – British Library

Donors' book: A vellum register of donations to the British Museum was begun in 1756. It was used to record gifts of all kinds, including books and manuscripts, and it continued in use until 1823. Thereafter a series of donation registers was kept, entitled 'Donations' until 1861, and 'Books of Presents' from 1862 onwards; the series continued down to 1973 (when a new filing system was introduced). Early volumes cover several years each; from 1875 onwards there is a separate volume for each year.

The Books of Presents record all gifts made to the Museum, except very minor ones. Each volume has an index of donors' names. Small gifts of books and manuscripts are usually described at individual item level; for larger gifts, only an indication of the size of the collection is given.

Additional information on major donations can sometimes be found in the Minutes of the Trustees (all gifts were reported at trustees' meetings), and in the volumes of Original papers relating to those meetings.

Although the British Library is now a distinct organisation, having been separated from the British Museum in 1973, the records of the Museum Trustees and Director's Office which relate to the Library before that date are maintained by the Museum, and enquiries relating to these documents should be directed to the Museum Archivist.

Edward Edwards's *Lives of the founders of the British Museum: with notices of its chief augmentors and other benefactors 1570-1870* (London, 1870) is an account of the growth of the Library (and other parts of the Museum collections) focussing on the owners and donors of the major collections received before 1870.

Manuscripts – The western manuscripts in the British Library are broken down into a number of named sequences, with major foundation collections (e.g. Cotton, Sloane) kept together, and the bulk of the general accessions outside these collections incorporated into a growing sequence of Additional manuscripts. The different collections and their major catalogues are summarised in M. A. E. Nickson, *The British Library: guide to the catalogues and indexes of the Department of Manuscripts*, 2nd edn, London, 1982, although this is now partly out of date (see the marked-up copy in the Manuscript Students' Room).

Various printed catalogues describing different collections have been published since the beginning of the nineteenth century. The Additional Manuscripts are described in a series of *Catalogues of additions to the manuscripts*, which began in 1843 and is still in progress. All these published catalogues include provenance information on the manuscripts covered, although the quality and fullness of the details varies considerably, depending on the date of compilation. An amalgamated index, created by interfiling the index sequences of the various published catalogues, has been issued:

Index of manuscripts in the British Library. 10v. Cambridge, 1984-86.

Former owners of manuscripts have entries to the extent that they are included in the textual descriptions in the published catalogues. The amalgamated *Index* covers collections acquired before 1950. There are two further published catalogues covering additions 1951-55, and 1986-90.

Manuscripts acquired since 1956 (e.g. Additional Mss.48989 onwards) are described in a series of binders kept in the Manuscript Students' Room, where an index to those descriptions, on cards, is also available.

The indexes to the separate printed catalogues include subject entries which were not reprinted in the amalgamated *Index*. These entries, which are available in an interfiled card index in the Department of Manuscripts ('Supplement to the subject catalogues'), include a number of sequences which may be useful, e.g. Bookplates and bookstamps.

The Class-catalogue of manuscripts, a subject index to the manuscript collections compiled 1867-73 with later additions, has a section on owners (corporate and individual), and donors (9 vols., class catalogue 102-104). It is made up of pasted-up slips taken from the descriptions of the mss. published in printed catalogues. Most, but not all, of the information it contains will be found in the amalgamated *Index*; the exceptions relate to collections with old printed catalogues whose indexing is less full than that found in later catalogues.

Printed books – The catalogue of printed books, most easily accessible in printed form as *The British Library general catalogue of printed books down to 1975* (London, 1979), includes some information on the provenance of particular items, but the great majority of entries include no provenance data. Notes were sometimes made to indicate autograph signatures, annotations, bookplates or armorial stamps of noteworthy collectors or scholars, but the guidelines for adding such notes were always highly selective, and subjective in interpretation. Occasionally added entries were included under the names of the owners or annotators, but this is usually not the case, and the user should be cautious of thinking that a sequence of entries for books owned by an individual is a comprehensive index of items thus noted in the *Catalogue* – the entry for Etienne Baluze, for example, includes a number of books owned by Baluze, but there are books noted in the *Catalogue* as having Baluze's signature which are not included in this list at the Baluze heading. There is no easy way of retrieving the provenance data from the printed catalogue (but see R. C. Alston's *Books with manuscript* listed below). Since 1975, new acquisitions have been listed in the automated catalogue which is available in the reading rooms and via BLAISE, but provenance data is not generally recorded and this continues to be an area of low priority in cataloguing policy.

The catalogue has been issued on CD-ROM (*The British Library general catalogue of books to 1975 on CD-ROM*, 1991) and this facilitates fuller retrieval of provenance information, using the keyword function. A search on au=baluze will find the books owned by Baluze which have added entries under Baluze in the printed catalogue, but a search on kw = baluze will find *both* those books and the other books which are noted as having Baluze's inscription but which are not given printed added entries under Baluze. The CD therefore offers a slight advance on the printed catalogue, but the fundamental problem remains that the great majority of records include no provenance information to retrieve.

In addition to the guides to the British Library's holdings that are either published or on open access in reading rooms, there are numerous lists and indexes which provide provenance details on parts of the collections, often compiled as working tools for staff and kept behind the public areas, but available to readers on request. Their scope is limited in all cases, but they may offer useful information which cannot be gleaned from other sources. A handlist of these indexes has been published:

R. C. Alston: *Handlist of unpublished finding aids to the London collections of the British Library*. London, 1991.

A. G. Watson: *Catalogue of dated and dateable manuscripts c. 700-1600 in the Department of Manuscripts, the British Library*. 2v. London, 1979.

> Provenances noted in the text; there is a separate name index which includes scribes and illuminators as well as owners.

C. E. Wright: *Fontes Harleianae. A study of the sources of the Harleian collection of mss. preserved in the Department of Manuscripts in the British Museum*. London, 1972.

> Comprises a detailed provenance index to the Harleian collection, with dates and biographical information. See also his 'Manuscripts of Italian provenance in the Harleian collection ... their sources, associations and channels of acquisition', in C. H. Clough (ed.): *Cultural aspects of the Italian renaissance: essays in honour of Paul Oskar Kristeller*, Manchester, 1976, pp. 462-484; and A. G. Watson's review of the main work in the *Journal of the Society of Archivists* 4 (1973), 603-9, which lists various corrections and additions.

A. Gould: *Named special collections in the Department of Printed Books [of the British Library, Humanities & Social Sciences]*. (Reader Guide no. 9, available free in the Reading Room.) London, 1981.

> A list of collections, both large and small, associated with particular individuals and still kept together in the Library. Arranged alphabetically by collector, with pressmarks of the collections or their catalogues.

R. C. Alston: *Books with manuscript: a short-title catalogue of books with manuscript notes in the British Library*. London, 1993.

> Created by extracting entries from the automated file of the *General catalogue* to 1975 which include notes relating to adversaria and manuscript additions. In part, therefore, an index to the provenance data included in GK, but not by any means a comprehensive catalogue of all the books on the British Library's shelves which might qualify for inclusion in such a listing.

Catalogue of books printed in the XVth century now in the British Museum. London, 1908-

> 11 parts have now been issued, covering books printed in most of Europe but not England; work is continuing on the remaining parts. Provenances are noted in the text, but not indexed (but see following item).

L. G. Clark: *Collectors and owners of incunabula in the British Museum: index of provenances for books printed in France, Holland and Belgium*. Bath, 1962.

> Lists inscriptions, bookplates, etc., giving brief biographical details where possible, and references to the main incunabula catalogue described in the preceding entry. Mrs. Clark also prepared provenance indexes to the Italian and German incunabula in the BL; these have never been published, but are held on slips, and can be examined on request.

A. E. C. Simoni: *Catalogue of books from the Low Countries 1601-21 in the British Library*. London, 1990.

> Provenances noted in the text and included in the general index (owners are denoted with asterisks in the index).

W. H. Weale: *Early stamped bookbindings in the British Museum: description of 385 blind-stamped bindings of the XIIth-XVth centuries*. London, 1922.

> Some provenances (mostly institutional) noted in the text; no index.

Three hundred notable books added to the Library of the British Museum under the Keepership of Richard Garnett. Edinburgh, 1899.

> Some provenances noted in the text, but not included in the index.

J. T. Payne & H. Foss: *Bibliotheca Grenvilliana; or, bibliographical notices of rare and curious books, forming part of the library of the Right Hon. Thomas Grenville*. 3v. London, 1842-72.

> Some provenances noted in the text, but not included in the indexes. The collection was bequeathed to the British Museum in 1846, and one of the British Library's copies of the catalogue (on open access at NL 21.c) is mounted and marked up with the present-day pressmarks.

M. M. Foot: *The Henry Davis gift: a collection of bookbindings*.
Vol. I *Studies in the history of bookbinding*. London, 1978.
Vol. II *A catalogue of north-European bindings*. London, 1983.
[Vol. III *South-European bindings*, yet to be published]

> Provenances noted in the text; separate indexes of owners.

T. A. Birrell: *The library of John Morris: the reconstruction of a seventeenth-century collection*. London, 1976.

> Morris's library of ca. 1500 volumes, collected mostly in the second quarter of the seventeenth century, passed into the Royal Library in 1661 and thence became part of the British Library. Professor Birrell's catalogue identifies the 1300 or so items still in the Library today, noting provenances prior to Morris in the text. Morris books which have been traced outside the BL are also listed, with their ownership history given as extensively as possible. There is a separate index of owners at the end.

G. M. Kahrl & D. Anderson: *The Garrick collection of old English plays. A catalogue with an historical introduction*. London, 1982.

> Provenances noted in the text; separate provenance index, with some biographical notes, at Appendix A.

London – College of Arms

L. Campbell & F. Steer: *A catalogue of manuscripts in the College of Arms collections.* Volume 1. London, 1988.

> Covers the older sections of the College's manuscript holdings (i.e. those which have been in the College since the seventeenth century or earlier). Provenances noted in the text; separate index of 'owners, scribes and annotators', with biographical notes.

F. Jones: *A catalogue of Welsh manuscripts in the College of Arms.* London, 1988.

> Provenances noted in the text, but not generally included in the index, unless owners were scribes, or donors to the College.

London – Doctor Williams's Library

Donors' book: A benefactors' register was begun in 1730 and continued in use until 1886. Lists donors' names, and titles of books given; also details of monetary gifts and the books subsequently purchased.

London – Dulwich College

Donors' book: there is no donors' book as such. An early manuscript catalogue of the Library, begun in 1729 and continued to 1832 as further books were acquired, includes details of some eighteenth- and early nineteenth-century gifts, interspersed in the general sequence.

London – Inner Temple Library

J. Conway Davies: *Catalogue of manuscripts in the Library of the Honourable Society of the Inner Temple.* 3v. Oxford, 1972.

> Provenances noted in the text and included in the general index. Appendix III in vol. 3 (pp. 1341-2) comprises a table of donors of miscellaneous mss, and the extensive introduction in vol. 1 includes a section on some of these donors (vol. 1, pp. 80-101), with biographical details.

London – Lambeth Palace Library

There is no separate provenance index. The author catalogue for the printed books (on cards) includes a limited amount of provenance information; where a book can be identified as having come from the collection of a particular archbishop (usually because his arms are stamped on the covers), this is noted on the card. Until recently, other provenances and inscriptions in the books were not noted, but such information is now being added to the cards and should be found on recently created catalogue entries. There is, however, no way of recovering the provenance information other than reading through the card catalogue. Plans for computerization include a field for the indexing of provenance.

M. R. James & C. Jenkins: *A descriptive catalogue of the manuscripts in the Library of Lambeth Palace*. Cambridge, 1930.

> Former owners and donors noted. No separate provenance index, but names of previous owners are included in the general index.

S. R. Maitland: *A list of some of the early printed books in the Archiepiscopal Library at Lambeth*. London, 1843.

> Covers continental and English books, 1460-1520, and English books 1520-1550. Some provenances noted in the text, but not indexed.

London – Leathersellers' Company Library

W. H. Black: *Bibliothecae Colfanae catalogus. Catalogue of the library in the free grammar-school at Lewisham*. London, 1831.

> Donors (only) noted in the text, and separately listed in Appendix IV on pp. xliv-xlvi. The library has been transferred from Colfe's School to Leathersellers' Hall, and requests for access should be directed to the Clerk there.

London – Lincoln's Inn Library

An appreciable proportion of the Library's early printed books have been recatalogued using an automated system, and provenances have been recorded.

J. Hunter: *A catalogue of the manuscripts in the Library of the Honourable Society of Lincoln's Inn*. London, 1838.

> Some provenances noted in the text, but not indexed. A copy of this catalogue, kept in the Library, has been annotated with some additional provenance information, and typescript descriptions of mss added since 1838 have been added, together with an index to the whole. A photocopy of this augmented copy has been deposited with the National Register of Archives.

London – National Art Library (Victoria & Albert Museum)

The recataloguing of the Library's special collections, in automated format, began in 1991 with the Clements Collection of armorial bindings. Since then, work has begun on other parts of the stock. Provenances are thoroughly recorded and are searchable through the Online Catalogue in the Reading Room. The catalogue entries also include indexed genre and physical features headings for different kinds of provenance evidence, so it is possible to search for e.g. book-plates of a certain century or date, as a group.

The draft Catalogue of Illuminated Manuscripts in the Library (compiled in 1957) is a typescript which is available in the Reading Room. The description of each manuscript includes a provenance section, but there is no index. The Bindings Collection is listed on a series of separate cards, with photographs, and the descriptive text in each case includes a provenance section, but again there is no index. The cards are available to readers on request.

A handlist of the contents of the Clements Collection is available, in which the names of the owners (as identified from the armorials – other provenances are not noted) are interfiled with the names of the authors of the books in one alphabetical sequence. See also D. Woodfield, *An ordinary of British armorial bookbindings in the Clements Collection*, 1963, and the further information on the Clements Collection in chapter IV above. The recataloguing work on this collection will supersede these older resources in due course.

Dyce Collection. A catalogue of the printed books and manuscripts bequeathed by the Reverend Alexander Dyce. 2v. London, 1875.

> Some provenances noted in the text, but not indexed.

Forster Collection. A catalogue of the printed books bequeathed by John Forster. London, 1888.

> Some provenances noted in the text, but only selectively included in the index.

R. F. Sketchley worked through the Dyce and Forster collections in the late nineteenth century using interleaved copies of the published catalogues, which he annotated copiously with provenance information not included in the printed text. Sketchley's copies are available on request. There is also a separate manuscript volume of indexes to these collections, compiled in the late nineteenth century, and presently kept in the Reading Room with the Dyce and Forster catalogues (labelled 'Dyce & Forster Collns. – Indices, various'). This includes indexes of 'autographs, autograph inscriptions and mss notes', and 'bookplates'.

London – National Maritime Museum Library

The Rare Book Collection of the Museum spans the years 1474 to 1850 and consists of approximately 7500 volumes. The entire Library of over 100,000 volumes has been recatalogued onto computer and is now available via two OPAC terminals situated in the Library. All inscriptions, signatures and bookplates have been noted in the catalogue and access to names listed is possible by keyword search.

London – Royal College of Physicians

The Library maintains several special indexes relating to provenance, held on cards; these cover the whole collection, not only antiquarian material:
i) autographs in books (6 drawers);
ii) bookplates in books (1 drawer; also separate catalogue for the Horace Barlow bookplate collection);
iii) association copies (1 drawer);
iv) bindings (1 drawer; largely armorial and other ownership stamps).

London – Royal College of Surgeons

A provenance index was begun in the 1930s, but has never been completed; the Library's manuscript collections include several lists of books bequeathed by individual benefactors.

London – Royal Society Library

Donors' book: A donations register begun in the eighteenth century (Ms.416), intended to be a comprehensive record of all objects given to the Society, is missing the sections on books and manuscripts (they may never have been compiled). Donations of books 1660-87 are recorded in Birch's *History of the Royal Society*, 1757 (embedded in the main text of the proceedings); donations 1769-1869 were printed in the *Philosophical transactions* for those years, and after 1869 in other Society journals. The Society's pre-1800 collections have been seriously depleted by a series of sales of non-scientific books.

R. F. Sharp & H. M. Mayhew: *Catalogue of a collection of early printed books in the Library of the Royal Society*. London, 1910.

> Some provenances noted in the text (particularly books from the library of Bilibald Pirckheimer), but not indexed. All the books in this catalogue were sold at Sotheby's, 4 May 1925; the sale catalogue contains a fuller record of provenances than the Sharp and Mayhew catalogue.

London – St. Paul's Cathedral

Donors' book: A donors' register (37.B.10) was begun in 1708; it records gifts, and some purchases, 1708-83 and 1862-75. A new register was begun in 1875, which has remained continuously in use to the present day. Donors' names, and titles of books given, are included. Much of the earlier register is taken up with details of Henry Compton's bequest (1713).

London – Sion College

Donors' book: Begun in 1629; lists benefactions to the Library from the College's foundation in 1624 down to the present day. Includes donors' names, and titles of books given; also lists books purchased with monetary gifts, where appropriate. The Library's entry in the *Directory of rare book and special collections* (1985) noted major benefactions, and the relevant page numbers in the Donors' Book.

W. Reading: *Bibliothecae cleri Londinensis in Collegio Sionensi catalogus*. London, 1724.

> A classified catalogue of the Library as it stood in 1724. The names of the donors of the books, when known, is added at the end of each entry; books given by major benefactors are signified by initials only, e.g. J.L. (John Lawson), E.W. (Edward Waple).

London – Society of Antiquaries

Donors' book: There are two separate donations registers covering gifts to the Library 1848-65, and 1865-77. In addition, gifts to the Library are recorded in the minutes of the Society's meetings, kept from the foundation in 1717 onwards. From 1782-1846 library gifts are printed in *Archaeologia* (vols. 6-31), from 1843 onwards they are printed in the *Proceedings of the Society of Antiquaries of London*. All these sources list donors' names, and titles of books given.

A card index (half a drawer) of bookplates found in books in the library is available; this does not cover the collection systematically, but includes bookplates which have been noticed in the course of recent cataloguing.

J. F. Clayton: Incunabula in the Library of the Society of Antiquaries of London: a handlist. *The Antiquaries Journal* 60 (1980), 308-319.

> Provenances noted in the text; separate index of donors (which does not include owners who were not donors).

London – University College

D. K. Coveney: *A descriptive catalogue of manuscripts in the library of University College, London*. London, 1935.

> Provenances noted in the text and included in the general index.

London – University Library

M. Canney & D. Knott: *University of London Library: catalogue of the Goldsmiths' Library of economic literature.*
Vol. 1: *Printed books to 1800*
Vol. 3: *Additions; manuscripts*
Vol. 4: *Index*
London, 1970-83.

> A few printed book provenances are noted in the text; the provenance of manuscripts is recorded more thoroughly. Provenances are not indexed.

The Sterling Library: a catalogue of the printed books and literary manuscripts collected by Sir Louis Sterling ... and presented by him to the University of London. [Cambridge], 1954.

> Provenances noted in the text, but not included in the index.

Exhibition catalogue: R. A. Rye & M. S. Quinn: *University of London: historical and armorial bookbindings exhibited in the University Library*. London, 1937.

> 83 items. A mixture of European fine bindings, 15th-19th centuries, and armorial bindings. Some provenances noted in the text, but not indexed.

London – Wellcome Institute for the History of Medicine Library

S. A. J. Moorat: *Catalogue of the western manuscripts on medicine and science in the Wellcome Historical Medical Library.*

I *Mss. written before 1650*
II *Mss. written after 1650*
London, 1962-73.

> Provenances noted in the text; separate indexes of owners, bookplates, etc.

F. N. L. Poynter: *A catalogue of incunabula in the Wellcome Historical Medical Library.*
London, 1954.

> Provenances noted in the text; separate index of signatures, and other marks of ownership.

A catalogue of printed books in the Wellcome Historical Medical Library.
I *Books printed before 1641.* London, 1962.
II *Books printed from 1641 to 1850. A-E.* London, 1966.
III *Books printed from 1641 to 1850. F-L.* London, 1976.
[Further parts yet to be published]

> Some provenances noted in the text, but not indexed.

London – Westminster Abbey

Donors' book: A benefactors' register was begun ca. 1650, with retrospective coverage back to 1623; it continued in use until 1750, with one later entry in 1911. Lists donors' names, and titles of books given; also the titles of books purchased with monetary gifts. A typescript summary of names, dates and gifts is kept with the register.

A provenance index on cards, which covers most of the Library, is available for consultation on application to the Library staff.

J. A. Robinson & M. R. James: *The manuscripts of Westminster Abbey.* Cambridge, 1909.

> Provenances noted in the text and included in general index I.

H. M. Nixon: *British bookbindings presented by Kenneth H. Oldaker to the Chapter Library of Westminster Abbey.* London, 1982.

> Provenances noted in the text, and included in the general index. The collection comprises 71 items, mostly dating from the middle of the eighteenth to the early twentieth century.

Manchester – Chetham's Library

Donors' book: A benefactions register was begun in 1694 and continued in use to 1853 (later gifts are recorded elsewhere). Lists donors' names, and titles of books given; also artefacts and curiosities given to the Library, such as shells, coins, and the tail of a rattlesnake.

A catalogue of the Library of the late John Byrom ... preserved at Kelsall Cell, Lancashire.
London, 1848.

> A catalogue of Byrom's collection with a few notable provenances noted in the text, but no separate provenance index. The collection was presented to Chetham's Library in 1870.

Manchester – John Rylands University Library

The John Rylands Library, founded at the end of the nineteenth century as a memorial to the Manchester merchant of that name, was merged with Manchester University Library in 1972. The Special Collections now comprise the combined wealth of the two libraries, including the Althorp Library of Earl Spencer and subsequent accretions (from the John Rylands Library), and a number of large and small collections from the University Library.

Partial access to provenances in the (pre-1972) John Rylands collections is provided by a series of indexes in sheaf binders: autographs and inscriptions (1 binder); book-plates (2 binders); armorial bindings (1 binder); illuminated arms in printed books (1 binder). Coverage is selective and incomplete in all these cases. The special collections originally belonging to the University, except the Christie Collection (which has its own printed catalogue, see below) are covered by a card catalogue. Provenances are sometimes noted on the entries but there is a separate card index (4 drawers, labelled University Manuscripts) which includes some cards for inscriptions and bookplates found in special collections printed books.

M. R. James: *A descriptive catalogue of the Latin manuscripts in the John Rylands Library at Manchester.* 2v. Manchester, 1921.

> Provenances noted in the text, and included in the index of 'place names, proper names, saints'.

M. Tyson: *Hand-list of the collection of English manuscripts in the John Rylands Library, 1928. (Bulletin of the John Rylands Library* 13 no. 1, 1929). Manchester, 1929.

> Provenances noted in the text and included in the general index. There are supplements, by M. Tyson and F. Taylor, covering the accession periods 1928-35 and 1937-51, published in 1935 and 1951.

C. W. E. Leigh: *Catalogue of the Christie collection ... bequeathed to the Library of the University of Manchester.* Manchester, 1915.

> Some provenances noted in the text; separate provenance index.

E. M. Parkinson & A. E. Lumb: *Catalogue of medical books in Manchester University Library 1480-1700.* Manchester, 1972.

> Some provenances noted in the text; no provenance index. This covers only the holdings of the University Library before the merger of 1972, not including the John Rylands Library.

More, Shropshire – Parish Library

C. Condren: More Parish Library, Salop. *Library History* 7 (1987), 141-162.

> A catalogue of the Library (238 items) is followed by an 'index of owners, donors and readers'.

Newcastle – City Library

J. C. Day: *A short title catalogue of books ... printed before 1701 in the Thomlinson Collection,*

Newcastle upon Tyne Central Library. Thesis submitted for Fellowship of the Library Association, 1970.

> Provenances noted in the text; no index.

Newcastle – University Library

W. S. Mitchell: *A list of the post-incunabula in the University Library, Newcastle upon Tyne.* Newcastle, 1965.

> Covers STC material 1501-1640, and continental material 1501-1600. Provenances noted in the text, but not indexed.

J. S. Emmerson: *Catalogue of the Pybus Collection of medical books … held in the University Library, Newcastle upon Tyne.* Manchester, 1981.

> Provenances noted in the text; separate provenance index.

[Appleby Grammar School Library] – A list of donors to the Library, 1739-1800, transcribed from contemporary parchment rolls which were originally displayed in the school, is printed in R. E. Leach, Transcript of old parchment rolls of benefactors to Appleby School Library, *Transactions of the Cumberland and Westmorland Antiquarian and Archaeological Society* 13 (1895), 20-36. The gifts are mostly monetary ones made by pupils when leaving the school.

E. Hinchcliffe: *Catalogue of the Bainbrigg Library of Appleby Grammar School.* Newcastle, 1977.

> Provenances noted in the text; separate provenance index. The Library was deposited at Newcastle in 1966.

[Kepier School Library] – R. W. Ramsey: Kepier School, Houghton-le-Spring, and its library. *Archaeologia Aeliana* n.s. 3 vol. 3 (1907), 306-333.

> Includes at end a list of books printed before 1600, which notes inscriptions in the books, and a list of provenances found in books printed after 1600. Kepier School was founded in 1574 and its Library was substantially augmented by the bequest of Thomas Griffith in 1776. The collection is now housed in Newcastle University Library.

[St. Bees School Library] – Manuscript catalogue entries, including provenance information, have been prepared for the books in this collection, which was acquired at Newcastle in 1966; these are available on application to the Special Collections staff. A *donors' register*, arranged as an alphabetical catalogue with donors' names added after the titles of the books, was begun in ca. 1690 and continued in use until 1737. It was acquired by W. A. Jackson in the nineteenth century and is now part of the Jackson Library in the Local Studies Collection of Carlisle Public Library (shelfmark M368).

Norwich – City Library

Donors' book: Now Ms.4228 in the Norfolk Record Office (at the Central Library, Norwich). Begun in 1608, when the Library was founded, and continued in use until 1737.

David Stoker's article 'Doctor Collinges and the revival of Norwich City

Library, 1657-1664', *Library History* 5 (1980), 73-84, includes a list of books purchased, sold and exchanged 1657-64, with the names of donors and buyers.

F. Kitton: *A catalogue of the books in the Library of the City of Norwich in the year 1883.* Norwich, 1883.

> The text of the catalogue is preceded by an alphabetical list of donors to the Library, with dates, although the books given are not identified.

Oscott – St. Mary's College

Recusant books at St. Mary's, Oscott 1518-1830. New Oscott, 1964-66.

> Some provenances noted in the text; no provenance index.

G. F. Pullen: *Catalogue of the Bible collection in the Old Library at St. Mary's, Oscott c. 1472-c. 1850.* New Oscott, 1971.

> Provenances noted in the text, but not indexed. Covers not only Biblical texts, but also commentaries, concordances, and other works relevant to Biblical scholarship.

Oxford

Paul Morgan's guide to *Oxford libraries outside the Bodleian* (see p. 185 above), which gives brief descriptions of the histories and holdings of the college and departmental libraries, contains a great deal of information about the major benefactors, upon whose gifts of books the growth of the college libraries has largely depended.

H. O. Coxe: *Catalogus codicum mss. qui in collegiis aulisque Oxoniensibus hodie adseverantur.* 2v. Oxford, 1852. (Vol. 1 reprinted, Wakefield, 1972.)

> Covers all the Oxford colleges founded before 1852, except Christ Church and Pembroke. Text in Latin; still the only source for descriptions of most of the manuscripts in the Oxford colleges. Provenances noted in the text, and included in the general index in vol. 2; there is also a separate list of 'Nomina benefactorum' at the beginning of each college's section of the catalogue.

J. J. G. Alexander & E. Temple: *Illuminated manuscripts in Oxford College libraries, the University archives, and the Taylor Institution.* Oxford, 1985.

> The description of each manuscript includes a provenance section; separate provenance index.

A. G. Watson: *Catalogue of dated and dateable manuscripts c. 435-1600 in Oxford libraries.* 2v. Oxford, 1984.

> Covers manuscripts in the Bodleian Library and the Oxford colleges. Provenances down to 1600 noted in the text, and included in the name index (which also includes scribes and illuminators).

D. E. Rhodes: *A catalogue of incunabula in all the libraries of Oxford University outside the Bodleian.* Oxford, 1982.

> Owners and donors noted in the text; separate provenance index, with biographical details and dates where possible.

Oxford – All Souls College

Donors' book: a donors' register was begun in 1604 (now L.R.5.l.10), covering benefactions retrospectively to the middle of the fifteenth century. Used exclusively for gifts to the Library 1604-41, but after 1660 it became a list of gifts of all kinds made to the college; continued in use into the 1960s. Lists donors' names and titles of books given, also has details of books bought for the college in the first half of the seventeenth century; a few later lists of books given are also included. There is an index at the end. Donations down to 1600 are chronicled in N. R. Ker, *Records of All Souls College Library* (Oxford Bibliographical Society Publication, new series 16), Oxford, 1971.

Oxford – Balliol College

Donors' book: The donors' register was begun in the seventeenth century, covering benefactions retrospectively to 1419, and beginning with lists of books of unknown origin. Covers the period 1419-1841, with donors' names and titles of books given. Includes an index of names.

R. A. B. Mynors: *Catalogue of the manuscripts of Balliol College, Oxford.* Oxford, 1963.

Provenances noted in the text; separate index of owners, donors and pledgers.

Oxford – Bodleian Library

Donors' book: A register of benefactors was begun in 1600, on the instructions of Sir Thomas Bodley, and it was used to record gifts to the Library (donors' names and titles of books given, or books bought with money given) from then until 1688. A second volume of the register was then begun, which covers the period 1688-1794. The first 90 pages of the first volume (covering 1600-04) are printed, the remainder is manuscript. Each volume has an index of donors' names; the second volume is less comprehensive in its coverage than the first. A microfilm copy of the register is available on open access in Duke Humfrey's Library, which those wishing to consult the register will normally be asked to use. Chapter XI (pp. 135-144) of G. W. Wheeler's book *The earliest catalogues of the Bodleian Library* (Oxford, 1928) is devoted to a description of the register of benefactors.

From 1780 until 1861 a series of annual lists of new accessions to the Library was printed, *A catalogue of books purchased for the Bodleian Library in 1780 [-1861]; with an account of monies collected for that purpose.* From 1796 onwards these lists include at the end lists of *Donations*, giving titles and donors' names. Separate annual lists of *Donations to the Bodleian Library* were printed 1862-85.

W. D. Macray's *Annals of the Bodleian Library*, 2nd edn, Oxford, 1890, is a chronologically arranged summary of noteworthy events in the Library's history, including the acquisition of significant items and collections by gift or purchase. Major donations are described in the text, and appendix III (pp. 419-430) comprises a 'List of all the recorded donors, from 1600 to 1700'. Macray's book contains a great deal of other information about the provenance of Bodleian books, and appendix VI (pp. 439-450) gives a 'List of mss. formerly in the possession of cathedrals, monasteries, colleges, and churches ... with some personal owners connected therewith'.

A provenance index on cards (4 drawers) is kept in Room 132, with various other Special Collections indexes. It covers early printed books from most of the Library's collections, but is obviously very far from comprehensive, and coverage is not systematic. It is largely based on a file created by Dr. D. M. Rogers, who noted provenances as books passed through his hands during his long career in the Special Collections Department. It includes facsimiles of inscriptions, bookplates and stamps, and some biographical information. The index is gradually being augmented, albeit not as a matter of priority, and entries will normally be added for any newly-catalogued material.

The Broxbourne Library (the collection of Albert Ehrman, acquired by the Bodleian in 1978) has separate, comprehensive card indexes of provenances and bindings; these are available on request to the Library staff.

There is also a separate catalogue of the incunabula in the Bodleian Library, compiled by L. A. Sheppard, which includes a provenance index. This too is available on request to Library staff. A project to produce a modern automated catalogue of the Library's incunabula is in progress, and will eventually supersede Sheppard's work.

It is worth adding that the Special Collections card indexes also include an index to consigners of books in Sotheby's auction catalogues, ca. 1900 to the present day (16 drawers, still being added to).

Since 1989, catalogue records for special collections items have been created on OLIS, the Library's on-line cataloguing system. Provenance details are included in these records, but they are not yet indexed or searchable through the public access catalogue.

Manuscripts in the Bodleian Library: The seven volume *Summary catalogue of the western manuscripts in the Bodleian Library* (7v., Oxford, 1895-1953) lists all western manuscripts acquired by the Library before 1916, and describes those which are not included in the series of Quarto Catalogues published in the nineteenth century. The Quarto Catalogues cover many of the important collections acquired in the seventeenth and eighteenth centuries – e.g. Laud, Digby, Rawlinson – and are still the standard guides for those collections. These catalogues (which are written in Latin) include some provenance details in the descriptions, and this information is usually included in the indexes. The 1973 reprint of the Quarto Catalogue of Laudian manuscripts includes a section of addenda, with much information on provenance, and a valuable introduction by R. W. Hunt which lists many of the owners prior to Laud. The Digby catalogue is being revised, for reprinting, by Professor A. G. Watson.

The Summary catalogue includes provenances within its descriptions, and there is a separate index of former owners at the end of vol. 7.

For manuscripts acquired 1916-75, see:

M. Clapinson & T. D. Rogers: *Summary catalogue of post-medieval western manuscripts in the Bodleian Library, Oxford: acquisitions 1916-1975.* 3v. Oxford, 1991.

This includes provenance information in the descriptions, and has a separate index of owners and donors. For manuscripts acquired since 1975, the card index which is kept in Duke Humfrey's Library must be consulted; this includes provenances.

O. Pacht & J. J. G. Alexander: *Illuminated manuscripts in the Bodleian Library, Oxford.* 3v. Oxford, 1966.

> Provenances noted in the text; separate indexes of owners, coats of arms, and mottoes.

D. Rogers: Francis Douce's manuscripts: some hitherto unrecognised provenances. In: *Studies in the book trade in honour of Graham Pollard* (Oxford Bibliographical Society publications, new series 18), Oxford, 1975, pp. 315-340.

> A series of notes on the provenance of certain mss. in the Douce collection, additional to (or making corrections to) the information available in the Summary catalogue.

A. de la Mare: *Catalogue of the collection of medieval manuscripts bequeathed to the Bodleian Library, Oxford by James P. R. Lyell.* Oxford, 1971.

> Provenances noted in the text; separate provenance index.

J. Sparrow: The earlier owners of books in John Selden's library. *Bodleian Library Quarterly* 6 (1931), 263-274.

> A list of books in Selden End, published before 1631, containing the inscriptions of 'eminent or interesting persons' (this is therefore a very selective provenance index only).
> * The list was compiled in the process of searching for books previously owned by John Donne, and those published after his death were not examined. Arranged by owners. The bulk of Selden's collection was given to the Bodleian Library in 1659.

W. M. Lindsay: Books (containing marginalia) of the Bibl. Heinsiana, now in the Bodleian. *Zentralblatt für Bibliothekswesen* 18 (1901), 159-163.

> A list of 52 items from the 1682 sale of the library of Nicolaus Heinsius, purchased by Edward Bernard and subsequently acquired by the Bodleian. Shelfmarks are given, together with notes on provenances prior to Heinsius.

*Elenchus librorum vetustiorum apud ** hospitantium.* [Oxford, 1911]

> A catalogue of the private collection of Professor Ingram Bywater, bequeathed to the Bodleian in 1914. Some provenances noted in the text; separate indexes of 'Books with arms on binding', 'Books with bookplates or other marks of ownership', 'Books with marginalia', and 'Autographs'.

H. M. Nixon: *Broxbourne Library: styles and designs of bookbindings from the twelfth to the twentieth century.* London, 1956.

> Detailed descriptions of selected books, with fine or interesting bindings, from the Broxbourne Library. Provenances noted in the text; separate indexes of owners and binders.

M. J. Sommerlad: *Scottish 'wheel' and 'herring-bone' bindings in the Bodleian Library: an illustrated handlist*. Oxford Bibliographical Society, Occasional Publication no. 1, Oxford, 1967.

> Provenances noted in the text; no index.

Exhibition catalogues: The Bodleian Library in the seventeenth century. Oxford, 1951.

> Includes sections on major 17th century donors, e.g. Laud, Selden; provenances noted.

Oxford college libraries in 1556. Oxford, 1956.

> A catalogue of the major texts acquired by Oxford libraries in the mid-16th century, with notes on their holdings in those libraries, and the donors where known.

English literature in the seventeenth century. Oxford, 1957.

> 'Books in English written and published during the 17th century, and read then or now for their literary merit'. Provenances noted.

Notable accessions 1945-1957. Oxford, 1958.

> Mss and printed books; provenances noted.

Fine bindings 1500-1700 from Oxford libraries. Oxford, 1968.

> A major exhibition of 240 fine and interesting bindings, British and continental, from the Bodleian and the college libraries. Provenances noted in the text; separate index of previous owners.

Duke Humfrey and English humanism in the fifteenth century. Oxford, 1970.

> An exhibition of surviving books from the collection of Humfrey, Duke of Gloucester (1390-1447), and other 15th century mss associated with England; drawn from many libraries in and around Oxford. Provenances noted.

Manuscripts at Oxford: R. W. Hunt memorial exhibition. Oxford, 1980.

> A selection of Oxford mss to honour the memory of R. W. Hunt, Keeper of Western Manuscripts at the Bodleian to 1975. Provenances noted, and included in the general index to the catalogue.

Duke Humfrey's Library & the Divinity School 1488-1988. Oxford, 1988.

> An attempt to convey some of the early history of the University Library by bringing togather mss, many now dispersed outside Oxford, which were once there. Mostly concerned with the period down to 1550. Provenances noted, and included in the general index to the catalogue.

N. K. Kiessling: *The legacy of Democritus Junior, Robert Burton*. Oxford, 1990.

> Mounted to celebrate the 350th anniversary of the death of the author of *The anatomy of melancholy*, drawn mostly from his books in the Bodleian and Christ Church. Provenances noted in the text, and included in the index; see also Kiessling's full catalogue of Burton's library (p. 246 below).

Oxford – Brasenose College

Donors' book: The donors' register was begun in 1657, to cover all kinds of gifts to the college (not just books); still in use today. No retrospective coverage before 1657; gives monetary values of gifts, but includes no details of books.

Major benefactions to the college are summarised, and the donors' register is largely transcribed, in A. J. Butler, *An account of the benefactions bestowed on the College*, Brasenose College Quartercentenary Monographs IV, Oxford, 1909.

The College archives include a small notebook begun by H. C. Wace (Librarian 1912-20) and continued by his successors down to 1961, comprising an index of donors of books to the Library.

Oxford – Christ Church

Donors' book: A donors' register was begun in 1614; covers benefactions (but not comprehensively) 1614-1841. No retrospective coverage before 1614; lists names of donors, and titles of books given. The Library contains a card index to the donors' book, arranged alphabetically by donor; this has appended to it a sequence of cards for donations 1841-97.

A provenance index (arranged alphabetically in an exercise book) covering about two-thirds of the Library's early printed books was compiled in the 1930s, and is available for consultation in the Library.

N. R. Ker: Books at Christ Church 1562-1602. In: J. McConica (ed.), *History of the University of Oxford, vol. 3: The collegiate University* (Oxford, 1986), 498-519.

> A list of 174 volumes in Christ Church bearing presentation inscriptions to the College, dated between 1562 and 1602. Arranged chronologically by date of gift, with press-marks given; also includes notes on bindings.

Oxford – Corpus Christi College

Donors' book: A College benefactors' register (now Corpus archives B/11/1/1) was begun in the late seventeenth century; it includes a section on gifts to the Library, covering the period 1660-1803. Donors' names are listed, with the monetary values of their gifts, but no titles of books are included. The archives also include a list of donations made to the Library, 1695-1824 (D/2/2); a list of books given, from the foundation of the College to the end of the seventeenth century, compiled by J. G. Milne ca. 1930 (D/2/1); and several other lists of individual bequests of books.

A loose-leaf catalogue of noteworthy bindings in the College Library (covering mostly sixteenth and early seventeenth century material) was compiled earlier this century. References are given to Gibson, Hobson, etc. where applicable. Previous owners and donors are noted in the catalogue, and there is a separate list of names at the beginning. It is kept with the College archives as ms. Add. 051/1.

A manuscript catalogue of incunabula and post-incunabula down to 1520 in the College Library, compiled by Robert Proctor ca. 1890, is now preserved as Arch.L.10; it includes at the end an index of donors and former owners.

Oxford – Exeter College

Donors' book: A donors' register was begun in 1703, to covers all kinds of gifts to the college (not just books); it is still in use today. Covers major benefactions retrospectively to 1567; lists donors' names, and monetary value of their gifts. A second donors' book (C.II.1), on paper, was begun about the same time, listing major benefactions from the time of the college's foundation to the bequest of John Barbon (d.1688). The contents of these registers are summarised in C. W. Boase, *Registrum Collegii Exoniensis: register of ... Exeter College*, Oxford, 1894, pp. 268-274; the biographical register on pp. 1-267 also includes details of gifts of books by members of the college, which do not feature in the donors' books (see Index, 'books', p. 379).

A provenance index on cards is available in the Library, covering most of the college's pre-1701 books; it is still being added to.

Wing titles in Exeter College Library [Typescript]. Oxford, 1986.

> A catalogue of all known copies of Wing titles (i.e. British books, 1641-1700) in the College Library. Provenances noted in the text, but not indexed. A copy is available in the Bodleian Library (2590.c.Oxf.60).

Oxford – Hertford College

Donors' book: Hertford College, founded in its present form in 1874, has a rather complicated ancestry based on two medieval halls, Hart Hall and Magdalen Hall. The only surviving donors' register comes from Magdalen Hall, where it was begun in 1656, without retrospective coverage, and continued in use until 1746. It records donors' names and titles of books given, or monetary sums (many of the later entries relate to admission fees).

The Library's older books are being recatalogued and provenances are being recorded. It is hoped that a provenance index will be available ca. 1995.

Oxford – Jesus College

Donors' book: The earliest Library benefactors' book (now Muniment Room shelf 17) was begun ca. 1630, to mark the building of the new Library about that time. It was actively used for the 1620s, 1630s and 1650s (down to 1662), listing donors' names and titles of books given. It was later used, in the eighteenth and nineteenth centuries, to list general benefactions to the College; it also includes a catalogue of the large collection of books bequeathed by Jonathan Edwards in 1712. A second benefactors' book (B.7.13) was begun in 1681, which lists Library gifts at one end and gifts of plate at the other. Library benefactions are listed retrospectively back to about 1630, with a summary of gifts down to the end of the seventeenth century, and fuller details, including titles of books given, from then until ca. 1750, when the last entry was made. A list of the manuscripts given by Sir John Price is in the College Register for 1602-04 (Muniment Room shelf 18); lists of the books given by Edward, Lord Herbert of Cherbury, and by Francis Mansell, are included in Mansell's Inventory of 1649 (Muniment Room shelf 17).

The card catalogue to the Old Library includes a section on 'autographs' noted in books (about half a drawer); this was compiled in the middle of the present century and coverage is not comprehensive, or systematic.

Oxford – Keble College

M. B. Parkes: *The medieval manuscripts of Keble College, Oxford: a descriptive catalogue.* London, 1979.

> Provenances noted in the text; separate index of 'persons and places connected with the manuscripts' (which includes binders, scribes, etc. as well as owners).

Oxford – Lincoln College

Donors' book: A benefactors' register was begun in 1676, with retrospective coverage back to 1620; it continued in use until 1755, listing donors' names and titles of books received.

Oxford – Magdalen College

Donors' book: A donors' register (Ms. 777) was begun in 1637 and continued to 1711. No retrospective coverage before 1637. Lists donors' names, and titles of books given.

W. D. Macray: *Register of the members of St. Mary Magdalen College, Oxford. New series II (Fellows, 1522-75).* London, 1897.

> Includes as Appendix II Notes of books in the Library bearing memoranda of ownership and donorship, etc.

R. T. Gunther: *Early British botanists and their gardens.* Oxford, 1922.

> Chapter III (pp. 197-232), on 'Goodyer's library', comprises a catalogue of ca. 240 books bequeathed to Magdalen College by John Goodyer in 1664. Owners previous to Goodyer are noted in the text; separate index of 'signatures or personal memoranda in Goodyer's books' on pp. 200-201.

Oxford – Merton College

Donors' book: The *Liber benefactorum* (28.H.10) was begun in 1692, but fell out of use shortly thereafter until revived earlier this century. Contains only a few pages of late seventeenth-century gifts to the Library, with donors' names and titles of books. No retrospective coverage before 1692.

There is a card index (one drawer) of owners and donors of books in the Library, incomplete, but added to occasionally.

P. S. Morrish: *Bibliotheca Higgsiana: a catalogue of the books of Dr. Griffin Higgs (1589-1659)*. (Oxford Bibliographical Society, Occasional Publications 22). Oxford, 1990.

> A catalogue of 678 items bequeathed to Merton by Griffin Higgs. Provenances prior to Higgs noted in the text, and included in a separate index sequence at the end. See also P. S. Morrish, 'Dr. Higgs and Merton College Library', *Proceedings of the Leeds Philosophical and Literary Society, Literary and Historical Section*, 21(2) (1988), 133-201.

Oxford – New College

Donors' book: A Library benefactions book (New College Archives 3582) was begun in 1617, to mark the major gift of Arthur Lake. Covers gifts retrospectively to 1386, and continued in use until 1909, listing donors' names and titles of books given. It includes an index at the end. Various other lists of benefactions to the College survive in the archives, including catalogues of particular bequests of books, and more general lists of gifts to the College over certain periods; see F. W. Steer, *The archives of New College, Oxford*, London, 1974, pp. 50-55 (Benefactions) and 91-92 (Library).

A provenance index on cards was begun some years ago, but it has never been possible to complete it; there are about 100 entries, whose coverage is rather unsystematic and far from comprehensive.

Oxford – Oriel College

Donors' book: A donors' register was begun ca. 1617, to cover all kinds of gifts to the college (not just books); no retrospective coverage before 1617. Lists donors and details of books given from 1617 to the beginning of the eighteenth century; continued in use until ca. 1775, but after 1700 gifts are mostly commencement fees, shown only as a monetary value. A ms. index, compiled early in the nineteenth century, is loosely inserted.

Oxford – Pembroke College

Donors' book: The College benefactors' book, begun in 1692, lists general gifts to the College from the seventeenth century to 1808. Gives monetary values only; no gifts of books are listed.

Oxford – Queen's College

Donors' book: A donors' register was begun in 1629 and copied out anew, arranged alphabetically by donors, in 1659 (Ms. 556; the original does not survive). Includes some retrospective coverage back into the 16th century, with brief notes on some earlier benefactors; continues down to 1691. Lists donors' names, and details of books given. Bodleian Library Gough Ms. Oxon. 15, part of a collection of mss. on the history of Queen's, compiled by Edward Rowe Mores (d.1778), includes a list of benefactors to the Library, derived either from this donors' register or from its predecessor; this list is transcribed and annotated in J. R. Magrath, *The Queen's College*, Oxford, 1921, v.2, pp. 267-278.

There is a provenance index on cards (2 drawers) available in the Library, although its coverage is not complete. Includes notes on the nature of the provenance evidence (inscription, bookplate, etc.); the large donations of Thomas Barlow, Theophilus Metcalfe and Joseph Williamson account for a sizeable proportion of the index.

Oxford – St. Edmund Hall

Donors' book: A benefactions register was begun ca. 1685, listing all kinds of gifts to the College, with retrospective coverage back to ca. 1659. It continued in use until 1855. It includes gifts to the Library, with donors' names and titles of books given, or monetary values, as appropriate. The register was described and illustrated by A. B. Emden in the *St. Edmund Hall Magazine* 1 (1923), 15-16.

Oxford – St. John's College

Donors' book: A Library benefactors' book was begun ca. 1620, listing gifts retrospectively back to the foundation of the College in 1555. Lists donors' names, and titles of books given; it continued in use until 1756. Includes an index at the end.

See also R. Hunt, St. John's College donors … 1611-1621 in R. W. Hunt et al (eds.), *Studies in the book trade in honour of Graham Pollard*, Oxford, 1975, 63-70, and the thesis by John Fuggles, *A history of the Library of St. John's College … to 1660*, Bodleian Library ms. B.Litt. c.360.

Oxford – Taylor Institution Library

A provenance index on cards was begun in 1970, and mostly covers material acquired since then. There is a sequence of provenances, and a separate sequence of bookplates, binders' tickets and other bibliographical miscellanea. These amount to two drawers of cards (currently kept in the Periodicals Reading Room).

Oxford – Trinity College

Donors' book: A Library benefactors' register was begun ca. 1625, covering gifts retrospectively back to the foundation of the College in 1555. Lists donors' names and titles of books given; it continued in use until 1849, although entries after about 1700 are patchy. It also includes lists of books purchased with monetary gifts (most notably, lists of books bought between 1675 and 1775 with the endowment bequeathed by Richard Rands in 1640).

A complete index of donors of books has been compiled, in shelfmark order, and is available as a typescript in the Library. A separate card index of donors (based on the typescript) is also available there. Owners, who were not donors, are also noted on the typescript, but these are not yet covered by an index.

Exhibition catalogue: R. Gameson & A. Coates: *The Old Library, Trinity College.* Oxford, 1988.

> 20 items, manuscripts and printed books. Provenances noted in the text, but not indexed. The introduction includes a brief history of the Library.

Oxford – University College

Donors' book: A donors' register was begun retrospectively in 1674; covers benefactions 1406-1678. A few later entries (1678-88) are loosely inserted in draft on a separate sheet of paper. Lists names of donors, and titles of books given.

Oxford – Wadham College

The older books in the Library have been recatalogued and arranged on the shelves by alphabetical order of donors. Donors' names are noted on the catalogue cards and a separate handlist of donors is available in the Library, noting the date of gift and the number of volumes involved. There are no indexes currently available covering owners who were not donors.

An incomplete list of bookplates found in Wadham Library, compiled ca. 1906, is also available there. See also J. Henderson Smith, 'The bookplates of Wadham College, Oxford', *Journal of the Ex Libris Society* 16 (1907), 27-30, which mentions some of the bookplates found in the Library.

H. A. Wheeler: *A short catalogue of books printed in England and English books printed abroad before 1641 in the Library of Wadham College, Oxford.* London, 1929.

> Donors, and some other provenances, noted in the text, but not indexed.

Oxford – Worcester College

Two provenance indexes to the College Library were compiled in exercise books by E. M. Girling at the beginning of this century, 'Catalogue of bookplates in Worcester College Library' (about 200 entries), and 'Catalogue of autographs' (about 380 entries). These are not comprehensive in their coverage. An earlier 'Catalogue of curious and valuable books' (1886) includes provenance sections. The College Library also has an interleaved copy of C. H. Wilkinson's 'Worcester College Library' (1927), with notes made by Wilkinson, some of which relate to provenance.

Denchworth Parish Library: C. H. Tomlinson: The Vicar's Library at Denchworth. *Supplement to the Denchworth Annual. 1875.* Wantage, 1875, 2-18.

> A catalogue of 147 items then in the Library (founded 1693), which is now deposited in Worcester College. The seven major donors are listed and their initials are used in the catalogue to indicate the source of each book; a few other provenances are noted in the text.

Peterborough – Cathedral Library

Donors' book: Begun in 1672, when the Library was refounded, and continued in use until 1879. Includes gifts to the Church (e.g. plate), as well as gifts to the Library. Lists donors' names, and titles of books given. The manuscripts and the pre-1801 printed books are all now deposited in Cambridge University Library, and the donors' book is available there as Peterborough Ms. 37.

Reading – University Library

The Library has for some years kept a provenance index on cards, although its coverage is incomplete and not systematic. It is however regularly maintained and updated as new material is acquired, and as existing items are recatalogued.

Catalogue of the Library, Overstone Park. 1867.

> Some provenances noted in the text; no index. The collection is mostly that formed by J. R. McCulloch (1789-1864); it was bequeathed to Reading University in 1920.

N. B. Eales: *The Cole Library of early medicine and zoology. Catalogue of books and pamphlets. Part I: 1472 to 1800.* Reading, 1969.

> Provenances are noted in the text, but are not indexed. See also Miss Eales's article 'On the provenance of some early medical and zoological books', *Journal of the history of medicine,* 24 (1969), 183-192.

Reigate – Cranston Library

The Library has been recatalogued and the new catalogue is available on microfiche. Owners and donors of the books are noted in the catalogue entries and there is a separate donors' index, available on cards in the Library, or on microfiche.

Ripon – Cathedral Library

J. E. Mortimer: The library catalogue of Anthony Higgin, Dean of Ripon (1608-1624). *Proceedings of the Leeds Philosophical and Literary Society,* 10 (1962), 1-75.

> The post-medieval library at Ripon was founded by the bequest of Dean Higgin in 1624. This edition of a ms. inventory of his books (758 vols.) identifies books still in the Cathedral Library; provenances are noted in the text and there is a separate provenance index.

Rochester – Cathedral Library

The Library has been recatalogued but some revision work is still in progress. The data is held on a computer at the University of Kent and the catalogue can be accessed on-line from Canterbury Cathedral Library. A print-out of the file is held at Rochester, and at Canterbury. Provenances were recorded, and a printed-out provenance index is kept at Canterbury Cathedral Library.

St. Andrews – University Library

Donors' book: There is no donors' book as such. A list of donations on the foundation of the Library in 1612 from Principal Howie's Book (St. Andrews University Muniments UY152/2, pp. 267-273) is printed as part of 'Inventories of buikis in the colleges of Sanctandrois', *Miscellany of the Maitland Club* v.1, Edinburgh, 1834, pp. 303-329. Apart from this, the University Muniments include several lists of important 17th century donations of books, and later gifts of books are listed selectively in the Senate minutes, 1696-1892, which are indexed.

A provenance index to the Library's printed books has been maintained for some time, in sheaf binders; its coverage is not comprehensive, but it currently occupies eight full binders.

St. Andrews University Library: catalogue of incunabula. (St. Andrews University publications, 53). St. Andrews, 1956.

> Provenances noted in the text; separate provenance index.

Salisbury – Cathedral Library

The Library is currently being recatalogued by Miss S. Eward, and a card index of donors is in process of compilation.

Shrewsbury – Shrewsbury School Library

Donors' book: A donors' register was begun in 1634 and continued in use until 1743. Coverage is retrospective back to 1596, using accession rolls for 1596-1634 (which still survive). Includes donors' names, and titles of books given. The names of donors were read out at the Town Hall at the annual town audit, and separate lists made for this purpose also survive, covering the period 1596-ca. 1736, although these are less detailed than the donors' book proper.

J. B. Oldham: Shrewsbury School Library: its history and contents. *Transactions of the Shropshire Archaeological Society* 51 (1941), 53-81.

> Includes at end an Index of bookplates and an Index of autographs found in books in the Library – pressmarks are given, but no other details of the books concerned.

J. B. Oldham: *Shrewsbury School Library bindings: catalogue raisonné.* Oxford, 1943.

> Some provenances noted in the text and partially included in the general index.

Southampton – King Edward VI School Library

P. Yeats-Edwards: *Catalogue of the Select Library, King Edward VI School, Southampton.* Southampton, 1967.

> Donors noted, from inscriptions in the books, but no other provenance information. No index.

Steeple Ashton, Wiltshire – Parish Library

W. Smith: The parochial library of Steeple Ashton in Wiltshire. *Library History* 6 (1983), 97-113.

> Includes lists of 'select items surviving from before 1828', 'additions since 1828', and 'books given to Magdalen College, Cambridge'; provenances noted in the text, but not indexed.

Suffolk

A. E. Birkby: *Suffolk parochial libraries: a catalogue.* London, 1977.

> Provenances are noted in the text; no index. There is an introduction giving brief histories of the libraries concerned, including details of notable donors, etc.

Swaffham – Parish Library

M. C. Lyons: *Swaffham Parish Library: a catalogue of printed books and manuscripts.* Dublin and Norwich, 1987.

> This separately published catalogue was originally compiled as part of a Loughborough University M.A. thesis. Provenances noted in the text, but not separately indexed.

Twickenham – Twickenham Reference Library

B. Reid: *Alexander Pope (1688-1744): catalogue of the Pope collection.* London, 1989.

> A catalogue of works by and relating to Pope, held in the Local Studies Collection at Twickenham Public Library. Provenances noted in the text, and included in the general index.

Wells – Wells Cathedral

Donors' book: A register of benefactors was begun in 1672 when the Library was refounded, and continued in use until 1734; it was also used between 1861 and 1914. Lists donors' names, and titles of books given, or values of monetary gifts. A separate library for the Vicars Choral at Wells was set up early in the seventeenth century and the remnants of this collection are now in the Cathedral Library. Its donors' register survives, which was begun in 1622 and continued up to 1644; most of the books were lost during the Civil War but the

Library was re-established after the Restoration and there is a second sequence of donations, ca. 1660-ca. 1700.

A provenance index is being compiled but it is expected that the work will take some years to complete.

Bath Abbey Library: Now deposited in Wells Cathedral Library.

Donors' book: Begun ca. 1619 when the Library was founded by Bishop Lake, and continued in use until 1715. Lists donors' names, and titles of books given.

Wimborne – Wimborne Minster

W. G. Wilkinson: *Catalogue of the books in the Minster Library, Wimborne.* Wimborne, 1863.

> A list of 185 books then surviving in the Library. Arranged in columns, with a separate column for donors' names, where known, and one for other former owners (as identified from inscriptions). Reprinted, with fuller bibliographical details, in W. Blades, *Bibliographical miscellanies* no. 2: *Books in chains: Wimborne Minster,* London, 1890.

Winchester – Cathedral Library

Donors' book: A donors' register was begun in 1686 (after the major bequest of George Morley), with no retrospective coverage; it continued in use until 1946. Lists donors' names, and titles of books given.

A provenance index on cards (1 drawer) was compiled 1989-91, and covers the entire library.

Winchester – Winchester College

Donors' book: A donors' register (shelfmark Z4) was begun in 1652, with retrospective coverage back to 1543; it continued in use until 1866. Includes donors' names, and titles of books given, although the major eighteenth-century benefaction of Alexander Thistlethwayte is not fully listed, and entries for the sixteenth century are probably incomplete.

Windsor – St. George's Chapel

M. R. James: The manuscripts of St. George's Chapel, Windsor. *The Library* 4th ser. 13 (1932), 55-76.

> This deals not only with the small handful of medieval mss. at Windsor in 1932, but also with the 75 or so given to the Bodleian Library by the Dean and Chapter of Windsor in 1612. Provenances noted in the text; although these are not separately indexed, the article includes (pp. 69-71) 'Note[s] on the provenance on the Windsor mss. at Oxford'.

J. Callard: *A catalogue of printed books (pre-1751) in the Library of St. George's Chapel, Windsor Castle.* Windsor, 1976.

> Provenances noted in the text; separate provenance index.

Wisbech – Wisbech and Fenland Museum Library

An author catalogue of the Library (which includes Wisbech Town Library), on cards, was completed in 1985. Some provenances (inscriptions and bookplates) are noted on the cards, but there is no separate provenance index.

Worcester – Cathedral Library

A provenance index for printed books covering Bishop Prideaux's collection (only) has been completed by Dr. B. S. Benedikz and Dr. V. Butcher; further work is in progress, but there is no anticipated completion date. Enquiries to Dr. Benedikz at Birmingham University Library.

J. K. Floyer & S. G. Hamilton: *Catalogue of manuscripts preserved in the Chapter Library of Worcester Cathedral*. Oxford, 1906.

> Provenances noted in the text, and (mostly) included in the general index. The manuscripts are mostly those which survive from the medieval monastic library. A revised edition of this catalogue is being prepared by Dr. Benedikz.

D. Wyn Evans: *Catalogue of bindings in Worcester Cathedral Library*. [Typescript with photographs], 1973.

D. Wyn Evans: *Catalogue of bindings with centre stamps in Worcester Cathedral Library*. [Typescript with photographs], 1973.

> These two catalogues describe sixteenth- and early seventeenth-century bindings in the Library; provenances are noted in the text, with a separate provenance index. Copies of both catalogues are available in the Heslop Room in Birmingham University Library.

Wye College, Kent – Crundale Rectory Library

The Library (which is largely the collection of Richard Forster, d.1728) has been recatalogued. The data is held on a computer at the University of Kent, and the catalogue can be accessed on-line from Canterbury Cathedral Library. Provenances were recorded, and a printed-out provenance index is kept at Canterbury Cathedral Library.

York – Minster Library

Donors' book: A donors' register was begun by Thomas Comber ca. 1685, and includes brief summary mentions of some earlier benefactions back to 1628. Continued in use 1686-1924, listing donors' names and titles of books given, but kept up only sporadically for much of the eighteenth century, when at least one major benefaction was not recorded.

A provenance index is held in sheaf binders, which currently runs to 50 binders and includes about 25,000 entries. An earlier provenance index is also available, on typed sheets; this ranges over the whole collection but its coverage is not systematic, or complete.

J. Raine: *A catalogue of the printed books in the Library of the Dean and Chapter of York*. York, 1896.

> Abbreviations are used in the text to identify books given by some of the Library's principal donors (Matthew, Fairfax, Fothergill, etc.), and a few other provenances are noted in the text; no index.

S. E. Boorman: *A catalogue of the Hackness Parochial Library*. (Study submitted in partial fulfilment of the requirements for the degree of M.A. in Librarianship, University of Sheffield). Sheffield, 1980.

> Provenances noted in the text, but not indexed; includes as Appendix III a transcript of the list of patrons mentioned in the parish benefactors' book. The Library is now in York Minster Library.

Catalogues with national coverage

[Seymour de Ricci's *Bibliotheca Britannica Manuscripta*]: In the mid-1930s, de Ricci evolved a plan to compile a union catalogue of all British manuscript collections, something along the lines of Ker's *Medieval manuscripts in British libraries* but rather more ambitious, and correspondingly less realistic, in scope. The project never approached completion, but as part of the preliminary work de Ricci compiled an index by reading through manuscript catalogues and all the Sotheby's manuscript sale catalogues from ca. 1890-1935. This index includes a provenance sequence, in which all provenances noted by de Ricci in the aforementioned catalogues were recorded. The entire index is now on open access in the Palaeography Room of the University of London Library, and the provenance slips fill 11 wooden drawers. This is clearly an imperfect tool, but it undoubtedly includes information on owners of certain manuscripts which is not easily obtainable elsewhere. A full account of the history of de Ricci's project has been published by J. Gibbs: 'Seymour de Ricci's Bibliotheca Britannica Manuscripta', in A. S. Osley (ed.): *Calligraphy and palaeography: essays presented to Alfred Fairbank*, London, 1965, pp. 81-91.

[*History of the Book in Britain* database]: Margaret L. Ford has compiled an automated database containing details of books with evidence of pre-1557 British ownership. The work was carried out in support of the third volume of the forthcoming *History of the book in Britain* and was funded by the Leverhulme Trust, with some help from the Pilgrim Trust. The database focusses on the period 1400-1557 but is primarily concerned with printed books from the second half of the fifteenth century, and the first half of the sixteenth. Evidence of ownership may be anonymous, such as an English binding, or the presence of marginal notes in an English hand, as well as relying on inscriptions. Where names of owners have been identified, brief biographical notes are included. The database was compiled partly through personal examination of books in libraries throughout Britain, and partly by abstracting information from published catalogues which include copy-specific information; by autumn

1993, it contained details of over 4200 books. Although the means of access and future development of this database have not yet been fully determined, it is expected to come under the aegis of the Early Collections Service (being established 1993-94) of the British Library in London, and enquiries should be directed there.

J. J. G. Alexander (ed.): *A survey of manuscripts illuminated in the British Isles.*
>   v. 1: J. J. G. Alexander: *Insular mss, 6th to the 9th century*, London, 1976.
>   v. 2: E. Temple: *Anglo-Saxon mss 900-1066.* London, 1966.
>   v. 3: C. M. Kauffman: *Romanesque mss 1066-1190.* London, 1975.
>   v. 4: N. Morgan: *Early gothic mss 1190-1250.* London, 1982; *Early gothic mss 1250-1285.* London, 1988.
>   v. 5: L. F. Sandler: *Gothic mss 1285-1385.* 2v. London, 1986.
>   v. 6: K. Scott: *Later gothic mss 1390-1490.* 2v. London, 1994.

>   The description of each manuscript includes a provenance section; provenances are included in the general indexes of some (but not all) the volumes.

N. R. Ker: *Catalogue of manuscripts containing Anglo-Saxon.* Oxford, 1957.

>   Provenances noted in the text; separate index of owners, divided into pre- and post-1540.

N. R. Ker: *Medieval libraries of Great Britain: a list of surviving books.* (Royal Historical Society Guides and Handbooks, no. 3) Second edition. London, 1964.
A. G. Watson: *Medieval libraries of Great Britain ... Supplement to the second edition.* (Royal Historical Society Guides and Handbooks, no. 15) London, 1987.

>   Arranged by libraries, with the present locations of surviving material given. Mostly concerned with manuscripts, naturally, but also includes printed books. Separate list of 'Donors, scribes and other persons concerned before 1540 with the books recorded'. Professor Watson's *Supplement*, which adds over 500 books to the original census, follows the same layout.

N. R. Ker & A. J. Piper: *Medieval manuscripts in British libraries.*
>   v. 1: London. Oxford, 1969.
>   v. 2: Abbotsford – Keele. Oxford, 1977.
>   v. 3: Lampeter – Oxford. Oxford, 1983.
>   v. 4: Paisley-York. Oxford, 1992.

>   These catalogues aim to give full descriptions of manuscripts which have not been adequately listed before, and references to other published catalogues where these exist. Provenances are recorded in the descriptions. There is no index as yet.

G. R. C. Davis: *Medieval cartularies of Great Britain: a short catalogue.* London, 1958.

>   A list of surviving cartularies, arranged alphabetically by place. Present and previous owners are noted in the text and there are separate provenance indexes for corporate and private owners past and present.

N. R. Ker: *Fragments of medieval manuscripts used as pastedowns in Oxford bindings.* (Oxford Bibliographical Society Publications, new series 5). Oxford, 1954.

>   A catalogue of manuscript fragments used in Oxford bindings, ca. 1480-1620, which also describes the tools used on the bindings. Lists relevant books identified by Ker in Oxford and elsewhere. Contemporary owners of the books are noted in the text and listed in a separate index, although the names of owners later than the date of binding are not recorded.

J. H. Baker: *English legal manuscripts volume II. Catalogue of the manuscript year books, readings, and law reports in Lincoln's Inn, the Bodleian Library and Gray's Inn.* London and Switzerland, 1978.

> A detailed catalogue of legal manuscripts in the named libraries. The description of each item includes a provenance section, and there is a separate index of owners. The book also includes notes on the dispersed libraries of John Selden, Charles Fairfax, and Henry Powle.

W. Carew Hazlitt: Autographs in books. *The Bibliographer* 6 (1884), 135-140 and 153-158.

> A series of short numbered notes on 95 books with interesting inscriptions or other association evidence, seen by Hazlitt. The introductory note states: 'It was formerly my custom to preserve a note of every book, having interesting associations with it in respect of prior ownership or some analagous point, which fell in my way in the course of my rather wide bibliographical researches, and the result is that I have by me a series of memoranda extending over about a quarter of a century. I shall in the following pages give only what appear to be the most important or curious'. Each note includes brief bibliographical information, and details of inscriptions or other provenance evidence. The notes mostly concern English owners from the 16th to the 19th centuries. Unfortunately, the locations of the books described are very seldom given – there are a few references to lot numbers in auction sales – so the usefulness of Hazlitt's documentation is very limited.

S. de Ricci: *A census of Caxtons.* (Bibliographical Society, Illustrated monographs, 15). Oxford, 1909.

> A catalogue of all copies of books printed by William Caxton, as located by de Ricci. The provenance of each copy is traced and described. Modern and previous owners are listed in a separate index.

S. Lee: *Shakespeare's comedies, histories, & tragedies ... containing a census of extant copies.* Oxford, 1902.

> Issued as a supplement to the facsimile edition of the first folio published in 1902. Comprises a list of identified surviving copies of the first folio; provenances noted in the text, and included in the index.

H. C. Bartlett & A. W. Pollard: *A census of Shakespeare's plays in quarto 1594-1709.* New Haven, 1939.

> A list of surviving copies of separate quarto editions of the plays, printed before 1710. Some provenances noted in the text, and included in the index.

W. S. Peterson: *A bibliography of the Kelmscott Press.* (Soho Bibliographies, 24). Oxford, 1984.

> Includes an 'Index of association copies of Kelmscott books'.

A. B. Emden: *A biographical register of the University of Oxford A.D. 1501 to 1540.* Oxford, 1974.

> Appendix B comprises lists of books known to have been owned by certain Oxford graduates (based partly on probate documents); when the present location of these books is known, this is indicated, with the relevant shelf-marks.

J. Durkan & A. Ross: Early Scottish libraries. Glasgow, 1961.

> A catalogue of printed books, printed between 1470 and 1560, which bear contemporary marks of ownership of Scottish libraries or collectors, and which survive today in the major Scottish libraries. Arranged in three alphabetical sections, bishops, individual owners, and

institutions. An invaluable work for which there is no English equivalent, beyond Ker's *Medieval libraries of Great Britain*, which deals only with institutions. It was originally published as the Spring 1958 issue (vol. 9, no. 1) of *The Innes Review*. Several supplements to Durkan & Ross have been published in *The Bibliotheck*, as follows:

v. 4 (1963-66), 13-24; 9 (1978-79), 13-20; 10 (1980-81), 87-98; 11 (1982-83), 29-37 and 57-58; 12 (1984-85), 85-90.

British Association Aberdeen Meeting 1885: guide to the exhibition of manuscripts, printed books ... and other exhibits in the Art Gallery and Museum, Schoolhill. Aberdeen, 1885.

600 items, three quarters of which are mss or early printed books. Largely drawn from the collection of the Earl of Crawford, and a few other noteworthy Scottish collectors of the late nineteenth century. Some provenances noted in the text, but not indexed.

J. F. K. Johnstone and A. W. Robertson: *Bibliographia Aberdonensis: being an account of books relating to or printed in the shires of Aberdeen, Banff, Kincardine, or written by natives ... or by ... alumni of the universities of Aberdeen ... 1472-1640 (1641-1700).* 2v. Aberdeen, 1929-30.

A detailed bibliography of Aberdeen-related printing of the fifteenth-seventeenth centuries, with locations of copies in nearly 200 libraries around the world. Physical characteristics of particular copies, including provenance, are sometimes noted in the text, and rather patchily included in the index.

Catalogue of an exhibition of books ... illustrative of the history & progress of printing and bookselling in England 1477-1800: held at Stationers' Hall, 25-29 June 1912, by the International Association of Antiquarian Booksellers. London, 1912.

1229 items. Some provenances noted in the text, but not indexed.

[Catalogues of parochial libraries]: In the course of preparing *The parochial libraries of the Church of England*, Dr. N. R. Ker gathered together numerous typed or handwritten lists and catalogues of parochial libraries, which he subsequently deposited in the Bodleian Library, where they are now available for consultation as MS.Eng.Misc.C360. Photocopies are also available in the Library of the Council for the Care of Churches in London. Several of these lists include provenance information; as they often run to only two or three pages of typescript they are not listed here separately, but examples are the lists of the parish libraries of Buckland (Berkshire), Prees (Shropshire), Marlborough (Wiltshire) and Sutton Courtenay (Berkshire).

M. Craig: *Irish bookbindings 1600-1800.* London, 1954.

Describes noteworthy Irish bindings now housed in various libraries. Some provenances noted in the text, but not indexed.

J. McDonnell & P. Healy: *Gold-tooled bookbindings commissioned by Trinity College, Dublin in the eighteenth century.* (Studies in the History of Irish Bookbinding, 1). Leixlip, 1987.

A catalogue of just over a hundred bindings, now located in private and institutional libraries on both sides of the Atlantic. The description of each binding includes a provenance section and there is a separate index of owners.

D. B. Quinn (ed.): *The Hakluyt Handbook. Volume II.* London, 1974.

Principally a bibliography of the works of Richard Hakluyt and the sources he used. 'The primary Hakluyt bibliography' (p. 461 ff) includes lists of surviving copies of Hakluyt's books, with provenances noted, and a series of title page reproductions of Hakluyt's source books, complete with early inscriptions of ownership.

Private collections, not subsequently absorbed entire by institutions

This list is restricted to catalogues which include details of ownership earlier than, or subsequent to, the collector whose library is being described.

J. J. G. Alexander & A. C. de la Mare: *The Italian manuscripts in the library of Major J. R. Abbey*. London, 1969.

> 63 items, mostly 15th-16th centuries. The description of each ms includes a provenance section; provenances included in the general index.

G. D. Hobson: *English bindings 1490-1940 in the library of J. R. Abbey*. London, 1940.

> Detailed descriptions of fine or interesting bindings selected from Abbey's collection. Provenances noted in the text; no provenance index. The collection was dispersed at Sotheby's between 1965 and 1978.

S. de Ricci: *A hand-list of a collection of books and manuscripts belonging to the Right Hon. Lord Amherst of Hackney*. Cambridge, 1906.

> Some provenances noted in the text and listed in a separate provenance index. Most of the collection was dispersed at Sotheby's in 1908-09.

G. P. Johnston: *Catalogue of the rare and most interesting books and manuscripts in the Library at Drummond Castle*. Edinburgh, 1910.

> Some provenances noted in the text; no index. Drummond Castle is the seat of the Earl of Ancaster.

D. E. Rhodes: *John Argentine Provost of King's: his life and his library*. Amsterdam, 1967.

> Argentine was a physician who ended his career as Provost of King's College, Cambridge, from 1501 until his death in 1508. Surviving books (printed and mss.) from his library are listed, with provenances previous to, and later than, Argentine noted in the text, but not indexed.

D. C. Baker & J. L. Murphy: The books of Myles Blomefylde. *The Library* 5th series 31 (1976), 377-385.

> Lists 21 books known to have belonged to Blomefylde (1525-1603), and 2 which possibly belonged to him. Provenances previous to, and later than Blomefylde noted in the text, but not indexed separately.

G. I. Ellis: *A catalogue of the manuscripts and printed books collected by Thomas Brooke, F.S.A. and preserved at Armitage Bridge House, near Huddersfield*. 2v. London, 1891.

> Some provenances noted in the text; no index.

N. K. Kiessling: *The library of Robert Burton*. (Oxford Bibliographical Society Publications, new series 22). Oxford, 1988.

> A catalogue of Burton's collection (over 1700 titles), most of which survives today in the Bodleian Library or Christ Church. Present day locations are given, with pressmarks. Provenances prior to, and later than Burton noted in the text, and indexed (with identifications where possible) in Appendix VI.

H. Collmann & G. A. Paternoster Brown: *The Britwell handlist: or short-title catalogue of the principal volumes ... formerly in the Library of Britwell Court Buckinghamshire*. 2v. London, 1933.

A record of the library of Sydney Christie-Miller, built up over several generations during the nineteenth and twentieth centuries, and dispersed at Sotheby's between 1908 and 1927. It was especially strong in early English books and constituted the largest single collection sold at Sotheby's this century. Major provenances noted in the text, using a series of abbreviations, but not indexed.

R. J. Coffman: *Coleridge's library: a bibliography of books owned or read by Samuel Taylor Coleridge.* Boston, 1987.

A catalogue of Coleridge's library based on extant books, Coleridge's published work, and other sources; includes books known to have been consulted, but not necessarily owned, by him. Provenances prior to, and later than Coleridge noted in the text, but not included in the index. The introduction includes an extensive section on the sources of his collection.

A. G. Watson: The manuscript collection of Sir Walter Cope. *Bodleian Library Record* 12 (1987), 262-297.

Sir Walter Cope (d.1614) amassed a collection of over 200 medieval manuscripts. The appendix to Professor Watson's article lists material which is known to have been in his library, identifying individual mss. where possible (he gave 47 mss. to the Bodleian Library in 1602; a few others can be traced in the British Library, and elsewhere). Provenances other than Cope noted in the text; no index.

A. L. Humphreys: *Catalogue of the library of Laurence Currie, 1 Richmond Terrace, Whitehall.* London, 1901.

Some provenances noted in the text; no index.

A. L. Humphreys: *Catalogue of the library of Laurence Currie, Minley Manor, Hants.* London, 1901.

Some provenances noted in the text; no index.

A. G. Watson: A sixteenth-century collector: Thomas Dackomb, 1496-c. 1572. *The Library* 5th series 18 (1963), 204-217.

Dackomb spent most of his life as Rector of St. Peter Colebrook, Winchester. Professor Watson identifies 19 mss. and 4 printed books from his collection, now housed in various libraries. Provenances previous to, and later than, Dackomb noted in the text, but not indexed separately.

J. Roberts & A. G. Watson: *John Dee's library catalogue.* London, 1990.

An annotated facsimile of Dee's 1583 catalogue, listing ca. 2500 books then in his possession. Surviving books from his collection are described in the editorial apparatus, noting owners previous to, and later than, Dee; index II covers 'owners and other persons, places and institutions'.

A. G. Watson: *The library of Sir Simonds d'Ewes.* London, 1966.

Sir Simonds d'Ewes (1602-50) built up a collection of about a thousand printed books and 600-700 manuscripts, all of which were absorbed into Robert Harley's library in 1705. Professor Watson's catalogue comprises annotated editions of contemporary lists of d'Ewes's library, or parts of it. Hardly any of the printed books can be located today, but most of the manuscripts are identifiable. Provenances prior to d'Ewes are noted in the text, and included in the general index. Most of this provenance information is, of course, reproduced in C. E. Wright's *Fontes Harleiani.*

G. Keynes: *A bibliography of Dr. John Donne.* Fourth edition. Oxford, 1973.

> Appendix IV ('Books from Donne's library') lists 218 volumes from Donne's collection which have been identified in various libraries in Britain and America (many are in the Middle Temple Library). Other provenances, previous to and later than Donne, noted in the text, but not indexed.

W. E. Moss: *Bindings from the library of Robt. Dudley, Earl of Leicester, K.G. 1533-1588.* Sonning-on-Thames, 1934.

> Includes a list of ca. 80 identified bindings, located in various collections; some provenances later than Dudley noted in the text, but not indexed.

A catalogue of a portion of the library of Charles Isaac Elton and Mary Augusta Elton. London, 1891.

> Some provenances noted in the text; no index. The collection was dispersed at Sotheby's on 1 May 1916.

Seventy five books from a library formed by E. Ph. Goldschmidt of Trinity College, Cambridge 1905-1909. Cambridge, 1909.

> A miscellaneous collection of fine and collectible books, 1478-1906. Some provenances noted in the text, and included in the index.

R. J. Lister: *A catalogue of a portion of the library of Edmund Gosse.* London, 1893.

> Mostly covers literary material, seventeenth-nineteenth centuries. The entry for each book includes a physical description and some provenances are noted. No index. Gosse's library was dispersed at Sotheby's in 1928-29.

Rariora: being some notes of the printed books, manuscripts, historical documents ... etc., collected (1858-1900) by John Eliot Hodgkin, F.S.A. 3v. London, [1902].

> Some provenances are noted in the catalogue of incunabula in vol. 2, but not included in the index. Hodgkin's library was dispersed at Sotheby's on 12-19 May 1914.

The Huth Library: a catalogue of the printed books, manuscripts, autograph letters, and engravings, collected by Henry Huth. 5v. London, 1880.

> Some provenances noted in the text, but not indexed.

J. D. Fleeman: *A preliminary handlist of copies of books associated with Dr. Samuel Johnson.* (Oxford Bibliographical Society, occasional publication 17). Oxford, 1984.

> Includes books referred to in sale catalogues and elsewhere whose present location is unknown, as well as identified books in British and American libraries. Provenances prior to, and later than, Johnson noted in the text and included in the general index.

D. McPherson: *Ben Jonson's library and marginalia: an annotated catalogue. Studies in philology: Texts and studies,* 1974. (Vol. 71, no. 5). Chapel Hill, North Carolina, 1974.

> A catalogue of surviving books from Jonson's collection which have been identified in libraries in Great Britain and North America. Inscriptions of owners other than Jonson are recorded in the text; no index.

S. de Ricci: *A handlist of the manuscripts in the Library of the Earl of Leicester at Holkham Hall.* Oxford, 1932.

> Provenances noted in the text; no index. Part of this collection has been dispersed by sale; a copy of the Handlist in the Students' Room of the Department of Manuscripts in the British Library is annotated to show the pressmarks of those which have been acquired by the BL.

B. F. Roberts: Edward Lhuyd's collection of printed books. *Bodleian Library Record* 10 (1978-82), 112-127.

> An account of the library of Edward Lhuyd (1660-1709), the Celtic scholar and Keeper of the Ashmolean Museum, followed by a list of identified books from his collection (mostly in the Bodleian Library). Provenances prior to, and later than, Lhuyd noted in the text; no index.

A list of printed books in the Library of Charles Fairfax Murray. [London], privately printed, 1907.

> A few provenances noted in the text; no index. The collection was dispersed at Sotheby's, 21 May 1920, 17 July 1922.

S. Strongman: John Parker's manuscripts: an edition of the lists in Lambeth ms. 737. *Transactions of the Cambridge Bibliographical Society* 7 (1977) 1-27.

> An annotated edition of the list of manuscripts belonging to John Parker (son of Archbishop Matthew Parker), found in Lambeth Palace ms. 737. Manuscripts which can be traced today are identified, with provenances prior to, and later than, Parker noted in the text; no index.

M. Mack: Pope's books: a biographical survey with a finding list. In M. E. Novak (ed.), *English literature in the age of disguise*, Berkeley, 1977, 209-305.

> A list of 176 items which can be identified as being from Alexander Pope's collection, mostly surviving today at Hartlebury Castle or in various American libraries. Provenances prior to, and later than, Pope noted in the text, but not indexed.

N. R. Ker: Sir John Prise. In *Books, collectors and libraries* [A collection of Ker's essays, ed. by A. G. Watson], London, 1985, 471-496 (originally published in *The Library* 5th series 10 (1955), 1-24; the reprint includes corrections).

> Prise (1502?-55) belonged to the first generation of manuscript collectors following the dissolution of the monasteries. Books from his collection are now found in Jesus College, Oxford, (ca. 40 mss.), Hereford Cathedral, (ca. 30 mss.) and elsewhere. Lists of identified books at the end of the article are followed by extensive notes which include details of provenances previous to, and later than, Prise; not separately indexed.

J. S. Dearden: John Ruskin, the collector: with a catalogue of the illuminated and other manuscripts formerly in his collection. *The Library* 5th series 21 (1966), 124-154.

> The catalogue lists 87 manuscripts known to have been owned by Ruskin. Provenances prior to, and later than, Ruskin noted in the text, but not separately indexed.

Catalogue of the Library at Broomhill, Tunbridge Wells. The property of Sir David Lionel Salomons, Bt.. [London], 1909-10.

> The collection was particularly strong in eighteenth century French books and nineteenth century illustrated books. A few provenances noted in the text, but not indexed.

A. G. Watson: *The manuscripts of Henry Savile of Banke*. London, 1969.

> An annotated edition of the catalogue of the collection of manuscripts formed by Henry Savile (1568-1617), based mainly on a list found in BL Add. ms. 35213. The manuscripts are now found in libraries around the British Isles (although many are in the BL) and are identified wherever possible. Owners previous to Savile are noted in the text, and included in the general index (which is 'primarily of authors, owners, and other persons and institutions connected with Savile's manuscripts').

[Dawson Turner]: British Library Additional Ms.23106 is a list of printed books in Dawson Turner's collection with autographs or inscriptions. Many relate to presentation or similar inscriptions in nineteenth-century books by nineteenth-century authors, but there are also entries for earlier collectors (e.g. Andrew Ducarel, Richard Farmer, Peter le Neve) where Turner had evidently acquired books from their libraries.

A. T. Hazen: *A catalogue of Horace Walpole's library*. 3v. Oxford, 1969.

> A reconstruction of Walpole's collection, based on his own catalogue, the 1842 Strawberry Hill sale catalogue, and other evidence; surviving books are identified where known. Provenances previous to, and later than, Walpole noted in the text; separate index of owners.

W. E. Moss: *The English Grolier: life, lineage, and library ... of Thomas Wotton*. Privately printed, 1941-52.

> A catalogue, with historical introduction (to be treated with caution), of surviving books from the library of Thomas Wotton, traced by Colonel Moss. Provenances subsequent to Wotton noted in the text, but not indexed.

UNITED STATES OF AMERICA

Directories listing whole collections

There is, unfortunately, no American equivalent for the British *Directory of rare book and special collections*. Both the works listed below are general directories which do not include the kind of historical details and emphasis found in the British *Directory*. As named collections are not covered by the index in either case, they cannot easily be used to check the whereabouts of such collections. These directories cover both the USA and Canada.

American library directory. 45th edn. New Providence, 1992.

> An annually published directory which covers all public, academic, government and special libraries. Libraries with substantial named collections previously belonging to particular owners or donors often have that information briefly noted in the 'Special Collections' section of their entries, but these names are not indexed.

B. T. Darnay & S. L. Stanton (eds.): *Directory of special libraries and information centers*. 8th edn. Detroit, 1983.

> More selective in coverage than the preceding entry; as before, named special collections are briefly noted, but the names are not indexed.

Alabama

University – University of Alabama

Rare books and collections of the Reynolds Historical Library: a bibliography. University, 1968.

> A large collection on medical history, 15th-20th centuries. Some provenances noted in the text, but not indexed.

California

Berkeley – University of California at Berkeley – Bancroft Library

The Bancroft Library contains a special collection of western Americana (the Bancroft Collection), together with the general rare book collections of the University of California at Berkeley (containing a wide range of material, 15th-20th centuries, as well as middle eastern papyri and medieval manuscripts). The two elements were merged ca. 1970 and a manual provenance file for the general rare book collections was maintained until ca. 1985, when a programme to computerise all the Bancroft Library catalogue records was begun. Provenance information is now recorded systematically for all holdings, and the manual file has been superseded by a separate browsable file of provenance headings available on the Library's OPAC.

Claremont – Claremont College Libraries

C. W. Dutschke & R. H. Rouse: *Medieval and renaissance manuscripts in the Claremont libraries*. (Medieval and renaissance manuscripts in California libraries, v. 1). Los Angeles, 1986.

> Covers the holdings of the six Claremont Colleges in California. Provenances noted in the text; separate index (VII) of 'Persons, institutions and places associated with the mss'.

Claremont – Francis Bacon Foundation

Provenance information is included in catalogue records held in the Library in loose-leaf binders, subdivided into several sequences by place of publication. A project to compile a provenance catalogue for all the Library's pre-1801 books was begun in 1991.

E. S. Wrigley: *Wing (Short Title Catalogue 1641-1700) numbers in the Library of the Francis Bacon Foundation, Incorporated*. Pasadena, 1959.

> Provenances noted in the text, but not indexed.

E. S. Wrigley: *Supplement to the Francis Bacon Library holdings in the Short title catalogue of English books*. Claremont, 1967.

> A catalogue of STC and Wing material acquired by the Francis Bacon Library between 1959 and 1967. Provenances noted in the text, but not indexed.

La Jolla – University of California at La Jolla

Provenance information for all material catalogued in the Special Collections Department is included in the automated catalogue records, but it is not always indexed. A number of collections of pre-1801 material have yet to be catalogued or recatalogued.

Los Angeles – University of California at Los Angeles

F. L. Finger: *Catalogue of the incunabula in the Elmer Belt Library of Vinciana.* Los Angeles, 1971.

> A small collection formed to bring together books in editions used by Leonardo da Vinci, or related to him in other ways. Now housed at the University of California at Los Angeles. Provenances noted in the text, but not indexed.

San Diego – University of California at San Diego

J. M. Edelstein: *A selected catalog of books from the library of Don Cameron Allen, Mandeville Department of Special Collections, University of California, San Diego.* San Diego, 1968.

> Only a small selection from a collection of ca. 5000 volumes, illustrating renaissance literature and culture. Provenances noted in the text, but not indexed.

San Marino – Huntington Library

Provenance information is often included in catalogue entries, and several sequences of provenance indexes on cards are available, covering different parts of the Library's collections. The index covering STC books is thought to be about 80% comprehensive, that covering Wing books rather less so. Both inscriptions and bookplates are recorded. There are also separate provenance indexes for pre-1801 American imprints, and for later printed books. The Manuscripts Department maintains its own provenance files.

C. W. Dutschke et al: *Guide to medieval and renaissance manuscripts in the Huntington Library.* 2v. San Marino, 1989.

> A catalogue of the 390 western mss in the Huntington Library. Provenances noted in the text; separate provenance index ('Index 3: persons and institutions, mainly owners').

Colorado

Boulder – University of Colorado at Boulder

The Special Collections Department maintains a series of provenance indexes, held as a donor file, former owner file, and provenance evidence file (bookplates, stamps, etc.). Coverage is very incomplete. Pre-1984 records are held on cards, those created after 1984 are held both on cards and on the Library's automated catalogue.

J. E. May: *Henry Pettit Edward Young Collection at the University of Colorado.* Boulder, 1989.

> A catalogue of 18th- and 19th-century editions of Young, mostly collected by Henry Pettit. Provenances noted in the text, but not indexed.

Connecticut

Hartford – Trinity College

A provenance index to the Library's collections is held on cards (5 drawers), although it is hoped that this will eventually be automated. New entries are now made by adding the information to the automated catalogue, rather than the manual file. Coverage is more complete for pre-1801 British imprints than for continental material.

New Haven – Yale University – Beinecke Rare Book and Manuscript Library

A provenance index is maintained on cards, currently running to 64 drawers. Entries have been made systematically for inscriptions, bookplates and marginalia for all books catalogued since ca. 1960; for material catalogued before then, coverage is only partial. Since 1980, books have been catalogued on ORBIS, the Yale Library on-line catalogue, and provenance information is both recorded and retrievable. Retrospective conversion of the card catalogue is planned. Provenance data is recorded for all manuscript material, although in the past this was seldom done for post-1600 manuscripts.

B. A. Shailor: *Catalogue of medieval and renaissance manuscripts in the Beinecke Rare Book and Manuscript Library, Yale University.* (Medieval & Renaissance Texts & Studies, 34, 48, 100). New York, 1984-92.

> The description of each ms includes a section on provenance; seperate index of provenances (index V).

Catalogue of the William Loring Andrews collection of early printed books in the Library of Yale University. New Haven, 1913.

> 36 items. Provenances noted in the text, but not indexed.

R. F. Metzdorf: *The Tinker Library: a bibliographical catalogue of the books and manuscripts collected by Chauncey Brewster Tinker.* New Haven, 1959.

> 2368 items, ms and printed, with an emphasis on significant editions of literary texts. The books are now in the Beinecke Library. Provenances noted in the text, and included in the general index.

I. MacPhail et al: *Alchemy and the occult. A catalogue of books and manuscripts from the collection of Paul and Mary Mellon.* 4v. New Haven, 1968-77.

> Vols. 1-2 cover printed books, and vols. 3-4 manuscripts. The description of each item includes a provenance section; separate provenance indexes in vols. 2 and 4.

New Haven – Yale University –
Harvey Cushing/John Hay Whitney Medical Library

A provenance index is held on cards (5 drawers); the entries relate mostly to books given by Harvey Cushing, John Fulton or Arnold Klebs and much of the material is post-1801.

Delaware

Newark – University of Delaware

A provenance index on cards was begun ca. 1975 and currently contains about 7500 entries, largely relating to 18th-19th century British or American printed books. Coverage is highly selective and tends to be restricted to former owners who are thought to be noteworthy. On-line cataloguing of the books began in the mid-1980s and selective provenance information has been included; it can be retrieved through the Library's OPAC.

District of Columbia

Folger Shakespeare Library

Separate provenance indexes on cards are maintained for printed books, and manuscripts. There are 50 drawers of cards for printed books, two for manuscripts, one for playbills and one for Shakespeare prompt-books. Entries are selective and may depend on identification of the former owner in question. The provenance index covers only material which has been catalogued; all the Library's STC holdings are catalogued, but there are appreciable holdings of post-1641 British material, and continental material of all periods, which are not catalogued.

Catalog of manuscripts of the Folger Shakespeare Library. 3v. Boston, 1988. *First supplement.* Boston, 1988.

> Reproduced from the Library's card catalogue; provenances noted in the text, but not indexed. The manuscript collections include many letters, family papers, promptbooks, diaries, commonplace books, etc.

Catalog of printed books of the Folger Shakespeare Library. 28v. Boston, 1970.
First supplement 3v. 1976.
Second supplement 2v. 1981.

> Reproduced from the card catalogue. Some provenances noted, but not indexed.

F. A. Bearman et al: *Fine and historic bookbindings from the Folger Shakespeare Library*. Washington, 1992.

> The description of each binding includes a provenance section; separate index (C) of former owners.

George Washington University

A provenance index, previously held on cards (ca. 1000 entries), has been automated and the data is available through the on-line catalogue. Coverage is selective and the great majority of the material concerned is 19th-20th century American printing.

Georgetown University

A provenance index on cards for the Library's Special Collections was begun in 1970, and by 1991 contained over 10,000 entries. The Library has several thousand pre-1801 printed books but many of these were catalogued before 1970 and are therefore not covered by the index; it is hoped that these will be re-catalogued over the next 15 years. There are plans to automate the index.

Library of Congress

A number of provenance indexes, on cards, have been created for Rare Book items catalogued between ca. 1980 and 1991. A provenance file (6 drawers) covers donors or previous owners of books whose collections were not established as special (separate) collections; an autograph file (4 drawers) covers manuscript signatures inscribed in books by contributors to the intellectual content or physical production of the books concerned; a presentation file (2 drawers) covers presentation inscriptions. There are separate provenance files for incunabula (3 drawers) and for the John Davis Batchelder Collection (3 drawers); there are also some older card file sequences covering gifts (4 drawers) and autographs (6 drawers). These card files are available in the Rare Book Division.

The card file sequences were all closed in 1991 when automated catalogue records began to be created for rare books, incorporating copy-specific information. It is now cataloguing policy in the Rare Book Division to provide added entries for former owners, using the evidence of inscriptions or bookplates, unless the individual concerned cannot be readily identified without special searching.

S. Schutzner: *Medieval and renaissance manuscript books in the Library of Congress. A descriptive catalog.*
 v. 1: *Bibles, liturgy, books of hours.* Washington, 1989.

> 64 mss covered. Provenances noted in the text; separate index of former owners.

E. M. Sowerby: *Catalogue of the library of Thomas Jefferson.* 5v. Washington, 1952-59.

> Jefferson's library of ca. 6000 books was purchased for the Library of Congress in 1815; ca. 2000 volumes remain today. Provenances prior to Jefferson noted in the text, and included in the general index in vol. 5.

F. W. Ashley: *Library of Congress: catalogue of the John Boyd Thacher collection of incunabula.* Washington, 1915.

> Comprises 840 items. Provenances noted in the text, but not indexed. A separate typescript provenance index to this catalogue was compiled by Paul Needham in 1992 and this is now shelved with the Reference Collection copy in the Library.

The Rosenwald Collection: a catalogue of illustrated books and manuscripts, ... 1150-1950, the gift of Lessing J. Rosenwald to the Library of Congress. Washington, 1954.

> Provenances noted in the text; separate provenance index.

H. Bartlett: *The Library of Congress: catalogue of early books on music (before 1800): supplement (books acquired by the Library 1913-1942)*. Washington, 1944.

> Provenances noted in the text, but not indexed. The earlier catalogue by J. Gregory (Washington, 1913) did not include provenance data.

Florida

Gainesville – University of Florida

A provenance index on cards, covering pre-1800 imprints, was maintained until 1983, when cataloguing was automated. Provenance information is included on post-1983 machine-readable records, although it has yet to be made indexable.

S. Ives (gen. ed.): *The Parkman Dexter Howe Library*. Gainesville, 1983-

> A detailed catalogue of this collection, devoted to New England authors, is being issued in parts. It is mostly concerned with nineteenth-century authors (e.g. Hawthorne, Whittier), but part I (1983) includes a catalogue of 'early New England books' by Roger Stoddard. Each fascicule has provenances noted in the text, and a separate provenance index.

Georgia

Atlanta – Emory University – Pitts Theology Library

A provenance index on cards covers about 2700 items in the Library's collections, but the bulk of the special collections material (upwards of 70,000 items) is not covered.

Illinois

Chicago – Newberry Library

An index of bookplates, on cards (2 drawers) was maintained until about 1960 but its coverage is far from complete and it includes only bookplates, not inscriptions. In about 1980 cataloguing was automated, and provenance information has been added more systematically to the records since then.

P. Saenger: *A catalogue of the pre-1500 western manuscript books at the Newberry Library*. Chicago, 1989.

> Provenances noted in the text; separate index of 'scribes, former owners, and selected codicological characteristics'.

Dictionary catalog of the history of printing from the John M. Wing Foundation in the Newberry Library. 6v. Boston, 1961.
First supplement. 3v. Boston, 1970.
Second supplement. 4v. Boston, 1981.

> Reproduces the card catalogue of the Wing Foundation collection (ca. 20,000 volumes by 1961), which illustrates the history of printing from the earliest times to the present day. Provenance (mostly bookplates) is included on main entry cards where known, with added entries provided sometimes, but not always, for owners.

Chicago – University of Chicago

E. J. Goodspeed & M. Sprengling: *A descriptive catalogue of the manuscripts in the libraries of the University of Chicago*. Chicago, 1912.

> 75 medieval mss described, mostly western. Provenances noted in the text, and included in the general index.

Urbana – University of Illinois at Urbana-Champaign

A provenance index on cards has been maintained for many years and currently runs to 7 drawers. Both manuscripts and printed books are covered, of all periods.

M. Harman: *Incunabula in the University of Illinois Library at Urbana-Champaign*. Urbana, 1979.

> 1083 items included. Provenances noted in the text, but not indexed.

Catalog of the rare book room, University Library, University of Illinois, Urbana-Champaign. 11v. Boston, 1972.
First supplement. 2v. Boston, 1978.

> Reproduced from the card catalogue. Some provenances noted, but not indexed.

J. L. Harner: *Ex libris F. S. Ferguson. A checklist of the F. S. Ferguson Collection of Scottish imprints and Scotica at the University of Illinois*. Urbana-Champaign, 1971.

> 296 items. Provenances noted in the text, but not indexed.

Indiana

Bloomington – Indiana University – Lilly Library

A provenance index on cards (the 'Association File', 3 drawers) has been maintained irrregularly for some years. Coverage is far from comprehensive; the criteria for inclusion have varied over the years, and have always been selective.

Exhibition catalogue: The first twenty-five years of printing, 1455-1480. An exhibition, The Lilly Library, Indiana University. Bloomington, 1967.

> Provenances noted in the text and included in the general index.

Notre Dame – University of Notre Dame

A provenance index on cards was begun in the 1980s and is still being added to, but with about 600 records it covers only a small proportion of the Library's Rare Book Collections (ca. 30,000 items, 15th-20th centuries, mostly British and European).

J. A. Corbett: *Catalogue of the medieval & renaissance manuscripts in the University of Notre Dame*. Notre Dame, 1978.

> 64 items described. Provenances noted in the text, and included in the general index.

A. Masin: *Incunabula typographica: catalog of fifteenth-century books held by the Memorial Library of the University of Notre Dame.* Notre Dame, 1979.

> Some provenances noted in the text, and included in the indexes.

Terre Haute – Indiana State University

A provenance index on cards has been maintained for some time, although its coverage is incomplete. Provenance information is now added to the Library's automated records, when applicable, although it is not fully searchable in the OPAC.

Kansas

Lawrence – University of Kansas

The Special Collections Department has maintained a provenance index on cards for some time, currently containing ca. 9900 entries. Coverage is not comprehensive, as cataloguing standards have varied in the past, but current practice is to record all provenance information as fully as possible.

R. M. Mengel: *A catalogue of the Ellis Collection of ornithological books in the University of Kansas libraries.* Lawrence, 1972-

> Being issued in parts covering sections of the alphabet. Largely 19th-20th century imprints, with some earlier material. Provenances noted in the text, but not as yet indexed.

Kentucky

Lexington – University of Kentucky

A provenance index on cards was begun in 1968 and is still being maintained, although only a small handful of entries relate to pre-1801 material. A separate card index of bookplates contains about 1000 entries.

Maryland

Baltimore – Johns Hopkins University

L. H. Fowler & E. Baer: *The Fowler architectural collection of the Johns Hopkins University: catalogue.* Baltimore, 1961.

> 448 items, mostly 16th-18th centuries. Provenances noted in the text, but not indexed.

Baltimore – Walters Art Gallery

L. M. C. Randall: *Medieval and renaissance manuscripts in the Walters Art Gallery.*
v. 1: *France, 875-1420.* Baltimore, 1989.
v. 2: *France, 1420-1540.* Baltimore, 1993.

> Provenances noted in the text; separate sequence of 'previous owners' in the general index.

Massachusetts

Boston – Boston Public Library

A card index of bookplates (12 drawers) has been maintained for some time, covering holdings of all periods down to the 20th century.

Boston – Boston University

Added entries for former owners began to be added to the catalogue records for Special Collections material in the 1970s, initially on cards and after 1979 on the machine readable records in the on-line catalogue. There is some pre-1801 European material in the Collections, which mostly comprise 19th-20th century American or British imprints.

Cambridge – Harvard University – Houghton Library

A provenance index on cards is maintained, currently running to 66 drawers, alhough it covers only material which has been catalogued or recatalogued since 1942. It is Houghton Library practice to classify books which come from the collections of recognised authors after that author's works, and in these cases entries are not made in the provenance file, but in the main catalogue sequence.

Catalogue of manuscripts in the Houghton Library, Harvard University. 8v. Alexandria, 1986.

> Reproduced from the card catalogue in the Houghton Library, which contains most (but not all) of the manuscript collections of Harvard University. The single alphabetical sequence includes entries for previous owners of early mss.

R. S. Wieck: *Late medieval and renaissance illuminated manuscripts 1350-1525 in the Houghton Library.* Cambridge, 1983.

> Prepared to coincide with an exhibition mounted in 1983. Provenances noted in the text; separate index of previous owners.

J. H. Baker: *English legal manuscripts vol. I. Catalogue of the manuscript year books, readings, and law reports in the library of the Harvard Law School.* Zug, 1975.

> Harvard Law School has the largest collection of English legal mss outside the British Isles. The description of each ms includes a provenance section; separate index of former owners.

J. E. Walsh: *A catalogue of the fifteenth-century printed books in the Harvard University Library.*
v. 1: *Books printed in Germany, German-speaking Switzerland, and Austro-Hungary.* (Medieval and Renaissance Texts and Studies, 84). New York, 1991.

> Provenances noted in the text; separate provenance index.

R. Mortimer: *Harvard College Library Department of Printing and Graphic Arts catalogue of books and manuscripts.*
Part I: *French 16th century books.* 2v. Cambridge, 1964.
Part II: *Italian 16th century books.* Cambridge, 1974.

> Provenances noted in the text, but not indexed.

Exhibition catalogues: A. Anninger: *Spanish and Portuguese 16th century books in the Department of Printing and Graphic Arts: a description of an exhibition.* Cambridge, 1985.

> Includes a catalogue of 210 items from the collection; provenances noted in the text, but not indexed.

A catalogue of an exhibition of the Philip Hofer Bequest in the Department of Printing and Graphic Arts. Cambridge, 1988.

> 100 exhibits. Provenances noted in the text; separate provenance index.

Cambridge – Harvard University – Francis A. Countway Library of Medicine

J. F. Ballard: *A catalogue of the medieval and renaissance manuscripts and incunabula in the Boston Medical Library.* Boston, 1944.

> Some provenances noted in the text, but not indexed.

Northampton – Smith College

The collections of the Rare Book Room (ca. 23,000 volumes) are covered comprehensively by a donor index and an association index, on cards. All provenances are recorded in the association index, including annotations, autographs, bookplates, initials, inscriptions and stamps.

Waltham – Brandeis University

D. S. Berkowitz: *A descriptive catalogue of the incunabula of the Brandeis University Library.* Waltham, 1963.

> Includes 22 items. Provenances noted in the text, but not indexed.

Wellesley – Wellesley College

The Special Collections Department maintains a bookplate and autograph index on cards for the English Poetry Collection. Since 1987, provenance information (bookplates, autographs, and donors) has been included in automated catalogue records, although the relevant note field has yet to be indexed.

A catalogue of early and rare editions of English poetry, compiled and presented to Wellesley College by George Herbert Palmer. Boston, 1923.

> A major collection of English poetry, from Chaucer to Masefield. Provenances noted in the text; separate indexes of 'Autographs, letters, inscriptions, &c.' and 'Bookplates'.

M. H. Jackson: *Catalogue of the Frances Taylor Pearsons Plimpton Collection of Italian books and manuscripts in the Library of Wellesley College.* Cambridge (Mass.), 1929.

> Ca. 1000 items, largely 15th-16th century Italian imprints, intended to illustrate the history of Italian literature of the 14th-16th centuries. Provenances noted in the text, but not indexed.

Williamstown – Chapin Library, Williams College

A provenance index on cards is maintained and all material catalogued since 1976 has been thoroughly documented. Items catalogued before then are less well covered, but older catalogue records are being upgraded as resources permit. Since 1983, provenance information has been included in the Library's automated catalogue.

L. E. Osborne: *The Chapin Library, Williams College: a short-title list*. Portland, 1939.

> A wide-ranging collection of ca. 12,000 volumes. Some provenances (where 'previous ownership is known and is of interest') noted in the text, but not indexed.

Worcester – American Antiquarian Society

A provenance index on cards, covering all pre-1801 imprints then in the Society's library, was compiled in 1922-24. This is still available in the Library; it contains about 1500 entries, but has not been added to since it was first made. Since 1980, automated records which include comprehensive provenance data have been created for all pre-1877 books catalogued at the AAS. The online catalogue holds added entries for former owners and donors in a separate index. All the Society's pre-1801 North American imprints (ca. 23,000 books) have been catalogued in this way, as part of the North American Imprints Program (NAIP), and a number of early British and European printed books have been covered too. The Society's automated file of provenance data is therefore large, and constantly growing.

Michigan

East Lansing – Michigan State University

A provenance index on cards is maintained (currently about 90 cm of cards), including bookplates and labels, autographs, inscriptions, and donors; this covers British, continental and American printed books down to the end of the nineteenth century.

Minnesota

Minneapolis – The Bakken

J. A. Overmier & J. E. Senior: *Books and manuscripts of the Bakken*. Metuchen, 1992.

> A catalogue of the library of The Bakken, a Museum of Electricity in Life, founded in 1969 by Earl Bakken and now based in Minneapolis. The collection is predominantly post-1801, but a number of relevant earlier works are included. Provenances are noted in the text and included in the index.

Minneapolis – University of Minnesota

A provenance index on cards is fairly complete for catalogued books published before 1700, and selective in its coverage of post-1700 material. Signatures, bookplates, stamps, etc. are recorded. Separate files are also maintained for signed bindings, armorial bindings, and letters bound with books. These provisions do not apply to material which is only partly catalogued, currently estimated at ca. 50,000 items.

Missouri

St. Louis – St. Louis Public Library

A provenance index on cards was maintained for special collections material from about 1970 until 1982, after which provenance data was added selectively to the Library's automated records. The special collections are chiefly concerned with the history and culture of the area around St. Louis, and it is thought that the Library's holdings of pre-1801 imprints runs to a little over 1000 items.

St. Louis – Washington University

A provenance index on cards was maintained up to 1978 (10 drawers, divided into former owners, and donors). Since then, provenance information has been added to the Library's automated catalogue records. A retrospective conversion project is being carried out, and by summer 1994 all provenance data, including that from the card catalogue, will be searchable through the OPAC.

New Hampshire

Hanover – Dartmouth College

A provenance index on cards was maintained ca. 1950-ca. 1965 and has about 3350 entries. It covers various kinds of evidence of former ownership, selectively, for a small proportion of the Library's stock of rare books (currently over 72,000 items, of which ca. 5000 are pre-1801 imprints). Automated cataloguing began in the 1980s and noteworthy provenance information is now added to the on-line records.

New Jersey

Princeton – Princeton University

A provenance index on cards currently has about 8000 entries, covering perhaps 10,000 books, but this covers only a small proportion of the 150,000 or so books in the Special Collections. It is still being maintained. A number of other finding aids are available in the Library, relating to particular collections, which may provide additional information on previous ownership.

New York

Ithaca – Cornell University

R. G. Calkins: *Medieval and renaissance manuscripts in the Cornell University Library. The Cornell Library Journal*, no. 13, 1972 (whole issue).

> 54 mss described. Provenances, mostly 19th century or later, noted in the text, but not indexed.

M. Bishop: *Petrarch: catalogue of the Petrarch Collection in Cornell University Library*. New York, 1974.

> Reproduced from catalogue cards; a major collection of material by and about Petrarch, 15th-20th centuries. Some provenances noted in the text, but not indexed.

New York – American Museum of Natural History

A provenance index was begun in 1985 but so far only covers a small proportion of the Library's holdings.

New York – Grolier Club

Exhibition catalogues: The catalogue of books from the libraries or collections of celebrated bibliophiles … with arms or devices upon the bindings: exhibited at the Grolier Club … January 1895. New York, 1895.

> 244 items, mostly continental collectors 16th-18th centuries. The index is in effect a provenance index.

Catalogue of an exhibition of renaissance bookbindings held at the Grolier Club. New York, 1937.

> 103 items. Some provenances noted in the text, and included in the general index.

New York – Hispanic Society of America

A provenance index for pre-1701 imprints was begun in 1985 but so far covers only about 1200 books acquired since 1984. An index covering pre-1984 accessions will be created in the future.

C. B. Faulhaber: *Medieval manuscripts in the library of the Hispanic Society of America*. 2v. New York, 1983.

> 780 items described. Provenances noted in the text; separate index (XI) of owners, and of coats of arms (VI), mostly Spanish.

New York – New York Public Library

The Rare Book Room has an extensive provenance and autograph file, which covers an appreciable proportion of the pre-1801 books acquired since the end of the nineteenth century. There are separate indexes for armorial bindings and bookplates, and some collections which are kept separately also have their own provenance files (e.g. Spenser, Arents). Provenance data is included in the Library's automated records for rare books, which are available through RLIN and OCLC. Some details of the Library's range of special indexes, including provenance files, will be found in the *Guide to the research collections of the New York Public Library*, by S. P. Williams et al, Chicago, 1975, p. 50.

S. de Ricci: Medieval manuscripts in the New York Public Library. *Bulletin of the New York Public Library* 34 (1930), 297-322.

> A handlist containing brief descriptions of 137 mss. Provenances noted in the text, but not indexed.

New York – New York University

Provenance data is being added to automated records which are being created for a collection of 19th century British books.

New York – Pforzheimer Library

The Carl H. Pforzheimer Library. English literature 1475-1700. 3v. New York, 1940.

> A detailed catalogue of 1105 English printed books. Provenances noted in the text; separate provenance index.

New York – Pierpont Morgan Library

The recording of provenance information has long been a priority for Pierpont Morgan cataloguers, and it is the Library's policy to identify and record all evidence of previous ownership, as far as this is possible. A provenance index on cards is maintained (currently 10 drawers), and provenance data is now input to, and retrievable from, the Library's automated catalogue. Coverage of the collections is extensive, but not complete.

M. R. James & A. W. Pollard: *Catalogue of manuscripts and early printed books from the libraries of William Morris, Richard Bennett, Bertram, fourth Earl of Ashburnham, and other sources, now forming portion of the library of J. Pierpont Morgan.* 4v. London, 1906-07.

> Some provenances noted in the text; vol. I (manuscripts, by M. R. James) has a separate index of 'owners, other names occurring, and literary contents'.

M. Harrsen & G. K. Boyce: *Italian manuscripts in the Pierpont Morgan Library: descriptive survey of the principal illuminated manuscripts of the sixth to the sixteenth centuries.* New York, 1953.

125 items described. Provenances noted in the text, and included in the general index (grouped together at heading: Provenance).

M. Harrsen: *Central European manuscripts in the Pierpont Morgan Library*. New York, 1968.

> 64 items described, 8th-17th centuries. Provenances noted in the text, and included in the general index (grouped together at heading: Provenance).

J. Plummer:*The Glazier collection of illuminated manuscripts*. New York, 1968.

> A catalogue of 69 medieval illuminated mss given to the Pierpont Morgan Library by William S. Glazier (d.1962). Provenances noted in the text, but not indexed.

A catalogue of a collection of books formed by James Toovey, principally from the library of the Earl of Gosford, the property of J. Pierpont Morgan. New York, 1901.

> Particularly strong in books from the Aldine Press in the 16th century, but covering European literature of all periods, and including many fine bindings. Some provenances noted in the text, but not indexed.

P. Needham: *Twelve centuries of bookbindings 400-1600*. New York, 1979.

> A detailed catalogue of 100 notable bindings from the Pierpont Morgan Library. Provenances noted in the text; separate provenance index.

H. M. Nixon: *Sixteenth-century gold-tooled bookbindings in the Pierpont Morgan Library*. New York, 1971.

> 66 items described. Provenances noted in the text; separate index of owners.

Exhibition catalogues: C. R. Morey et al: *The Pierpont Morgan Library: exhibition of illuminated manuscripts held at the New York Public Library*. New York, 1934.

> Detailed descriptions of 152 exhibits. Provenances noted in the text, and included in the general index.

Books and manuscripts from the Heinemann collection. New York, 1963.

> A selection of items from the collection of D. N. Heinemann (d.1962), deposited in the Pierpont Morgan Library, particularly strong in French and German literature of the 18th and 19th centuries, and musical mss. Provenances noted in the text, but not indexed.

New York – University of Buffalo

A selection of books and manuscripts in the Lockwood Memorial Library of the University of Buffalo. New York, 1935.

> Some provenances noted in the text, but not indexed.

Rochester – University of Rochester

An incomplete provenance index on cards (ca. 6500 entries) exists for bookplates and association copies of printed books. Added entries for noteworthy former owners are now provided in automated catalogue records.

North Carolina

Chapel Hill – University of North Carolina at Chapel Hill

A provenance index on cards, covering both printed books and medieval or renaissance manuscripts, was begun in the mid-1970s, and covers material catalogued since then.

Durham – Duke University

A provenance index on cards has been maintained for some time, although coverage of the collections is not complete. Since 1988, the card file has been closed and provenance data is included in the on-line catalogue; it can be retrieved through the OPAC.

Greensboro – University of North Carolina at Greensboro

A provenance index is maintained on cards, which covers all the Library's rare book collections; only a few hundred of these entries relate to pre-1801 European imprints.

Ohio

Cleveland – Case Western Reserve University

A provenance file was begun in 1980; since that time, provenance data appears in the Special Collections card catalogue and in the Library's online catalogue.

Columbus – Ohio State University

A provenance file to cover the rare book collections was begun in the 1980s, but it is as yet very incomplete. Provenance data is added selectively to on-line catalogue records, although an indexing system has yet to be developed. An annotated handlist of the University's incunabula is in preparation, in which provenances are being recorded.

Kent – Kent State University

Provenance information has been recorded for some time when cataloguing books and manuscripts in the Department of Special Collections, and provenance data can be retrieved from the Library's on-line catalogue, which includes several thousand provenance tracings.

Pennsylvania

Carlisle – Dickinson College

M. E. Korey: *The books of Isaac Norris (1701-1766) at Dickinson College.* Carlisle, 1976.

> 1902 items. Provenances noted in the text; provenance index, with biographical details.

Haverford – Haverford College

An 'ex libris' index on cards (ca. 700 entries) covers previous ownership of books in the Magill Library; an additional 'autographs' file (ca. 1250 entries) includes signatures by authors or illustrators, and also covers provenance.

C. W. Miller: *A descriptive catalogue of the William Pyle Philips Collection.* Part II of *William Pyle Philips Collection in the Haverford College Library*, Haverford, 1952.

> A small collection of renaissance literature, mainly English (58 items described). Some provenances noted in the text, but not indexed.

Latrobe – St. Vincent College

V. L. Cassidy: *A descriptive catalog of the incunabula in St. Vincent College and Archabbey Library*. Pittsburgh, 1976.

> 83 items. Some provenances recorded in the text.

Philadelphia – College of Physicians of Philadelphia

A provenance index for the rare book and manuscript collections was begun earlier this century, but not continued. A new file was begun in 1989 but so far covers only material catalogued since then.

Philadelphia – Free Library of Philadelphia

A provenance file on cards covers the collection of Early American Children's Books, and the Hampton L. Carson Collection on common law. These represent only a small proportion of the Library's total rare book collections, many of which are only partially catalogued.

E. Wolf: *A descriptive catalogue of the John Frederick Lewis collection of European manuscripts in the Free Library of Philadelphia.* Philadelphia, 1937.

> Comprises 199 medieval mss. Each description includes a section on provenance; separate index of former owners.

Philadelphia – Library Company of Philadelphia

A provenance index on cards (ca. 20,000 entries) covers most of the Library's pre-1801 imprints, although indexing is selective with an emphasis on previous American owners. Provenance data is also included in on-line catalogue records. The Library's accession records are useful in determining provenance for the several large collections of books which were acquired in the 18th and 19th centuries. Some of the more noteworthy provenances on the Library's shelves are described in 'Some books of early English provenance in the Library Company of Philadelphia', by Edwin Wolf, in *The Book Collector* 9 (1960), 275-284. Wolf's card index on books previously owned by Benjamin Franklin (ca. 3000 entries, two thirds of the books being held at the Library Company) was given to the Library when Wolf died in 1991, and it is now available for consultation there.

E. Wolf: *The library of James Logan of Philadelphia 1674-1751*. Philadelphia, 1974.

> The bequest of the books of James Logan, a little over 2000 volumes, formed the foundation collection of what is now the Library Company of Philadelphia. Provenances noted in the text; separate index of former owners and correspondents, with biographical details. Includes an introductory essay on the formation and subsequent history of Logan's library.

E. Wolf: *A check-list of the books in the Library Company of Philadelphia in and supplementary to Wing's Short-title catalogue 1641-1700*. Philadelphia, 1959.

> Donors and (to a limited extent) previous owners noted in the text; separate provenance index.

Philadelphia – Temple University

A small provenance index on cards is maintained for the Special Collections, and provenance data is also included selectively on on-line catalogue records.

Philadelphia – University of Pennsylvania

A provenance index on cards is maintained by the Special Collections Department, although its coverage is incomplete; provenance data is included and indexed in catalogue records created in the on-line catalogue.

N. P. Zacour & R. Hirsch: *Catalogue of the manuscripts in the libraries of the University of Pennsylvania to 1800*. Philadelphia, 1965.

> Provenances noted in the text, and included in the index.

Pittsburgh – Carnegie-Mellon University – Hunt Institute

J. Quinby & A. Stevenson: *Catalogue of botanical books in the collection of Rachel McMasters Miller Hunt*.

v. 1: *Printed books 1477-1700.*
v. 2: *Printed books 1701-1800.*
Pittsburgh, 1958-61.

> Provenances noted in the text, and included in the general index. The collection is now housed in the library of the Hunt Institute for Botanical Documentation of Carnegie-Mellon University.

Rhode Island

Newport – Redwood Library Company

M. McCorison: *The 1764 catalogue of the Redwood Library Company at Newport, Rhode Island.* New Haven, 1965.

> An edition of the 1764 printed catalogue of the Redwood Library (867 items), with notes on copies which survive in the Library today. Provenances noted in the text, and included in the general index. The Library was founded by Abraham Redwood in 1747, and his donation was used to buy books from London through the agency of the London merchant John Thomlinson.

Providence – Brown University

A. W. Pollard: *Catalogue of books mostly from the presses of the first printers ... collected by Rush C. Hawkins ... and deposited in the AnnMary Brown Memorial at Providence, Rhode Island.* Oxford, 1910.

> Provenances largely noted in the text, but not indexed. Includes a list of incunabula in the John Carter Brown Library and the General Library of Brown University, outside the Hawkins collection.

Bibliotheca Americana: catalogue of the John Carter Brown Library in Brown University.
v. 1 (imprints to 1599) Providence, 1919
v. 2 (imprints 1600-1658) Providence, 1922
v. 3 (imprints 1659-1674) Providence, 1931
v. 4 (imprints 1675-1700) Providence, 1973

> Provenances noted in the text, but not indexed.

South Carolina

Columbia – University of South Carolina

A provenance index on cards has been maintained for some time. Since 1989, provenance data has been added to the Library's on-line catalogue records, although the card file is still kept up selectively. The G. Ross Roy Collection of Burnsiana and Scottish verse is currently being catalogued and provenance is being recorded; a published catalogue is planned ca. 1995.

D.-J. Stribling Ridge: *Rare book collection in the McKissick Memorial Library, University of South Carolina.* Columbia, 1966.

> A catalogue of the contents of the Rare Books Room as it stood in 1966. 2277 items described. Provenances noted in the text, but not indexed.

Texas

Austin – Harry Ransom Humanities Research Center, Universty of Texas

Since ca. 1975, a provenance index on cards has been maintained for all books catalogued, with a view to recording provenance data as fully as possible; before 1975, provenance data was often added to main entry catalogue cards, but no separate provenance index file was generated. It is thought that about 25% of the collections of pre-1801 material are currently covered by the provenance index.

Utah

Provo – Brigham Young University

A provenance index on cards is maintained for the Special Collections (12.5 linear feet of cards); cataloguing is now automated, and provenance data is included.

Virginia

Richmond – Virginia Historical Society

A provenance file on cards is maintained (the association file, ca. 5700 entries), covering inscriptions and bookplates; it is not kept in the Reading Room, but is available on request. Inclusion is selective and is biased towards former owners from Virginia.

Williamsburg – College of William & Mary

A provenance index on cards was maintained for some time, although provenance data is now added to on-line catalogue records instead. Most of the material covered by the provenance file is Americana and Virginiana.

Wisconsin

Milwaukee – University of Wisconsin-Milwaukee

M. A. Mikolajczak: *A selected catalog of books in the seventeenth century research collection of the University of Wisconsin-Milwaukee*. University of Wisconsin, 1982.

> Ca. 250 items described. Bookplates, but not inscriptions, noted in the text, but not indexed.

Catalogues with national coverage

S. de Ricci & W. J. Wilson: *Census of medieval and renaissance manuscripts in the United States and Canada.* 3v. New York, 1935-40.
C. O. Faye & W. H. Bond: *Supplement to the census.* New York, 1962.

> An attempt to produce a union catalogue of pre-1600 western manuscripts in North American libraries, public and private. Provenances noted in the text, although not exhaustively; both the *census* and the *Supplement* have separate indexes of previous owners. The *Supplement* includes corrections to the original *Census*, as well as additional material.

The National Union Catalog: pre-1956 imprints. 685v. + supplements. London & Chicago, 1968-81.

> The *NUC* brings together in one sequence the holdings of pre-1956 western printed material from many hundreds of research libraries in North America. Entries are based on the cards or other reports submitted by the various libraries and in many cases copy-specific notes, relating to the copy on which the *NUC* entry is based, are reprinted in the form in which they were reported. Provenance information is therefore scattered throughout the catalogue, but is is not accessible or retrievable in any useful way.

J. H. Baker: *English legal manuscripts in the United States of America: a descriptive list.*
vol. 1: Medieval and renaissance. London, 1985.
vol. 2: 1558-1902. London, 1990.

> Provenances noted in the text and included in the index. The holdings of about 35 major U.S. libraries are covered.

D. Dutschke: *Census of Petrarch manuscripts in the United States.* (Censimento dei codici Petrarcheschi, 9). Padua, 1986.

> Provenances noted in the text; separate index of owners.

The history of bookbinding 525-1950 A.D. An exhibition held at the Baltimore Museum of Art 1957-58. Baltimore, 1957.

> 718 items, drawn from a number of U.S. institutional and private libraries. Provenances noted in the text, and partially included in the index.

Private collections, not subsequently absorbed entire by institutions

S. de Ricci: *A catalogue of early English books in the library of John L. Clawson, Buffalo.* Philadelphia & New York, 1924.

> 926 items described. Some provenances noted in the text, but not indexed. Most of the books were sold in 1926.

Catalogue of the library of Charles Templeton Crocker. Hillsborough, 1918.

> Strong in literature and American history, largely 19/20th century, but including some earlier material. Some provenances noted in the text, but not indexed. The bulk of his collection is now divided between the California Historical Society, the University of California at Los Angeles, and the University of Virginia.

C. Shipman: *A catalogue of books in English later than 1700: forming a portion of the library of Robert Hoe.* 3v. New York, 1905.

C. Shipman: *A catalogue of books printed in foreign languages before the year 1600, forming a portion of the library of Robert Hoe*. New York, 1907.
C. Shipman: *Catalogue of books in foreign languages published after the year 1600: forming a portion of the library of Robert Hoe*. 4v. New York, 1909.
C. Shipman: *A catalogue of manuscripts: forming a portion of the library of Robert Hoe*. New York, 1909.

> Some provenances noted in the text, but not indexed. The collection was sold at auction, 1911-13.

H. A. Morrison: *The Leiter Library: a catalogue of the books manuscripts and maps principally relating to America collected by the late Levi Ziegler Leiter*. Washington, 1907.

> Includes many British and continental imprints. Some provenances noted in the text, but not indexed. The collection was sold at auction, 1933.

Catalogue of a collection of books formed by William G. Medlicott, of Longmeadow, Mass. Boston, 1878.

> 3667 entries; strong in English literature and history. Some provenances noted in the text, but not indexed.

D. H. Hook and J. M. Norman: *The Haskell F. Norman Library of science and medicine*. 2v. San Francisco, 1991.

> A detailed catalogue of a distinguished contemporary private collection, containing over 2500 first editions of significant scientific and medical works, 15th-20th centuries. Provenances noted in the text; separate provenance index.

CANADA

New Brunswick

Sackville – Mount Allison University

L. McCann: *The Edgar and Dorothy Davidson Collection of Canadiana at Mount Allison University*. Sackville, 1991.

> A collection of ca. 600 items, 16th-19th centuries, relevant to the history of Canada. Provenances noted in the text.

Ontario

Hamilton – McMaster University

A provenance index on cards was begun in 1980, and since then its coverage has been extended to cover all the Library's pre-1801 collections (ca. 30,000 volumes). The index contains about 5400 entries.

Kingston – Queens' University Libraries

A provenance file on cards was methodically collected when the Special Collections Unit was established in 1964, and since then provenance information has been recorded for all pre-1801 material and other Special Collections material where appropriate. Since 1980, cataloguing has been automated, and provenance data is included. Records entered since 1988 are searchable in the on-line system. Automated provenance records include the entire library system holdings as well as those in the Special Collections Unit.

Ottawa – National Library of Canada

Provenance data for pre-1801 books has been included in the Library's automated catalogue records for some time, although it is not at present searchable and there are no separate provenance indexes.

Toronto – Thomas Fisher Rare Book Library, University of Toronto

The Library maintains three types of provenance file – autographs, associations, and bookplates. The autograph file, for inscriptions, is restricted to people who can be identified in standard reference works, and no records are kept for unidentified autographs. Bookplates are recorded more thoroughly and every effort is made to identify them where necessary (and also to identify armorial stamps and ciphers). Xerox copies of bookplates are kept and filed. The association file covers those cases where books are known to have belonged to a particular individual, but the bookplate or other identification was not put into the book by the individual concerned. The files are available on cards, but added entries are also made on the Library's automated catalogue records, and these headings can be searched through the OPAC.

Exhibition catalogue: Twenty-five years: an exhibition in celebration of the twenty-fifth anniversary of the founding of the Department of Rare Books and Special Collections, the Thomas Fisher Rare Book Library, University of Toronto. Toronto, 1980.

> 35 selected highlights from the collections, 13th-20th centuries. Provenances noted in the text, but not indexed.

Quebec

Montreal – McGill University

A provenance index on cards was begun by the Rare Books Department in 1969, and all material catalogued since then has had provenance data recorded. Cataloguing is now automated, and provenances are included, and searchable, in the on-line system. There is no access to provenance information for material catalogued before 1969, although the old shelf-list cards sometimes had a note added about famous former owners.

VIII

HERALDRY; PALAEOGRAPHY; BIOGRAPHY; WORKS ON BOOK COLLECTING & LIBRARY HISTORY

This chapter aims to bring together a range of material which relates to the deciphering of provenance evidence, the identification of names, and placing the information in the context of existing published work.

Introduction and basic terminology

The researcher looking at ownership evidence in early books will not go far before encountering a coat of arms or other heraldic device. The continued extensive use of coats of arms by corporations, such as universities and local councils, ensures that they remain familiar everyday objects, although the use of heraldic insignia by individuals is much less common than was once the case. The importance of a coat of arms as a status symbol has declined. The heralds no longer spend their time making county visitations to record the arms of all the families entitled to use them, to challenge people to prove their right where necessary, and to publish lists of those whose right is not established, who are thus forbidden to call themselves gentlemen. This does not mean that heraldry is not taken seriously by those whose business it is to do so, and the College of Arms, which has been described as the only part of the English establishment never to have been reformed by Parliament, continues to monitor the use of arms much as it did in the sixteenth century.

The use of heraldry has been immensely popular as a means of designating ownership, and it is manifested in books as bookplates, armorial book stamps, or painted-in coats of arms. Because an heraldic achievement is (at least in theory) a unique pictorial device applicable to only one individual or family, it should always be possible to identify an owner from his or her arms, and the regular use of arms without a name attached, in both bookplates and book stamps, makes some knowledge of heraldry a *sine qua non* for the student of provenance. It cannot be denied that it sometimes appears to be a complicated science, and one with a language of its own which immediately proves a barrier to the uninitiated. The terminology of heraldry developed in the middle ages when Anglo-Norman was the language of the English court, and the words which were in everyday use then have remained fixed in the heraldic amber while all else has changed. One does not speak of a red shield with a blue bar across the middle, with three gold stars on the bar, but of *Gules a fess azure three estoiles or.* This constancy does however mean that heraldry has remained a fairly consistent science for many centuries, with clearly defined rules which have changed very little since the sixteenth century and earlier, and once the basics have been mastered and the language is understood, it should be possible to decipher a wide range of armorial bearings.

This section attempts a simple explanation of the most fundamental elements of British heraldry, outlining the principal features which appear on coats of arms and the way in which they are described, and lists a number of standard textbooks and reference books where further information will be found. It must be stressed that a brief account like this cannot possibly be a substitute for the detailed information which will be found in the textbooks, whose perusal is strongly recommended.

The origins of heraldry are not altogether clear and have been the subject of debate; the traditional and immediately obvious explanation, based on the need to distinguish armour on the battlefield, can be challenged on a number of counts, and it has been suggested that coats of arms developed from patterns on seals used as early as the eleventh century. Whatever the origins, the practice of adopting distinctive designs on shields as identifying symbols of particular families can be traced spreading across Europe by the middle of the twelfth century. The earliest designs were very simple, but as time passed they grew more complicated and distinctive national characteristics developed. The rules and terminology which govern heraldry today began to emerge in the thirteenth century. At first, adoption of arms was a fairly arbitrary process which was not governed by any central regulatory body, but the fifteenth century saw a number of changes and the Crown, acting through the heralds who comprise the College of Arms, exercised stricter control over their use. Then, as now, arms could only be used by people with a grant of arms from one of the Kings of Arms, or by those who could prove descent from someone entitled to bear arms. The registration of arms became an important function of the heralds, and between 1530 and 1688 they travelled around the country on visitations, recording arms and issuing new grants where appropriate. Since the beginning of the sixteenth century, many hundreds of grants of arms have been made. The use of arms is not restricted to the aristocracy and armorial families have proliferated in the ranks of the gentry and the professional classes.

Armorial bearings and the right to use them are legal property which pass by inheritance from generation to generation. Children are entitled to use their father's arms, and they pass them on to their children, possibly in an altered form (see *marks of cadency* and *marshalling of arms* below). A coat of arms on a shield constitutes the central focus and the most important part of any grant of arms, but a full **heraldic achievement** normally comprises a shield surmounted by a helmet with a crest on top (sitting on a wreath known as a torse), with mantling flowing round the shield and the possible addition of supporters at each side, a badge and a motto. Fig. 8.1 reproduces a late seventeenth-century representation of the achievement of George Savile, Marquis of Halifax (1633-95), which displays most of these features. The shield bearing his arms (argent on a bend sable three owls of the field) is flanked by his supporters (two talbots argent ducally gorged per pale gules and or), has his motto 'Be fast' at the base, and has his crest (an owl argent), torse, helmet and mantling above. The coronet between the shield and the helmet is an additional feature often found in the arms of the English aristocracy, and its shape indicates the bearer's rank of Marquis (see p. 282 below). Women do not use a crest, helmet or mantling and

Fig. 8.1 The heraldic achievement of George Savile, Marquis of Halifax (1633-95), as shown in *The art of heraldry*, London, 1693.

when unmarried or widowed they display their arms on a lozenge, rather than a shield. A spinster bears her father's arms, on a lozenge, and a married woman bears her husband's arms on a shield (these will be a mixture of the arms of the two families, as determined by the rules for marshalling). A widow continues to use her husband's arms, but reverts from the shield to the lozenge. Some of these points may be seen illustrated in the armorial binding stamp of Barbara Yelverton, Viscountess de Longueville (fig. 8.2). She was born Barbara Talbot ca. 1671, and in 1689 she married Henry Yelverton (d.1704), who was created Viscount de Longueville in 1690. This binding was made after her husband's death, so her arms are those of the Viscount, impaling Yelverton (argent three lions rampant and a chief gules) with Talbot (gules a lion rampant within a bordure engrailed or), displayed on a lozenge (as usual, the armorial stamp makes no attempt to reproduce the tinctures).

An individual's coat of arms should be unique, and that uniqueness is defined not in any particular representation of the arms, but in the language used to describe them. There is no one correct shape of shield, or shade of colouring which must always be used for particular arms, and there is no single defined pattern for portraying any of the many objects which may appear on shields. Coats of arms are described according to a strict set of rules and it is the written description or **blazon** which uniquely defines a particular achievement. Any legitimate representation of a blazon will constitute an acceptable depiction of the coat of arms concerned.

A coat of arms comprises either a pattern formed with geometrical divisions, or a group of objects arranged in a particular way, or a combination of the two. Each part of the shield also has a defined colour, or **tincture** in heraldic terminology. Strictly speaking, tinctures are not just colours, but also include metals and furs which may be used in constructing real shields; in the two-dimensional black-and-white representations which are normally found in books, metals, furs and colours are all depicted according to a system of shading which is shown in the chapter on bookplates on p. 68 above. Tinctures are always referred to in blazons according to their correct heraldic name. The list of permitted tinctures has varied somewhat over the centuries, and different heraldic writers have introduced peculiarities of their own, but there is a basic core of nine tinctures which have been in common use for many centuries:

Metals	*Term of blazon*
Gold	Or
Silver	Argent

Colours	
Blue	Azure
Red	Gules
Black	Sable
Green	Vert
Purple	Purpure

Fig. 8.2　Armorial binding of Barbara Yelverton, Viscountess de Longueville: National Art Library Clements FF17, G. Stanhope, *The paraphrase and comment on the epistles and gospels*, 1705-08. (Reduced from 20 × 12 cm.)

Furs

Ermine	Ermine
Vair	Vair

Animals and other objects which are meant to be painted in their natural colours are referred to as *proper*. Ermine is the winter fur of the stoat, white with a black tail, and it is depicted as white with a speckled black pattern. Vair is grey squirrel fur, which was sewn up in the middle ages using belly and back fur to create a kind of chequered design. It is depicted in coats of arms using a two-tone pattern of alternating cup- or bell-shapes, normally blue and silver (i.e. azure and argent). There are a number of variations on the furs which will be found described in any of the standard heraldic textbooks.

A blazon of a coat of arms describes the shield and its features according to a particular predefined order. The first element will normally be the tincture of the surface or main background of the shield (the **field**), followed by a description of its other characteristics; the order is as follows:

  i) the tincture of the field;
 ii) the principal charge, or group of charges, and its/their tinctures;
iii) secondary charges, and tinctures;
 iv) objects placed on any of the charges, and tinctures;
  v) charges on the field not occupying a central position, and tinctures;
 vi) objects placed on any of these non-central charges, and tinctures;
vii) marks of cadency.

If the shield is quartered, i.e. divided up into a number of equal segments, the blazon will begin with the word 'Quarterly', and will describe the segments according to a standard numerical order. A **charge** is any object borne on a coat of arms. References to sinister and dexter, i.e. left and right, are given as though the spectator was *behind* the shield, not in front of it, a rather confusing point as one is invariably facing it. Some writers recommend that a blazon should not include punctuation, in order to avoid any possible ambiguity.

Shields which are divided into compartments may use straight lines or a variety of wavy or indented lines, which have their own heraldic names (e.g. nebuly, embattled); it is always assumed that plain lines are used, unless an alternative is specified in the blazon. There are a number of standard geometrical patterns for the division of shields, each with a defined descriptive term; for example, a shield divided into two with a horizontal line across its centre is divided *per fess*, one divided into four by a St. Andrew-shaped cross is divided *per saltire*. A shield thus divided may have different tinctures and charges in its subdivisions. As well as division by lines into compartments, there are numerous common patterns imposed on shields, such as vertical stripes (a *pale* if there is one broad stripe down the centre of the shield, *pallets* if there are several narrower stripes), or one of the many possible forms of cross; these are known as **ordinaries**. Certain **sub-ordinaries** are also defined, including the fret and the lozenge.

In addition to the abstract and geometrical decorations which may be used on shields, a potentially endless range of **charges** has been used, drawn from the real world. Animals, men, fish, shells, stars, insects, trees, flowers, bells, horns, wheels, ships and weapons are all fairly common possibilities. There are also charges drawn from an imaginary world; fabulous beasts like griffins, dragons and unicorns are sometimes used. Animals may be depicted in a variety of forms – sitting, standing, leaping, facing outwards or to the side – and a standard terminology has been developed to cover the possibilities. A lion *rampant*, for example, has one hind paw on the ground, the other three raised, and the tail erect; a lion *statant* is standing with all its paws on the ground, and its tail curved over its back. It is important to recognise the heraldic posture of such charges as well as their tincture; the full range of terms for charges, ordinaries and sub-ordinaries will be found in the heraldic textbooks. The choice of charges may be arbitrary, but many families have arms incorporating objects which make some punning allusion to their names.

Arms are sometimes amended by the addition of **augmentations of honour**, which are granted by the sovereign as recognition for outstanding services. The augmentations sometimes reflect the achievement; when the Lane family arms were augmented, because Jane and John Lane helped Charles II to escape in 1651, the augmentation included (as a crest) the horse on which the dangerous ride to freedom took place. A study of augmentations of honour, as they appear on bookplates, was published by Peter Allpress in *The Bookplate Journal* vols. 5 and 6 (1987, 1988), pp. 53-89 and 84-93.

Cadency

Arms are inherited by all legitimate male heirs in a family; if a man has three sons, they are all entitled to bear their father's arms. Inevitably, such a system leads to confusion when families proliferate over the generations and different branches become established in different localities. To overcome this problem, *marks of cadency* were developed so that sons added to their fathers' arms small charges denoting their relationship within the family. These marks are normally added at the head of the shield (i.e. *borne in chief*), unless the shield is quartered, in which case they are superimposed at the centre where the quarters meet. The standard system of cadency marks is shown in fig. 8.3.

These marks became established around the beginning of the sixteenth century, and before then a variety of other means of differencing arms within families was used, such as the reversal of tinctures or the transposition of charges. The eldest son retains his mark of cadency only during his father's lifetime, after which he adopts his father's arms without the label, but the marks for the subsequent sons remain a permanent feature of their arms and their sons take over the arms with the cadency mark, to which they add further marks of their own. Cadency marks are not used by sisters, as they have equal rank. The crescent for difference borne by Francis Bacon (1561-1626), the second

	The Elder Brother du-ring the Life of his Father.	Label.
	The Second Brother.	Crefcent.
	The Third Brother.	Mullet.
	The Fourth Brother.	Mertlet.
	The Fifth Brother.	Annulet.
	The Sixth Brother.	Flower-delis.
	The Seventh Brother.	Rofe.
	The Eighth Brother.	Crofc. Moline
	The Ninth Brother.	Double Cater-foile.

Fig. 8.3 Marks of cadency, as represented in M. A. Porny's *The elements of heraldry*, London, 1765.

son of Sir Nicholas Bacon (1509-79) by his second marriage, may be seen in the armorial binding stamp based on his crest, illustrated in fig. 4.15 above.

Crests

Crests originated as decoration at the top of medieval helmets; the first crests were painted fan-shaped plates or arrangements of feathers, but these evolved into leather models of animals and birds. Crests became an accepted element in heraldic achievements, and they have long been included in grants of arms. Ideally, crests should be unique to particular families in the way that coats of arms are, but the more restricted scope which is available in their design sometimes makes for difficulties in distinction (in Scotland, there is no rule against different families using the same crest, which means that Scottish crests tend to be simpler than English ones, but less distinct from one another). A wide variety of beasts, birds and objects has been used, and a number of fanciful crests have been created which could not possibly be used to decorate a real helmet. Because they are relatively small and easy to reproduce, crests have been widely used on their own as marks of ownership, separate from full coats of arms; they lend themselves to spine decoration, but they are also found on bookplates, and armorial stamps on boards. A standard reference work on crests alone has been published, *Fairbairn's book of crests* (see p. 286 below).

In an heraldic achievement, the crest sits on top of the helmet, which is placed at the top of the shield of arms, and between the crest and the helmet is the *torse* or crest-wreath, representing the coloured ribbon or scarf which was often wound round real helmets to hide the join between the crest and the helmet. Heraldic rules govern the tinctures used in the torse, which are normally related to those in the shield. Before the beginning of the seventeenth century, there were no rules about the shape of the helmet which should be depicted in a coat of arms, but since then a system of ranking has been employed which helps in identification (see fig. 8.4). The arms of the sovereign or princes of the blood should have a gold helmet, barred and affronty (i.e. facing outwards from the page); those of peers should have a silver helmet with gold bars, in profile (i.e. seen from the side); those of knights and baronets should have a steel helmet, affronty, with a raised visor; and those of esquires and gentlemen should have a steel helmet, in profile, with a closed visor.

Many examples of crests may be seen in the bookplates illustrated in chapter III; see also the section on crests and badges in chapter IV, p. 104. The bookplate of Richard Hopton, for example (fig. 3.8), incorporates his crest: out of a ducal coronet a griffin's head, in mouth a bleeding hand. The crest rests on a esquire's helmet.

Bishops and archbishops do not use crests but their shields are ensigned with a mitre, as shown in the bookplates of Henry Compton or George Jones (figs. 3.7, 3.13).

Crowns and coronets

The arms of the English aristocracy are often decorated with coronets signifying rank within the peerage. The use of coronets as insignia of nobility

Fig. 8.4 The helmets appropriate to different ranks, as shown in *A short introduction to heraldry*, by H. Clark and T. Wormull, London, 1775.

began in the fourteenth century, but the system of defining patterns of coronets appropriate to the five orders of the peerage was not fully regularised until the seventeenth century. In achievements of arms, coronets are usually included above the shield, sometimes circling the base of the helmet; an example may be seen in fig. 8.1. The correct identification of coronets is an important factor in deciphering a coat of arms; the conventions are as follows:

Dukes: a coronet, chased as though jewelled, with eight stylized strawberry leaves, of which five are seen in the normal sideways-on representations.

Marquesses: a coronet, with four gold strawberry leaves alternating with four silver balls, the latter slightly raised on points above the rim; three leaves and two balls are seen in representations.

Earls: a coronet with eight tall rays, each topped with a silver ball, with a gold strawberry leaf between each ball; five rays are seen in representations.

Viscounts: a coronet with sixteen silver balls touching one another; nine seen in representations.

Barons: a coronet with six large silver balls; four seen in representations.

Marshalling of arms

Many of the difficulties which are encountered in the interpretation of heraldry arise because arms do not remain simple, but become compounded when people marry and arms are joined together. The rules are relatively straight-forward, but the process becomes cumulative as the generations pass and more and more elements are added to a shield. A fondness for intense (and some-times dubious) genealogical research in the sixteenth and seventeenth centuries produced elaborately quartered shields with which people of middling rank hoped to demonstrate their status and lineage.

The conventions for the marshalling of arms, like everything else in heraldry, developed gradually and there are exceptions and precursors to the present rules. For detailed guidance, one of the textbooks of heraldry should be consulted; it is only possible to give here an outline summary of the most common practice.

Arms may be combined by *impaling, quartering,* or using an *escutcheon of pretence.* An impaled shield is one divided into two equal halves by a vertical line

Fig. 8.5 Coronets of rank, as shown in *A short and easy introduction to heraldry,* by H. Clark and T. Wormull, London, 1775.

down the middle, with two distinct coats of arms on either side. A quartered shield may be, as its name suggests, one divided into four equal quarters by one vertical and one horizontal line, but the term also applies to shields divided up into any number of equal segments; it is quite feasible to have 20 or more quarters. An escutcheon of pretence is a small shield placed at the centre of the main shield, bearing the separate coat of arms.

When people marry, the arms of the husband and wife are impaled, with his arms on the dexter side and hers on the sinister. These then become the arms of both husband and wife. If the wife has brothers or deceased brothers with issue, this arrangement continues in force during the wife's lifetime, but the impaled arms are not passed on to the children of the marriage, who inherit the father's original arms. It is only when the wife has no male relations to inherit her family arms that the situation becomes more complicated. The wife is then an *heraldic heiress* and her arms become a permanent feature of her children's heraldic achievements. A man who marries an heraldic heiress impales his arms with hers while her father is alive, but once her father dies he adopts his own arms again with the wife's arms on an escutcheon of pretence at the centre. (The terminology reflects the fact that he is pretending to represent the wife's family, as the nearest thing to a male heir.) The children of the marriage then inherit a shield which is divided into four quarters, with the father's arms in quarters one and four (top left-hand and bottom right-hand, as you look at the shield), and the mother's in quarters two and three (top right-hand and bottom left-hand). This process can continue down the generations, gradually increasing the number of quarterings. There are a number of possible complications and the diagrams in *Boutell's heraldry* (1983 edition, p. 141ff.) help to explain some of them. The rules for marshalling have always been subject to individual whims and preferences, and a man is not obliged to use all the quarterings to which he is entitled.

It might be added that impaling is used by office-holders such as bishops, deans, and heads of colleges, who place their personal arms on the sinister side and the arms of the see, cathedral or college on the dexter; the arrangement ends with the death or resignation of the office-holder, and the official element in the impaled arms is not inherited by his descendents.

Examples of marshalled arms may be seen in the arms of Viscountess de Longueville (fig. 8.2), and in many of the bookplates illustrated in chapter III.

Identifying a coat of arms

The way to identify a given coat of arms is to blazon it following the guidance outlined above and expanded upon in the standard works by Boutell, Fox-Davies and others, listed below. The blazon may then be sought through Papworth's armorial (if it is English), which should lead to the family name; biographical and genealogical sources may then be needed to work out the family member in question.

Further sources on heraldry

The details given above comprise only a minimal outline of a sophisticated subject, and a fuller exposition will be found in the standard works on heraldry listed here, and (if necessary) in the bibliographies they contain.

Dictionaries of arms

J. Papworth: *Papworth's ordinary of British armorials*. London, 1874; reprinted Bath, 1977.

> First published as *An alphabetical dictionary of coats of arms*, this is a very extensive list of known British coats of arms arranged by blazon in a classified system. To quote from J. P. Brooke-Little's introduction to the 1977 reprint: 'It is the only book in which the amateur … can essay to identify a coat of arms. The only skill the searcher needs is the ability to blazon arms'. There is no index to family names, so it is only possible to work from arms to families, and not vice versa.

Sir B. Burke: *The general armory of England, Scotland, Ireland and Wales*. London, 1884; reprinted London, 1961.

> The revised edition of a work first published in 1842. A dictionary of all known armigerous families, with their arms described in blazon; works from families to arms, so like Papworth in reverse. Supplemented by C. R. Humphery-Smith: *General armory two: Alfred Morant's additions and corrections to Burke's General armory*, London, 1973.

J. B. Rietstap: *Armorial général: précédé d'un dictionaire des termes du blason*. 2nd edn. Gouda, 1884-87, and later supplements, reprinted London, 1965.

> The standard armorial for European arms, arranged alphabetically by family names. The original work was not illustrated, but a series of illustrations appeared separately; the third edition of the plates (V. and H. Rolland, *General illustrated armorial*, Lyons, 1953) was reprinted in London in 1967 as *Illustrations to the Armorial général of J. B. Rietstap*.

G. Briggs: *Civic and corporate heraldry: a dictionary of impersonal arms of England, Wales & N. Ireland*. London, 1971.

> An ordinary of British corporate arms, concerned with current bodies which were in existence in 1971. Many illustrations.

Standard textbooks

A. C. Fox-Davies, rev. J. P. Brooke-Little: *A complete guide to heraldry*. London, 1985.

> The standard guide, first published in 1909 and revised several times; more substantial than Boutell, and well illustrated.

J. P. Brooke-Little (ed.), *Boutell's heraldry*. London, 1983.

> The latest revision of a standard textbook first published in 1950; well illustrated, covers all the basic ground, and includes a selective bibliography.

T. Woodcock & J. M. Robinson: *The Oxford guide to heraldry*. Oxford, 1988.

> An excellent first introduction to the subject, more narrative in style than Fox-Davies and Boutell, and handsomely illustrated.

R. Marks & A. Payne: *British heraldry from its origins to* c. *1800*. London, 1978.

> The catalogue of a major exhibition at the British Museum. Includes short essays on various aspects of heraldry, as well as descriptions of the exhibits; well-illustrated, and useful in showing the wide range of artefacts which have been used for the display of heraldry.

Sir T. Innes, rev. M. R. Innes: *Scots heraldry*. London, 1978.

> The revised edition of the standard introduction to Scots heraldry, which differs from English heraldry in some respects; originally published in 1934.

Dictionaries of terminology

J. Parker (ed.): *A glossary of terms used in heraldry*. Oxford, 1894, reprinted Newton Abbot, 1970.

> Fairly comprehensive and helpfully illustrated.

A. G. Puttock: *A dictionary of heraldry and related subjects*. London, 1970.

> More approachable than Parker, but less detailed.

J. Franklyn & J. Tanner: *An encyclopaedic dictionary of heraldry*. London, 1970.

> Includes heraldic terminology in the major European languages as well as English.

S. Friar: *A new dictionary of heraldry*. London, 1987.

> A well-illustrated and up-to-date guide which covers the standard heraldic terminology and also has sections on the various uses of heraldic insignia (e.g. a four-page section on bookplates).

Crests and mottoes

J. Fairbairn: *Fairbairn's book of crests of the families of Great Britain and Ireland*. 2v. 4th edn. London, 1905, reprinted London, 1983.

> The expanded version of a work first published in 1859. Volume 1, of text, lists family names with their crests and mottoes; volume 2, of plates, illustrates all the crests, in a thematic arrangement.

R. Pinches (ed.): *Elvin's handbook of mottoes revised*. London, 1971.

> First published in 1860 by C. N. Elvin; an alphabetical list of mottoes, with the names of the families who used them.

PALAEOGRAPHY

Introduction and historical overview

Reading the handwriting of other people, no matter when it was written, can present problems, related to the interpreter's familiarity with the letter forms and conventions of the script, and to the writer's care and consistency in forming the letters. As a general rule, inscriptions of the Tudor and early Stuart periods are more likely to create problems for the student of provenance in printed books than those nearer our own time, but there are plenty of sixteenth-century inscriptions in clear bold hands, and nineteenth-century inscriptions in careless spidery hands, to prove exceptions. Palaeographical skill is largely a matter of practice, aided by knowledge of basic letter forms and the way they have changed as handwriting has developed over the centuries. There are a number of guides to the history of writing in Britain, coupled with facsimiles of documents with accompanying transcripts, which will offer help when faced with difficult inscriptions.

The development of handwriting can be traced back ultimately to the invention of the alphabet by the near eastern civilisations, sometime before 1000 B.C. It was adopted by the Greeks ca. 900 B.C., and was developed through the Greek and Roman cultures to become the basic building block of written communication in the western world. Many of the letter forms in use today can be seen as descended from the square capitals used by the Romans for inscriptions carved in stone. The earliest surviving British manuscripts are written in uncials and half-uncials, the latter being the attractive rounded letter-forms familiar to many people from the Book of Kells and the Lindisfarne Gospels. Uncial book hands gave way to the script known as Caroline minuscule, which developed in France during the eighth and ninth centuries, and came to England during the tenth. Minuscule letter forms developed an increasing angularity and compression from the twelfth century onwards, mutating into the Gothic scripts of the high and late middle ages. There are many works on early handwriting, and the palaeography of the period before 1500 has been studied and written about much more than that of more modern times. As users of this Handbook are not likely to have to decipher many tenth century ownership inscriptions, it seems unnecessary to go into further detail here on early scripts; fuller information on the development of these hands will be found in Bernhard Bischoff's *Latin palaeography: antiquity and the middle ages* (Cambridge, 1990), and in some of the references at the end of this section, if desired.

Palaeographers distinguish hands by function into *book hands* (sometimes called text hands), used for literary or liturgical manuscripts, and *business hands* (sometimes called charter or court hands), used for legal and business documents, letters, and more general purposes. The use of separate hands for these different functions becomes noticeable in England during the twelfth century, and from then on the distinctions grew. The term 'court hand' reflects the fact that the various courts of law developed their own characteristic business hands for the engrossing of documents (the Exchequer was the first court to do so, during the twelfth century), and some formal court hands remained in use, changing very little after the beginning of the sixteenth century, until the reforms of George II's reign when the use of English was made standard for recording legal proceedings. English court hands developed from cursive scripts used for business purposes, becoming more angular and upright. As time progressed, the handwriting used for business and everyday purposes tended to become more cursive in style, and often (to the modern eye) less legible. The 'free' hands of the fifteenth century evolved into the *secretary hand* of the sixteenth century, the general business hand of the Tudor and early Stuart period. While the secretary hand was flourishing and being developed by the writing masters of the period, there was at the same time an increasing use of the italic or 'humanist' hands, whose birth and spread across Europe was one of the products of Renaissance education. The growing use of Roman typefaces for printed books during the sixteenth century was a closely allied movement. The occurrence of Italic script in English documents is increasingly common from about 1550 onwards, and many English scholars of the period learnt to write both secretary and Italic hands. It is not uncommon to find a late sixteenth- or early seventeenth-century book with contemporary ownership inscriptions written in both styles by the same man; fig. 8.6 shows an example from the library of Sir Thomas Knyvett (ca. 1539-1618). The two hands gradually cross-fertilised each other and the major development in English handwriting during the seventeenth century was the growing fusion of the characteristics of secretary and Italic to produce the 'round hand' which is the direct ancestor of the handwriting in use today.

One of the problems attached to deciphering difficult inscriptions is that one usually has very little text to work with. Uncertainties with particular letters can often be resolved by looking for recurrences of the same letter in other words, where the context may help with interpretation, but a simple signature may be too brief to make this technique possible. The examples show a series of inscriptions from the middle of the fifteenth century to the middle of the eighteenth, to help illustrate the way in which handwriting has evolved during that time. Fig. 8.7 shows a mid-fifteenth century book-hand, dating from the 1440s, as written by Edmund Shenley, a monk at St. Albans. The inscription of Bartholomew Otford of Christ Church, Canterbury, (fig. 8.8) which dates from 1540, is typical of the evolving secretary hand of the early sixteenth century; it reads: Thys boke pertaynythe to master otford mownke of crystys churche yn canterbury an[no] d[omi]ni m^{o}v^{c}xl. The inscription 'Thomas Cantuarien[sis]' (fig. 8.9) written in Thomas Cranmer's books (probably not by the Archbishop himself, but by one of his chaplains), is another example of a secretary hand of much the same period. The letter-forms here have a number of similarities which are characteristic features of secretary hand, such as the descending left-turning loop of the h, and the terminal s like a small o with a rising stroke at the top left-hand side. A slightly later example of sixteenth-century secretary hand may be seen in the inscription of Stephen Chesby shown in fig. 8.22. John Dee (1527-1608, fig. 8.10) wrote his name in his books in a clear and upright cursive Italic hand; the inscription of John, Lord Lumley (1534?-1609, fig. 8.11) also reflects a preference for Italic letters for ownership marks, common in the later sixteenth century. The inscription of Sir Nathaniel Bacon (d.1622, fig. 8.12) is based on a business hand sometimes called an engrossing hand, such as would be used for titles and headings in contemporary documents. As

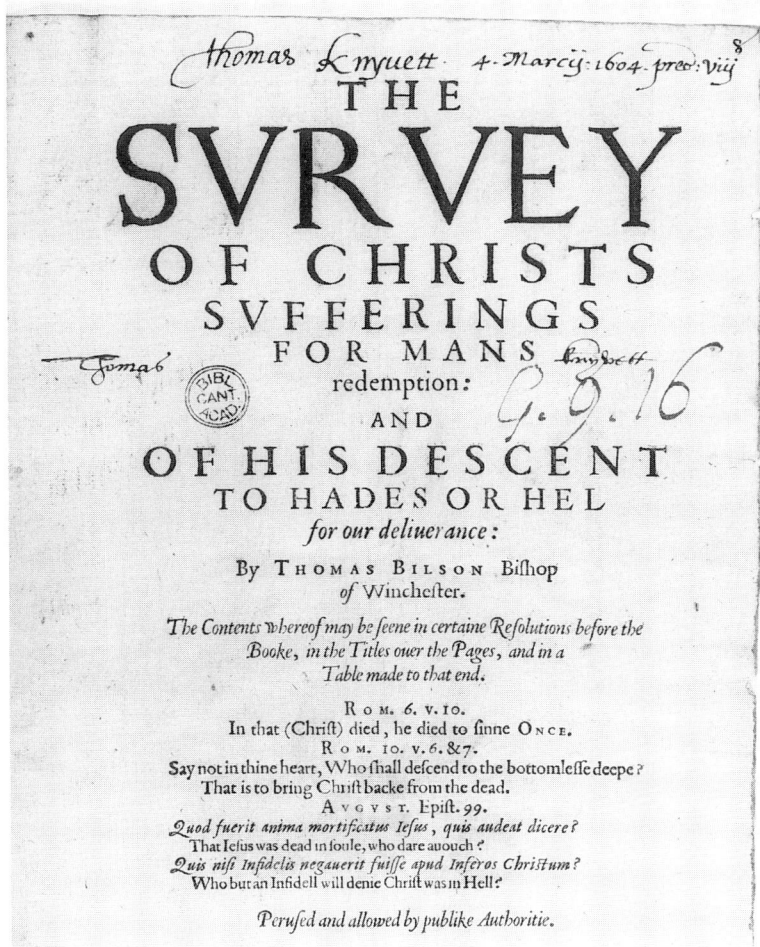

Fig. 8.6 Sir Thomas Knyvett's inscriptions, in both italic and secretary hand, on one titlepage: Cambridge University Library G.9.16, T. Bilson, *The survey of Christs sufferings*, 1604.

we move through the generations the Italic letter-forms win the day, but they become smaller and more rounded. The hand of Isaac Casaubon (1559-1614, fig. 8.13) is quite modern in appearance, but retains some aspects of older customs such as the poor distinction between the n and u at the end of the surname. The seventeenth century saw the emergence of i and j as truly separate letters, but the same letter-form is used for the capital I of Isaac Casaubon as for the capital J of John Hacket (1592-1670, fig. 8.14). The lower-case e like a Greek epsilon, or a reversed numeral 3, seen in the

Fig. 8.7 Mid fifteenth-century inscription, Liber d[omi]ni edmu[n]di shenley: Cambridge University Library Ms.Dd.6.7, Geoffrey of Monmouth, *Historia Britonum*, written between 1440 and 1448.

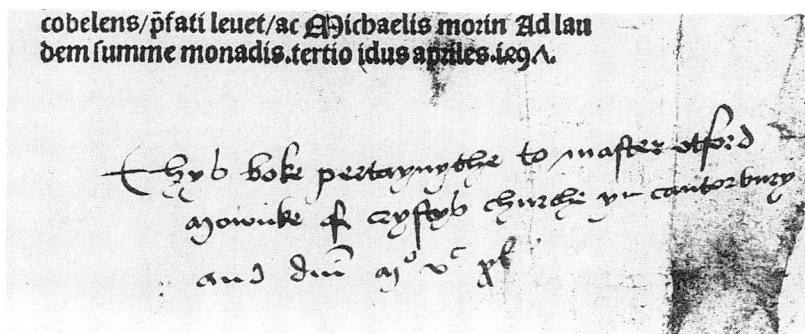

Fig. 8.8 Early sixteenth-century inscription of Bartholomew Otford: British Library 748.d.19, an album of title pages and stray leaves of various dates.

Fig. 8.9 Mid sixteenth-century inscription 'Thomas Cantuarien', as written in Thomas Cranmer's books: British Library 1505/333, J. B. Folengius, *In psalmos commentaria*, 1540.

Fig. 8.10 Inscription of John Dee, dated 1556: Peterhouse, Cambridge H.6.1, J. Stobaeus, *Sententiae*, 1543.

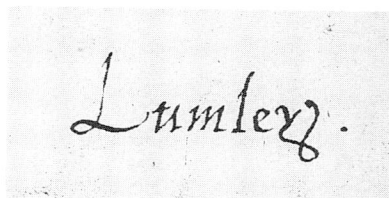

Fig. 8.11 Late sixteenth-century inscription of John, Lord Lumley: British Library 1505/333, J. B. Folengius, *In psalmos commentaria*, 1540.

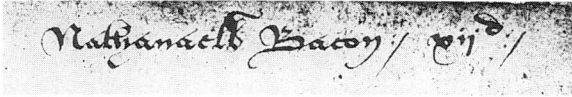

Fig. 8.12 Late sixteenth-century/early seventeenth-century inscription of Sir Nathaniel Bacon: British Library 1492.ff.18, A. Ambrogini, *Epistolae*, 1542.

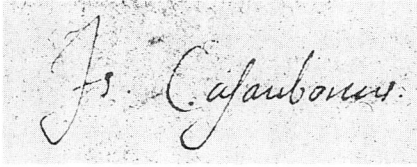

Fig. 8.13 Late sixteenth-century/early seventeenth-century inscription of Isaac Casaubon: British Library 1505/253, H. Estienne, *Glossaria duo*, 1573.

Fig. 8.14 Mid seventeenth-century inscription of John Hacket: British Library 3166.f.22, P. Vermigli, *In primum librum Mosis ... commentarii*, 1569.

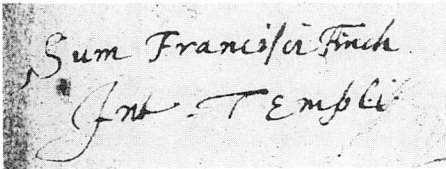

Fig. 8.15 Early/mid seventeenth-century inscription of Francis Finch: British Library 1482.h.14, *Novellarum constitutionarum Dn. Iustiniani*, 1541.

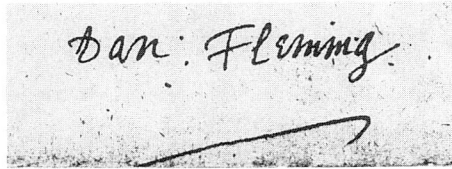

Fig. 8.16 Late seventeenth-century inscription of Sir Daniel Fleming: British Library 1509/1370, *A seasonable treatise*, 1678.

Fig. 8.17 Late seventeenth-century/early eighteenth-century inscription of Charles Bernard: British Library 3127.h.19, T. Malvenda, *De paradiso voluptatis*, 1605.

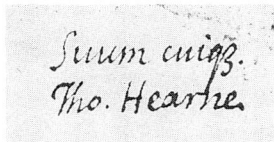

Fig. 8.18 Late seventeenth-century/early eighteenth-century inscription of Thomas Hearne: British Library 1492.dd.10, *Pro Daniele Heinsio adversus Ioannis Croii calumnias apologia*, 1646.

inscriptions of Francis Finch (b.1586, fig. 8.15), John Hacket, and Sir Daniel Fleming (1633-1701, fig. 8.16), is a common seventeenth century feature (although it will be noted that Hacket used two forms of e within his short inscription). By the time we come to the end of the seventeenth century and the beginning of the eighteenth – as, for example, with the inscriptions of Charles Bernard (1650-1711, fig. 8.17) or Thomas Hearne (1678-1735, fig. 8.18) – many of the letter-forms being used are even closer to those in common use today.

As mentioned earlier, the legal world had developed a number of distinctive hands which were used when writing out formal documents, and different courts (e.g. Chancery, Common Pleas) had their own individual styles. The use of court hands, clearly based on medieval letter forms, continued until 1733 and book owners involved in the legal profession sometimes used these hands when inscribing their books. It is not uncommon to find seventeenth- or early eighteenth-century inscriptions in these rather strange-looking hands, particularly, as might be expected, in law books. Fig. 8.19 shows a late seventeenth-century example of an inscription in court hand, which reads 'Car Whitaker possidebt [sic] 1685 pcm xiij^s'. The standard palaeographical textbooks include examples of court hands, which can be tricky to decipher.

Abbreviations

The deciphering of inscriptions is sometimes complicated by the fondness of earlier generations for the use of abbreviations. Words may be shortened in a variety of ways, by leaving out letters at the end or in the middle, and by signifying the missing text using a variety of devices such as punctuation, superscript letters, or abbreviation symbols. The problem is most acute for students of medieval palaeography, as scribal conventions of the middle ages

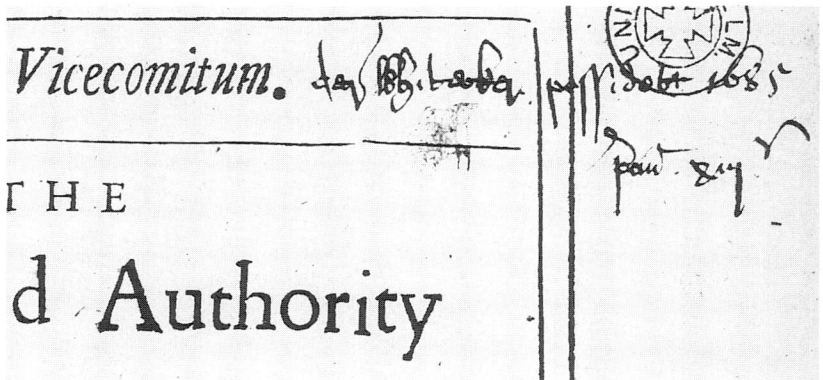

Fig. 8.19 Inscription of Charles Whitaker, in court hand, dated 1685: Durham University Library +ELCA.C82D, M. Dalton, *The office and authority of sheriffs*, 1682.

evolved a very extensive system of abbreviations. The standard manual on the subject, Capelli's *Lexicon*, illustrates over 14,000 examples of abbreviated forms, mostly selected from manuscripts of the twelfth to the fifteenth centuries. Abbreviation saved time, and also space, an important consideration when writing materials were expensive. By the sixteenth and seventeenth centuries, with increasing numbers of documents written in the vernacular, the system had become less formal, but abbreviations based on the inherited traditions were still common.

Abbreviations have, of necessity, been much studied by palaeographers and categorised by types. As stated above, there is a standard reference work which is based on the reproduction of many examples:

A. Capelli: *Lexicon abbreviaturarum*. 3rd edn. Milan, 1929.

A useful English translation of Capelli's introductory text has been published (A. Capelli, tr. D. Heimann and R. Kay: *The elements of abbreviation in medieval Latin palaeography*, Lawrence, University of Kansas Libraries, 1982). An alternative, but less extensive, list of abbreviations will be found in C. T. Martin, *The record interpreter*, 2nd edn, London, 1910, pp. 1-163. L. C. Hector's book on *The handwriting of English documents* (2nd edn, London, 1966) has a good chapter on abbreviations (ch. III, pp. 29-39), which provides a helpful brief overview of the subject.

Fig. 8.20 Inscription of Sir Clement Throkmorton: Cambridge University Library Pet.E.5.59, H. Cole, *The true copies of the letters*, 1560.

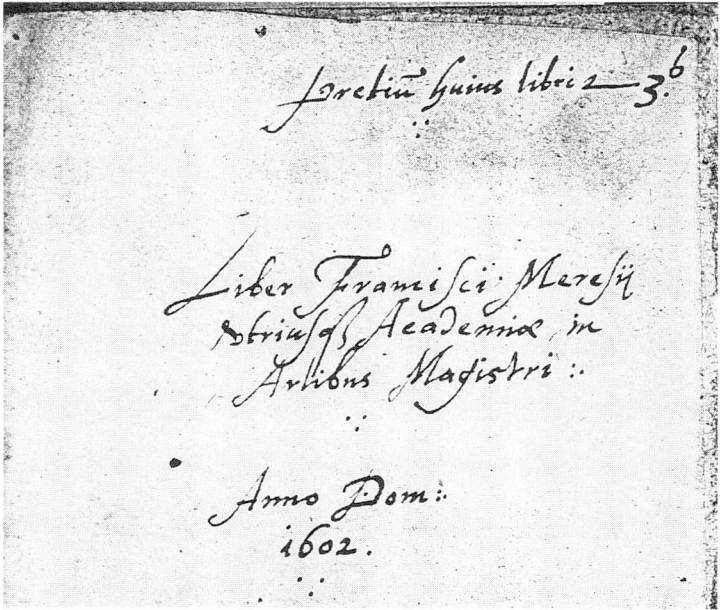

Fig. 8.21 Inscription of Francis Meres, dated 1602: Cambridge University Library Pet.B.1.43, J. Brandmuller, *Conciones funebres*, 1596.

Fig. 8.22 Inscription of Stephen Chesby, Archdeacon of Winchester (d.1571): Cambridge University Library Pet.A.7.22, M. Bucchinger, *Historia ecclesiactica nova*, 1560.

The range of abbreviations likely to be experienced in deciphering ownership inscriptions is, obviously, quite limited and resort to Capelli is not often necessary. Many abbreviations comprise truncated words marked with a full stop or colon, rather than any more technical siglum of abbreviation, and expansion of the word is often straightforward. See, for example, figs. 2.2, 2.21 or 8.15 (where Int. stands for Interioris – Francis Finch of the Inner Temple). Abbreviations occur more often in Latin inscriptions than English ones. A commonly encountered abbreviation mark is a bar over a letter or letters;

according to the formal conventions, this should signify a missing m or n, and it can be seen in operation in this way in figs. 8.20 – Throkmorto[n] – and 8.21 – Pretiu[m]. A bar may also be used more loosely to indicate a missing section of a word, as in fig. 8.9 (Cantuarie[nsis]), or fig. 8.22, where the final word should read 'Wintoniensis'. Fig. 8.22 also shows another standard abbreviation mark; the last character of the penultimate word, like an arabic numeral '9', normally stands for a final -us, but in this case stands for rather more (Archidi[aconus], i.e. Archdeacon). Latin words ending in -que were sometimes abbreviated by substituting a mark like a loose figure 3 for the final -ue, and this can be seen in Francis Meres's inscription (fig. 8.21 – vtriusq[ue] Academiae). Thomas Hearne was using this abbreviation mark as late as the early eighteenth century (see fig. 8.18).

Many of the abbreviations in ownership inscriptions relate to names or places. The expansion of abbreviated christian names is usually obvious, especially as the range of first names commonly used in earlier centuries is much more limited than that which we are used to today. Ant., Dan., Fran., Geo., Hen., Matt., Ro., Sam., and Tho. are all frequently encountered truncations which present no challenge. Charles is latinised as Carolus and William as Gulielmus or Guilielmus, so the truncations are Car. and Gul. or Guil. Jo. may stand for John/Joannes or Joseph/Josephus; Jno. is another shortened version of Joannes. College names are often truncated also, but terms like Magd., Pemb., Trin. are usually straightforward to identify. C.C.C.C., which is occasionally found, may be expanded in apropriate contexts to read Collegium Corporis Christi Cantabrigiensis, i.e. Corpus Christi College, Cambridge.

It may be useful to summarise the abbreviations which commonly occur in the Latin ownership inscriptions of English book owners, and a selective list follows.

A.B.	Artium Baccalaureus, i.e. B.A.
A.M.	Artium Magister, i.e. M.A.
a^o	anno
Arm.	Armiger
Aul.	Aula, i.e. Hall in the university sense of Magdalen Hall, Oxford
Can.	Canonicus (in the ecclesiastical sense)
Cant. Cantab. Cantabr.	Cantabrigia/Cantabrigiensis, i.e. Cambridge
Col. Coll.	Collegium
Com.	Comes, Comitis
d.d.	dono dedit
Dni. Dns.	Domini, Dominus

Eccl.	Ecclesia/Ecclesiae
empt.	emptum
Epi. Epus.	Episcopi, Episcopus
Gen. Gener.	Generosus
lib.	liber, libris
Mil.	Miles/Militis
Mri.	Magistri
Oxo. Oxon.	Oxonia/Oxoniensis, i.e. Oxford
pr. pret.	pretium
Soc.	socius, i.e. fellow in the collegiate sense

See also F. B. Williams, An initiation into initials, *Studies in bibliography* 9 (1957) 163-178, which is concerned with the identification of initials and other abbreviations found in English books of the STC period (particularly pseudonymous authors). Inspiration for decoding abbreviations not in the list above may be sought in one of the numerous published dictionaries of abbreviations, e.g. J. Paxton, *Everyman's dictionary of abbreviations*, 2nd edn, London, 1986 (which includes many ancient abbreviations among the host of modern ones).

Palaeographical textbooks and collections of examples

Most palaeographical guidebooks comprise facsimiles of documents with adjacent transcriptions and commentaries on the handwriting, with more or less by way of historical introduction and overview. In addition, there are many detailed studies of particular hands, scriptoria, or groups of manuscripts. The books listed here comprise only a brief selection of some of the standard works, designed for the general student rather than the palaeographical specialist, although many of them include bibliographies with references to a wider range of material. This section is biased in favour of guides which cover the hands of the fifteenth, sixteenth and seventeenth centuries, as these are most likely to be relevant to users of this Handbook, and many of the textbooks which are primarily concerned with the medieval period are therefore excluded.

M. P. Brown: *A guide to western historical scripts from antiquity to 1600.* London, 1990.

> Mostly an extensive selection of facsimiles, well laid out with notes and transcriptions. The emphasis is very much on the medieval period and before, but there is also a useful and up-to-date classified bibliography of other palaeographical works.

G. E. Dawson & L. Kennedy-Skipton: *Elizabethan handwriting 1500-1650.* London, 1968, repr. 1981.

A particularly useful book for help with the sixteenth century hands which can prove the most troublesome for students of provenance who are primarily concerned with printed books. Includes 50 plates of examples, with transcripts, and a brief history of the secretary hand.

N. Denholm-Young: *Handwriting in England and Wales*. Cardiff, 1954.

A standard textbook on the history and development of English handwriting. Includes 30 plates of illustrative examples, from the 7th to the 17th century.

H. E. P. Grieve: *Examples of English handwriting 1150-1750*. Chelmsford, 1954.

A simply-produced collection of illustrations and transcripts, taken from archives in the Essex Record Office.

L. C. Hector: *The handwriting of English documents*. Second edition. London, 1966.

A standard introductory textbook on the development of handwriting in England, from the earliest times to the post-medieval period, with 36 plates, 8th-19th centuries.

H. Jenkinson: *The later court hands in England from the fifteenth to the seventeenth century*. 2v. Cambridge, 1927.

The major work on the specialised court hands of the period, which also deals with the other hands in use (e.g. secretary and Italic). It follows on from an earlier work written by Jenkinson in collaboration with Charles Johnson, *English court hand A.D. 1066 to 1500* (Oxford, 1915).

J. F. Preston & L. Yeandle: *English handwriting 1400-1650: an introductory manual*. New York, 1992.

Reproduces and transcribes 31 manuscripts from the Folger Shakespeare Library, showing (among other things) the development of the secretary hand through the Tudor and Stuart periods. Many of the transcripts are accompanied by extensive reproductions of the individual letter forms used in the manuscripts.

BIOGRAPHY

The range of biographical sources which may be useful in the context of provenance research is virtually endless, and it is not limited to formal biographical dictionaries and similar compilations. Once a person has been identified and is known to have lived or died in a particular locality, been educated at a particular school or university, or held a particular job, all kinds of secondary sources may be worth investigating to flesh out the details of his or her life, and it is not possible to compile a bibliography to cover all foreseeable needs. But at the initial stage, the researcher often has no more than a name, an inscription on a title page or a name on a bookplate, and the first job is to trace bearers of that name and pinpoint the one who owned the book.

Here again, of the making of many lists there has been no end, and a comprehensive bibliography is out of the question. But there is a core of standard material within which it is usually sensible to begin, and this section aims to list only the most important or major sources, with pointers to more extensive bibliographies. An appreciable proportion of British book owners were educated to degree level, and we are fortunate in possessing biographical dictionaries or printed registers from most of the British universities founded before 1800; these are often good places to start. There are also directories or lists which cover many of the major professions, such as lawyers, clergymen, medics or artists. The pedigrees of the aristocracy and gentry are recorded in print, and the heraldic visitations carried out down to the end of the seventeenth century provide much information about families over many generations.

The following section lists, first, **bibliographies and consolidated indexes** which cover a wide range of biographical sources; **national and international biographical dictionaries**; directories and lists which cover **education**, and particular **professions**; **genealogical** sources including pedigrees of both aristocratic and non-aristocratic families; and a number of other important and wide-ranging sources which may prove useful.

Bibliographies and consolidated indexes

G. E. Armytage (ed.): *Obituary prior to 1800 ... compiled by Sir William Musgrave.* (Publications of the Harleian Society, v.44-49). 6v. London, 1899-1901.

> An amalgamated index to a wide range of biographical sources, including some 18th century periodicals, collected by Sir William Musgrave (1735-1800). Printed from his ms. index now in the British Library (Add.ms.25403).

P. M. Riches: *An analytical bibliography of universal collected biography.* London, 1934.

> An index to biographical information found in over 3000 published sources (mostly collections of lives of various sorts), with over 50,000 index entries. Covers English language material published in Britain and America.

A. M. Hyamson: *A dictionary of universal biography.* 2nd edn. London, 1951.

> An amalgamated index to the entries in 23 of the major biographical dictionaries, e.g. the *Dictionary of National Biography*, *Nouvelle biographie universelle*, *Dictionary of American biography*.

Index bio-bibliographicus notorum hominum. Osnabruck, 1972-

> An international biographical index on an ambitious scale, being published in parts (surnames beginning A-D had been covered by 1992). The bibliography of works cited (part B) lists over 5000 biographical dictionaries and sources; part C, the alphabetical list of persons covered, refers back to the sources in part B, where the full biographical details will be found.

Bio-base: a periodic cumulative master index on microfiche to sketches found in about 500 current and historical biographical dictionaries. Detroit, 1984.
Supplement, containing an additional 1,235,000 citations to 175 biographical sources. Detroit, 1988.

> Covers a wide range of material, international in scope. The printed guide which accompanies the microfiche index lists the sources indexed.

R. B. Slocum (ed.): *Biographical dictionaries and related works: an international bibliography of more than 16,000 collective biographies.* 2nd edn. 2v. Detroit, 1986.

> International in coverage, as the title implies, with arrangements both by country or area, and by subject or vocation.

National and international biographical dictionaries

The emphasis in this section is on dictionaries which are likely to be useful in identifying British and Irish collectors down to the end of the nineteenth century. It does not include any of the numerous American biographical dictionaries, for which a good place to start is the *Historical biographical dictionaries master index*, by B. McNeil and M. C. Herbert (Detroit, 1980), which lists and indexes a wide range of American sources.

L. Stephen & S. Lee (eds.): *Dictionary of national biography*. 63v. London, 1885-1900.

> Reissued in 22 vols. at the beginning of this century and reprinted several times since in this form, together with supplements covering decades. The standard chronicle of the lives of the most significant people in British history, in all walks of life. The one-volume *Concise dictionary of national biography*, first issued in 1903, forms a handy summary and index to the whole. A supplementary volume, C. S. Nicholls (ed.), *The Dictionary of national biography: missing persons*, Oxford, 1993, adds a little over a thousand names for people omitted first time round.

F. Boase: *Modern English biography: containing many thousand concise memoirs of persons who have died since the year 1850*. 6v. Truro, 1892-1921.

> An extensive collection of short biographies of noteworthy nineteenth-century men and women, which naturally includes many people born in the second half of the eighteenth century.

L. Baillie & P. Sieveking (eds.): *British biographical archive*. London, 1989. On microfiche.

> 'A one-alphabet cumulation of 324 of the most important English-language biographical reference works originally published between 1601 and 1929'. A brochure accompanying the fiche lists the biographical works whose entries are reproduced on the fiche. A printed index is available which lists all the people covered by biographical entries in the *archive* (ca. 170,000 names in all): D. Bank & A. Esposito: *British biographical archive*. 4v. London, 1990. This gives names, dates, occupations, reference sources, and frame numbers on the fiche.

J. E. Lloyd & R. T. Jenkins (eds.): *The dictionary of Welsh biography down to 1940*. London, 1959.

> Contains about 3500 entries; the criterion for inclusion is that the subject, or one of his/her parents, should have been born in Wales.

H. Boylan: *A dictionary of Irish biography*. 2nd edn. Dublin, 1988.

> More selective than the preceding dictionary (ca. 1000 entries), and more concerned with distinctive achievement; allows inclusion on the basis of Irish birth, descent, or adoption.

Educational lists and registers

There is a wide range of printed lists and transcribed registers from schools, colleges and universities. It is impossible to list them all here, but fortunately there is a bibliography which covers them:

P. M. Jacobs: *Registers of the universities, colleges and schools of Great Britain and Ireland*. London, 1964.

The works listed below constitute only the most important lists from the seven British universities in existence before 1800; there are a number of useful biographical registers relating to particular Oxford and Cambridge colleges, which often supplement the details given in Foster or Venn, and there are other lists from all the universities. Details of these will be found in Jacobs's bibliography.

Cambridge

A. B. Emden: *A biographical register of the University of Cambridge to 1500.* Cambridge, 1963.

J. & J. A. Venn: *Alumni Cantabrigienses: a biographical list ... from the earliest times to 1900.* 10v. Cambridge, 1922-54.

C. H. & T. Cooper: *Athenae Cantabrigienses.* 2v. Cambridge, 1858-61.

> Covers members of the University 1500-1609; less comprehensive than Venn in terms of names, but has fuller biographical details.

Oxford

A. B. Emden: *A biographical register of the University of Oxford to A.D.1500.* 3v. Oxford, 1957-59.

A. B. Emden: *A biographical register of the University of Oxford A.D.1501 to 1540.* Oxford, 1974.

J. Foster: *Alumni Oxonienses: the members of the University of Oxford 1500-1714 (1715-1886).* 8v. Oxford, 1891.

A. à Wood, ed. P. Bliss: *Athenae Oxonienses. An exact history of all the writers and bishops ... To which are added the fasti.* 4v. London, 1813.

> First published 1691-92, edited and expanded by Bliss, and still worth consulting for 16th and 17th century names.

Aberdeen

P. J. Anderson: *Officers and graduates of University & King's College, Aberdeen 1495-1860.* Aberdeen, 1893.

> A transcript of the registers with limited biographical annotations.

P. J. Anderson: *Roll of alumni in arts of the University and King's College of Aberdeen 1596-1860.* Aberdeen, 1900.

Edinburgh

A catalogue of the graduates in the faculties of arts, divinity, and law, of the University of Edinburgh, since its foundation. Edinburgh, 1858.

> A transcript of the registers, from 1587, without any additional biographical detail.

Glasgow

W. Innes Addison: *A roll of the graduates of the University of Glasgow from 31st December, 1727 to 31st December, 1897, with short biographical notes*. Glasgow, 1898.

W. Innes Addison: *The matriculation albums of the University of Glasgow from 1728 to 1858*. Glasgow, 1913.

A transcript of the registers with some biographical notes added.

St. Andrews

J. M. Anderson: *Early records of the University of St. Andrews*. Scottish History Society, 3rd series, vol. 8, 1926.

Contains the graduation roll, 1413-1579, and the matriculation roll 1473-1579.

J. M. Anderson: *The matriculation roll of the University of St. Andrews 1747-1897*. Edinburgh, 1905.

An unannotated transcript.

Trinity College, Dublin

G. D. Burtchaell & T. U. Sadleir, *Alumni Dublinenses: a register of the students, graduates, professors and provosts of Trinity College ... Dublin (1593-1860)*. Rev. edn. Dublin, 1935.

Clergy

The standard listing of the upper ranks of the clergy in the established Church in England is John le Neve's *Fasti ecclesiae Anglicanae*, first published in 1715 but revised more than once. It is arranged by dioceses and lists archbishops, bishops, deans and stall-holders in cathedral chapters. The most satisfactory edition is the latest revision which was begun in 1955 and issued in separate volumes; it is complete for the period 1300-1541, but only six volumes covering the period 1541-1857 have appeared:

J. le Neve, rev. J. M. Horn et al: *Fasti ecclesiae Anglicanae 1300-1541*. 12v. London, 1962-67.

J. le Neve, rev. J. M. Horn et al: *Fasti ecclesiae Anglicanae 1541-1857*. London, 1969-

(Six volumes only to date, covering St. Paul's, London; Chichester; Canterbury, Rochester & Winchester; York; Bath & Wells; and Salisbury).

For dioceses not yet covered by this edition, the 1854 revision must be used:

J. le Neve, rev. T. Duffus Hardy: *Fasti ecclesiae Anglicanae, or a calendar of the principal ecclesiastical dignitaries in England and Wales*. 3v. Oxford, 1854.

This covers the period from the earliest times to 1854. Le Neve deals only with the upper strata of the established church, and does not list the incumbents and curates at parish level who constituted the major proportion of the clergy, nor does he cover nonconformists and recusants. There are two substantial published lists which cover rectors, vicars and perpetual curates across whole dioceses; one deals with the diocese of London, the other with the diocese of Peterborough:

G. Hennessy: *Novum repertorium ecclesiasticum parochiale Londinense, or London diocesan clergy succession from the earliest time to the year 1898.* London, 1898.

> This is partly based on Richard Newcourt's *Repertorium* of 1708-10; it includes biographical notes on many of the clergy.

H. I. Longden: *Northamptonshire and Rutland clergy from 1500.* 16v. Northampton, 1938-52.

> Published in parts, in alphabetical order by clergy surnames. The final volume contains addenda, corrigenda, and an index.

An attempt to produce a nationwide historical listing of clergy was made by Joseph Foster, based on bishops' certificates of institutions to livings, but the scheme was never completed and the only portion of his *Index ecclesiasticus: or, alphabetical lists of all ecclesiastical dignitaries in England and Wales since the Reformation* to be published covers the period 1800-1840 (Oxford, 1890).

Much useful information on mid-seventeenth century clergymen (and also laymen) will be found in the two standard works on those who were ejected by the puritans during the Civil War, and and on those who subsequently suffered the same fate once the Crown was restored:

A. G. Matthews: *Walker revised: being a revision of John Walker's Sufferings of the clergy during the grand rebellion 1642-60.* Oxford, 1988.

A. G. Matthews: *Calamy revised: being a revision of Edmund Calamy's Account of the ministers and others ejected and silenced, 1660-2.* Oxford, 1988.

Roman Catholics

D. A. Bellenger: *English and Welsh priests, 1558-1800.* Bath, 1984.

> 'Intended to provide as complete a list as possible of Roman Catholic priests ordained between the years 1558 and 1800 who either worked on the English and Welsh mission or who were members of English religious communities abroad'. Only a list of names with summary biographical information added, but includes an extensive bibliography of other biographical sources for British Roman Catholics.

J. Gillow: *A literary and biographical history, or bibliographical dictionary of the English catholics.* 5v. London, 1885-1902.

> A detailed biographical dictionary of prominent English catholics, both ordained and lay, from 1534 to the end of the nineteenth century. Coverage is more comprehensive in the first half of the alphabet. A separate index volume, compiled by J. Bevan, was published in 1985.

Scotland and Ireland

The clergy of the Church of Scotland, of all ranks, are covered by the following, which has biographies of all clergymen attached to the Church of Scotland from the middle of the sixteenth century to the beginning of the twentieth:

H. Scott: *Fasti ecclesiae Scoticanae: the succession of ministers in the Church of Scotland from the Reformation.* Rev. edn. 7v. Edinburgh, 1915-28.

For senior Scottish Roman Catholics, including bishops, vicars apostolic and prelates, see:

J. Darragh: *The catholic hierarchy of Scotland, a biographical list 1653-1985.* Glasgow, 1986.

The clergy of the Church of Ireland are partly covered by the following, which is like Le Neve and only includes the upper ranks of the clergy:

H. Cotton: *Fasti ecclesiae Hibernicae. The succession of the prelates and members of the cathedral bodies in Ireland.* 5v. plus supplement. Dublin, 1845-78.

Lawyers

J. Foster: *The register of admissions to Gray's Inn, 1521-1889.* London, 1889.

Students admitted to the Inner Temple. 1547-1660. [London, 1877].

> There is unfortunately no published listing of Inner Temple admissions after 1660.

The records of the Honorable Society of Lincoln's Inn. 2v. London, 1896.

> Includes admissions, 1420-1893.

H. A. C. Sturgess: *Register of admissions to the Honourable Society of the Middle Temple from the fifteenth century to the year 1944.* 3v. London, 1949.

J. B. Williamson: *The Middle Temple Bench book.* 2nd edn. London, 1937.

> Contains fuller biographical details of Middle Temple members who became Masters of the Bench.

G. D. Squibb: *Doctors' Commons: a history of the College of Advocates and doctors of law.* Oxford, 1977.

> Appendix III (pp. 118-203) comprises a complete list of members during the College's existence (ca. 1495-1865), with brief biographical details.

E. Foss: *Biographia juridica: a biographical dictionary of the judges of England ... 1066-1870.* 2v. London, 1870.

F. Elvington Ball: *The judges in Ireland, 1221-1921.* 2v. London, 1926.

> Includes short biographies of all Irish judges within the stated period, as well as a narrative history of the Irish judiciary.

Register of the Society of Writers to Her Majesty's Signet. Edinburgh, 1983.

> A complete list of all known members of the Society down to modern times, with biographical details where possible.

F. J. Grant: *The Faculty of Advocates in Scotland 1532-1943, with genealogical notes.* Edinburgh, 1944.

> Lists all known advocates, with short biographical notes.

E. Keane, P. B. Phair & T. U. Sadleir: *King's Inns admission papers 1607-1867.* Dublin, 1982.

A fuller bibliography of works relating to the Inns of Court, including many which are rich in biographical detail and which relate to long-disbanded institutions as well as surviving ones, will be found in D. S. Bland, *A bibliography of the Inns of Court and Chancery*, London, 1985 (Selden Society supplementary series, 3).

Officers of state, and Members of Parliament

E. B. Fyde, D. E. Greenway, S. Porter & I. Roy: *Handbook of British chronology*. (Royal Historical Society, Guides and Handbooks, 2). 3rd edn. London, 1986.

> Contains lists of British officers of state from the earliest times down to 1986, also bishops and archbishops, and the senior members of the aristocracy. Also includes (pp. xxiii-xxxix) a bibliographical guide to lists of English office-holders.

J. Haydn: *The book of dignities containing lists of the official personages of the British Empire.* 3rd edn. London, 1894.

> Contains lists of names of British office-holders of all sorts – ecclesiastical, legal, diplomatic and military. Useful for its coverage of categories not included in the *Handbook of British chronology*, such as heralds, judges, and orders of knighthood.

The series *The History of Parliament*, broken up into separate chronological divisions, includes biographies of all M.P.s who sat at Westminster. Volumes for periods not yet covered are in preparation:

J. S. Roskell, L. Clark & C. Rawcliffe: *History of Parliament: the House of Commons 1386-1421*. 4v. Stroud, 1993.

J. C. Wedgwood & A. D. Holt: *History of Parliament: biographies of members of the Commons House 1439-1509*. 2v. London, 1936.

S. T. Bindoff: *The history of Parliament: the House of Commons 1509-1558*. 3v. London, 1982.

P. W. Hasler: *The history of Parliament: the House of Commons 1558-1603*. 3v. London, 1981.

B. D. Henning: *The history of Parliament: the House of Commons 1660-1690*. 3v. London, 1983.

R. Sedgwick: *The history of Parliament: the House of Commons 1715-1754*. 2v. London, 1970.

Sir L. Namier & J. Brooke: *The history of Parliament: the House of Commons 1754-1790*. 3v. London, 1964.

R. G. Thorne: *The history of Parliament: the House of Commons 1790-1820*. 5v. London, 1986.

J. Foster: *Members of Parliament, Scotland ... 1357-1882*. 2nd edn. London, 1882.

> A single alphabetical listing, with brief biographical details supplied where possible.

Medics and scientists

C. H. Talbot & E. A. Hammond: *The medical practitioners in medieval England: a biographical register*. London, 1965.

Covers the period from the earliest times to 1518, and includes men whose careers extended into the sixteenth century. Intended to complement Munk's Roll, but there is a little overlap.

W. Munk: *The roll of the Royal College of Physicians of London*. 2nd edn. 3v. London, 1878.

Contains short biographies of all members of the Royal College of Physicians licensed to practice between 1518 and 1825; a volume covering 1826-1925 (by G. H. Brown) was published in 1955, and other 20th century supplements have appeared.

R. W. Innes Smith: *English-speaking students of medicine at the University of Leyden*. Edinburgh, 1932.

A directory with brief biographical details, covering the period 1575-1875. An important source for tracing English medical practitioners, many of whom obtained their first degrees at British universities before proceeding to medical degrees at Leyden.

J. H. Bloom & R. R. James: *Medical practitioners in the diocese of London, licensed under the act of 3 Henry VIII, c.11: an annotated list 1529-1725*. Cambridge, 1935.

Mostly surgeons.

J. H. Raach: *A directory of English country physicians, 1603-1643*. London, 1962.

Based on surviving ecclesiastical records and other manuscript sources, as well as the printed university lists and other medical directories.

P. J. & R. V. Wallis: *Eighteenth century medics (subscriptions, licences, apprenticeships)*. 2nd edn. Newcastle-upon-Tyne, 1988.

A very extensive list of medical practitioners of all sorts, 1701-1800, based on apprenticeship records, book subscription lists and various other sources; each entry is restricted to a few brief details.

E. G. R. Taylor: *The mathematical practitioners of Tudor & Stuart England*. Cambridge, 1954.

E. G. R. Taylor: *The mathematical practitioners of Hanoverian England*. Cambridge, 1966.

A substantial section in each book is devoted to short biographies of mathematicians and scientific professionals (e.g. instrument makers, surveyors); the overall period covered in 1485-1840.

P. J. Wallis: *Biobibliography of British mathematics and its applications: part II: 1701-1760*. Letchworth, 1986.

Lists mathematical writers, 1701-60, with brief biographies and lists of their publications.

The aristocracy and gentry

G. E. Cokayne: *The complete peerage of England, Scotland, Ireland, Great Britain and the United Kingdom, extant, extinct or dormant*. New edn. 12v. 1910-59. Reprinted in compact form, 6v., 1984.

First published 1887-98. The standard comprehensive work on the peerage, tracing genealogies and giving brief biographical details of all past members of the peerage.

G. E. Cokayne: *Complete baronetage*. 6v. London, 1900-09. Reprinted in 1v. in compact form, 1983.

The equivalent work for members of the baronetcy.

Genealogy, family history, and other sources

There is a very wide range of historical sources which will provide varying amounts of biographical information: parish registers, electoral registers, poll books, directories, and census returns are only some of the most obvious. Many of these sources will provide only the briefest of glimpses of an individual's life – for example, that he was baptized on a particular day in a particular place, or that he was living in a certain town and eligible to vote in a certain year – but they may be essential for serious research into the identification or history of a particular collector. Family pedigrees may be found in printed histories of individual families – a surprising number of such histories have been produced – and also in the records of heraldic visitations, which are particularly useful for the more significant families of the sixteenth and seventeenth centuries. Many heraldic visitations have been printed by the Harleian Society. Most of these sources have been quarried for many years by the growing army of genealogists, and there are a number of bibliographical guides, designed primarily for family historians, which may also prove useful to provenance researchers. These provide indexes to other biographical sources, list the whereabouts of archival material, or point the way to explanations of the working of certain categories of source material.

C. R. Humphery-Smith: *A genealogist's bibliography*. 2nd edn. Chichester, 1985.

> Covers a wide range of sources likely to be useful to genealogists, arranged by county and by types of source within county; also includes a general bibliography at the end. Inspired by an earlier bibliography which is also useful: *A select bibliography of English genealogy*, by H. G. Harrison, London, 1937.

J. W. Moulton: *Genealogical resources in English repositories*. Columbus, Ohio, 1988.

> A selective brief summary of the holdings of English record offices which are likely to be particularly relevant to genealogists, listing categories of material and dates covered.

G. W. Marshall: *The genealogist's guide*. Guildford, 1903.
J. B. Whitmore: *The genealogical guide: an index to British pedigrees*. London, 1953.
G. B. Barrow: *The genealogist's guide. An index to printed British pedigrees and family histories, 1950-1975*. London, 1977.

> Alphabetical lists of family names with references to published pedigrees in a wide variety of sources, including the heraldic visitations printed by the Harleian Society, etc. Whitmore's guide is a continuation of Marshall's, and Barrow's follows on from Whitmore's.

T. R. Thomson: *A catalogue of British family histories*. London, 1980.

> The revised version of a guide first published in 1928. An attempt to compile a comprehensive list of family histories published in book form.

There is a series of handy short guides for genealogists, compiled by Jeremy Gibson and others, and published by the Federation of Family History Societies. Particularly useful are:

J. Gibson: *Unpublished name indexes in record offices and libraries*. 2nd edn. 1977.

J. Gibson: *Marriage, census and other indexes for family historians.* 2nd edn. 1986.
J. Gibson: *A simplified guide to probate jurisdictions: where to look for wills.* 3rd edn. 1986.

Scottish genealogy

M. Stuart: *Scottish family history: a guide to works of reference on the history and genealogy of Scottish families.* Edinburgh, 1930.
J. P. S. Ferguson: *Scottish family histories.* Rev. edn. Edinburgh, 1986.

> Ferguson's book supplements Stuart's by printing a union list of printed and manuscript resources for Scottish family history, based on the holdings of 53 Scottish libraries, together with references to relevant periodical articles published after 1930.

Irish genealogy

W. Clare: *A simple guide to Irish genealogy.* 3rd edn, revised by R. ffolliott. Ipswich, 1966.
D. F. Begley: *Irish genealogy: a record finder.* Dublin, 1981.

WORKS ON BOOK COLLECTING AND LIBRARY HISTORY

The study of book collecting and library history, both private and institutional, has generated a very extensive literature. Much of this comprises books and articles about particular collectors or libraries, and a comprehensive bibliography of such material is beyond the scope of this *Handbook*. There are however a number of bibliographies which cover this area, and these are listed in the final section below.

In addition to the numerous studies of individual collections, there is a smaller corpus of works which deal with the history of book collecting in a wider sense, and a selection of such material is given here. Outside the early medieval period, there is no satisfactory historical directory of British book collectors. There are several books like de Ricci's *English collectors* (which is probably the most frequently cited guide to the history of British collecting), or Quaritch's *Dictionary*, which provide a brisk trot through the more spectacular collections formed over the last 400 years, but they are extremely selective in scope. A series of dictionaries based on surviving books, wills, donation registers and other evidence, like Susan Cavanaugh's directory for 1300-1450, but covering later centuries, would be extremely useful, but until they are created we have only the older works to rely on. The compilation of directories of contemporary book collectors began towards the end of the nineteenth century, and a section on these directories is included below, as they may provide useful information on collections formed and dispersed since then.

The increasing interest in the importance and use of provenance research which has developed over the last few decades, and the growing recognition of its place within the framework of bibliographical studies, has generated a number of articles on the general subject of provenance, and a list of these is given first.

Articles on the study and use of provenance

F. B. Adams: *The uses of provenance.* [Lecture given in Los Angeles, 1969, as the ninth annual Zeitlin & Ver Brugge lecture in bibliography] Berkeley, 1969.

F. B. de Marez Oyens: ISTC and provenance in L. Hellinga & J. Goldfinch (eds.), *Bibliography and the study of 15th-century civilisation* (British Library Occasional Papers 5), London, 1987, pp. 216-227.

N. B. Eales: On the provenance of some early medical and biological books, *Journal of the history of medicine* 24 (1969), 183-192.

W. McCann: The study of provenance in older printed books: some examples from the Henry Davis collection, *An Leabharlann* ns 1(3) (1984), 73-85.

R. Nikirk: Looking into provenance in H. G. Fletcher (ed.), *A miscellany for bibliophiles*, New York, 1979, pp. 15-45.

J. A. Overmier: Medical rare book provenance. *Bulletin of the Medical Library Association* 75 (1987), 14-18.

J. Sparrow: *Association copies: an essay with examples drawn from the author's own collection.* Los Angeles, 1978.

I. R. Willison: The treatment of notes of provenance and marginalia in the *Catalogue of books printed in the XVth century now in the British Museum* (BMC) in *Buch und Text im 15. Jahrhundert*, Wolfenbüttel, 1978, pp. 169-177.

Studies of book collecting and book collectors

This section does not include works which are concerned with one particular collector or library (for which see the section on Bibliographies covering book collecting and collectors below, p. 314). The emphasis here is on British collectors, but a couple of important and wide-ranging works on American collectors have also been included (Cannon, Dickinson).

The medieval period

Works which include coverage of the medieval period but are predominantly concerned with post-Reformation collectors are listed in the next section.

M. Lapidge: Surviving booklists from Anglo-Saxon England. In M. Lapidge & H. Gneuss (eds.), *Learning and literature in Anglo-Saxon England: studies presented to Peter Clemoes*, Cambridge, 1985, 33-89.

> A survey of surviving evidence for book ownership, both personal and institutional, ca. 775-1100.

S. H. Cavanaugh: *A study of books privately owned in England 1300-1450.* Unpublished Ph.D thesis, University of Pennsylvania, 1980.

A list of people known to have owned books in the period, with biographical information and details of the books they are known to have owned, based on wills, donation registers, surviving books and other sources. A survey of about 8000 wills formed the nucleus of the study, and the bibliography includes many sources of printed wills. The location of surviving books is also given.

K. Harris: Patrons, buyers and owners: the evidence for ownership and the role of book owners in book production and the book trade. In J. Griffiths & D. Pearsall (eds.), *Book production and publishing in Britain 1375-1475*, Cambridge, 1989, pp. 163-199.

Surveys the different kinds of evidence for book ownership in late medieval England, and links patterns of ownership with the known facts about the ways in which books were produced and traded.

K. W. Humphreys: The library of John Ergholme and personal libraries of the fourteenth century in England. *Proceedings of the Leeds Philosophical and Literary Society: Literary and Historical Section* 18 (1982), 106-123.

K. W. Humphreys: Books in private hands in England in the first half of the fifteenth century. In A. Horodisch (ed.), *De arte et libris: festschrift Erasmus 1934-1984*, Amsterdam, 1984, 237-248.

These two articles follow the same pattern and the second is designed as a continuation of the first. Although the earlier one concludes with a brief study of a particular collection of books, i.e. the 220 or so volumes given to the Augustinian Convent of York by John Ergholme ca. 1375, the bulk of the article comprises a survey of known 14th century personal collections of books. The later piece begins with a list of people who died between 1420 and 1455 who are known to have had 20 or more books, then summarises the books known to have been in private hands in smaller collections using a table, classified by subject, and further broken down to show owners based in Oxford, Cambridge, or elsewhere. It concludes with an analysis of the library of Humphrey, Duke of Gloucester (1391-1447).

R. Weiss: The private collector and the revival of Greek learning, in F. Wormald & C. E. Wright (eds.), *The English library before 1700*, London, 1958, pp. 112-135.

Not concerned only with Greek books, but rather an attempt to survey the growth of the private library in England in the medieval period.

S. G. Bell: Medieval women book owners: arbiters of lay piety and ambassadors of culture. *Signs: journal of women in culture and society* 7 (1982), 742-768.

A brief overview of patterns of book ownership among European women, including a statistical table of 'Identified European laywomen owning books, A.D.800-1500'.

From the end of the medieval period to the present day

A. Besson: *Classification in private library catalogues of the English renaissance, 1500-1640.* Unpublished Ph.D thesis, University College, London, 1988.

Focussed on classification and the organisation of knowledge, but based on a study of the inventories of 36 English private libraries compiled between 1521 and 1640; includes transcripts of 9 hitherto unpublished inventories.

G. A. E. Bogeng: *Die grossen Bibliophilen: geschichte der Büchersammler und ihrer Sammlungen.* 3v. Leipzig, 1922.

International in coverage; ch. VII of v.1 (pp. 379-466) attempts a chronological narrative of the major book collectors in England from medieval times to the nineteenth century.

Particularly useful for its illustrations; v.2 consists entirely of plates with pictures of collectors, libraries, book stamps, etc.

C. L. Cannon: *American book collectors and collecting from colonial times to the present*. New York, 1941.

A chronologically arranged survey of the major American collectors.

J. Carter: *Taste and technique in book collecting*. Rev. edn. London, 1970.

An overview of the development of book collecting in Britain and America in the nineteenth and twentieth centuries, with an emphasis on changing patterns of conoisseurship.

W. Clarke: *Repertorium bibliographicum; or, some account of the most celebrated British libraries*. London, 1819.

An account of 27 institutional and 53 private libraries; the approach is very much based on lists of noteworthy items in the various collections. The private libraries are divided between those of contemporary living collectors (e.g. Heber, Grenville) and those dispersed at auction in the late eighteenth and early nineteenth centuries (with notes on a few earlier collections). There is a final section comprising a 'select list of some rare books in minor sales, or in private collections'.

R. C. Cole: Private libraries in eighteenth-century Ireland. *Library Quarterly* 44 (1974), 231-247.

A brief study of the professional standing of 198 Irish collectors, and of the contents of their libraries.

K. Dent: The private library of the landed classes: its role in informal education in the eighteenth century. In K. S. Dent (ed.), *Informal agencies of education: proceedings of the 1977 annual conference of the History of Education Society of Great Britain*, Leicester, 1979, 37-59.

An attempt to estimate the extent to which the eighteenth century English gentry engaged in 'serious' reading, and the extent to which their libraries played an educational, rather than a recreational, role. Includes studies of two particular libraries (of the Isham and St. Quintin families), looking at content, growth patterns, and the evidence of use in surviving books.

S. de Ricci: *English collectors of books & manuscripts (1530-1930) and their marks of ownership*. Cambridge, 1930, reprinted London, 1960, and New York, 1969.

The Sandars lectures for 1929-30. A survey of major English collectors, 16th-19th centuries, with numerous illustrations of characteristic inscriptions and bindings.

D. C. Dickinson: *Dictionary of American book collectors*. New York, 1986.

A biographical dictionary covering 359 significant American collectors who died before 1984; includes extensive coverage of 20th century collectors, but earlier centuries are not neglected. Includes references to sale catalogues and to published catalogues and articles relating to particular collectors.

T. F. Dibdin: *The bibliomania, or, book-madness*. London, 1809.
The bibliographical decameron. 3v. London, 1817.

Dibdin's *Bibliomania* represents the first serious attempt to compile a history of book collecting in Britain and the bulk of the text comprises a chronologically-arranged account of noteworthy collectors from the middle ages to the beginning of the nineteenth century. The *Decameron* is more of an overview of bibliography in general but the third volume (chapters 9 and 10) includes much detailed material on English collectors and book sales. The main text of both books is cast as a dialogue between imaginary characters and Dibdin's florid style drives most modern readers demented; the footnotes, which occupy more space than the text, are more factually and straightforwardly written. Both books have useful indexes through which the names of collectors can be traced. Enlarged editions of *Bibliomania* appeared in 1811 and 1842; the 1842 edition was reprinted in 1876.

W. Y. Fletcher: *English book collectors*. London, 1902, reprinted New York, 1969.

Short biographies of 100 major collectors, Matthew Parker – William Morris, arranged chronologically.

W. C. Hazlitt, *A roll of honour: a calendar of the names of over 17,000 men and women who throughout the British Isles and in our early colonies have collected mss. and printed books from the XIVth to the XIXth century*. London, 1908.

A curious and frustrating work which does indeed list many thousands of British collectors, but most entries comprise only a name, sometimes with dates, addresses or qualifications, and only occasionally with very brief notes about their libraries or bookplates. The gravest omission is the total lack of information as to the whereabouts of the books in which Hazlitt found the inscriptions. The British Library has Hazlitt's own copy, interleaved by him and extensively annotated, with the addition of cuttings from sale catalogues (shelfmark 1655/4); unfortunately, his notes continue the conventions of the printed text and give little information on the locations of items.

A. Hyatt King: *Some British collectors of music c.1600-1960*. Cambridge, 1963.

As well as offering a general historical treatment of music-collecting in this country, incorporating much biographical information, this book includes as appendix B 'classified lists of past collectors'.

M. McKisack: *Medieval history in the Tudor age*. Oxford, 1971.

The general theme of this book is the development of medieval historical studies in the sixteenth century, and although it is partly about the writers of history it is also very much concerned with collectors. It contains much valuable material on the collectors of manuscripts in the first few generations following the dissolution of the monasteries. Similar ground is covered in C. E. Wright's essay on 'The dispersal of the libraries in the sixteenth century' in F. Wormald and C. E. Wright (eds.), *The English library before 1700*, London, 1958, 148-175.

A. N. L. Munby: *Conoisseurs and medieval miniatures, 1750-1850*. Oxford, 1972.

A study of the collecting of illuminated manuscripts, which inevitably touches on book collecting in a wider sense, and mentions many of the important names of the late eighteenth and early nineteenth centuries.

A. N. L. Munby: *The cult of the autograph letter in England*. London, 1962.

Like the preceding title, this is concerned with a specialised field rather on the fringes of, but related to, mainstream book collecting. Largely devoted to two major 19th century collectors, but includes details of numerous others, and deals with the trade in autographs and manuscripts.

A. N. L. Munby: *Essays and papers*. London, 1977.

This book brings together 18 short pieces by Munby, mostly concerned with particular book collectors (e.g. Heber, Macaulay), or with book collecting in general; note particularly 'The libraries of English men of letters' (pp. 101-120), an overview of known facts on the collections of English literary figures from the late sixteenth to the early nineteenth centuries, with extensive references to sale catalogues.

R. Myers & M. Harris (eds.): *Property of a gentleman: the formation, organisation and dispersal of the private library, 1620-1920.* Winchester, 1991.

> A collection of essays on various aspects of book-collecting; includes a survey by T. A. Birrell in 'the place of light literature in some gentlemen's libraries of the 17th century', and an article by Brian North Lee on 'Gentlemen and their bookplates'.

D. Pearson: The libraries of English bishops, 1600-1640. *The Library* 6th ser 14 (1992), 221-257.

> A survey of book ownership across a particular professional grouping in the first half of the seventeenth century.

B. Quaritch (ed.): *Contributions towards a dictionary of English book-collectors as also of some foreign collectors.* London, 1892-1921, reprinted New York, 1968.

> A series of essays originally issued in parts; rather biased towards 19th century collectors, and highlights of sale catalogues.

E. Sangwine: The private libraries of Tudor doctors. *Journal of the History of Medicine and Allied Sciences* 33 (1978), 167-184.

> A brief analysis of the books listed in surviving inventories of six English physicians who died between 1500 and 1593.

R. J. Schoeck: The libraries of common lawyers in Renaissance England: some notes and a provisional list. *Manuscripta* 6 (1982) 155-167.

> A list of 45 known private legal libraries, 1500-1650, with brief summaries and introductory remarks.

N. Ni Sheaghdha: *Collectors of Irish manuscripts: motives and methods.* (Richard Irvine Best Lecture, 1984.) Dublin, 1985.

> A short chronological survey of major collectors, 17th-20th centuries.

J. L. Thornton & R. I. J. Tully: *Scientific books, libraries and collectors.* 3rd edn. London, 1971.

> Chapter X, 'Private scientific libraries', pp. 339-353, is a brief summary account of major scientific collectors since the beginning of the sixteenth century. The information given here is expanded in *Scientific books, libraries and collectors ... Supplement 1969-75,* by Thornton and Tully, London, 1978, pp. 104-112.

A. Besson (ed.), *Thornton's medical books, libraries and collectors.* Aldershot, 1990.

> A thoroughly revised version of a book first published by J. L. Thornton in 1949. The chapter by Alain Besson on 'Private medical libraries' (ch. 9, pp. 267-300) is a more thorough treatment of the subject than the equivalent chapter in *Scientific books, libraries and collectors,* and it has an extensive and up-to-date bibliography in the form of the footnotes.

E. B. Wells: Scientists' libraries: a handlist of printed sources. *Annals of Science* 40 (1983) 317-389.

> A list of sale catalogues, exhibition catalogues, published catalogues and articles relating to the libraries of about 880 scientists, arranged alphabetically by surnames.

J. Yeowell: *A literary antiquary. Memoirs of William Oldys.* London, 1862.

> Includes (pp. 58-109) a section on 'London libraries'. comprising notes made by Oldys and John Bagford on noteworthy London collections of the eighteenth century. Largely

concerned with institutional libraries, but it includes a section on private collections, giving details of 20 important private libraries formed in the late seventeenth or early eighteenth centuries.

Directories of book collectors

During the twentieth century, several series of directories of current collectors have been compiled, on both sides of the Atlantic, aimed at booksellers and the collectors themselves, to spread information about collecting interests, and perhaps also to satisfy vanity. As these directories grow older they gain some value as historical records of possibly dispersed collections. Also included here are a number of accounts of private libraries which were published in the second half of the nineteenth century, mostly in America, which are not so much general directories of collectors as descriptions of selected major collectors within a particular locality. It should be added that *The Book Collector* has, since its inception in 1952, run a series on 'Contemporary collectors' which had by 1994 included over 50 accounts of noteworthy collections of the second half of the twentieth century.

The British Isles

T. Mason: *Public and private libraries of Glasgow*. Glasgow, 1885.

> Includes descriptions of 13 private collections.

R. & J. Sheppard: *International directory of book collectors 1976/77*. Beckenham, 1977.

> The first issue in a series, with a new edition published every few years (latest edition, 1993). Lists names, addresses, and collecting interests.

United States of America

L. Farnham: *A glance at private libraries*. Boston, 1855.

> An essay on major mid-19th century collections in and around Boston.

J. Wynne: *Private libraries of New York*. New York, 1860.

> Describes 51 collections.

F. H. Apponyi: *The libraries of California*. San Francisco, 1878.

> Includes descriptions of 89 private libraries.

H. Rogers: *Private libraries of Providence*. Providence, 1878.

> 8 collections described.

J. A. Holden: *A list of private book collectors in the United States and Canada*. New York, 1919.

> An expanded and separately published version of a list first printed in the *American Library Journal* for 1912-13. Later editions appeared in 1922, 1925, 1931, 1936 (*Holden's private book collectors*, comp. B. E. Weston & A. C. Frasca), 1948 (*Private book collectors in the United States and Canada*).

International

G. Hedeler: *List of private libraries.* Leipzig, 1897-98.
 I United States and Canada
 II Great Britain
 III Germany

> Parallel text in three languages, English, French and German, listing collectors with brief notes on their interests, and the sizes of their collections.

Bibliographies covering book collecting and collectors

Many studies of particular private libraries, and of book collecting in general, have appeared in journals and monographs; fortunately, there are a number of bibliographies which provide consolidated indexes to a wide range of material.

There is one particularly useful series of bibliographies, published by the Library History Group of the Library Association, which provides an annotated listing of monographs, pamphlets, periodical articles and theses published since 1962:

D. F. Keeling: *British library history: a bibliography 1962-1968.* London, 1972.
D. F. Keeling: *British library history: bibliography 1969-1972.* London, 1975.
D. F. Keeling: *British library history: bibliography 1973-1976.* London, 1979.
D. F. Keeling: *British library history: bibliography 1977-1980.* London, 1983.
D. F. Keeling: *British library history: bibliography 1981-1984.* London, 1987.
D. F. Keeling: *British library history: bibliography 1985-1988.* Winchester, 1991.

> The scope of this series is 'the history of libraries, librarianship and book collecting in Great Britain and Ireland from the earliest times to the present day', and each volume has a section on 'Libraries: private', which is particularly relevant to provenance research as it lists studies of individual collectors as well as material with a wider range. The main focus is on British publications, but some overseas material is included as well. For an American equivalent, see:

D. G. Davis, jr., & J. M. Tucker: *American library history: a comprehensive guide to the literature,* Santa Barbara & Oxford, 1989.

> Section 3, pp. 35-54, is devoted to 'Private libraries and reading tastes'.

A number of other indexes, specifically devoted to bibliographical publications, are also important:

G. W. Cole: *Index to bibliographical papers ... 1877-1932.* Chicago, 1933.

> An index to articles published in *the Library,* the *Library Association Record,* and various other publications issued by the Bibliographical Society or the Library Association between 1877 and 1932.

Index to selected bibliographical journals 1933-1970. London, 1982.
J. Feather: *An index to selected bibliographical journals 1971-1985.* (Oxford Bibliographical Society, Occasional Publication 23). Oxford, 1991.

> These two works attempt to provide comprehensive indexes to a range of major bibliographical journals published in Britain and America. An addendum to the first index,

covering *The Library* for 1964, was published by C. B. L. Barr in *The Library* 6th ser 9 (1987), 44-52.

ABHB: annual bibliography of the history of the printed book and libraries. The Hague, later Dordrecht, 1973-

> An international bibliography which aims to index 'all books and articles of scholarly value which relate to the history of the printed book'. Each annual volume is devoted to the publications of a particular year (volume 1 dealt with material published in 1970), and is arranged in a classified order; section H deals with bibliophily and book collecting.

Bibliographie der Buch- und Bibliotheksgeschichte (BBB). Bad Iburg, 1982-

> An annually published bibliography, compiled by Horst Meyer, which indexes the articles appearing in a wide range of journals covering bibliographical topics. The scope is international and about 800 separate journal titles are indexed. Each volume is devoted to the publications of a particular year (e.g. volume 10, issued in 1992, indexed journals published in 1990).

F. A. Schmidt-Künsemüller: *Bibliographie zur Geschichte der Einbandkunst von den Anfängen bis 1985.* Wiesbaden, 1987.

> This is the major international bibliography on the literature of bookbinding, which indexes nearly 200 journals and also covers monographs. Section 9 (pp. 79-95) is devoted to 'Bibliophilie (fur Einbande)' and lists studies which focus on particular collectors and their bindings. There is also a separate index of collectors at the end.

Anyone concerned with owners who may have been connected with cathedral libraries should be aware of the following bibliography:

E. A. Read: *A checklist of books, catalogues and periodical articles relating to the cathedral libraries of England.* (Oxford Bibliographical Society, Occasional Publication 6). Oxford, 1970.

> A supplementary listing was published in *Library History* 4 (1978), 141-163.

Some bibliographies with a wider remit should also be mentioned:

G. Watson et al (eds.): *The new Cambridge bibliography of English literature.* 5v. Cambridge, 1969-77.

> The sections on 'Book production and distribution' in vols. I and II (600-1660 and 1660-1800 respectively) include selective bibliographies on Book collectors and collecting, listing general works and significant studies of individual collectors. A revised edition of the *NCBEL* is in preparation.

T. H. Howard-Hill: *Bibliography of British literary bibliographies.* Oxford, 1971-

> A massive bibliographical project whose primary focus is English literature (books and articles about particular authors), but which includes extensive general apparatus devoted to the production, distribution, and acquisition of books. Volume 4 (1979, covering material published 1892-1969), includes a big section (pp. 199-285) on 'Book collecting and libraries'. It is indexed in volume 5. Volume 7 (1992), covering material published 1970-79, has a similar section on pp. 117-134.

Beyond these sources, which are specifically focussed on historical bibliography, there is a vast range of material which deals with related disciplines, such as literature or history, or with humanities research in general. It is beyond the scope of this book to cover this ground, but there are several excellent research guides which describe the available resources in a structured way. One of the best places to begin is:

A. J. Walford: *Walford's guide to reference material*
   v.3: *Generalia, language & literature, the arts.* 5th edn, ed. by A. Chalcraft, R. Prytherch, & S. Willis. London, 1991.
   v.2 (*Social and historical sciences, philosophy and religion,* 5th edn, ed. by A. Day and J. Harvey, London, 1990) is also relevant.

APPENDIX:
DESCRIBING PROVENANCE
IN CATALOGUES

A substantial portion of this book is devoted to provenance indexes – i.e. indexes to library catalogues of various sorts which reveal the previous ownership of books. Such indexes play a major part in making provenance research possible and the growing tendency among rare book librarians to record provenance information in detail is clearly one to be encouraged. It will be clear from chapter VII that there are still a number of important libraries who pay scant attention to copy-specific data when creating new catalogue entries for antiquarian material. The situation is not helped by the lack of any widely agreed standards for the recording of provenance.

Library catalogues are compiled according to cataloguing codes, which are normally followed strictly. It will come as no surprise to observe that older codes pay little attention, or less, to questions of provenance. Their emphasis has been based firmly on the text of the book being catalogued. The British Museum cataloguing rules, formulated in the nineteenth century but followed by many libraries well into the twentieth, allow only for the presence of 'manuscript notes' in books to be recorded in catalogue entries, 'to be shown by the words MS. NOTES, with FEW or COPIOUS prefixed, if applicable, and, when known, the addition in brackets of the name of the writer'.[1] There is no provision for noting the names of owners who do not add adversaria; the interest is considered to be justified only if the copy-specific additions have a relevance to the study of the text as a text. The *Rules for the author-catalogue of books published in or after 1920* promulgated by the Bodleian Library in 1923 include no mention of copy-specific data of any kind.

Many British and American libraries now use the *Anglo-American cataloguing rules* as the cornerstone of their cataloguing practice. The first edition of this code appeared in 1967 but it was superseded in 1978 by the second edition, commonly known as AACR2, which has gained widespread acceptance.[2] AACR2 is principally concerned with the cataloguing of modern books but it does include a section on antiquarian material (2.18). Provenance is briefly

---

1. *Rules for compiling the catalogues in the Department of Printed Books in the British Museum*, London, 1900, rule 19.
2. M. Gorman & P. W. Winkler (eds.), *Anglo-American cataloguing rules. Second edition, 1988 revision*, London, 1988.

mentioned here (rule 2.18F1: 'make notes on special features of the copy in hand. These include ... provenance'), and the implication, correctly, is that this *should* be recorded (not that it *might* be recorded), but the two examples of notes which could be given are far from satisfactory in their presentation.

It has been widely recognised that AACR2, like any code of general application for current library materials, cannot be expected to meet the needs of rare book cataloguers, and a number of more specialised codes have been developed during the last twenty years. They are generally intended to be used within the wider framework of an AACR2 cataloguing environment, but to lay down detailed rules for the additional information which is appropriate for rare book records. Three such codes have gained wide acceptance in the English-speaking world: the *International standard description of older books (antiquarian)*, generally known as ISBD(A), the rare books code developed by the International Federation of Library Associations (IFLA); *Descriptive cataloguing of rare books* (DCRB), the code used by the Library of Congress; and the *Eighteenth-Century Short Title Catalogue cataloguing rules*, developed for the ESTC project but widely used by others too.[3]

As far as the student of provenance is concerned, all these codes have major shortcomings. They are strongly rooted in the traditional text-centred approach to library cataloguing and their directions regarding copy-specific information are weak. The ESTC rules do not touch on copy-specific data, other than imperfections (which is reasonable in the context of the ESTC database). ISBD(A) includes a tiny section (7.9) on 'Notes relating to the copy in hand' and gives one not very good instance of a provenance note; there are no instructions as to when, or how extensively, such notes should be included in catalogue records. DCRB likewise has a very small section (7C18) on copy-specific notes, which should be included 'when they are considered important'. Provenance is one example of 'features which may be brought out here', but the tone throughout is that this is very much an optional extra, less important than the mandatory directions about the transcription and recording of edition-specific details. In this respect, the emphasis is less satisfactory than that found in AACR2, and the two examples of provenance notes which might be given are very poor (one of them repeats the AACR2 example, 'Signed: Alex Pope' and endeavours to improve upon it by expanding it to read 'Signed in ms.: Alex Pope'; it still carries no indication of the date of the inscription).

Many library catalogues are now automated, and in order to facilitate record exchange between libraries, standardised formats have been devised to ensure that the field structures of the automated records used by different libraries are the same; in other words, the same elements of information (e.g. author, title)

3. *ISBD(A): International Standard Bibliographic Description for older monographic publications (antiquarian)*, 2nd rev. edn, Munich, 1991; *Descriptive cataloging of rare books*, 2nd edn, Washington, 1991; J. C. Zeeman (ed.), *The Eighteenth Century Short Title Catalogue: the cataloguing rules*, 2nd edn, London, 1986.

are input in the same way in fields which carry the same numerical tags. A number of these formats, called MARC formats, have been developed (MARC = MAchine Readable Cataloguing), specific to particular countries; there is a UKMARC format, widely used in British libraries, and a USMARC format, used in North America. As regards making provision for copy-specific data, the MARC formats of the English-speaking library world are rather more advanced than the cataloguing codes which are meant to go with them. The USMARC format was adapted in the 1980s to provide a structure for the sophisticated recording of such data, and the UKMARC format was similarly augmented in 1992. Cataloguers using UKMARC now have three recommended fields in which to enter provenance data: 561, for free-text notes describing provenance evidence; 700/710, to provide added entry points for the names of former personal and institutional owners; and 755, another indexing field, which allows different kinds of evidence to be categorised and retrieved accordingly. The use of the 755 field is facilitated by the existence of a thesaurus of standard terminology, issued by the Association of College and Research Libraries: *Provenance evidence: thesaurus for use in rare book and special collections cataloguing* (Chicago, 1988). The UKMARC rare book fields are listed in full in the *Rare Books Newsletter* 43 (1993), 41-49.

The library catalogues and provenance indexes listed in chapter VII vary greatly in their level of detail regarding provenance data and it may be worth suggesting some guidelines for basic standards when compiling catalogue entries. In the MARC context, these suggestions apply to the free-text notes used in field 561.

Inscriptions should ideally be documented in a way which incorporates a transcript of the wording as it appears in the book, and an indication of position. 'Inscription at top-right hand corner of titlepage: Su[m] Gulielmi Chark' is better than 'with signature of William Chark', or similar. Ink colour should certainly be noted if unusual, or if the writing medium is pencil or crayon. It is particularly important to include some indication of *date*; this is one of the most common failings of provenance cataloguers. 'Inscription on flyleaf in 17th century hand: Thomas More' is, for obvious reasons, much more useful than 'Inscription on flyleaf: Thomas More'. Handwriting is not always easy to date, but an approximation by century is much better than nothing at all. Inscriptions which include dates should, obviously, be transcribed as such. If full transcription is not a feasible option, summary descriptions should include the name or names, the date (however approximate), and any additional information to help with identification (e.g. places, degrees).

Bookplates should similarly be recorded as fully as is reasonably possible, e.g. 'Bookplate on title leaf verso, mid-18th century, Franks 5497: William Chaloner Esqr of Gisborough in Cleveland'. A reference to Franks or some other standard reference work on bookplates is obviously a desirable inclusion if feasible. An additional possibility is the inclusion of the style of the plate (e.g.

armorial, pictorial, bookpile) or description according to the standard classification scheme for bookplates (Early Armorial, Jacobean, Chippendale, etc.), but, as with inscriptions, a rough date is probably the most important element of information, after the owner's name. Additional details which could be given are physical dimensions – in this case, the area being measured should be clearly stated (e.g. total plate area, or extent of inked area).

Armorial stamps may present more difficulties, not least because the owner may not be readily identifiable. Armorials may be described in the context of the binding to which they are applied, e.g. 'Early 17th century plain calf binding with late 17th century gilt armorial stamp of Ralph Sheldon at the centres of the boards'. If the armorial cannot be identified, the arms should be described as accurately as possible according to the correct heraldic nomenclature. As with other forms of evidence, dating is important; is the armorial contemporary with, or later than, the binding to which it is applied?

Catalogue entries for books which carry different kinds of provenance evidence, or evidence of more than one previous owner, should describe each piece of evidence equally systematically. They should make it possible to reconstruct the chain of provenance, as far as the evidence permits, and to make connections between different owners as appropriate.

INDEX

This index covers **individual collectors**, named in various contexts throughout the book, and **libraries** where reference is made to their historic practices (e.g. use of stamps). Library entries in the list of provenance indexes in chapter VII are not indexed under library name, as the listing there is already alphabetical. Entries for **auctioneers** and **booksellers** are mostly restricted to a single reference to their main descriptions in chapter V. **Subjects** are not covered by this index: use the contents pages instead. **Authors** of catalogues and works cited in the text are not indexed.